W9-DEY-060

Promoting Postsecondary Education for Students with Learning Disabilities: A Handbook for Practitioners

Promoting Postsecondary Education for Students with Learning Disabilities

A Handbook for Practitioners

Loring C. Brinckerhoff
Stan F. Shaw
Joan M. McGuire

with a Foreword by
Charles T. Mangrum II
and Stephen S. Strichart

pro·ed
8700 Shoal Creek Boulevard
Austin, Texas 78757

pro·ed

© 1993 by PRO-ED, Inc.
8700 Shoal Creek Boulevard
Austin, Texas 78757-6897

Library of Congress Cataloging-in-Publication Data

Brinckerhoff, Loring Cowles.
    Promoting postsecondary education for students with learning
disabilities : a handbook for practitioners / Loring C.
Brinckerhoff, Stan F. Shaw, and Joan M. McGuire.
    p.   cm.
    Includes bibliographical references (p.   ) and index.
    ISBN 0-89079-589-4
    1. Learning disabled—Education (Higher)—United States—
Handbooks, manuals, etc.   2. Special education—United States—
Planning—Handbooks, manuals, etc.   3. Special education—Law and
legislation—United States—Handbooks, manuals, etc.   I. Shaw, Stan
F.   II. McGuire, Joan.   III. Title.
LC4818.5.B75   1993
371.9—dc20
                                                            93-9576
                                                            CIP

Publisher's Note: The photographs used in this book do not represent any individual
with a known disability, and no such inference is intended or should be drawn.

This book is designed in Trump Mediaeval, with Univers.

Production Manager: Alan Grimes
Production Coordinator: Adrienne Booth
Art Director: Lori Kopp
Reprints Buyer: Alicia Woods
Editor: Helen Hyams
Editorial Assistant: Claudette Landry

Printed in the United States of America

2   3   4   5   6   7   8   9   10   97   96   95   94

Contents

Foreword   *xi*
CHARLES T. MANGRUM II and STEPHEN S. STRICHART

Preface   *xiii*

Chapter 1
An Introduction   *1*

Differences Between High School and College • 5
Promoting Postsecondary Education • 8

Chapter 2
**Judicial Intent and Legal Precedents:
Shaping Policy for Students with
Learning Disabilities**   *19*

Legal Foundations • 21
Implications of Federal Laws • 27

Comparing the IDEA, Section 504, and the ADA:
  Implications for Higher Education • 42

The Canadian Perspective • 50

Relevant Court Cases in the United States • 54

Developing Practical Guidelines Based on Legal
  Precedent • 64

Conclusion • 64

Chapter 3
Issues in Defining the Population 67

Challenges in Defining Learning Disabilities • 68

An Operational Definition of Learning Disabilities • 73

Differentiating Learning Disabilities from Other
  Conditions • 81

Should We Label? • 86

Conclusion • 87

Chapter 4
Issues in Assessment and Diagnosis 89
PATRICIA L. ANDERSON

Difficulty in the Assessment of Adults with Learning
  Disabilities • 91

Identifying the Purposes of LD Assessment • 101

The Assessment Process • 103

Components of the Assessment Process • 109

Referral Procedures • 111

Screening Options • 113

Diagnostic Testing • 118

Obtaining Appropriate Diagnostic Testing • 126

Interpreting and Applying Diagnostic
  Information • 132

Conclusion • 136

Chapter 5
Psychosocial Characteristics and Issues of Adults with Learning Disabilities — *137*
LYNDA PRICE

The Importance of Psychosocial Issues in Postsecondary Education • 139

Definition of Psychosocial Issues • 141

Limitations in the Current Research • 147

Theoretical Rationale for Psychosocial Service Delivery • 148

Using a Team Approach and Making Referrals • 152

Addressing Psychosocial Issues with Support Groups • 158

Addressing Psychosocial Issues with Individual Counseling Techniques • 160

Working with Resistant Students • 162

Caveats for Practitioners in Postsecondary Education • 163

Conclusion • 167

Chapter 6
Issues in Program Development — *169*

Administrative Issues: Laying the Groundwork • 170

Service Delivery Issues • 178

Garnering Administrative Support • 182

Developing a Summer Transition Program • 191

Challenges in Service Delivery • 199

Conclusion • 201

Chapter 7
Issues in Staffing and Personnel Development — *203*

Staffing Needs • 204

Personnel Development Needs • 208

Approaches to Personnel Development • 215
Conclusion • 220

Chapter 8
Issues in Determining Academic Adjustments at the Postsecondary Level   *221*

Administrative Considerations in Program
Modifications • 222
Service-Delivery Options and Considerations • 236
Providing Academic Adjustments, Technological Aids,
and Support Services • 238
Adapting or Modifying Methods of Instruction • 251
Conclusion • 258

Chapter 9
Determining Program Effectiveness   *259*

The Impetus for Measuring Program Effectiveness • 260
An Approach to Postsecondary LD Program Evaluation • 264
An Illustration of Program Evaluation: The University of
Connecticut • 268
Challenges in Evaluating Programs • 277
Conclusion • 278

Chapter 10
Future Directions in Postsecondary Learning Disability Programming and Service Delivery *279*

Fostering Successful Outcomes • 281
Developing Professional Standards • 282
Proactive or Reactive Service Delivery • 284
Knowledge Base • 285
Integration into the Postsecondary Community • 286
Becoming a Change Agent • 288

Appendix A   Department of Education, Office for Civil Rights, Regional Civil Rights Offices   *291*

Appendix B   Resources on Diagnosing Adults with Learning Disabilities   *295*

Appendix C   Information to be Addressed During the Screening Process   *301*

Appendix D   Tests Frequently Used for Diagnosing Adults with Learning Disabilities   *309*

Appendix E   Guidelines for Documentation of a Specific Learning Disability   *315*

Appendix F   Regional Learning Disability Contact Persons in the United States and Canada   *319*

Appendix G   Application Forms with Optional Checkoff Boxes   *323*

Appendix H   Follow-Up Letter to Prospective Applicants   *327*

Appendix I   Sample Nondiscrimination Statement, University of Connecticut   *331*

Appendix J   Academic Accommodations Policy Statement, University of California at Berkeley   *335*

Appendix K   Course Substitution Policy Statement, University of Connecticut   *341*

Appendix L   Policy Issues Relating to Accommodations for Students with Learning Disabilities: A Step-by-Step Approach, Boston University   *345*

Appendix M   Postsecondary Learning Disability Resources for Professional Development   *349*

Appendix N Tape-Recording Agreement Form, Ball State University *373*

Appendix O Procedures for Obtaining Exam Testing Assistance, Ohio State University *375*

Appendix P Alternative Testing Request Form, Ohio State University *379*

Appendix Q Effective Instructional Handouts, Western Carolina State University *383*

Appendix R User-Friendly Course Syllabus, Boston College *387*

References *391*

Index *427*

About the Authors *439*

Foreword

When the first edition of our book, *College and the Learning Disabled Student*, was published in 1984, we sensed that college opportunities for students with learning disabilities would significantly increase over the next several years. We are pleased that this indeed has been the case. The growth of opportunities was largely made possible by the work of dedicated professionals such as Loring Brinckerhoff, Stan Shaw, and Joan McGuire, the authors of this new book. They have worked tirelessly to create exemplary college programs for students with learning disabilities. As they developed these programs, they gained important empirical knowledge about what these students need to succeed. In this book, they share this knowledge so that others can replicate and build upon their efforts.

You will find a wealth of valuable information in this book. The discussion of the judicial and legal foundations of services for students with learning disabilities at the college level extends to the recently enacted Americans with Disabilities Act. Important emphasis is given to the psychosocial problems these students experience in the college setting, with accompanying recommendations for helping them make appropriate adjustments. Practical issues such as assessment and diagnosis, program development, and staffing are comprehensively discussed. The forms and guidelines presented in the appendixes are a particularly valuable resource in this regard. Perhaps the most indicative sign that the movement to provide college opportunities for students with learning disabilities has come of age is the chapter describing the ways to determine the effectiveness of programs. In 1984, programs were in an incipient stage, with little data available concerning their effectiveness. Today, we are at a point where concern has shifted from just getting programs started to issues of their quality.

The information throughout this book provides you with everything you need in order to initiate or refine college programs for students with learning disabilities. We are confident that you will find the book as valuable as we do, and that its publication will further the opportunities for students with learning disabilities to enter and succeed in college.

Charles T. Mangrum II, EdD
University of Miami

Stephen S. Strichart, PhD
Florida International University

Preface

Through tenacity and hard work, students with learning disabilities, with the support of caring parents and dedicated teachers, have been graduating from high school in growing numbers. In the past, those students who sought postsecondary education typically encountered a lack of understanding, limited support, and obstacles from admission to graduation. Thanks to the efforts of Barbara Cordoni, Charles Mangrum, Harriet Sheridan, Stephen Strichart, Susan Vogel, Gertrude Webb, Eleanor Westhead, and other pioneers in the field of postsecondary education for students with learning disabilities, significant change has occurred. By the 1990s, most colleges and universities had at least some personnel and services to support students with learning disabilities in their pursuit of higher education.

This book was developed to enhance the ability of postsecondary personnel to move from this baseline of service delivery to state-of-the-art efforts based on research, current interpretation of legislative intent, and recent litigation. The authors have been on the front line of service delivery as coordinators of learning disability efforts at five colleges including 2- and 4-year public and private institutions of higher education. During the last 10 years, they have implemented state, regional, and national technical assistance initiatives that helped them to identify the problems, issues, and concerns facing practitioners of postsecondary learning disabilities. Through these efforts at technical assistance, some very creative solutions to service delivery have emerged from college deans and faculty and from the students themselves. This book has also given the authors an opportunity to search the literature (educational, psychological, legislative, and judicial) and communicate with numerous professionals to assemble current and comprehensive information about identification, diagnosis, program and policy development, and service delivery regarding students with learning disabilities at the postsecondary level.

We gratefully recognize the contributions of many dedicated and talented individuals who supported the completion of this book. Chapter contributors Patricia Anderson and Lynda Price provided content that is critical to the needs of practitioners. Audrey Ald, Steve Bigaj, Joseph Cullen, Rich Goldhammer, Salome Heyward, Vivienne Litt, Jean Ness, Kay Norlander, Kip Opperman, Barbara Rhein, and Patricia Tomlan provided resources, ideas, and assistance. Carrol Waite, who prepared much of the manuscript, is a consummate professional with incredible creativity, accuracy, and diligence. We appreciate the continued support and encouragement of our editor, Jim Patton. We thank Don Hammill for his vision and his often-expressed desire to have the manuscript completed yesterday. Without doubt, the countless college and graduate students with learning disabilities we have had the opportunity to work with have energized our efforts and expanded our horizons. To them, we extend our respect and admiration. Finally, we gratefully acknowledge the encouragement, patience, and unwavering support of friends, both personal and professional, and family who helped us maintain our sense of perspective during the production of this work.

Loring C. Brinckerhoff
Boston University

Stan F. Shaw
University of Connecticut

Joan M. McGuire
University of Connecticut

CHAPTER 1
An Introduction

By most accounts, the field of postsecondary service delivery to students with learning disabilities is about two decades old. In 1970, Dr. Gertrude Webb began the first full-time college program for students with learning disabilities at Curry College in Milton, Massachusetts. The first substantive paper on the topic of successful college programs for students with learning disabilities was published by the HEATH Resource Center in 1981 and it listed only nine programs in the United States (Hartman, 1992). One of the earliest surveys of first-year college students, *The American Freshman: National Norms*, was conducted by the American Council on Education (ACE) in 1978. At that time, only 2.6% of all full-time first-year college students reported having *any* type of disability. A follow-up survey by ACE in 1991 indicated that the percentage of first-year students reporting a disability had more than tripled (Henderson, 1992).

Since 1985, the percentage of college students citing learning disabilities as the primary disabling condition has grown the fastest of all individuals with disabilities, from 15% to 25%. Presently, there are over 1.6 million full-time first-year students attending more than 3,200 institutions of higher education in the United States. It is estimated that over 35,000 of these students have identified learning disabilities (Henderson, 1992). The most recent edition of *Peterson's Colleges with Programs for Students with Learning Disabilities* (Mangrum & Strichart, 1992) listed nearly one thousand institutions with services for students with learning disabilities in the United States. In response to these increasing numbers, the number of postsecondary learning disability (LD) service providers has expanded at a phenomenal rate. Hartman (1992, p. vi) stated: "As students became better prepared, as their aspirations were raised by supportive parents and teachers, and as colleges and universities came to understand the strengths and potential that such students add to campus life, the number of such programs multiplied."

Shaw, McGuire, and Brinckerhoff (in press) indicated that this upsurge of interest is due to many factors that have affected both secondary and postsecondary institutions.

1. Public Law (P.L.) 94-142, which was implemented in 1978, has required mandated special education services for recent high school graduates with learning disabilities throughout their

public school experience. These students have often succeeded in school and expect that success to continue in college with the help of support services.

2. Emphasis on placing students with disabilities in the least restrictive environment has resulted in many students with learning disabilities taking sufficient academic coursework to qualify for 4-year colleges.

3. More than half (50.1%) of the students with learning disabilities who exited school in 1988–89 graduated with a diploma (*Thirteenth Annual Report to Congress on the Implementation of the Education of the Handicapped Act*, 1991). This cohort of more than 66,000 students has become increasingly attractive as a viable student market to college admissions offices since the number of high school graduates has plummeted in recent years.

4. Awareness of college options has resulted from the efforts of advocacy groups such as the Learning Disabilities Association of America and publication of postsecondary college guidebooks such as *Peterson's* and *Lovejoy's*. Students and their parents are effective advocates for program development because they know their needs and their rights. As many as 66% of young adults diagnosed as having learning disabilities want to extend their education beyond high school (Mangrum & Strichart, 1992).

5. States whose laws require individual transition plans (Texas, Kansas, Connecticut, Minnesota, and Utah) have helped students focus on college early enough in their secondary program to take the necessary prerequisite courses for competitive 4-year colleges. Recent amendments to P.L. 94-142, now the Individuals with Disabilities Education Act (IDEA), have extended this requirement to all states.

6. The increasing availability of computers and other compensatory technology has fostered academic success.

7. Increasing numbers of high school special education programs have moved away from the remedial or content-tutoring models to instruction in the learning strategies, metacognition, self-advocacy, and social skills necessary for college success

(Phillips, 1990; Shaw, Brinckerhoff, Kistler, & McGuire, 1991; Spector, Decker, & Shaw, 1991). In addition, regular classroom teachers who are working with these students in high school content classes are beginning to develop effective instructional skills with a focus on problem solving and training for independence (K. Decker, Spector, & Shaw, 1992).

8. Section 504 of the Rehabilitation Act of 1973 is a civil rights statute that provides equal access and reasonable accommodations for "otherwise qualified" college students with disabilities (Scott, 1990). In recent years, case law and decisions by the Office for Civil Rights based on Section 504 have provided the impetus for 4-year colleges, graduate schools, and professional schools to revise admission policies, provide accommodations, and develop support services (Brinckerhoff, Shaw, & McGuire, 1992; Scott, 1991).

9. The Americans with Disabilities Act (ADA) expands access beyond the campus and into the private sector. Disability support staff need to be knowledgeable about the act and its requirements concerning the availability of accommodations or auxiliary aids in employment, transportation, public accommodations, state and local governmental activities, and communication. Under the ADA, college students with disabilities will be affected by policies regarding certification and licensure and job hiring practices after graduation.

These significant events have all contributed to the rapidly changing profile that characterizes service delivery to students with learning disabilities in higher education. As more colleges and universities, as well as graduate and professional schools, develop and publicize support services for students with learning disabilities, enrollment will grow throughout the 1990s despite demographic trends indicating a continual decline in the number of traditional college-age students. Another factor that has contributed to the rapid expansion of services to college students with learning disabilities has been the availability of federal grant monies through the Office of Special Education and Rehabilitative Services. During the 1980s, approximately 50 model demonstration projects for college students with learning disabilities as well as programs that promoted the transition from high school to college of students with learning disabilities were federally supported (Hartman, 1992). Many of these model programs have served as blueprints for services that are now being offered in the United States and Canada and are highlighted in this book.

DIFFERENCES BETWEEN HIGH SCHOOL AND COLLEGE

Before one can address the needs of college students with learning disabilities, it is important to reflect back upon the secondary setting that has shaped these young adults. Research has shown that high school students with learning disabilities often find the transition from high school to college to be a source of anxiety and panic (Fass, 1989). This sense of "panic" is frequently due to the fact that they feel unprepared for the rigors of college life (Aase & Price, 1987; Aune & Ness, 1991a). They may not have experienced college preparatory classes in high school, either because they were "tracked" in lower-level courses or because they were taking academic courses in the resource room (McGuire, Norlander, & Shaw, 1990).

Making a successful transition from secondary to postsecondary settings may be difficult for any student, but for students with learning disabilities these changes can be particularly dramatic (Dalke & Franzene, 1988; Trapani, 1990). The inherent differences in the structure of these two settings are illustrated in Table 1.1. High school students are in class about six hours a day. In comparison to high school, the opportunities for direct teacher contact are much more limited in college settings. For example, it is not unusual for a college professor to be available to meet with students who need additional help for only 2 to 3 hours a week during office hours. Students in high school may spend a limited amount of time completing homework assignments. In contrast, many college students spend only 12 hours per week in class, but invest 3 to 4 hours per day in studying. Studying in high school is often synonymous with doing homework. In college, studying may mean rewriting lecture notes, paraphrasing information from reading assignments, and integrating information gleaned from a variety of sources (e.g., texts, class lectures, or library assignments). While high school students are tested frequently, sometimes weekly, on course material, college students may have only two or four tests

TABLE 1.1. **Differences Between High School and College Requirements**

	High School	College
Class Time	6 hours *per day,* 180 days Total? 1,080 hours!	12 hours *per week,* 28 weeks Total? 336 hours!
Study Time	Whatever it takes to do your homework! 1–2 hours per day?	Rule of thumb: 2 hours of study for 1 hour of class. 3–4 hours per day?
Tests	Weekly; at the end of a chapter, frequent quizzes.	2–4 per semester; at the end of a four-chapter unit; at 8:00 A.M. on the Monday *after* Homecoming!
Grades	*Passing* grades guarantee you a seat!	Satisfactory academic standing = C's or above!
Teachers	Often take attendance May check your notebooks Put information on the blackboard Impart knowledge and facts	Rarely teach you the textbook Often lecture nonstop Require library research Challenge you to think
Freedom	*Structured* defines it most of the time! Limits are set: by parents, by teachers, or by other adults	The single greatest problem most college students face! Should I go to class? Should I plan on 4, 5, 6, or 10 hours of sleep?

From "Preparing Students with Learning Disabilities for Postsecondary Education: Issues and Future Needs" by S. F. Shaw, L. C. Brinckerhoff, J. Kistler, and J. M. McGuire, 1991, *Learning Disabilities: A Multidisciplinary Journal, 2,* 21–26. Reprinted with permission.

per semester, making it more difficult for students and faculty to monitor academic progress. Furthermore, college students are expected to be much more independent than high school students in matters of class attendance and completion of assignments. While it may be sufficient for high school students to memorize facts, college professors often require students to think analytically, as well as to synthesize abstract information (Shaw et al., 1991).

High school students find that their time is structured by limitations set by parents and teachers. In contrast, college students are faced with the freedom to make their own decisions about scheduling time. Along with the demand for self-motivation in academic areas, college students with learning disabilities must also be responsible for making their accommodation needs known. This contrasts with high school, where a student is rarely responsible for determining and requesting accommodations for his or her special needs. In addition to the increased academic demands on students with learning disabilities in postsecondary education, a new environment away from the familiar support of family and friends may heighten already-existing problems with self-concept and social or interpersonal skills. Clearly these dramatic differences between the demands of high school and those that characterize higher education create a backdrop of challenge and change for students with learning disabilities.

The system has often "handicapped" these students from becoming active participants in their own futures. P.L. 94-142 stresses the role of the parent as the decision maker, not the student. Parents in turn often relinquish their rights in shaping program goals for their son or daughter, feeling intimidated by professionals they regard as "experts" who know what is best. The student with a learning disability is often left out of this process. The parents unquestioningly sign the Individualized Education Program (IEP), guidance counselors select courses that won't be too challenging, and well-meaning resource room teachers often teach content material instead of learning strategies and computer literacy skills. These prevailing practices must change so that high school students are better prepared for the rigors of postsecondary education. Many of the goals established in the IEP should be developed by the student so that he or she can become an active member in the decision-making process. Since self-advocacy is an essential skill for prospective college students with learning disabilities (Goldhammer & Brinckerhoff, 1992; Michaels, 1988; Ryan & Price, 1992), it is critical that these skills become sharpened while students are still in high school. Aune and Ness (1991a) have developed a comprehensive transition-related curriculum for high school students with learning disabilities that includes units on enhancing students' understanding of learning disabilities, interpreting information from initial diagnostic reports into everyday language, understanding the IEP, and actively planning for the future in vocational and postsecondary settings.

High school students with learning disabilities must also learn that they have fundamental rights under both P.L. 94-142 and Section 504 and that services or academic adjustments (e.g., taped textbooks, laptop computers, or extended time on exams) offered at the postsecondary level should be "tried out" first while they are still in the more protective and structured setting of high school. The student, not the parent, should call the LD service provider at the college and inquire about the services that are offered at the institution. Parents need to realize that conducting the college search, arranging for the campus tour and interview, and even writing a thank-you note for their son or daughter to the LD service provider after the interview does little to foster independence and independent decision making.

With this backdrop illustrating the contrasts in these two educational settings, it is logical to address the formidable role that postsecondary LD service providers play in bridging the transition from high school to college. Not only do the service providers need to be aware of the legal, social, political, and academic demands inherent in the two educational settings, but they must also work concurrently to build stronger linkages between high school teachers, vocational rehabilitation counselors, parents, and future consumers, as they establish internal support with campus administrators, faculty, and staff. By effectively networking at both the secondary and the postsecondary levels, LD service providers will be better able to promote postsecondary education for students with learning disabilities. The goal of this book is to facilitate that process. The following section will present chapter highlights of the critical issues that need to be addressed by the year 2000.

PROMOTING POSTSECONDARY EDUCATION

Chapter 2: Judicial Intent and Legal Precedents

Chapter 2 presents an overview of the IDEA, Section 504 of the Vocational Rehabilitation Act of 1973, and the ADA. Each of these three legal mandates is reviewed and implications for serving students with learning disabilities are offered. Since the impact of Section 504 on postsecondary settings is significant, the chapter focuses primarily on what colleges may and may not do under this civil rights legislation. Specific examples of academic adjustments or accommodations that may be necessary to ensure full participation in higher education by persons with learning disabilities are cited. The ADA of 1990 is considered by many to be the most sweeping piece of federal civil rights legislation in history. Its impact has already been felt in public and private employment settings and will become increasingly more visible in undergraduate and graduate programs as students with learning disabilities are faced with meeting competency-based curriculum standards and passing examinations for licensure and certification. Included in this chapter is a comparison of the three laws as well as an accompanying chart (Table 2.1) that succinctly illustrates similarities and differences in such areas as scope, coverage, and enforcement. This section concludes with a review of the Canadian equivalent of Section 504, the Charter of Rights and Freedoms. Key provisions of the charter are discussed and comparisons are made between provincial laws and those in the states.

The second part of the chapter shifts the focus to a number of recent test cases that help to clarify the parameters of "reasonableness" as they apply to accommodations at the postsecondary level. Five significant cases are reviewed, followed by a discussion of their potential impact in shaping educational policy for college students with learning disabilities. These cases should give LD service providers additional insights as they seek to make informed judgments about admissions, service delivery, and academic adjustments for college students with learning disabilities. The chapter concludes with potential areas of future litigation.

Chapter 3: Defining the Population

Donald Hammill (1990, p. 74) stated that "few topics in the field of learning disabilities have evoked as much interest or controversy as those relating to the definition of this condition." Chapter 3 begins by addressing these concerns and by offering some reasons why it is critical for the field to adopt a definition of learning disabilities that is appropriate at the postsecondary level. One approach to defining this population is to survey current definitions and to determine which elements within them are germane to adults. The definition of the National Joint Committee on Learning Disabilities (NJCLD) is cited for its many advantages, including the fact that it has been endorsed by representatives of nine national organizations that have a major interest in learning disabilities. It is suggested that if more postsecondary service providers would adhere to this functional definition, the field would not be faced with the rampant overidentification and misidentification of adults with learning disabilities.

Building on the work of the NJCLD, the authors point to the need to establish an operational definition in a manner that will allow individuals with little formal training in learning disabilities and diagnosis to make clear decisions about service eligibility. Four levels of investigation are offered. Level I involves the identification of significant difficulties and relative strengths in any one of six skill areas. Level II requires verification that the learning disability is intrinsic to the individual. The disability may be the result of either central nervous system dysfunction or an information-processing problem in one of three areas: (a) executive functioning, (b) cognitive processing, or (c) a knowledge base of general information. Level III involves the identification of concomitant limitations such as a lack of psychosocial skills or physical or sensory abilities that must not be viewed as elements of the learning disability, but as related problems that may or may not be associated with a learning disability. Level IV addresses alternative explanations for a learning disability. Factors cited include a lack of motivation; environmental, cultural, or economic influences; inappropriate instruction; or the possibility that the primary disability is not a learning disability (for example, it might be a psychological disorder or a health impairment). The model is then applied and illustrated with a variety of typical college student profiles that serve to delineate the more subtle differences between individuals with learning disabilities and those classified as "slow learners" or as having attention deficit–hyperactivity disorders or traumatic brain injuries.

Chapter 4: Assessment and Diagnosis

The intent of Chapter 4 is twofold: to help postsecondary service providers to become knowledgeable consumers in obtaining useful diagnostic reports for students with learning disabilities and to help them interpret diagnostic reports and translate results into recommendations regarding appropriate and effective accommodations. Since eligibility guidelines tend to vary from state to state under the IDEA, it is often difficult to determine which students are in fact eligible for services. Postsecondary service providers will find little guidance on this matter, since most guidelines concerning LD eligibility standards are based on the needs of students in grades K–12.

There are numerous reasons for conducting an LD evaluation. Some of the most common are to diagnose the disability, to determine eligibility for services under Section 504, and to assist in the development of reasonable accommodations in coursework. Ideally, the evaluation should provide the student with both documentation of the learning disability and specific recommendations for compensating for the disability, either in coursework or on the job. After establishing a rationale for conducting an evaluation, the assessment process is reviewed. This process includes establishing policies and procedures for referrals, conducting an initial screening or intake interview, conducting the diagnostic evaluation, interpreting the diagnostic report, and using diagnostic data for program decision making.

Difficulties in determining eligibility for services are compounded at the postsecondary level because there are few diagnostic test instruments that adequately measure the performance level of adults. Consequently, the most complete evaluations include a variety of formal and informal assessment data. Formalized evaluation data typically included in diagnostic reports at the college level may come from the *Wechsler Adult Intelligence Scale–Revised (WAIS-R)*, or the *Woodcock-Johnson Psycho-Educational Battery–Revised (WJPEB-R)*. Informal assessment data may include a review of the student's class notes or an evaluation of the student's reading comprehension using a class textbook. The most common types of diagnostic evaluations available to postsecondary institutions are psychological (or psycho-educational) and neuropsychological reports. The diagnosticians who most often prepare these reports are psychologists, neuropsychologists, school psychologists, or special educators. LD service providers need to be aware of the wide diversity in the focus, training, and backgrounds of these professionals when reviewing diagnostic reports. The available data in these reports may provide documentation for the diagnosis of a learning disability, but they typically do not provide enough specific information to identify appropriate support services needed by the student. The final section includes useful information on identifying the appropriate tools for diagnosing a learning disability, a listing of frequently used tests, and considerations concerning test construction (e.g., reliability and validity).

Chapter 5: Psychosocial Characteristics

Chapter 5 is premised on the fact that *both* the academic and psychosocial needs of students with learning disabilities require consideration. Unfortunately, the diverse psychosocial needs of these students often are not fully met in postsecondary settings. Providing academic support without psychosocial assistance may not be enough to meet student needs. A concise definition of psychosocial issues is presented along with a listing of several characteristics that have implications for counseling adults with learning disabilities. Specific areas addressed include (a) self-concept, (b) lack of social skills, (c) dependency on others, (d) stress and anxiety, and (e) various negative behaviors.

Dr. Abraham Maslow's theory regarding the stages of human development through the life span is used as a theoretical rationale for discussing the self-actualization process for students with learning disabilities. The overriding theme of the self-actualization model is the process of personal growth and movement as one moves toward wholeness and fulfillment in life. The author notes that employers are often looking for social skills similar to those proposed by Maslow. A recent report from the U.S. Department of Labor identified various psychosocial skills that are critical to employment; not surprisingly, they are also critical to academic success in college for adults with or without disabilities.

Because few postsecondary LD service providers have specific training in the components of psychosocial service delivery, the author offers numerous practical suggestions that can be applied in such diverse settings as a community college, a technical college, or a university. Emphasis is placed on collaborative team approaches to service delivery and to ways of effectively networking with limited campus or community resources.

Chapter 6: Program Development

Chapter 6 sets the stage for program development by offering postsecondary service providers some practical suggestions on how to best position LD support services on the campus. Whether services are designed from scratch or broadened to include components specifically related to the nature of the disability, familiarity with the organizational structure of the institution is critical. The authors discuss how LD coordinators can lay the groundwork for fledgling services that are in keeping with the institution's mission. A comparative model discusses the relative benefits, limitations, and ramifications of locating LD support services within academic affairs or student affairs. Clarification is also provided concerning the differences between LD support services and a traditional "LD program" model with respect to consumer expectations and service-delivery outcomes. Since no single approach will serve all students with learning disabilities, a developmental continuum of service-delivery models is presented. The purpose of this chapter is not to present readers with a "cookbook" approach to service delivery, but rather to present information that can guide postsecondary practitioners as they work to tailor services to meet the unique and diverse needs of students on their campus.

This chapter is designed both for newcomers to the field of postsecondary service delivery and for seasoned professionals. Newcomers are shown how to garner initial administrative support and how to prioritize core services with limited resources. Veteran service providers may find this section a welcome review of what may already exist on their campuses. Several recommendations are also offered on ways to maintain and enhance service delivery. As an example, the development of a summer transition program may bear many direct and indirect benefits for an institution. Numerous practical suggestions are presented for developing an orientation program that will facilitate the transition of students with learning disabilities from high school to a postsecondary setting. Several caveats are offered in regard to expanding services effectively, avoiding professional staff burnout, and establishing campus networks without duplicating services. The chapter also references in Appendix M an extensive listing of books, articles, videotapes, and sources of computerized technology that can assist LD service providers in developing or expanding services.

Chapter 7: Staffing and Personnel Development

This chapter addresses five key questions related to staffing and personnel development. Suggestions are offered on ways to effectively staff a program or support services office. Consideration is given to the different types of training that can be offered and the professional development opportunities that need to be available to administrators, direct service personnel, and faculty. After implementing initial in-service training efforts, service coordinators may need to determine what types of additional, ongoing professional development activities will be necessary.

Many service providers may see the benefits of providing in-service training to faculty about learning disabilities, but unless this is an ongoing effort and not a one-shot in-service event, little substantive attitudinal change will occur. The most effective training efforts are those that are conducted over time and that are tailored to the multi-faceted needs of the audience. It is clear that requiring a large number of staff and faculty to attend a mandatory in-service training session is not the most effective approach. Different constituencies at an institution of higher education will have different needs depending on their entry-level knowledge and degree of involvement with students with learning disabilities. Several suggestions from a position paper by the NJCLD (National Joint Committee on Learning Disabilities, 1988a) are offered on beginning a personnel development program.

The authors emphasize that the choice of postsecondary LD service-delivery models may have far-reaching implications for staff training. It is important to determine which service-delivery model would be best suited for meeting the needs of the consumers to be served. One model should not be selected over another based on the training style of initial personnel or the professional bias of an administrator. Staff should be hired who can diminish the impact of a learning disability by training the student in self-advocacy skills, writing skills, and learning strategies.

Direct service personnel, whether part-time or full-time, may need training regarding the program's mission, the service-delivery model, office operating procedures, and ways to approach faculty. It is recommended that such training efforts be extended over several days prior to the start of the academic year. Suggested training topics for in-house professional development activities are also included in this section. Higher education administrators need to understand and be supportive of the front-line efforts of LD service providers. These key individuals, who set policy, address concerns about curricular modifications, and may strongly influence funding patterns, need to be kept abreast of LD support service activities on a regular basis and not just at the end of the current fiscal year. Deans' meetings or executive councils can provide an opportunity for LD service coordinators to win support and to build further awareness of disability-related issues. Finally, suggestions are offered on developing a comprehensive, multi-faceted approach to ongoing personnel development on campus.

Chapter 8: Determining Academic Adjustments

The purpose of this chapter is to provide postsecondary LD support staff with suggestions on ways to develop campus policies and to establish clear guidelines for service delivery. The chapter builds on information presented in Chapter 2 concerning legal issues and in Chapter 6 concerning service-delivery considerations. These two chapters serve as the foundation for Chapter 8 as the authors implement the notion of "reasonable accommodations" at the postsecondary level.

Case law and subsequent litigation often necessitate the development of academic and administrative policies that can address day-to-day issues concerning service-delivery provisions. Unfortunately, many postsecondary LD service coordinators must try to make reasonable judgments about student access to educational opportunities without the benefit of administrative guidelines or knowledge of prevailing practices on other campuses. This chapter addresses many of the policy-related issues faced by service providers, such as establishing alternative admission procedures, developing course substitutions in mathematics or foreign language areas, assuring appropriate testing accommodations, and considering the impact of part-time versus full-time enrollment status on financial aid. Additional examples of ways to develop procedural guidelines for accommodating students with learning disabilities across a range of academic dimensions are given in the text and reinforced by sample policy statements in Appendixes J through L.

The remainder of the chapter focuses on the service-delivery provisions mandated under Section 504 and instructional accommodations that faculty can make to enhance the learning of *all* students. A range of essential academic adjustments and auxiliary aids designed to meet the intent of Section 504 are discussed in detail, including tape-recorded textbooks, readers, note-taking modifications, testing modifications, and assistive technology (e.g., word processors, spell-checkers, and reading machines). When academic adjustments are coupled with solid pedagogical practices, students with learning disabilities are in the best position to compete equitably with their nondisabled peers. The chapter concludes with several well-researched instructional techniques that can be employed by tutors or faculty when instructing college students with learning disabilities.

Chapter 9: Determining Program Effectiveness

Chapter 9 establishes the need for conducting a program evaluation at the postsecondary level. Unfortunately, the effectiveness of most LD support services models at the postsecondary level has not been well documented. This may be due to the fact that postsecondary LD service delivery is a relatively recent phenomenon and the divergent approaches to service delivery that are employed at the postsecondary level have not yet been carefully studied to determine their effectiveness. In a nationwide survey of coordinators of services for college students with learning disabilities conducted by Bursuck, Rose, Cowen, and Yahaya (1989), only 10% of the respondents were able to report on the graduation rates of these students. The authors of this study expressed their concern regarding the absence of data in this area and pointed to the critical need for follow-up research on college students' subsequent vocational and life adjustment. Program outcome data on the success rate of students with learning disabilities in completing college can assist service providers with future programmatic decision making.

One evaluation approach that seems well suited for adaptation to postsecondary LD programs is the context, input, process, and product evaluation (CIPP) model (Stufflebeam, 1988). An illustration of how the CIPP model can be used in postsecondary settings with limited LD support services is given, as well as a discussion of its application with comprehensive LD programs. The authors demonstrate how this program evaluation model has been used effectively for documenting and evaluating the ongoing activities of The University of Connecticut Program for College Students with Learning Disabilities. Various components of the evaluation plan are highlighted; they illustrate that flexibility is the key to "individualizing" evaluation activities that meet instructional and setting needs. By adapting this step-by-step approach to planning a program evaluation, readers will be able to develop their own agenda for program evaluation. However, postsecondary LD service providers need to keep in mind that the question of whether student success in achieving goals is related to program intervention is very complex and cannot be considered without a careful research design. By clearly planning the program evaluation, selecting appropriate measures, and systematically collecting data, service providers can address this question with greater certainty.

Chapter 10: Future Directions

The intent of Chapter 10 is to identify critical issues facing service providers and to encourage readers to seize opportunities for growth and change that are within reach. Service providers need to discriminate between services that foster student autonomy and those that do not. They also need to evaluate the extent to which their services undermine student self-determination and to seek alternative methods of fostering student empowerment at the postsecondary level.

Personnel new to the field of learning disabilities often bring with them a wealth of skills from a variety of related disciplines such as clinical psychology, social work, speech and language, and vocational education. When staffing and personnel standards are established for LD postsecondary service providers, everyone will benefit. Postsecondary institutions will be assured of employing staff who know how to develop state-of-the-art services rooted in "best practices," and students who access these services will be given support by professionals who have the necessary training and expertise. It is hoped that these individuals will become the future leaders in the field by refining program models, gathering research data, and sharing their research findings with others. Clearly, there is a pressing need to study the effectiveness of specific teaching interventions at the postsecondary level and to evaluate the utility of specific academic adjustments and auxiliary aids. The authors of this book challenge readers to become change agents so that disability rights can be furthered, higher education opportunities can be expanded, and the dignity of students with learning disabilities can be preserved.

Judicial Intent and Legal Precedents: Shaping Policy for Students with Learning Disabilities

I t has been nearly 20 years since the passage of P.L. 94-142 and Section 504 of the Rehabilitation Act of 1973. During this period, the field of special education has witnessed rapid change due, in part, to a variety of court cases, consumer lobbying efforts, and legal mandates that have directly altered the manner in which services are provided to individuals with disabilities. The recent passage of the Americans with Disabilities Act (ADA) is a further reflection of this trend, which ensures that individuals with disabilities are granted full participation in society.

These legal advances have already affected the lives of many individuals with disabilities in the United States, but nowhere is the potential for empowering more individuals greater than in the area of learning disabilities. Currently, children with learning disabilities represent 50.5% of the students with disabilities from ages 6 to 21 who are receiving special education in our schools (*Fourteenth Annual Report to Congress on the Implementation of the Education of the Handicapped Act*, 1992). This disability group alone accounts for over 4.5% of total school enrollment. Over 66,000 identified students with learning disabilities are graduating from high school every year, and of these, nearly half are pursuing some type of postsecondary program (*Tenth Annual Report to Congress on the Implementation of the Education of the Handicapped Act*, 1988). College students with learning disabilities are the fastest-growing disability group, with almost 60% of these students attending 2-year campuses, while another 40% are enrolled in 4-year settings (Henderson, 1992). Since 1985 the percentage of first-year college students with disabilities who indicated that they had a learning disability has increased from 15% to 25% (Henderson, 1992). Jarrow (1991) believes that this figure may underrepresent the actual number of students with learning disabilities, who now account for 35% to 50% of the postsecondary disability population on many college campuses. Given this rapid increase in the number of self-identified students with learning disabilities who are seeking services, it has become increasingly important for secondary and postsecondary teachers, administrators, and support staff to have a working knowledge of the rights, responsibilities, and subsequent policies for serving this population.

The purpose of this chapter is to (a) present an overview of the key provisions of P.L. 94-142, Section 504 of the Rehabilitation Act of 1973, and the ADA; (b) demonstrate how these three legal corner-stones compare and contrast and how they affect service delivery to students with learning disabilities at the secondary and postsecondary levels; (c) cite selected court cases that have helped to shape and define the scope of the law; and (d) lay a foundation, based on both the legislation and court cases, that can be used to develop guidelines, policies, and procedures, which will be discussed in Chapter 8.

LEGAL FOUNDATIONS

Public Law 94-142

Historically, the underpinnings of P.L. 94-142 rest in previous litigation involving two landmark cases: *Pennsylvania Association for Retarded Citizens (PARC) v. Commonwealth of Pennsylvania* (1971) and *Mills v. The Board of Education of the District of Columbia* (1972). These two class-action suits outlined several important substantive and procedural rights that were later incorporated into P.L. 94-142. Both were premised on the principle of "equal educational opportunity" that was first articulated by the Supreme Court in *Brown v. Board of Education of Topeka* (1954), which held that "separate but equal" was not enough. Through these early judicial mandates, future legislation evolved and culminated in the establishment of uniform standards for providing equal educational opportunity to children with disabilities.

The Education for All Handicapped Children Act, P.L. 94-142, was signed into law in 1975 and provides the guidelines and regulations for special education service delivery throughout the United States. Its major purpose, as stated in the Act, is as follows:

> to assure that all handicapped children have available to them . . . a free appropriate public education which emphasizes special education and related services designed to meet their unique needs, to assure that the rights of handicapped children and their parents or

guardians are protected, to assist States and localities to provide for the education of all handicapped children, and to assess and assure the effectiveness of efforts to educate handicapped children. (P.L. 94-142, 1975, Sec. 601c)

It is important that postsecondary service providers become familiar with P.L. 94-142 for several reasons. Many high school students with learning disabilities and their parents have the expectation that aspects of P.L. 94-142, including educational programs and services offered in high school, will continue in college. Since this is not the case, it is important to note the differences between the two educational settings as they relate to legal rights, access to services, and programming options. P.L. 94-142 guarantees that all children, regardless of disability, are entitled to a free, appropriate public education in the least restrictive environment. This entitlement is supported by the use of federal funds according to a payment formula that takes into account the national average expenditure per public school child and the number of students with disabilities receiving special education in each state (Ballard, Ramirez, & Zantal-Wiener, 1987). Since P.L. 94-142 is a grant statute and since federal funds are conditional on performance and compliance, it is very specific in its requirements for service provision. Under P.L. 94-142, two criteria must be met to establish eligibility: (a) a student must actually have one or more of the disabilities defined under the act and (b) such a student must require special education and related services. If these two conditions are met, the student is ensured appropriate, public education in the least restrictive setting at no expense to the parent or guardian. The six primary components of P.L. 94-142 provide for the legislative definition of a free, appropriate public education (Turnbull, Strickland, & Brantley, 1982, pp. 2–11). These components are:

1. *Zero-reject:* Prohibits schools from excluding any student from an education because he or she has a disability. States must provide full educational opportunities to all children with disabilities between the ages of 3 and 21, or in accordance with state law. In addition to providing for the educational placement of all children with disabilities, the local education agency (LEA) must provide students with disabilities all the related services (e.g., counseling and transportation) so that they can benefit fully from special education.

2. *Nondiscriminatory evaluation:* Requires that children be provided with a full educational evaluation prior to being placed in a special education program. More than one test must be used and the tests must be administered and scored in an unbiased way. The interpretation of the evaluation data must be conducted by a multidisciplinary team that can determine each child's eligibility and need for special education and related services.

3. *Individualized Education Program:* Stipulates that the child's education must be tailored to meet his or her unique needs. The Individualized Education Program, or IEP, is the document that spells out those needs. It includes the student's current level of functioning, annual goals, short-term objectives, documentation of the types of special education or related services to be provided, and an indication of the amount of time the child will be participating in the regular education setting. The IEP is subject to an annual review by parents and teachers.

4. *Least restrictive educational placement:* Mandates that, to the greatest extent possible, children with disabilities are to be educated with their nondisabled peers. Removing children with disabilities from the regular education setting should only occur when the nature or the severity of the disability prevents them from being successfully educated in regular classes with the use of supplemental aids and services.

5. *Procedural due process:* Provides parents with the opportunity to consent or object to the referral, assessment, program, or placement of their child. Safeguards may include the right to a due-process hearing, independent educational evaluations, parent notice, parent consent, and the appointment of surrogate parents.

6. *Parent participation:* Provides parents with the opportunity to participate in and have full knowledge of their child's educational program. These rights often include access to educational records and information, as well as involvement in the development of the IEP.

The Education of the Handicapped Act Amendments of 1990 (P.L. 101-476) included many provisions to strengthen P.L. 94-142 ("Summary of Major Changes," 1990). Its new title, Individuals with Disabilities Education Act (IDEA), more accurately reflects the preference for emphasizing person-first terminology and the current practice of using the term *disability* instead of *handicap* (Maroldo, 1991). The 1990 amendments made many significant changes. The law now includes autism and traumatic brain injury as protected disabilities under the scope of the IDEA. Initial plans for also including attention deficit disorder (ADD) as a disability category under the act were amended following public comment and clarification by the Office of Special Education and Rehabilitative Services (OSERS). Current policy stipulates that children with ADD who require special education and related services can meet eligibility under already-existing categories such as "other health impaired" (Davila, Williams, & MacDonald, 1991). Related services, such as rehabilitation counseling and social work services, are also covered in the revised legislation.

Of particular relevance to the postsecondary arena is the emphasis the law places on providing for transition services. Transition services are a set of coordinated activities designed to facilitate the student's move from high school to a variety of postsecondary activities including, but not limited to, higher education, vocational training, and adult education. Specific one-time grant monies have been earmarked for state education agencies and vocational rehabilitation agencies to "develop, implement, and improve systems to provide transition services for youth with disabilities from age 14 through the age they exit school" (Sec. 14.25 [3]). The IDEA also mandates that the IEP include a transition plan for students no later than age 16, but earlier whenever appropriate. These significant changes in special education law will facilitate the transition from high school to college for many students with learning disabilities. Since the IDEA requires that students have a transition plan, it is important that the plan be a realistic reflection of the rigors and realities of college life. Because P.L. 94-142 applies only to individuals with disabilities between the ages of 3 and 21 (or until high school graduation) who are receiving special education or related services, close coordination has not been maintained by the courts between the provisions in the IDEA and the regulations under Section 504 of the Rehabilitation Act of 1973, which is more typically applied to adults.

Section 504 of the Rehabilitation Act of 1973

Section 504 of the Rehabilitation Act of 1973 (P.L. 93-112) was the first federal civil rights legislation designed to protect the rights of individuals with disabilities. Unlike P.L. 94-142, which is very detailed in its provisions, Section 504 is brief in actual language, yet the regulation applies to both children and adults with disabilities from preschool through adult education. The statute states in part: "No otherwise qualified handicapped individual in the United States shall, solely by reason of his or her handicap, be excluded from participation in, be denied the benefits of, or be subjected to discrimination under any program or activity receiving federal financial assistance." (29 U.S.C. 794)

As stated, the regulation applies to persons with disabilities who are viewed as "otherwise qualified" to participate in and benefit from any program or activity that is receiving federal financial assistance. Recipients of federal funds may include state education agencies, elementary and secondary school systems, colleges and universities, libraries, vocational schools, and state vocational rehabilitation agencies. In order to be granted protections afforded to a person with a disability under Section 504, individuals must meet the following eligibility criteria: they must (a) have a physical or mental impairment that substantially limits one or more major life functions, (b) have a history of such impairment or (c) be regarded as having such an impairment, and (d) be deemed to be "otherwise qualified" despite the disability.

The specific classes of persons protected under Section 504 include anyone with a physical or mental impairment that substantially limits one or more major life activities, such as caring for oneself, performing manual tasks, walking, seeing, hearing, speaking, breathing, learning, or working. A disability means impediments to communication, mobility, learning, or earning a living (Percy, 1989). Determination of a "substantial limitation" could be documented by the history of a disability, or by the belief on the part of others that a person has such a disability. For example, a college student with a history of treatment for a psychiatric disability in junior high school would still be considered as disabled because he or she was previously identified and treated as "handicapped." A person born with a cleft palate or a burn victim is protected under Section 504 because he or she would be perceived by others as having a disability.

The intent of Congress in including both individuals with a record of an impairment and those who are regarded as having a disability as part of the definition was to extend the statutory protections beyond the actual existence of a disability. Heyward (1992) points out that these provisions address the subjective attitudes that often lead to discriminatory treatment. Disabilities covered under this regulation include, but are not limited to, the following:

Alcoholism	HIV-positive status
Attention deficit disorder	Mental retardation
Blindness or visual impairments	Multiple sclerosis
Cancer	Muscular dystrophy
Cerebral palsy	Orthopedic impairments
Contagious diseases	Perceptual handicaps such as dyslexia, developmental aphasia, and specific learning disabilities
Deafness or being hard of hearing	
Diabetes	
Drug addiction	Speech impairments
Epilepsy	Traumatic brain injury
Heart disease	Visual impairments

It should be noted that although alcoholism and drug addiction are considered "handicapping conditions," the 1978 amendments to the Rehabilitation Act stated that individuals with a history of alcohol or drug abuse come under the scope of Section 504 only if the individual is enrolled in a treatment program. An individual who is unable to perform the necessary duties of the job, or whose employment, by reason of current alcohol or drug use, would constitute a direct threat to the property or the safety of others, is not granted protection under Section 504. Because only rehabilitated or rehabilitating drug abusers and alcoholics are protected under Section 504, it has been held that an employer's mandatory drug or alcohol testing of employees does not violate the law, at least where safety is an integral part of the job in question (Tucker & Goldstein, 1991). Additional provisions regarding substance abuse disorders are discussed in relation to the ADA in a later section.

IMPLICATIONS OF FEDERAL LAWS

Impact of Section 504 on Elementary and Secondary Settings

The prevailing influence of P.L. 94-142 is reflected in the statutory provisions of Section 504. P.L. 94-142 requires that children with disabilities receive a free and appropriate education, to the greatest extent possible, in settings with nondisabled students (Percy, 1989). Heyward, Lawton, and Associates (1991c) observed that many people do not realize that Section 504 can have broad and sweeping implications for elementary and secondary settings that go beyond the limited reach of P.L. 94-142. For example, Section 504 would apply to a child with diabetes who does not require special education and can attend a regular class if he or she is provided with snacks at regular intervals and if school personnel are available to administer blood-sugar-level tests and injections of glucagon. Under these circumstances, the child can fully participate in the regular setting with "reasonable accommodations." Section 504 mandates not only that children with disabilities must be afforded access to an appropriate educational setting, but that they must be given the opportunity for full participation in nonacademic and extracurricular activities as well.

Impact of Section 504 on Postsecondary Settings

Subpart E of Section 504 is applicable to all postsecondary educational programs and activities that receive federal funding. Any college or university that receives federal financial assistance "may not, on the basis of handicap, exclude any qualified handicapped student from any course, course of study or other part of its education program or activity" (34 C.F.R. Sec. 104.43[c], 1989). College students with learning disabilities are clearly protected under Section 504 and must be granted an opportunity to compete with their nondisabled peers. Furthermore, these students may expect to be provided modifications or "academic adjustments" that will assist them in compensating for their learning disability (Rothstein, 1986).

Section 504 also stipulates that "a recipient shall operate each program or activity . . . so that the program or activity, when viewed in its entirety, is readily accessible to handicapped persons" (34 C.F.R. Sec. 104.22[a]). Not only does this provision apply to physical facilities on campuses, but it also covers all aspects of student life including admissions, recruitment, academic programs and adjustments, treatment of students, and nonacademic services (34 C.F.R. Sec. 104.42–104.44; 104.47). In brief, colleges and universities must be free from discrimination in their recruitment, admissions, and treatment of students. Treatment of students can take many forms, including access to housing, student health services, financial aid, athletic or cultural facilities, and campus transportation systems.

The impact of Section 504 on postsecondary settings is significant and extensive. Under its provisions, a college or university may *not:*

1. Limit the number of students with disabilities admitted.

2. Make preadmission inquiries as to whether or not an applicant has a disability.

3. Use admission tests or criteria that inadequately measure the academic level of applicants with disabilities, unless the measures used have been validated as a predictor of academic success in the education program or activity in question.

4. Give students with disabilities access to examinations that are not administered in the same frequency as tests given to nondisabled students. In addition, any admission test given to an applicant with a disability must be in an accessible location.

5. Give tests and examinations that do not accurately reflect the applicant's aptitude and achievement level without the interference of disability-related factors (e.g., providing additional time on exams or the use of a reader).

6. Limit access or excuse a student with a disability who is "otherwise qualified" from any course of study solely on the basis of his or her disability.

7. Counsel students with disabilities toward more restrictive careers than are recommended for nondisabled students. However, counselors may advise students with disabilities about strict licensing or certification requirements in a given profession.

8. Institute prohibitive rules that may adversely affect students with disabilities such as prohibiting the use of tape recorders or laptop computers in the classroom. Auxiliary aids, such as four-track tape recorders and hand-held spell-checkers, must be permitted when they are viewed as appropriate academic adjustments that will help to ensure full participation by students with disabilities.

9. Refuse to modify academic requirements that would afford qualified students with disabilities an opportunity for full educational participation. Permitting additional time to meet degree requirements or allowing a student to receive a course substitution for a foreign language requirement are examples of such actions.

10. Provide less financial assistance to students with disabilities than is provided to nondisabled students, or premise financial aid decisions on information that is discriminatory on the basis of disability, thereby limiting eligibility for assistance.

11. Provide housing to students with disabilities that is not equivalent and accessible and at the same cost as comparable housing available to nondisabled students.

12. Prohibit full participation in campus services or activities that are nonacademic in nature, such as physical education, athletics, or social organizations (adapted from Brinckerhoff, 1985, p. 93).

Under Section 504, institutions are required to respond by making modifications in academic requirements as necessary to ensure that such requirements do not discriminate or have the effect of discriminating against a qualified applicant with a disability (34 C.F.R. Sec. 104.44[a]). Many of the modifications or adjustments listed above are readily achievable without being too time-consuming or costly. It should be noted that the provision of accommodations for college students with disabilities need not guarantee them equal results or achievement; accommodations must merely afford them with an *equal opportunity* to achieve equal results (Biehl, 1978). Mangrum and Strichart (1988) further noted that the intent of the law is not to grant students access because of the disability, but simply to prevent exclusion because of it.

Potential Areas for Litigation Under Section 504

Within the postsecondary arena, it is likely that future litigation will be initiated in areas involving admission to a college and issues regarding the provision of reasonable accommodations to students after they are admitted. Scott (1990) noted that typical admission criteria are potentially discriminatory for applicants with learning disabilities. Standardized test scores, high school grade-point average, and class rank are not necessarily solid predictors of college success for students with learning disabilities. In order to be admitted, the student with a learning disability has to demonstrate that he or she can meet the academic and technical standards requisite for admission and participation in the college's programs or activities. Since many students with learning disabilities do not test well, and often have transcripts with great variability in performance levels, it is difficult for them to demonstrate that they are "otherwise qualified" for admission. Consequently, it is important for prospective college applicants to self-identify and to describe any inconsistencies in their transcript, such as course waivers or low Scholastic Aptitude Test scores, in a cover letter that accompanies their admission application. For example, if a college applicant was recently identified as having a learning disability in the junior or senior year of high school, the grades achieved prior to that time may not accurately reflect the student's true potential for college success. If the applicant self-identifies as having a learning disability on the application form, then he or she must be prepared to provide documentation of the disability for admission officers so that they can determine whether or not the applicant is otherwise qualified for admission. It is important to keep in mind that educational institutions may require reasonable physical qualifications for admission, but they are not obligated to eliminate requirements that are a necessary part of the curriculum (Heyward, Lawton, & Associates, 1990).

After being accepted to college, students with learning disabilities may request adjustments that will enable them to compete more fairly with their nondisabled peers. These accommodations are called *academic adjustments* in the educational arena and *reasonable accommodations* in the work setting. Academic adjustments may include adaptations in the manner in which specific courses are conducted, the use of auxiliary equipment, and modifications in degree requirements (Brinckerhoff, 1985). Requests for academic adjustments may be subjected to scrutiny as the institution weighs the merits of the request against such issues as a professor's right to academic freedom or concerns that the accommodation requested may substantially alter the program or be an undue administrative or financial burden. Specific examples of academic adjustments may include changing the length of time permitted for completion of a degree, substituting specific courses, administering an exam with additional time in a private room, or permitting a student to tape-record lectures. In addition to academic adjustments, auxiliary aids must also be provided as necessary to ensure that a student with a disability is "not denied the benefits of, excluded from participation in, or otherwise subjected to discrimination in any educational program or activity" because of the absence of auxiliary aids (34 Sec. 104.44 [d]). Typically, auxiliary aids for students with learning disabilities include access to taped textbooks, readers, computers, lecture notes, and other effective methods for making oral or written information available in an alternative form. It is the responsibility of the institution to be sure that the appropriate aids are available and are available at the proper time (*Handicapped Requirements Handbook*, 1985).

Given these regulations and the absence of funding mechanisms for Section 504 implementation, the following questions need to be posed: Who will pay for these accommodations provided to a college student with a disability? If vocational rehabilitation services are available to the student under Title I of the Rehabilitation Act, should the state department of rehabilitation, rather than the college or university, take the responsibility of paying for the accommodations? When monies are not available from the state department of rehabilitation or the student does not meet its service criteria, then is the college required to pay for the services and *essential* auxiliary aids? Future litigation will undoubtedly address some of these questions. Present interpretation of the law indicates that the costs associated with essential auxiliary aids or services cannot be passed on to the student, regardless of the student's ability to pay. For example, a student with a hearing impairment may not be asked to pay for the services of an interpreter. A student with a learning disability may not be asked to pay for the costs associated with taping textbooks, hiring a note taker, or hiring a proctor for an examination. Some institutions and vocational rehabilitation offices have agreed to share the expenses with students for more costly auxiliary aids that are determined to be augmentative in nature, but not essential, such as laptop computers or assistive listening devices.

It is important that postsecondary LD service providers have a thorough understanding of Section 504 so that they can be better prepared to address future areas of litigation on their campuses. Furthermore, if service providers are knowledgeable about the regulations under Section 504, they will have a solid basis for understanding many of the concepts, terminology, and analyses that will guide interpretation and application of the ADA (Bureau of National Affairs, 1990). The regulations promulgated under the act serve to clarify Section 504 case law with regard to individuals with disabilities and to resolve previously unanswered questions (Tucker & Goldstein, 1991). The following section may assist higher education personnel and LD service providers to achieve voluntary compliance with the requirements of the law as it pertains to individuals with disabilities.

The Americans with Disabilities Act

Senator Robert Dole commented upon the signing of the ADA by saying, "Forty-three million disabled Americans deserve to be brought into the mainstream of American life—to enjoy a meal at a restaurant, to see their favorite movie, to travel to a job on public transportation, to communicate by telephone, or to cheer at a ball game. The ADA's message to America is that inequality and prejudice are unacceptable. The ADA's important message to people with disabilities is that your time has come to live independently with dignity, to exercise your rights to participate in all aspects of American life" (Bureau of National Affairs, 1990).

The ADA was signed into law on July 26, 1990, as P.L. 101-336. Its intent is to provide equal opportunities for persons with disabilities. The ADA does not replace Section 504, but it draws much of its substantive framework from both Section 504 and the Civil Rights Restoration Act of 1987. The ADA expands the provisions in Section 504 to the private sector. Essentially, it prohibits discrimination against the same population and in many of the same areas as Section 504 but now includes areas that were not covered under Section 504, such as private businesses, nongovernment-funded accommodations, and services provided by state or local governments.

The definition of an individual with a disability under the ADA is identical to the definition previously outlined in Section 504. This individual is one who has a physical or mental impairment that substantially limits one or more major life activities, has a record of such an impairment, or is regarded as having such an impairment—even if he or she does not, in fact, have such an impairment. For example, an individual who is presently cured from cancer, but is still perceived by others as having a disability, is protected under the act. Specific learning disabilities are included as an impairment under the ADA, since learning is viewed as one of the major life activities. It is also unlawful to discriminate against an individual, whether disabled or not, because of a relationship or association with an individual with a known disability.

The most difficult challenge in establishing ADA eligibility appears to be for applicants with a history of substance abuse or alcoholism who claim to be rehabilitated (Bashook & Dockery, 1992). This is particularly true in the health care professions, where individuals who claim to be rehabilitated may have ready access to psychoactive substances. The law states that such individuals cannot be excluded from ADA eligibility if they have successfully completed a supervised drug rehabilitation program and are no longer engaging in illegal use of drugs or are otherwise rehabilitated successfully (Bashook & Dockery, 1992). There is a distinction made between the use of a controlled substance and addiction. A person who is addicted to drugs but is not actively using them is considered to be a person with a disability and is covered by law (Jarrow, 1992a).

The ADA is divided into five sections, or "titles," which are concerned with nondiscrimination on the basis of disability within a certain scope of activities. The five areas are:

Title I: Employment

Title II: Public services, including state and local government and transportation

Title III: Public accommodations

Title IV: Telecommunications relay services

Title V: Miscellaneous provisions

Key provisions from the U.S. Department of Justice publications (*ADA Requirements Handbook*, 1991) are briefly presented for each of the five title areas. Additional discussion addresses the implications these titles may have on individuals with learning disabilities in higher education settings.

Title I: Employment

Title I covers the area of employment. It specifies that an employer with 25 or more employees may not discriminate against an individual with a disability in hiring, promotion, benefits, and any other employment-related activity, if the person is qualified to perform the essential functions of the job, with or without accommodations. On July 26, 1994, the provision extends to employers with 15 to 24 employees. It should be pointed out that all higher education settings, both public and private, are bound by this title, except for entities that are wholly owned or operated by the U.S. government. As a result, the postsecondary service academies (e.g., the U.S. Naval Academy, Air Force Academy, and Military Academy) are not covered under ADA regulations (Jarrow, 1992b). Under the ADA, a prospective employee must be able to meet the employer's requirements for the job, such as level of education, employment experience, or licensure. Employers may ask about an applicant's ability to perform a job, but they cannot ask if someone has a disability or subject the applicant to tests that tend to screen out people with disabilities. An employer cannot require a prospective employee to take a medical examination before being offered a job. The employer cannot reject an employee because of information about a disability that was subsequently revealed by a medical examination, unless the reasons for rejection are job-related and necessary for the conduct of the business. The employer cannot refuse to hire an employee because the disability prevents the individual from performing duties that are not essential to the job. It should be noted that the ADA does not require an employer to hire an applicant with a disability over other applicants merely because the person has a disability. It only prohibits discrimination on the basis of a disability.

Once an individual with a disability is hired, the employer is required to provide "reasonable accommodation" in the workplace. This may include job restructuring, part-time or modified work schedules, modification of exams or training materials, taped texts, provision for readers or interpreters, and modification of equipment so that it is readily accessible. The costs associated with the needed accommodations are assumed by the employer. However, employers need not provide accommodations that are of a personal nature or that impose an "undue hardship" on business operations. An undue hardship is defined as "an action requiring significant difficulty or expense" when it is considered in light of a variety of factors, which include the nature and cost of the accommodation in relation to the size, resources, nature, and structure of the employer's operation. If the cost of the needed accommodation would be an undue hardship, then the employee must be given the choice of providing the accommodation or paying for the portion of the accommodation that causes the undue hardship.

In general, a larger employer would be expected to make accommodations requiring greater effort or expense than would be required of a smaller employer. However, an employer may require that applicants or employees not pose a "direct threat" to the health and safety of themselves or other persons. Jarrow (1992a) stated that a direct threat must include evidence that there is a significant risk of substantial harm to the individual or others that cannot be eliminated or reduced by reasonable accommodation. The direct threat must be shown to be real and must be based on present abilities, not conjecture about future circumstances. Such determinations must be made on an individual basis in light of reasonable medical judgment.

It is unlawful for an employer to retaliate against an employee for asserting his or her rights under the ADA. Data from several studies conducted by federal agencies indicated that only 22% of employees with disabilities need accommodations at the work site at all. In another study, less than one-quarter of all employees with disabilities needed accommodations and nearly 70% of such accommodations cost less than $500 per disabled employee (Eastern Paralyzed Veterans Association, 1991, p. 5).

Title II: Public Services and Transportation

Title II is divided into two subparts. Subpart A requires that state and local governmental entities and programs be accessible to individuals with disabilities and Subpart B addresses transportation services provided to the general public. Subpart A of the act also requires institutions covered under Section 504 to conduct a self-evaluation plan. In a higher education setting, a self-evaluation plan must have been conducted by January 26, 1993. The purpose of the plan is to determine what programs or activities on campus need to be made accessible and to establish a time frame for change (up to 3 years). If modification is necessary, the institution must develop a transition plan. If modification is not going to occur, then individuals with disabilities must be provided with alternative ways to effectively access the program. Institutions already covered under Section 504 that have previously conducted a self-evaluation need only do another self-evaluation that reflects any changes in policies and procedures since the initial evaluation (56 Fed Reg. 35718 [1991]). However, the Department of Justice strongly encourages public entities to review their full range of programs and services, since most Section 504 self-evaluations were conducted more than a dozen years ago and few have been monitored on an ongoing basis. For specific suggestions on how to conduct a self-evaluation plan in a postsecondary setting, readers are encouraged to consult *Title by Title—The ADA's Impact on Postsecondary Education* (Jarrow, 1992b).

Subpart B requires public entities that purchase or lease new buses, rail cars, or other vehicles to ensure that those vehicles are accessible to and usable by individuals with disabilities, including people in wheelchairs. These vehicles must be equipped with lifts, ramps, and wheelchair spaces or special seats unless the carrier can show that such equipment is unavailable despite its good-faith efforts to locate it (Bureau of National Affairs, 1990). All new public-transit buses must be accessible to individuals with disabilities. Transit authorities must provide comparable paratransit or other special transportation services to individuals with disabilities who cannot use fixed-route bus services, unless an undue burden would result. Existing rail systems must have one accessible car per train by July 26, 1995. All new cars and new bus and train stations must also be accessible. Key stations in rapid, light, and commuter rail systems must be made accessible by July 26, 1993, with extensions up to 20 years for commuter rail (30 years for rapid and light rail). All existing Amtrak stations must be accessible by July 26, 2010. The ADA also includes commercial aircraft that are covered by the Air Carriers Access Act.

Title III: Public Accommodations

This title ensures that goods, services, privileges, advantages, or facilities of any public place be offered "in the most integrated setting appropriate to the needs of the individual," except when the individual poses a direct threat to the health or safety of other people (*ADA Requirements Handbook*, 1991, p. 2). Private entities such as restaurants, hotels, retail stores, places of education, parks and zoos, and recreation sites such as bowling alleys, health clubs, or golf courses may not discriminate against individuals with disabilities. Private institutions of higher education are clearly covered under the protections of Title III unless they are wholly owned and operated by a religious organization. This exemption applies to entities controlled or operated by religious organizations, such as day care centers or nursing homes, that are open to the public. Auxiliary aids and services must be provided to individuals with disabilities, unless an "undue burden" would result. "Undue burdens" may include access to qualified interpreters, readers, assistive listening devices, audio recordings, large-print materials, or speech synthesizers, or the modification of equipment. In a postsecondary setting, attendant care, personal readers, specialized equipment for independent-study purposes, or individually prescribed devices such as wheelchairs or hearing aids would not need to be provided by the institution.

As a result of the ADA, all new construction and alterations of existing facilities must be accessible. Physical barriers in existing facilities must be removed, if removal is "readily achievable." "Readily achievable" means "easily accomplishable and able to be carried out without much difficulty or expense" (*ADA Requirements Handbook*, 1991, p. 5). Examples include simple ramping of a few steps, the installation of grab bars, lowering of telephones, or other modest adjustments. Jarrow (1992b) stated that barrier removal is not just a one-time obligation. Institutions are required to engage in readily achievable barrier removal whenever and wherever instances of architectural, communication, or transportation barriers are identified. If barrier removal is not readily achievable, institutions must make the program and activities available through alternative methods to guarantee full participation by individuals with disabilities.

One of the most delicate issues faced by postsecondary service providers involves the licensure of students with disabilities for the professions. Title II and Title III of the ADA contain sections that pertain to testing, licensing, and certification that may be particularly relevant to postsecondary service providers. Both state and local governments, as well as private entities, are barred from discriminating against qualified individuals with disabilities in licensing and certification programs. The ADA requires examinations (and the application process leading to examination) for licensure and certification to be accessible to persons with disabilities, regardless of who is doing the actual test administration. The agency administering the exam must provide any modifications or auxiliary aids at no expense to the test taker. The law also stipulates that the same accommodation may be used by individuals with different disabilities and that individuals with the same disability may need different accommodations (Jarrow, 1992b). If the test is administered by a state or local government, discrimination on the basis of disabilities is prohibited under Title II; if it is administered by a private entity, it is covered by Title III. In preparing the final rules for implementation of the ADA, the Department of Justice, the enforcement authority for Titles II and III, made the following point:

> Some commenters who provide examinations for licensing or certification for particular occupations or professions urged that they be permitted to refuse to provide modifications or aids to persons seeking to take the examinations if those individuals, because of their disabilities, would be unable to perform the essential functions of the profession or occupation for which the examination is given, or unless the disability is reasonably determined in advance as not being an obstacle to certification. The Department (of Justice) has not changed its rule based on this comment. An examination is one stage of a licensing or certification process. An individual should not be barred from attempting to pass that stage of the process merely because he or she might be unable to meet other requirements of the process. (Department of Justice, as cited in King & Jarrow, 1991, pp. 3–4)

The ADA regulations offer two standards for licensing boards to use in decisions about accommodations for eligible board candidates. One standard defines the limit of accommodations to allow boards to reject an examination accommodation request if it will result in an undue burden to the board because of additional expense and effort in creating and/or administering the modified examination. The second standard allows boards to reject an accommodation if it will fundamentally alter the measurement of skills or knowledge that the examination was designed to measure (Americans with Disabilities Act, 1990, Sec. 309 [b][3]).

Title IV: Telecommunications Relay Services

Title IV requires that telecommunications services be made accessible to persons with hearing and speech impairments. It states that companies offering telephone service to the general public must offer telephone relay services to individuals who use telecommunications devices for the deaf (TDDs) or similar devices. These services permit people with hearing or speech impairments to communicate with hearing individuals by using TDDs or other nonvoice terminal devices and by providing operators who relay messages between TDD users and nonusers (Bureau of National Affairs, 1990). The operator relay services must be available 24 hours a day, 7 days a week, by operators who will maintain the confidentiality of the messages, and users of the services are to pay functionally equivalent rates for voice-communication services. All public service announcements produced or funded in whole or in part with federal money must include closed captioning for viewers who are deaf.

Title V: Miscellaneous Provisions

Title V contains miscellaneous provisions that apply to all of the other titles and ensure that the ADA does not limit or invalidate other federal or state laws that provide equal or greater protection for the rights of individuals with disabilities. However, states are subject to the provisions of the ADA, and courts may provide the same remedies against a state as against any other private or public entity (Bureau of National Affairs, 1990).

The ADA's Impact on College Campuses

It is anticipated that the ADA will bring about several changes in the higher education setting. Certainly the passage of the act is resulting in an increase in attention given to instructional and programmatic access for students with disabilities, and it is most likely to result in increasing numbers of students with disabilities choosing to seek higher education. Their increased participation in higher education will help focus on the rights of college students with disabilities and will renew the focus on disability access in general (Jarrow, 1991).

Since the ADA increases access to employment, public accommodations, transportation, and telecommunications, it will undoubtedly have a ripple effect in expanding opportunities for postsecondary students with disabilities. The ADA should also help to foster a qualified pool of college-educated workers who can assist in alleviating the anticipated labor shortages in the next decade. It is likely that disability service providers on college campuses will become key resource personnel concerning public accommodations and ADA implementation issues both on and off campus. The new law probably does not add or change much of what is required under Section 504 in higher education settings, but its explicit requirement that structural barriers be removed in all existing public facilities, such as student unions, athletic arenas, and museums on college campuses, may require changes at some institutions (Rothstein, 1991). Since the ADA clarifies employment requirements for private colleges and reiterates the prohibition against discrimination by public entities such as state colleges and universities, it may ultimately result in increased costs for postsecondary institutions (Jarrow, 1991).

Rothstein (1991) pointed out that, for the most part, the law does not mandate many changes for colleges or universities but it has heightened disabled people's awareness of their rights, thus increasing the likelihood of litigation under both statutes. She expanded on this point by noting that "many colleges have probably been violating Section 504 for years by not removing architectural barriers, or by not providing accommodations such as reduced course loads or modifications of examinations in appropriate situations" (p. B10). Rothstein concluded that institutions have escaped being sued in the past, but that those days are probably over with the passage of the ADA.

College students with learning disabilities may find the provisions of the ADA comforting as they look for additional legal backing for accommodation requests in coursework, clinical internships, or practicums. Potential barriers to higher education for students with learning disabilities are often programmatic in nature and may include foreign language or mathematics requirements or faculty members who try to prohibit use of auxiliary aids in the classroom. Classroom settings that are noisy or visually distracting may be particularly troublesome to students with learning disabilities and

ADDs. Rigid requirements that prohibit time extensions or alternative test formats for examinations may be discriminatory for students with visual-processing deficits. Scott (1990) pointed out that some components of the traditional class format of lecturing, reading, and writing may pose great difficulties for a student with a learning disability. Course adaptations that reach the same intellectual and skill goals should be considered. Since the ADA does not permit exclusion of persons with disabilities on the basis of disability factors, these students may not be excluded from any program or activity that is open to the general student population. Jarrow (1992a) observed that an institution may not decide to limit admission to 25 students with learning disabilities each year because they have only set aside the resources to provide support to that number of students. The institution may develop special programs for students with learning disabilities and may limit enrollment, as long as students who do not qualify for the program receive nondiscriminatory consideration for admission and ultimately receive all mandated support services after admission.

Rothstein (1991) stated that in light of both the ADA and recent litigation under Section 504, every institution should give a high priority to setting up a campus committee to evaluate current policies and practices for dealing with people with disabilities and to consider what new responsibilities the campus may have. This is particularly true for students with learning disabilities who may need the protection of campus-wide policies that allow for flexibility in the use of the curriculum and in instructional practices. She added that failure to make mandated changes could result in significant financial liability, costly litigation, loss of public image, and, most important, loss of the valuable contributions that individuals with disabilities can make to any academic community.

In closing, the ADA has helped to expand public awareness of disability issues both on and off campus. It reinforces the provisions set forth in the Rehabilitation Act and it gives service providers additional clout with faculty and administrators when they seek to secure necessary academic adjustments for students in their coursework. For many employers, the ADA opens the door to an expanding work force and provides at least a third layer of enforcement with respect to disability discrimination (*ADA Requirements Handbook*, 1991).

COMPARING THE IDEA, SECTION 504, AND THE ADA: IMPLICATIONS FOR HIGHER EDUCATION

The IDEA and Section 504

The IDEA and Section 504 of the Rehabilitation Act complement each other in a variety of ways to assure equal access to educational opportunities. For example, most of the major principles of due process are embodied in P.L. 94-142 and are clearly presented in Section 504 (Ballard et al., 1987). However, it should be noted that P.L. 94-142 is very precise in its regulations and offers few opportunities for broader interpretation. Table 2.1 provides a comprehensive overview comparing the IDEA, Section 504, and the ADA in a number of areas.

The definition of "qualified handicapped individuals" is much narrower under the IDEA, which includes a specific listing of the disabilities covered under the act. Under the IDEA, students from 3 to 21 years of age are eligible for services. Section 504 regulations do not refer to a specific age group per se, but to public elementary, secondary, and postsecondary education. Section 504 is deliberately broad, resulting in more children being referred for services. For example, children with AIDS or orthopedic impairments are protected under Section 504 but may not be viewed as "educationally handicapped," which would allow them to receive special education services under the IDEA. For a student to be served under the IDEA, he or she "must be of an age during which non-handicapped persons are provided services or be of an age during which it is mandatory under state law to provide such services to a handicapped person" (Maroldo, 1991). Although the definition of an "appropriate education" under the IDEA is tightly bound to the need for special education services, Section 504 is not restricted just to special education. Section 504 also provides that an appropriate education may consist of an education in regular classes or an education in regular classes with the use of supplementary aids and services (34 C.F.R. Section 104.33). A student with a disability that requires only related services may be eligible for protections under Section 504, but may not be eligible for services under the IDEA. The IDEA states that related services may not be provided without special education, whereas Section 504 permits the provision of related services to a student who is not eligible for special education ("Section 504 of the Rehabilitation Act," 1991).

The IDEA is primarily concerned with issues in the elementary and secondary arena and has no impact on postsecondary service delivery. Unlike the IDEA, Section 504 imposes no obligation on postsecondary institutions to provide a free appropriate education to all qualified handicapped individuals. Section 504 simply states that institutions may not discriminate against "qualified handicapped persons" (Heyward, Lawton, & Associates, 1992a). Consequently, Section 504 regulations are quite different in their specifications regarding identification, assessment, and service delivery. P.L. 94-142 stipulates that the LEA is responsible for identifying, assessing, and serving students with disabilities at no cost to the parent. In contrast, college students with learning disabilities have the responsibility to self-identify by notifying the appropriate institutional representative or LD service provider of their disability. The student also has the responsibility for providing documentation of the learning disability and for working with the LD service provider to determine what academic adjustments may be necessary to compensate for the learning disability (Brinckerhoff, et al., 1992). Students who were not actively involved in decision making under P.L. 94-142 often find themselves ill-prepared for assuming their new responsibilities under Section 504, such as contacting the professor and making arrangements for accommodations independently. Jarrow (1992a) emphasized that both the request for accommodation and the provision of support must be "appropriate and timely and the institution is not required to jump through hoops" to meet the needs of students who fail to give adequate notice of their accommodation needs.

Scott (1991) also pointed out that one major difference between the IDEA and Section 504 concerns the manner in which accommodations are secured in higher education settings. Support services and auxiliary aids are mandated requirements under the IDEA. In higher education, support services and auxiliary aids are viewed as an array of options that may or may not be utilized by students with disabilities. Jarrow (1991) stated that Section 504 requires students with disabilities to receive appropriate accommodations upon request. However, if students choose not to identify themselves as disabled, the institution is under no obligation to search them out and offer support. Section 504 does not impose any obligation on colleges to admit and rehabilitate students with disabilities who are not otherwise qualified, or to make major changes in an academic program in order to accommodate a student with a disability.

TABLE 2.1. Comparisons Between the IDEA, Section 504, and the ADA

	The IDEA	Section 504	The ADA
Mission	To provide a free, appropriate, public education (FAPE) in the least restrictive environment.	To provide persons with disabilities, to the maximum extent possible, the opportunity to be fully integrated into mainstream American life.	To provide all persons with disabilities broader coverage than Section 504 in all aspects of discrimination law.
Scope	Applies to public schools.	Applies to any program or activity that is receiving federal financial assistance.	Applies to public or private employment, transportation, accommodations, and telecommunications regardless of whether federal funding is received.
Coverage	Only those who are educationally disabled, in that they require special education services, ages 3–21 years.	All qualified persons with disabilities regardless of whether special education services are required in public elementary, secondary, or postsecondary settings.	All qualified persons with disabilities, and qualified nondisabled persons related to or associated with a person with a disability.
Disability Defined	A listing of disabilities is provided in the act, including specific learning disabilities.	No listing of disabilities provided, but inclusionary criteria of any physical or mental impairment that substantially limits one or more major life activities, having a record of such an impairment, or being regarded as having an impairment.	No listing of disabilities provided. Same criteria as found in Section 504. HIV status and contagious and noncontagious diseases recently included.

Identification Process	Responsibility of school district to identify through "Child Find" and evaluate at no expense to parent or individual.	Responsibility of individual with the disability to self-identify and to provide documentation. Cost of the evaluation must be assumed by the individual, not the institution.	Same as Section 504.
Service Delivery	Special education services and auxiliary aids must be mandated by Child Study Team and stipulated in the Individualized Education Program.	Services, auxiliary aids, and academic adjustments may be provided in the regular education setting. Arranged for by the special education coordinator or disabled student services provider.	Services, auxiliary aids, and accommodations arranged for by the designated ADA coordinator. Requires that accommodations do not pose an "undue hardship" to employers.
Funding	Federal funds are conditional to compliance with IDEA regulations.	No authorization for funding attached to this Civil Rights statute.	Same as Section 504.
Enforcement Agency	Office of Special Education and Rehabilitative Services in U.S. Department of Education.	The Office for Civil Rights (OCR) in the U.S. Department of Education.	Primarily the U.S. Department of Justice, in conjunction with the Equal Employment Opportunity Commission and Federal Communications Commission. May overlap with OCR.
Remedies	Reimbursement by district of school-related expenses is available to parents of children with disabilities to ensure a FAPE.	A private individual may sue a recipient of federal financial assistance to ensure compliance with Section 504.	Same as Section 504 with monetary damages up to $50,000 for the first violation. Attorney fees and litigation expenses are also recoverable.

Adapted from *Handicapped Requirements Handbook*, January 1993, Washington, DC: Thompson Publishing Group. Adapted with permission.

Heyward, Lawton, and Associates (1991a) pointed out that one of the most common mistakes made at the elementary and secondary levels is assuming that a student who is not entitled to protections under the IDEA is also not protected under Section 504. In fact, many states or school districts have sought to avoid complying with Section 504 by arguing that the IDEA is the exclusive remedy for those alleging disability discrimination in the elementary and secondary arena. School districts must comply with both Section 504 and the IDEA. This was substantiated under a congressional action in 1986 with the Handicapped Children's Protection Act of 1986 (P.L. 99-372, 20 U.S.C. § 1415 [1986]), which indicates that all the rights, protections, or remedies provided under Section 504 and other federal statutes are also available to students covered by P.L. 94-142. The 11th Circuit Court of Appeals recently rejected the argument of a school district that the department of education does not have jurisdiction to conduct investigations under Section 504 and the IDEA (Heyward, Lawton, & Associates, 1991a). The school district lost its federal funding in September 1990 for refusing to comply with the court of appeals' decision (*Rogers v. Bennett*, 1989).

Another major difference between the IDEA and Section 504 concerns the availability of supportive personnel. Students with learning disabilities in elementary and secondary schools are often surrounded by a team of special educators, speech and language specialists, counselors, and teachers. Institutions of higher education are not required to provide special programs and few higher education settings have the luxury of providing comprehensive support services to students with learning disabilities (Brinckerhoff, 1991). Consequently, students entering college for the first time must learn the differences between these two pieces of legislation so they can act responsibly and effectively self-advocate for the services they need.

Section 504 states that postsecondary institutions cannot discriminate on the basis of disability, but it does not detail what needs to be accomplished for an individual to achieve meaningful access. Heyward, Lawton, and Associates (1991b, p. 2) noted that in seeking to interpret the "reasonable accommodation standard" under the Rehabilitation Act, courts have noted that "no standard for determining the reasonableness of an accommodation has been formulated" (*Dexler v. Tisch*, 1987). The determination of what academic adjustments are appropriate must be made on an individual case-by-case basis and are not typically included in a formal document such as an

IEP. At the postsecondary level, testing accommodations or other selected academic adjustments should provide the institution with a measure of the students' knowledge and skills that is equivalent, or at least similar, to those used to assess all other students. It is important to keep in mind that the faculty members' right to academic freedom may not outweigh the students' right to a needed accommodation (King & Jarrow, 1991). The following list includes a variety of considerations used in determining action under Section 504 in postsecondary settings:

1. Is the institution public or otherwise covered by state accessibility or accommodation statutes?

2. Is the institution a recipient of federal funds?

3. Does the applicant have a "handicapping condition" that is protected under Section 504?

4. Is the applicant "otherwise qualified" for admission? Despite the disability, are the academic and technical standards for admission to the institution being met?

5. Once admitted, does the proposed accommodation represent an appropriate academic adjustment?

   a. Can the student perform the essential functions that the program requires?

   b. If not, would there need to be a fundamental change in an essential element of the program in order to accommodate the student?

   c. Does the proposed accommodation pose an "undue hardship" on the institution?

   d. Does the proposed accommodation pose patient health or safety concerns to others?

The IDEA, the ADA, and Section 504

As noted in Table 2.1, unlike the IDEA, Section 504 and the ADA are civil rights statutes that merely include some general compliance guidelines. They contain no authorization for funding. Heyward,

Lawton, and Associates (1990) aptly pointed out that both Section 504 and the ADA do not provide a "monetary carrot" like the IDEA; instead, compliance is dictated by a "punitive stick"—that is, if an institution does not comply with the law, federal financial assistance will be lost. Rothstein (1991) noted that the major difference between the ADA and Section 504 is that the ADA is broader in its application and covers more programs and services than Section 504. Under Section 504, no specific mention is made regarding the eligibility for disability-related support services of persons with temporary disabilities. Several case law interpretations have indicated that persons with temporary disabilities are not covered under Section 504 (Jarrow, 1992b). The Department of Justice has said that coverage of a person with a temporary impairment is determined by whether or not the impairment substantially limits one or more major life activities. Kincaid (1992) pointed out that the ADA fills in some of the gaps in Section 504 by offering more sweeping protections, especially in the areas of the latest assistive technology. For example, it protects members of the general public with disabilities who attend activities at an educational facility, even if they are not employees or enrolled as students. The ADA regulations specifically mention a variety of auxiliary aids and services not previously cited in Section 504. These may include qualified interpreters, computer-aided transcription devices, telephone headset amplifiers, closed-caption decoders, and voice-activated computers.

Another critical difference between the IDEA, Section 504, and the ADA concerns enforcement and procedures for addressing alleged discrimination claims. The Office for Civil Rights (OCR) within the Department of Education is charged with enforcing Section 504 and OSERS is the agency charged with enforcing the IDEA. Depending on the title, the ADA is enforced both publicly and privately by the Department of Justice or the Equal Employment Opportunity Commission (EEOC). The U.S. attorney general has the authority to institute lawsuits when there is "reasonable cause" to believe that "any person or group of persons is engaged in a pattern or practice of discriminating against individuals with disabilities, or to institute a suit when any person or group of persons has been discriminated against under (Title III) and such discrimination raises an issue of general public importance" (ADA Sec 308 [b] [1] [B], 43 USCA).

Under Section 504, if an applicant believes that he or she has been discriminated against on the basis of disability in a program that is receiving federal financial assistance, a complaint can be filed with the OCR through the regional office that services the state in which the discrimination allegedly took place (Appendix A). The complaint must be in writing and filed within 180 days of the date the alleged discrimination occurred. The complaint should be specific in its scope; otherwise, a simple complaint investigation can turn into an overall compliance review visit ("Section 504 of the Rehabilitation Act,"1991). An extension for filing may be granted by the regional OCR director for good cause. The letter of complaint must be signed and should explain who was discriminated against, by whom or by what institution, when the discrimination took place, who was harmed, and who can be contacted for further information about the alleged discriminatory act. The OCR regional office may be contacted for assistance in preparing a complaint. Kincaid (1992) observed that recently, the Department of Justice advised the OCR that "it was turning over ADA complaints filed against institutions of higher education to OCR for enforcement purposes" (p. 4).

The ADA adopts all of the power, remedies, and procedures in Title VII of the Civil Rights Act of 1964. These provisions require that complainants file charges with the EEOC, the enforcement agency for the law. The EEOC, the attorney general, and the Office of Federal Contract Compliance Programs are required to issue regulations coordinating procedures under the Rehabilitation Act and the ADA in order to eliminate duplication of effort and inconsistent or conflicting standards under the two laws (Bureau of National Affairs, 1990). Complainants must file charges of alleged discrimination with the EEOC within 180 days of the alleged discriminatory act, or within 300 days in states with approved enforcement agencies. The EEOC has 180 days after a charge has been filed to investigate and to sue the employer or issue a right-to-sue letter to the complainant. The complainant then has 90 days to file a lawsuit. The EEOC also has a referral agreement with the OCR. Under the ADA, Title II may be enforced by the attorney general or by private lawsuit. The attorney general must investigate complaints and undertake compliance reviews. Title III's remedies and procedures are identical to those outlined above in the section on Title II of the Civil Rights Act of 1964. Courts may also order monetary damages to aggrieved persons and may seek civil penalties of up to $50,000 for a first violation and $100,000 for subsequent violations (Bureau of National Affairs, 1990).

Despite these three substantive pieces of legislation, within the educational arena, it is most likely that future litigation will be initiated in one or more of the following areas: (a) admission to a college or university, (b) provision of reasonable accommodations for college students with disabilities, and (c) access to nonacademic programs or services at a college or university (Tucker & Goldstein, 1991). These three areas have been fertile ground for courtroom debate during the last few years and certainly continue to attract the interest of advocates, consumers, and service providers. Section 504 is the launch pad and testing ground for many of the concepts and principles that have developed in disability nondiscrimination law since 1973 (Bureau of National Affairs, 1990).

Before leaving the area of legislation, some interesting comparisons between the Canadian and American viewpoints on serving students with learning disabilities will be drawn. Following the section on Canadian perspectives, five U.S. court cases will be highlighted that have direct implications for serving college students with learning disabilities.

THE CANADIAN PERSPECTIVE

Kendall and Wong (1987) reviewed Canadian policies related to learning disabilities and found that children with learning disabilities comprised 4.4% of the school population. Although hard data are lacking at the postsecondary level, a 1987 survey by the Learning Disabilities Association of Canada of services available at the postsecondary level indicated that of the 122 colleges and universities that responded to the survey, over 85% had "made some allowances and accommodations" for students with learning disabilities (Golick, 1988, p. 9). However, an analysis of the responses revealed a lack of understanding of the problems of these students. For example, only 18% of the respondents had a written definition and only 16% had an official policy in place, and a few institutions confused learning disabilities with a physical disability or mental retardation (Learning Disabilities Association of Canada, 1988). Wiener and Siegel (1992) noted that services for adults with learning disabilities are at a preliminary stage in most of Canada. Although many universities and community colleges have special needs offices, until recently the focus of these offices has been to provide accommodation for students with some sort of physical disability.

Ontario was one of the first if not the only province to receive special funding for providing special services in a higher education setting. As a result, these programs have expanded rapidly in Ontario, but according to Wiener and Siegel (1992), expansion has been so rapid that it has been difficult to find appropriately trained leaders and front-line personnel to meet these demands. Some provincial governments have recently provided funding for special projects for services at specific universities or colleges, but special purpose funding has not been made available to all institutions. Some provinces have provided funds to community colleges but not to universities (e.g., Quebec), or to universities but not to colleges (e.g., Manitoba). In other provinces (e.g., New Brunswick, Saskatchewan, Prince Edward Island) there are no special funding mechanisms in place. In general, colleges tend to be funded through provincial government departments of education and/or advanced education, whereas universities are really quite autonomous although they may receive grants from provincial governments and money from supplemental tuition fees (J. Backman, personal communication, March 26, 1993). It should also be pointed out that 2-year colleges in Canada are different from community colleges in the United States. In Canada, the primary focus of 2-year colleges is on teaching students specific occupational, vocational, or trade skills as opposed to providing a liberal arts curriculum. As a result, the two settings often attract very different student clientele and differences in funding patterns ultimately effect policy development and procedures for serving students with learning disabilities.

Like their American counterparts, Canadians have made strides in the field of special education in ensuring equal educational opportunities to students with learning disabilities. The most notable achievement in furthering this end was the passage of the Canadian Charter of Rights and Freedoms in 1982. The Charter is a constitutional act that guarantees Canadians with disabilities some fundamental rights similar to those afforded under Section 504 of the Rehabilitation Act. In fact, the passage of Section 504 in the United States was a major impetus behind the passage of the charter in Canada. During the early 1980s, members of provincial associations were key players in drafting and implementing mandatory special education legislation (Wiener & Siegel, 1992).

The Canadian Charter is the supreme law of Canada and it governs over all areas of government action and policy.

Wiener and Siegel (1992, p. 344) noted that the equality provision in Section 15 of the Charter states: "Every individual is equal before and under the law and has the right to the equal protection and equal benefit of the law without discrimination, and in particular, without discrimination based on . . . mental or physical disability."

Under Section 15, Canadians are guaranteed four basic rights:

1. The right to equality before the law—that is, the law is to be impartially administered and applied;

2. The right to equality under the law—that is, the right to equality in respect to the substance of the law;

3. The right to equal protection under the law—that is, the right to equality of opportunity and equality of results;

4. The right to equal benefit of the law—that is, the right to unequal distribution of resources in the case of unequal need (Henteleff, 1990, p. 1).

Section 15 of the Charter also prohibits public universities, colleges, and employers from discriminating against students and employees with learning disabilities and requires these institutions to provide reasonable accommodations for students and employees with disabilities. Section 15 further stipulates that basic rights shall be enjoyed without discrimination. Discrimination has been defined by the Supreme Court of Canada as being "the withholding or limiting of access from individuals of the opportunities, benefits and advantages available to other members of society" (Henteleff, 1991, p. 7). Rulings of the court have determined unequivocally that individuals who are disadvantaged in a social, political, and legal sense are covered under Section 15. Henteleff (1990) believed that students with learning disabilities are clearly a group who are socially, legally, and politically vulnerable; by virtue of several recent Supreme Court decisions, he has determined that "they would fall within the ambit of Section 15" (p. 7). In his keynote address to the LDAC, Henteleff (1990, p. 8) stated:

> Provincial Governments must pay immediate heed to the clear directions given by the Charter of Rights and Freedoms, as determined by the most recent judgments of the Supreme Court of Canada and

other high courts in our land. These decisions give me great confidence that if litigation must be the means to assure compliance with the Charter of Rights and Freedoms, then sooner than they may think the provincial Governments and school boards will be compelled to provide to learning disabled children an education specifically related to individual needs. It is their duty to act now and avoid destructive confrontation which can only serve to widen the gulf between the governing and the governed.

It is important to note that public education is exclusively a matter that is determined within each province. As a result, legislation, policies, and procedures for serving students with disabilities vary from province to province. According to Poirier, Goguen, and Leslie (1988), all but three provinces have mandatory special education legislation. The three provinces without such legislation are Prince Edward Island, Alberta, and British Columbia. In these provinces, special education is not yet mandatory. Although precedents under the federal charter suggest that exceptional children in these provinces do have a right to an education and parents to due process, the charter does not set, and the courts have not required, specific standards for that education (Wiener & Siegel, 1992). Only in Manitoba and Quebec is the right to an education universal.

Nova Scotia and some other provinces have recently expanded upon the rights guaranteed under the charter. The Human Rights Act of 1991 includes a provision for individuals with learning disabilities. This new act is particularly important because it provides, for the first time, specific protection for individuals with learning disabilities (Trainor, 1992). The definition used in the act is also deliberately broad in its coverage so that it can include all forms of learning disabilities. It states that "a learning disability or a dysfunction in one or more of the processes involved in understanding or using symbols or spoken language" qualifies for the protections under the Human Rights Act (Trainor, 1992, p. 6). Another feature of the Human Rights Act, as with Section 504, is that if someone is "perceived" to have a mental disability, including a learning disability, and discrimination results from that perception, whether it is intended or not, the individual is still protected under the act. In general, the Human Rights Act (HRA) covers the same things in the same way as the Charter. The Human Rights Act was influenced by the Charter but its scope is broader and it applies to public and private relationships. For example, the HRA covers private activities and university actions. Although these actions by the Nova Scotian government are very important because they may ultimately help to shape educational policy throughout Canada, the actual impact of this human rights legislation on individuals with learning disabilities remains to be seen.

RELEVANT COURT CASES IN THE UNITED STATES

Determining What Is "Otherwise Qualified"

The first case addresses the issue of what constitutes "otherwise qualified." In *Southeastern Community College v. Davis* (1979), a student with a hearing impairment was denied admission to a nurses' training program because the college held that she could not safely participate in the clinical training program that was required. Her application was rejected based on the belief that her hearing disability made it impossible for her to safely participate in the normal clinical training program and care for patients. On the basis of the audiologist's report, the court held that the respondent was not an "otherwise qualified" student since her performance was dependent on lipreading, which was not sufficient in clinical settings that might necessitate the use of a surgical mask. Since lipreading would not be possible in an operating room setting, she was not deemed to be "otherwise qualified" for the program. Davis suggested that a reasonable accommodation would be to allow her to substitute additional academic courses for the clinical component or to provide her with the individual attention of a nursing instructor. The case was initially reviewed by the Federal District Court, then was reviewed by the Fourth Circuit Court of Appeals. Clerc (1985) observed that the Court of Appeals ruled in favor of the college by stating that an institution cannot be expected to substantially alter admissions requirements on the basis of the disability. The court concluded that "Section 504 imposes no requirement upon an educational institution to lower or to effect substantial modifications of standards to accommodate a handicapped person" (pp. 410–412).

The intent of Section 504 is not to require postsecondary institutions to disregard program requirements for individuals with disabilities; it simply requires decisions to be based on actual abilities, rather than on the prejudicial assumption that people with handicaps are in all respects less capable than others (case brief 89-1607). Assuming that the cost of the requested accommodations is not unduly burdensome and the accommodations do not require a fundamental alteration of any essential aspects of the program, postsecondary institutions are legally required to provide these services (Rothstein, 1990). If, however, the institution can demonstrate that academic adjustments requested by the student infringe on a core program of instruction or are directly related to licensing requirements, such actions may not be viewed as discriminatory. Clerc (1985) noted that each program needs to define the physical and technical requirements that students must demonstrate for successful program completion. This point is pertinent to college students with learning disabilities who may possess the physical requirements necessary for a degree but who, because of their learning disabilities, may not have the technical skills to complete a course of study. For example, a student with a learning disability who is enrolled in a physical therapy program may possess the physical skills requisite for the course of study but may have difficulty remembering the sequential steps in a given therapy regimen even with reasonable accommodations. Certainly future litigation will seek to resolve this issue further for individuals with hidden disabilities. The scope of Section 504 in higher education was further defined in *Grove City v. Bell* (1984), described in the next section, and in accompanying legislation in the Civil Rights Restoration Act that delineated exactly which programs or activities are required to follow the Section 504 mandate.

Determining the Scope of Section 504 in Higher Education

The second case, *Grove City v. Bell* (1984), helped to define what constitutes a "program or activity" and who are the "recipients" of federal financial assistance. It was the most widely publicized case that addressed these two questions and involved a small church-run institution in Pennsylvania that claimed exemption from federal nondiscrimination statutes because it received no federal monies for its programs. The administration at Grove City College maintained that since it did not receive direct federal aid to its programs it was exempt from complying with Section 504 standards. The Department of Justice regulations provide several examples of financial assistance, including any grant, loan, or contract by which the agency or institution provides or makes available assistance in the form of funds, services of federal personnel, or real and personal property or any interest in such property (C.F.R. Sub. 41.3 [1989]). When the college refused to sign a statement issued by the U.S. Department of Health, Education, and Welfare, promising that the college would comply with Title IX of the Education Act amendments of 1973, the Department of Education moved to cut off financial aid to the college (Percy, 1989). Even though the college did not receive direct federal aid to its programs, it did have large numbers of students who received Basic and Supplemental Educational Opportunity Grants and guaranteed student loans through the financial aid office.

The U.S. Supreme Court ruled that since Grove City College students financed their education with Pell grants, then in fact, the college was an indirect recipient of aid from the federal government and was bound by Section 504. Unfortunately, the Supreme Court ruling was extremely narrow; it stated that since the financial aid office received direct funding from the federal government, only that particular office at the college was bound by the regulations. The financial aid office could not discriminate against students with disabilities, but the rest of the institution could. The Supreme Court ruling that *only* the specific program that received direct or indirect federal financial assistance within an entity or institution must comply with the applicable antidiscrimination mandate was viewed by many as a step back rather than a step forward (Tucker & Goldstein, 1991). Almost immediately legislation was promulgated in Congress to address the narrowness of the Grove City ruling (Tucker & Goldstein, 1991). Jarrow (1991) stated that this decision drew considerable concern throughout the civil rights community, and nowhere was that concern greater than in the disabilities rights movement and in the enforcement of Title IX cases. Fortunately, the legislation introduced at the federal level interpreted the law to mean that the entire facility is subject to the nondiscrimination clause regardless of what part of the college receives federal monies. The nondiscrimination clause passed in February 1987 as the Civil Rights Restoration Act.

The Civil Rights Restoration Act

After several years of debate, Congress enacted the Civil Rights Restoration Act of 1987 (P.L. 100-259) and expanded the scope of Section 504 coverage by clearly defining the phrase "any program or activity." The act prohibited discrimination on the basis of disability throughout the entire agency or institution if any part of the institution is receiving federal financial assistance. At a college or university, this would mean that the entire university or college is bound by the federal statute. Although the Civil Rights Restoration Act was vetoed by President Ronald Reagan, both houses of Congress voted to override the presidential veto, thus establishing (or in the view of some, reestablishing) the institution-wide approach to enforcement of non-discrimination policies (Percy, 1989). Jarrow (1991) observed that the Civil Rights Restoration Act restored the "teeth" to all federal civil rights statutes by ensuring that if *any* part of an institution received federal support, the entire institution was responsible for nondiscrimination under existing federal laws.

Providing Additional Time on Examinations

The third case, *Campbell A. Dinsmore v. Charles C. Pugh and the Regents of the University of California* (1989), was a civil suit involving a mathematics professor at the University of California, Berkeley, who refused to provide a dyslexic student with additional time on an examination. When the student requested accommodations in testing, the professor rejected the request on the grounds that "there was no such thing as a learning disability" (W. Newmeyer, personal communication, December 10, 1990). Essentially, the professor maintained that the student was using the disability as a ruse for securing additional time on the examination. Additional negotiations with the professor proved to be unsatisfactory, resulting in the student filing suit against the professor and the Regents of the University of California, Berkeley.

The plaintiff acknowledged that the Disabled Students Program and the university had attempted to rectify the problem but were "powerless" to change the professor's mind. The student demanded that the university develop policies and procedures to address future situations in which a faculty member might refuse to provide academic adjustments despite adequate documentation of a disability. The student also sought monetary damages against the professor for not providing the accommodations requested and for the emotional distress caused by making the case public. The professor was directed by members of the university's administration to provide the student with additional time to take a final examination in class, but the professor ignored the directive and would not permit the examination to be administered with the accommodations. The professor contended that granting extra time was unfair to the other students in the course. He said, "There are fast students and slow students . . . I think all students should be tested equally" (Link, 1989, p. B-2). He also maintained that his academic freedom was being encroached upon.

The university promptly settled the case out of court and developed a comprehensive policy for accommodating the academic needs of students with disabilities. The professor's claim of having his academic freedom usurped was not supported and he was required to pay monetary damages. Jarrow (1992a) commented on the Dinsmore case, noting that "the faculty member's right to academic freedom does not supersede the student's right to an accommodation." The outcome of this case may assist other service providers who are confronted with similar situations where faculty members believe they are in a position to dictate what they will and will not provide to students with disabilities. Chapter 8 contains a more detailed discussion of this case and the policy and procedures subsequently developed as part of the settlement.

Ensuring the Availability of Auxiliary Aids and Services

The fourth case, *United States v. Board of Trustees of the University of Alabama* (1990), involved a variety of claims by students with different disabilities who felt that the university violated their rights under Section 504 in the following areas: (a) implementing a policy regarding the provision of auxiliary aids that included a financial means test and restriction of auxiliary aids to students enrolled in the regular program, (b) offering classes to mobility-impaired students in a segregated setting rather than making its business education program accessible, (c) failing to make its swimming pool accessible, and

(d) failing to provide transportation services to a student with a disability that was comparable to those provided for nondisabled students. The complaints were filed by students with mobility impairments who were seeking access to campus transportation services and the swimming pool and by several deaf students at the University of Alabama at Birmingham who were required to request "all major or costly accommodations" in writing prior to the beginning of the school term.

The U.S. District Court for the Northern District of Alabama determined that the University violated Section 504 of the Rehabilitation Act when it denied auxiliary aids to students with disabilities. In addition, aids were only provided to students who were enrolled in degree-granting programs. Special students, such as postgraduates, temporary students, and students enrolled in nondegree programs, were not considered eligible for free aids or services. The district court concluded that the financial means test violated Section 504, which precludes such tests as criteria for providing auxiliary aids. On appeal, the 11th U.S. Circuit Court of Appeals affirmed the district court's ruling that the University of Alabama may not deny auxiliary aids to students with disabilities based on their ability to pay or their enrollment in nondegree programs. It concluded that the University of Alabama must provide auxiliary aids to students with disabilities regardless of financial need or full-time status (*Handicapped Requirements Handbook*, 1990). In addition, the court held that the university's actions regarding the business program and the swimming pool failed to make reasonable accommodations for students with disabilities (Heyward, Lawton, & Associates, 1991a).

This case may help to set a precedent requiring an institution to accept the responsibility for securing the funds necessary to provide essential services for students with disabilities regardless of their financial need or enrollment status. Extending this case to students with learning disabilities, it can be assumed that they are entitled to receive the same types of services that are available to all other students at no additional cost. D'Amico (1989) observed that if tutoring and counseling are available to nondisabled students without charge, the institution may not impose an additional fee on a student with a learning disability for the same services. It is permissible, however, for the institution to charge an additional fee to students with learning disabilities if these services go beyond the generic campus support services available to all other students. Examples of such services may include specialized tutorial support or diagnostic testing that is offered exclusively to students with learning disabilities. Personal academic adjustments are not necessarily the responsibility of the institution. The hiring of attendants, individually prescribed devices, or readers for personal use are not covered under Section 504. Rothstein (1989) concurred, noting that colleges are probably not required to pay for readers for personal reading, specialized tutoring programs, or other programs specifically for students with learning disabilities.

Modifying the Test Format to Accommodate a Learning Disability

The last case, *Wynne v. Tufts University School of Medicine* (1992), was heard in the First Circuit U.S. District Court of Appeals in April 1990 and was remanded in April 1992. The case involved a first-year medical student who, after failing eight out of fifteen courses, was subsequently tested at university expense and found to be dyslexic. He claimed that after he was identified as having a learning disability, the university unlawfully discriminated against him based on his handicap, in violation of Section 504, when it refused to modify testing methods to accommodate his learning disability (Jaschik, 1990). The student requested that he be given an alternative type of test, preferably an oral exam, but this suggestion was rejected by school administrators. He also sought unsuccessfully to take a reduced course load during his second attempt at the first-year program.

The Tufts Medical School did take some steps to address Wynne's difficulties. He was permitted to repeat the first year and received special tutoring in all subjects he had failed, the use of note takers in his classes, and assistance with a learning-skills tutor to improve his study habits. In his second attempt in the first-year program, he passed all but two of the subjects he had previously failed. He was permitted to retake those two examinations, passing one but failing biochemistry for the third time. Following the third failure, he was dismissed from the medical school. He filed suit, claiming that because of his learning disability, he was unable to demonstrate his knowledge of course content with a conventional multiple-choice format. Specifically, he argued that a different format of the test would "give him meaningful access to the medical education" (Handicapped

Requirements Handbook, 1992, App. IV, p. 254). Tufts attempted to dismiss Wynne's claim, comparing it to the decision in *Southeastern Community College v. Davis* by pointing out that because Wynne was unable to meet an essential requirement for a Tufts medical degree (e.g., passing all of his courses), he was not otherwise qualified. Tufts' affidavit stated, in part, that:

1) multiple choice tests are used to measure a student's ability to understand and assimilate relevant material;

2) modern diagnostic and treatment procedures require physicians to be able to read and assimilate complex data and immediately render important decisions in stressful situations; and

3) in the judgment of the medical educators setting Tufts' academic standards, these demands are best tested by multiple choice examinations (732F 2d 19 1991).

Initially, a decision in Tufts' favor was issued by the district court without a trial. Subsequently, the case was appealed and the full bench of the court of appeals granted Tufts' request for a rehearing and permitted other institutions to participate as *amici curiae*. The court was sharply divided on the issue of granting summary judgment on the claim involving discrimination based on handicap (the disability). It was the finding of the court of appeals that insufficient evidence had been presented to support the university's assertion that "changing the testing method would result in a 'fundamental alteration' in the program." The court concluded that the district court erred in granting summary judgment for Tufts, and the present record demonstrated that "Tufts may not select the one technique that poses an insurmountable barrier to dyslexic students."

The court of appeals remanded the case to the district court in 1991 after concluding that the university had failed to adequately support its position that altering its test format would fundamentally alter the program of medical education it offers (Heyward, Lawton, & Associates, 1992b). On remand, Tufts submitted additional explanations to the district court to support its position that changing the format of the exam from multiple-choice to a written essay would be burdensome. With this information at hand, the court agreed that altering the test format would in fact compromise the test's ability to show a future doctor's "ability to make subtle distinctions based on seemingly small but significant differences in written information"

(Heyward, Lawton, & Associates, 1992b, p. 7). The court of appeals held that the university had an obligation to "seek suitable means to reasonably accommodate a handicapped person and to submit a factual record indicating that it conscientiously carried out this statutory obligation." In addition, it was determined by the court that Tufts "clearly evaluated alternatives" and made a "professional academic judgment" in deciding not to provide alternative tests to the student (Heyward, Lawton, & Associates, 1992b, p. 7). Tufts was able to present convincing proof that the testing method is an integral component of the medical curriculum and added that the university had met its obligation to "seek suitable means to reasonably accommodate a handicapped person and to submit a factual record indicating that it conscientiously carried out this statutory obligation." The court also added that Tufts had reasonably accommodated the dyslexic medical student by permitting him to repeat the first-year curriculum and by paying for note takers, tutors, and taped lecture material.

Heyward, Lawton, and Associates (1991a) stated that the district court was persuaded by additional information provided by Tufts University that reflected (a) reasons why multiple-choice exams were superior to oral exams, (b) the faculty's dissatisfaction with its prior experience with essay questions, and (c) the difficulty of changing the test format without "compromising the test's function as a measure of a future doctor's ability to make subtle distinctions based on seemingly small but significant differences in written information." Professor Rothstein, associate dean for student affairs at the University of Houston Law Center, commented on this case, noting that "there should be limits on what colleges are required to do for learning disabled students" (Jaschik, 1990, p. A20). She felt that it could be "terribly burdensome" to faculty members if courts required them to develop new tests for students with learning disabilities. Rothstein looks to the courts to provide additional clarification on this matter in the years ahead. Runyan and Smith (1992, p. 327) commented on the case and noted that "it will be important to observe whether other courts adopt the standard set forth in *Wynne* and, if so, whether they will follow the lead of the majority or dissenting opinion in applying the standard." Heyward, Lawton, and Associates (1991c, p. 6) noted that "this decision is important because it is the first time that a court has stated in such specific detail what the burden of proof is regarding the decisions of postsecondary institutions to deny accommodations to disabled individuals. Institutions will not be permitted to simply perform cursory reviews."

A related case involved a student with a learning disability at Cabrillo College, California (1 NDLR 307) who requested an unlimited number of index cards during an exam or an open-book test and the use of a scientific calculator. The OCR ruled that allowing the use of two index cards and a four-function calculator satisfied the college's duty to accommodate. There will undoubtedly be additional cases such as these that will strive to further define what constitutes a reasonable academic adjustment under Section 504. These cases and others to follow will help to build legal precedent region by region. For example, the OCR in Region VI recently ruled that Southwest Texas State University (*Southwest Texas State University v. Region VI*, Case No. 06902084) was in violation of Section 504 when it denied a student with a learning disability in math, reading, writing, and spelling an academic adjustment to substitute one course for an algebra class. However, because algebra was a requirement for all students pursuing a bachelor's degree, a student majoring in geography would need to take 6 hours of math or computer science. Kincaid (1992) noted that the university did not provide evidence that substitution of the algebra course requirement would substantially alter the nature of the bachelor's degree or pose an excessive burden. Thus, the OCR concluded that the university had violated Section 504.

Each of the cases presented in this chapter helps to sharpen the picture of what constitutes "reasonableness" for college students with disabilities. Viewed together, these cases suggest that colleges and universities are in a state of transition in their attempts to respond to the unique needs of students with learning disabilities. Future cases will build on these foundations and should offer additional guidance in the form of institutional policies that will assist service providers who are now facing more complex issues. Potential areas for litigation are likely to involve the implementation of non-biased identification procedures for non-English-speaking college students with learning disabilities, accommodation in testing and coursework of college students with traumatic brain injuries, and disputes regarding access and full participation in campus services or activities that are nonacademic in nature. In addition, there are concerns about students with learning disabilities who are denied participation in intercollegiate athletics because the academic performance criteria used were inherently discriminatory. For college students with learning disabilities, physical barriers are not typically at issue; attitudinal barriers are the primary hurdle.

DEVELOPING PRACTICAL GUIDELINES BASED ON LEGAL PRECEDENT

Many postsecondary service providers are concerned about developing written policies or establishing guidelines concerning service provisions for students with learning disabilities. This process should involve careful planning and must be rooted in the legal principles discussed in this chapter in light of the IDEA, Section 504, and the ADA. As policy decisions are shaped on campus, new court cases can offer service providers additional guidance as to the parameters of the law. For example, policy issues concerning course substitutions or petitions for course extensions for students with disabilities must guarantee these individuals the rights to due process established under the IDEA. In keeping with established precedents under Section 504, campus policies will need to specify which students are "otherwise qualified" for admission and, once they are admitted, how academic adjustments can be provided so that full participation is guaranteed. The ADA will undoubtedly shape future campus policies by ensuring that architectural, telecommunications, and transportation facilities on campuses are readily accessible. Furthermore, under the ADA, a program or activity must be accessible for individuals with disabilities when viewed in its entirety, regardless of whether the institution is public or private.

CONCLUSION

It has taken over two decades to bring legislative intent more in line with practice for individuals with disabilities in higher education. The laws and court cases discussed in this chapter should give service providers the background they need to make informed judgments about admissions, service delivery, and accommodation standards for students with learning disabilities. By carefully balancing the institutional mission with the rights of these students, along with the rights of faculty members, guidelines can be established that will foster academic freedom in a climate of nondiscrimination. Several areas that seem to be particularly ripe for policy development include issues relating to admissions, recruitment, academic programs and adjustments, and treatment of students. Guidelines and policies that build upon the legal precedents described in this chapter are fully discussed in Chapter 8.

CHAPTER 3

Issues in Defining the Population

The problem of defining the term *learning disabilities* has challenged the field since Sam Kirk's first attempt in 1962 (Kirk, 1962). The fact that the definitional controversy has not been resolved is evidenced by a recent issue of *Learning Disability Quarterly* (Swanson, 1991a), which was devoted to articles on definitions of learning disabilities. Although most definitions have been developed primarily for children in public schools, some do have sufficient breadth to make them relevant to adults (Mellard, 1990). It would, therefore, be counterproductive to attempt to develop a new definition at the postsecondary level. Institutions of higher education must establish criteria for eligibility under Section 504 based upon an operational definition of learning disabilities.

This chapter will address the following definitional issues regarding the adult postsecondary population:

- Identifying appropriate definitions of learning disabilities

- Establishing an operational model for determining the presence of a learning disability

- Differentiating learning disabilities from other disabling conditions or other learning difficulties

- Deciding when to label or whether or not to label students with learning disabilities

CHALLENGES IN DEFINING LEARNING DISABILITIES

Institutions of higher education must recognize the population of students who are guaranteed protection under Section 504 of the Rehabilitation Act. Although Section 504 does not define learning disabilities, it does specify that if an individual has a physical or mental impairment that substantially limits one or more major life functions *or* has a history of such an impairment *or* is regarded as having such an impairment *and* meets the academic and technical standards required for admission or participation in a college's programs or activities, *then* that student must be ensured equal educational opportunity.

Students with apparent sensory disabilities or physical limitations are relatively easy to identify. It is more difficult to make a determination of eligibility for students with hidden disabilities such as a learning disability. In communicating with prospective and current students, as well as with faculty and staff, it is necessary to specify the process by which eligibility for protections under Section 504 is determined. Institutions are in compliance when they request documentation of a specific learning disability (Heyward, Lawton, & Associates, 1990). Yet nowhere in the regulations is there a definition, leaving postsecondary institutions clamoring for assistance in interpreting what constitutes adequate documentation. In addition, clearly defining the population is essential when attempting to garner administrative support (political and fiscal) and relating service to these students with the overall institutional mission.

Hammill (1990) recently conducted a comprehensive discussion and review of 11 major definitions of learning disability. The conceptual elements identified in those definitions include:

1. *Existence throughout the life span:* This is a critical element for those working with adults. Many early definitions focused on children, since manifestations of a learning disability were typically seen in school. It was then hoped that the learning disability would be remediated or "cured," or would disappear by adulthood.

2. *Intraindividual differences:* This terminology was chosen since it describes differences in performance *within* the individual (i.e., an individual might be above average in math, below average in writing) rather than an aptitude-achievement discrepancy. The latter descriptor may be problematic in identifying college students, since they may have learned to successfully compensate for learning difficulties, thus diminishing any discrepancy. In addition, many diagnostic instruments are not scaled beyond high school or normed on adults, making the determination of an aptitude-achievement discrepancy problematic with adults.

3. *Central nervous system dysfunction:* Some definitions cited by Hammill (1990) indicate that a problem in the central nervous system (CNS) is the cause of learning disabilities. Although this may be the case in many with severe learning disabilities, it has not yet been proved across the entire spectrum of individuals with learning disabilities (Hynd, Marshall, & Gonzeles, 1991).

4. *Problems with learning processes:* Some definitions suggest that disruptions in the processes of memory, attention, or cognition make proficient performance in some skill or ability areas difficult for students with learning disabilities. This is a critical component for definitions regarding adults, since poor teaching, diminished motivation, or educational disadvantage can also cause learning problems.

5. *Specification of academic, language, or conceptual problems as potential learning disabilities:* Most definitions specify that academic problems (e.g., reading, writing, spelling, or math), language problems (e.g., listening, speaking, or writing), or conceptual problems (e.g., thinking or reasoning) can be manifestations of learning disabilities.

6. *Other conditions as potential learning disabilities:* Some definitions have identified difficulties with social skills, spatial orientation, or integration of motor abilities as learning disabilities. There has been persistent controversy over the years regarding the relevance of defining these problems as learning disabilities (Myers & Hammill, 1990).

7. *Coexisting or excluded disabilities:* Some definitions distinguish between primary and secondary disabilities (e.g., a learning disability may be the primary disability while a psychological disorder could be a secondary disability). Many adults with learning disabilities do have coexisting disabilities. Psychological problems may manifest themselves as social misperceptions or in ongoing frustration in individuals with learning impairments, health problems, or psychiatric disorders.

Keeping these seven points in mind will help professionals as they attempt to determine an appropriate definition of learning disabilities.

The definition of learning disabilities used in public schools was promulgated under P.L. 94-142, the Education for All Handicapped Children Act:

> The term "specific learning disability" means a disorder in one or more of the basic psychological processes involved in understanding or in using language, spoken or written, which may manifest itself in an imperfect ability to listen, speak, read, write, spell, or to do mathematical calculations. The term includes such conditions as percep-

tual handicaps, brain injury, minimal brain dysfunction, dyslexia, and developmental aphasia. The term does not include children who have learning disabilities which are primarily the result of visual, hearing, or motor handicaps, or mental retardation, or emotional disturbance, or environmental, cultural, or economic disadvantage. (U.S. Department of Education, 1977, p. 65083)

Documentation of a learning disability provided by a public school will typically be based on some form of this definition. Although the definition does imply that learning disabilities occur at all ages, its use of the term *children* makes it inappropriate for use with adults. Other concerns include the use of the ambiguous term *psychological processes*, inclusion of spelling as a learning disability, and use of obsolete terms such as *perceptual handicap* (Myers & Hammill, 1990).

The National Joint Committee on Learning Disabilities (NJCLD), composed of nine organizations with a major interest in learning disabilities including the Association on Higher Education and Disability (AHEAD), American Speech-Language-Hearing Association, Council for Learning Disabilities, and National Association of School Psychologists, developed its own definition:

Learning disabilities is a general term that refers to a heterogeneous group of disorders manifested by significant difficulties in the acquisition and use of listening, speaking, reading, writing, reasoning, or mathematical abilities. These disorders are intrinsic to the individual, presumed to be due to central nervous system dysfunction, and may occur across the life span. Problems in self-regulatory behaviors, social perception, and social interaction may exist with learning disabilities but do not by themselves constitute a learning disability. Although learning disabilities may occur concomitantly with other handicapping conditions (for example, sensory impairment, mental retardation, serious emotional disturbance) or with extrinsic influences (such as cultural differences, insufficient or inappropriate instruction), they are not the result of those conditions or influences. (National Joint Committee on Learning Disabilities, 1988b, p. 1)

The NJCLD definition addresses many of the conceptual issues cited in Hammill's review (1990) in a way that is appropriate for adults. It is important to reiterate that use of the aptitude-performance discrepancy model is not advisable because:

1. Diagnostic instruments are often not normed or scaled adequately for adults nor do they include items to assess skills approaching college level.

2. Adults may have had years of training to help them gain proficiency or compensatory strategies in problematic skill areas.

3. At the postsecondary level, learning disabilities often manifest themselves in ways other than deficiencies in basic skill levels.

4. Some non-learning-disabled college students have superior aptitude scores that could result in a discrepancy in skill levels when determined by norm-referenced tests.

For the following specific reasons, the NJCLD definition would seem to be the definition of choice at the postsecondary level:

1. It has a broad base of support including that of the AHEAD.

2. It is consistent with the concept of intraindividual differences in a broad range of areas including reasoning.

3. It clearly specifies that learning disabilities exist throughout the life span.

4. It does not require identification of CNS etiology.

5. It recognizes that problems with related psychosocial skills may exist but does not include them as part of the definition.

6. Although it acknowledges possible concomitant disabling conditions, it deals with learning disabilities as the primary condition.

7. It does not rule out the possibility that learning disabilities can occur in people with superior intellectual functioning.

In the conclusion of his review, Hammill (1990, p. 82) noted that the NJCLD definition "is probably the best descriptive statement about the nature of learning disabilities."

Subsequent to the first NJCLD initiative to address the issue of definition in 1981, the Interagency Committee on Learning Disabilities (ICLD), which included personnel from a range of federal agencies, put forth a definition that was intended to be similar to but an improvement on the NJCLD definition. Social skills are identified as a specific manifestation of learning disabilities in the ICLD definition (Interagency Committee on Learning Disabilities, 1987). Although there is no doubt that the recognition of concomitant social-skills deficits is important (Greenspan, Apthorp, & Williams, 1991), including social skills in the definition would cause considerable overlap with the category of individuals with psychological disorders. For that reason, the ICLD definition should be considered with extreme caution.

Each postsecondary institution needs to first adopt a definition of learning disabilities. The NJCLD definition is clearly the one to choose. It is then necessary for professionals at each institution of higher education to determine how to identify "significant disabilities" that are "intrinsic to the individual" so that they can obtain an operational definition to assist them in determining which students are entitled to services under Section 504. The following section will attempt to provide some guidance.

AN OPERATIONAL DEFINITION OF LEARNING DISABILITIES

Since personnel at most postsecondary institutions do not have the training and expertise in LD classification and diagnosis (Norlander, Shaw, & McGuire, 1990), it is particularly critical for them to be in consensus regarding a clear and functional operational definition of learning disabilities. Kavale, Forness, and Lorsbach (1991) recommended an ordered and sequenced operational interpretation that is based on a definition of learning disabilities. They reinforced the need for a single definition of learning disabilities by noting that the concept of an aptitude-achievement discrepancy has become virtually the only criterion for the determination of a learning disability even though it is *not* mentioned in most definitions.

Although a definition of learning disabilities has been provided, the heterogeneous nature of students with learning disabilities must be reiterated. Even within the relatively narrow focus of college students with learning disabilities, considerable variability is expected.

Figure 3.1 illustrates a process for developing an operational interpretation of learning disabilities based on the NJCLD definition using the paradigm suggested by Kavale et al. (1991). In this model there are four levels of investigation, beginning with the most critical issue: identifying intraindividual discrepancies.

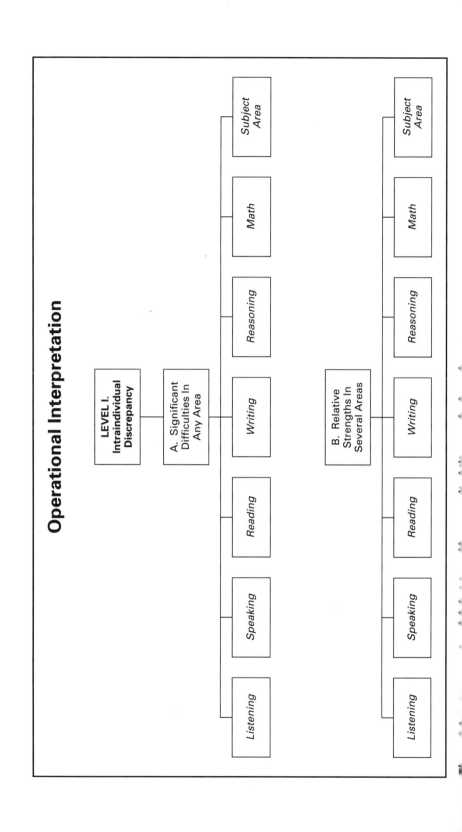

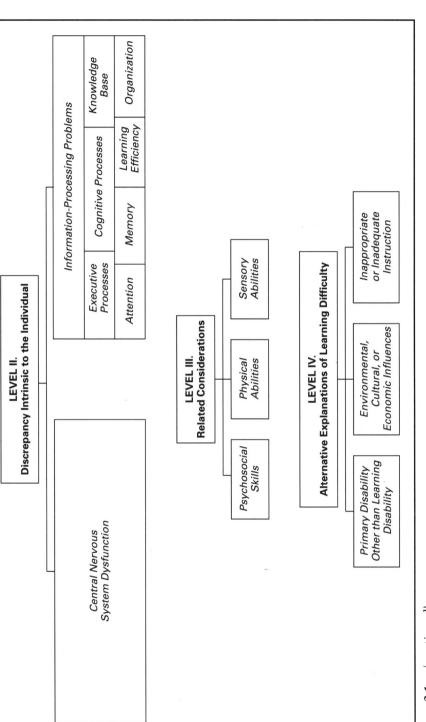

Figure 3.1. (continued)

Level I

Level I (intraindividual discrepancy) involves two steps: identifying a significant difficulty in any of the specified skill areas listed and identifying successful performance in several other skill areas. A subject-area category has been added to the six skill areas identified in the NJCLD definition in order to accommodate our focus on college students. Information gleaned at Level I may be used to identify a learning problem and to eliminate students with mental retardation or those who are slow learners. Yet, Level I alone is not sufficient to determine the presence of a learning disability.

Level II

Level II (discrepancy intrinsic to the individual) requires verification that the learning difficulty is intrinsic to the individual. This could involve a determination of CNS dysfunction or specification of deficits in information processing (Kolligian & Sternberg, 1987; Swanson, 1987) that are related to the skill deficits identified in Level I.

As noted previously, it is difficult to identify specific areas of CNS dysfunction in most individuals with learning disabilities. Only those with the most severe problems or with apparent organic impairment will be identified in this way. On the other hand, students with learning disabilities are seen as having deficient information-processing mechanisms. In addition, identifying CNS dysfunction typically requires a medical orientation, while identifying information-processing problems in memory, organization, or learning efficiency is within the province of educators. Therefore, an information-processing perspective can help us "understand students' learning processes and the factors that affect learning processes" (Ariel, 1992, p. 196). Information processing is conceptualized as an individual's acquisition, storage, and utilization of information (Swanson & Watson, 1982).

The three major components (Mercer, 1991; Swanson, 1987) of information processing are described in a very basic fashion as:

1. *Executive processes:* Higher-order processes used to plan, monitor, and evaluate learning and performance

2. *Cognitive processes:* Strategies or processes that enable students to learn and solve problems (e.g., verbal rehearsal, classification, summarization, and integration)

3. *Knowledge base:* Available information in long-term memory applied to help learn new information (e.g., select, integrate, or compare information)

Information-processing theory suggests that learning problems are caused by individuals' inability to organize their thinking skills and systematically approach learning tasks (Swanson, 1987). In other words, these students need to learn how to learn. Deshler, Schumaker, Lenz, and Ellis (1984) have demonstrated that students who have a learning disability can profit from instruction that teaches them *how* to learn. Individuals with learning disabilities have exhibited difficulties in short- and long-term memory (Swanson & Cooney, 1991), attention to task (Hallahan & Reeve, 1980), strategic production (Torgeson, 1982), strategic learning (Swanson, 1987), and development of automaticity of skills and strategies (Kolligian & Sternberg, 1987). Students with learning disabilities also experience difficulties in executive control or self-regulation, resulting in poor selection, monitoring, evaluation, and modification of strategies (Wong, 1991).

Level II allows for any one or more of a broad spectrum of factors that may explain or account for the deficits identified in Level I. The model, however, does not focus exclusively on any single element, such as CNS dysfunction, as a required condition of a learning disability. Assessment data must provide an *intrinsic* explanation for the learning difficulty. Chapter 4 will discuss the issues and instruments for this kind of assessment. The interaction between Levels I and II yields the most critical data for identifying a learning disability because it demonstrates that the learning difficulties are, in fact, a result of an information-processing problem within the individual. The final critical piece of information is in Level IV—determining whether there is an alternative explanation for the intrinsic learning difficulties identified in Levels I and II that can be attributed to non-LD (extrinsic) factors.

Level III

Level III (related considerations) involves the identification of concomitant limitations in areas such as psychosocial skills and physical or sensory abilities. These are *not* elements of a learning disability but may be viewed as related problems that may be associated with a learning disability. Although a student can be identified without any related deficits, this level has two important purposes:

1. It provides for the specification of additional problems that may need to be addressed for program planning purposes.

2. It may identify deficits that relate to the determination of alternative explanations of learning difficulties identified in Level IV.

For example, the area of psychosocial deficits is often a problem for college students with learning disabilities. Deficiencies may stem from social misperception, learned helplessness, or poor self-concept (see Chapter 5 for a detailed discussion). If psychosocial problems have become predominant, however, classification in another category of disability (psychological disorder) may be more appropriate.

Level IV

Level IV (alternative explanations of learning difficulty) addresses exclusions or alternative explanations for a learning difficulty. Application of this level provides an opportunity to specify a primary disability other than a learning disability or to identify an alternative explanation of the deficits identified in Level I. For example, a student who is not motivated to learn (i.e., who does not complete homework or attend class) may have learning difficulties that are not related to a learning disability. A more complex example is that of a student who is under the influence of drugs. That student's intraindividual discrepancy may not be intrinsic if it only occurs *while* he or she is under the influence of drugs, or it may be intrinsic if permanent damage has resulted from drug abuse. In either case, the diagnostic process may result in the determination of a primary disability of "other health impaired" or "psychological disorder." These determinations will require professional judgment based on this model.

Postsecondary administrators, service-delivery personnel, and related service personnel required to render eligibility or classification decisions can apply this model to review available data or implement diagnostic procedures in order to make consistent, valid, and defensible decisions about which students have learning disabilities, which do not qualify for services, and why. This model is presented to stimulate discussion and alternative approaches to providing operational definitions of learning disabilities at the same time that it gives practitioners a basis for action.

Figure 3.2 is provided to illustrate the heterogeneity that is characteristic of students in postsecondary settings. In addition to depicting the range of strengths and weaknesses indicated by the term *learning disabilities*, the figure exemplifies the divergent ability levels that may characterize students in various postsecondary settings. The profile depicting a student with a learning disability at an open-enrollment community college indicates average skills in math and reasoning, below-average skills in listening and reading, and significant deficits in writing and speaking. The profile of a student with a learning disability at a 4-year college demonstrates below-average scores in math and a subject skill (calculus) that are significantly discrepant from the student's average and above-average scores in all other skill areas. The profile of a student with a learning disability at a professional school indicates reading and writing scores in the average range that are significantly discrepant from all other scores, which are above-average or well-above-average. In spite of the variability in the range and level of abilities in these three profiles, they all demonstrate the intraindividual discrepancy necessary for Level I consideration as a student with a learning disability.

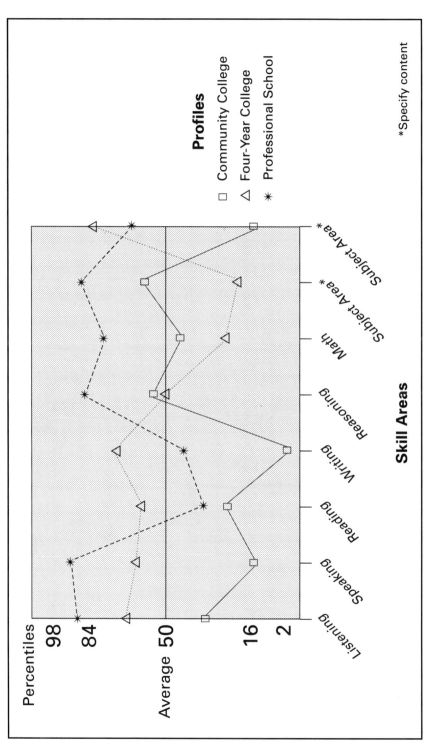

Figure 3.2. LD profiles.

DIFFERENTIATING LEARNING DISABILITIES FROM OTHER CONDITIONS

Learning Disability or Other Disability?

Given the heterogeneous nature of learning disabilities, the problem with definition and the difficulty of determining eligibility, there have been concerns about labeling for a long time (Dunn, 1968; G. O. Johnson, 1962). Over the last 20 years, public schools have seen a dramatic increase in the percentage of students identified as having learning disabilities and a concomitant decrease in the percentage of students identified as having many other disabling conditions (U.S. Department of Education, 1990). Of particular note is the "disappearance" of many students with mild mental retardation during the time of the sharpest growth in the LD population. In a similar vein, there have been huge discrepancies from district to district and state to state in the ratio of students with learning disabilities compared to those with emotional disturbances (U.S. Department of Education, 1990).

Postsecondary institutions need to be particularly careful about classification because of the differences in P.L. 94-142 and Section 504. The former provides a free, appropriate education for all students with disabilities, while the latter only requires access for "otherwise qualified" students with disabilities. It is also important to note that regulations regarding P.L. 94–142 define a learning disability while regulations for Section 504 do not. Therefore, it is even more imperative that postsecondary institutions specify their operational definition.

Mental Retardation or Learning Disability?

Many laypersons, including some college faculty, perceive anyone with a learning disability as having mental retardation. In order to maintain the integrity of support services and justify the presence of students with learning disabilities in postsecondary education, particularly in competitive settings, differentiation from students with limited intellectual ability is critical. Using the operational definition depicted in Figure 3.1, Levels I and IV provide the information necessary to differentiate students with learning disabilities from those with mental retardation. At Level I, college students with learning disabilities typically demonstrate several areas of significant difficulty and many areas of relative strength. Students with mental retardation often demonstrate many areas of difficulty and only a few isolated areas of relative strength. As indicated in Figure 3.3, students with learning disabilities demonstrate an uneven profile with significant peaks and valleys, while students with mental retardation typically demonstrate a rather flat profile with weaknesses that extend across skill areas.

According to the model, Level I would not yield evidence of intra-individual differences for a student with mental retardation. Level IV stipulates exclusions including the student's having a primary disability other than a learning disability. The diagnostic data alone or classification indicated by diagnosticians could exclude a student from identification as a student with a learning disability because of significantly below-average performance across most indicators.

Psychological Disorder or Learning Disability?

Students with psychological disabilities are seeking access to postsecondary institutions in ever greater numbers (Unger, 1991). Differentiating students with learning disabilities from students with psychological disorders at the postsecondary level creates the same difficulties that public school personnel have dealt with for many years. This is not to suggest that the problem is just a bureaucratic issue of labeling. It can often be critical for the student, faculty, and staff to understand the primary disability in order to determine appropriate services and accommodations.

Using the operational interpretation in Figure 3.1 on students with psychological disorders, Level I might not differentiate a learning disability from a psychological disorder, since both have a similar uneven profile. However, Level II might differentiate the two diagnostic categories, because it is likely that none of the intrinsic impediments to learning would be apparent in students with psychological disorders. Level III provides an opportunity to consider other problem areas. Problems with psychosocial skills will usually become evident as major conditions, leading to Level IV and an alternative explanation for learning difficulties.

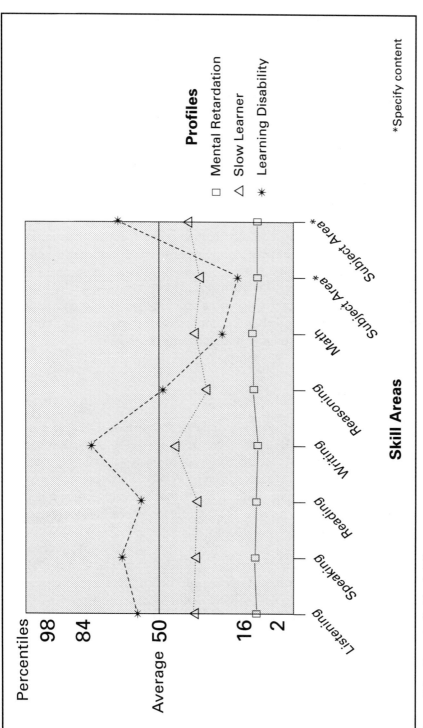

Figure 3.3. Intra-individual differences.

Learning Disability or Other Learning Difficulty?

There is little doubt that many postsecondary institutions, particularly those with open-enrollment policies, are experiencing increasing numbers of students at risk for encountering learning problems. Some of these students have learning disabilities, but the majority are slow learners because of less-than-average ability or limited educational opportunities. Others may have presumed or documented CNS dysfunction. Some students with *presumed* CNS dysfunction are now described as having an attention deficit disorder (ADD) or attention deficit–hyperactivity disorder (ADHD). Those with *documented* CNS dysfunction may have an impairment called traumatic brain injury (TBI) or acquired brain injury, which may result from an external event (accident or fall) or an internal event (tumor or disease). Table 3.1 provides a framework, using the four levels of operational interpretation, for determining if students with these learning problems are also qualified students with learning disabilities.

Slow Learners

Slow learners (i.e., students with less-than-average ability) may appear to have learning disabilities, but upon careful analysis they can be distinguished relatively easily. Table 3.1 indicates that both Level I and Level II demonstrate clear differentiations. Slow learners typically have a flatter profile, indicating primarily below-average performance in most areas, unlike the significant peaks and valleys of students with learning disabilities (see Figure 3.2). Nor do they exhibit specific learning deficits other than limited intellectual aptitude to explain their performance. As indicated in Figure 3.3, slow learners can be differentiated from individuals with mental retardation because their ability level is not as low and they tend to demonstrate more variability than is seen in the extremely flat profile of individuals with mental retardation.

Attention Deficit Disorder

Students with ADD have been identified under a variety of names. These students were first discussed more than a half-century

TABLE 3.1. Differentiating Learning Disabilities from Other Learning Difficulties

Operational Definition of a Learning Disability	Slow Learner	Attention Deficit Disorder (ADD)	Traumatic Brain Injury (TBI)
Level I Intraindividual Discrepancy	Few Intraindividual differences Flat profile	May have typical LD profile	Likely to have pronounced LD profile of strengths and weaknesses
Level II Intrinsic	No indication of specific learning problems other than limited ability	Will typically have attention, perceptual, and/ or learning dysfunctions	Obvious central nervous system dysfunction and possibly other significant problems
Level III Related Considerations	Usually no specific related conditions	Psychosocial deficits are likely	Many related conditions including physical and emotional concerns
Level IV Alternative Explanations	May be excluded because of environmental, cultural, economic, or educational disadvantage	Based on a September 1991 OSERS[a] policy, the primary disability for ADD students may be "other health impaired" or "seriously emotionally disturbed" (psychological disorder)	Primary disability could be "other health impaired" depending on the severity of the conditions identified in Level III

[a]OSERS = Office of Special Education and Rehabilitative Services.

ago (Strauss & Lehtinen, 1947). Diagnostic labels used to identify this group have included Strauss syndrome, brain damage, minimal brain dysfunction, and hyperactivity. The condition was last described in 1987 as attention deficit–hyperactivity disorder (American Psychiatric Association, 1987). Children with ADHD are typically impulsive, hyperactive, and inattentive (Reeve, 1990). Adults with ADHD are more likely to manifest disorganization, restlessness, problems with authority, frustration, poor self-esteem, and relationship problems (Landi, 1991). Table 3.1 indicates that many students with ADHD will fulfill Levels I, II, and III of the operational definition of learning disabilities. As noted in a recent policy decision from OSERS, they may have a primary disability other than a learning disability (Davila, 1991) and thus meet the criteria for "other health impaired" or "seriously emotionally disturbed" as their primary disability and thereby be eligible for services under those categories.

Traumatic Brain Injury

Students with TBI have had a severe injury involving parts of the brain that often creates physical, mental, and emotional difficulties (Bigler, 1990). As indicated in Table 3.1, they may also fit the operational definition of learning disabilities with one notable exception. At Level I students with TBI will most often demonstrate severe deficits that are likely to have resulted from areas of injury, and strengths in areas that were not affected. Application of Levels II and III will yield evidence of significant CNS dysfunction that may affect many learning processes and cause related problems in a variety of areas. However, students with TBI may be distinguished from students with "conventional" learning disabilities in Level IV, where they may exhibit any of a variety of other disabilities depending on the nature of their injuries. Other primary disabilities could include sensory impairments or chronic health problems.

SHOULD WE LABEL?

After defining learning disabilities, providing an operational interpretation of that definition, and distinguishing learning disabilities from other conditions, it is logical to ask if and when it is appropriate or necessary to label students. The issue of labeling is not new (Dunn, 1968; G. O. Johnson, 1962). Some professionals focus on the benefits to a protected class that receives special programs and services (Kaufman,

1989). Others have documented the stigma, isolation, and lack of utility associated with the use of categorical labels (Reynolds, 1984; Ysseldyke, 1987). In a recent statewide planning effort in Connecticut, it was determined that categories of disability need to be maintained to protect students but that labels were not productive in determining service delivery or types of accommodations (P. Campbell & Shaw, 1992).

At the postsecondary level it is necessary to determine which students have learning disabilities whether or not this information is important for service delivery. Every institution must know who has specific rights under Section 504 of the Rehabilitation Act, but given the many at-risk students in addition to those with disabilities, institutions may meet the needs of all students and provide equal access without categorical programs that separate students with disabilities from other students. This may be possible at open-enrollment, 2-year colleges where significant numbers of students will be in need of generic accommodations and support from general learning centers. Programs that serve only students with documented disabilities, on the other hand, will need to focus on eligibility requirements.

CONCLUSION

The NJCLD definition and its operational interpretation should provide personnel at institutions of higher education with the tools to determine which students have learning disabilities. Personnel at postsecondary institutions should be able to implement the four-level model process:

Level I   Determining if there is an intraindividual discrepancy

Level II   Identifying elements indicating whether the discrepancy is intrinsic to the individual

Level III   Specifying related considerations

Level IV   Determining possible alternative explanations of the learning difficulties

The following chapter provides more detailed information on the diagnostic data used to make that decision.

CHAPTER 4

Issues in Assessment and Diagnosis

Patricia L. Anderson

T he assessment and diagnosis of traditional college-age students and adults with learning disabilities is one of the most controversial topics in the area of postsecondary LD service delivery. The growing number of self-identified students with learning disabilities who are enrolling in colleges across the country (Henderson, 1992) as well as an increasing number of referrals of students with suspected but undiagnosed learning disabilities (Jarrow, 1991) create challenges for postsecondary personnel. Additional concerns include the heterogeneity of the LD population (Algozzine & Ysseldyke, 1986; Bursuck, et al., 1989); inconsistent criteria for defining learning disabilities (Hammill, 1990; D. J. Johnson, 1987a; Mercer, 1987); multiple purposes for identification (D. J. Johnson, 1987a; Keogh, 1987); the complex nature of diagnosing adults with learning disabilities (Blalock, 1981; Cohen, 1984; Vogel, 1985); and a lack of adequate tests and trained professionals (Carlton & Walkenshaw, 1991; Gregg & Hoy, 1990; D. J. Johnson, 1987b; Norlander et al., 1990; Shepard & Smith, 1983; Vogel, 1987a, 1987b). For LD service providers, most of whom do not provide diagnostic services on their campuses, the most significant concerns include the use of assessment information to determine eligibility for services under Section 504, the relevancy of data for assisting students to make appropriate programming choices, and the utility of assessment for determining effective academic adjustments and/or the auxiliary aids that are necessary to assure equal educational opportunity at the postsecondary level.

Although research abounds on the assessment of school-age students with learning disabilities, the paucity of information on the assessment of the adult population suggests that this field is in its infancy. There is a growing literature on data-based profiles of college students with learning disabilities (Cordoni & Goh, 1989; Dalke, 1988; Gajar, Salvia, Gajria, & Salvia, 1989; Morris & Leuenberger, 1990; Vogel, 1986); programs and institutions providing LD assessment (Beirne-Smith & Deck, 1989; Block et al., 1986; Carlton & Walkenshaw, 1991; Gregg & Hoy, 1990); and recommendations for diagnosing adults and college students with learning disabilities (Hawks et al., 1990; D. J. Johnson, 1987b; Mellard, 1990; Vogel, 1989; Whyte, Kovach, & Vosahlo, 1991). However, limited information exists to help service providers to collect, understand, and apply assessment information in order to plan appropriate support services for qualified college students with learning disabilities.

This chapter will attempt to fill the gap between assessment and educational planning, while also highlighting the concerns that exist in the field of adult LD assessment for both diagnosticians and service providers. Specifically, this chapter identifies assessment procedures and tools to assist service providers in developing a systematic process for (a) obtaining useful diagnostic information when making referrals to off-campus diagnosticians, (b) helping students plan or choose appropriate programs, (c) identifying effective academic accommodations (based on assessment data), and (d) using diagnostic information to help students understand their learning disability. Interpretation and application of technical diagnostic information will be discussed in reference to program planning; however, the specifics of administering a diagnostic evaluation to identify a specific learning disability are beyond the focus of this chapter. For more in-depth discussion of LD assessment procedures that can be implemented with adults, see the diagnostic resources listed in Appendix B.

DIFFICULTY IN THE ASSESSMENT OF ADULTS WITH LEARNING DISABILITIES

The Dilemma of Definition

The assessment and diagnosis of adults with learning disabilities at the postsecondary level is a complicated process, compounded by numerous issues. One of the first questions service providers and diagnosticians face is What is a learning disability? As discussed in Chapter 3, the definitional controversy within the field has yet to be resolved, although some suggest that a consensus is near (Hammill, 1990). In the meantime, service providers must have some mechanism to determine which students are eligible for services under Section 504. To this end, it is recommended that each postsecondary institution should first adopt a definition of learning disabilities like the one developed by the NJCLD (National Joint Committee on

Learning Disabilities, 1988b), which is the most relevant for adults. Hammill (1990, p. 83) noted that the NJCLD definition "has obtained a high level of acceptance among multiple national associations and individuals and is arguably the best one that is presently available."

California is the first and only state to develop a formal model to diagnose and determine the eligibility for services of adults with learning disabilities in a postsecondary system. As the result of 5 years of research and development, the California Community College system implemented a comprehensive eligibility model for students with learning disabilities (Mellard, 1990). According to Mellard, this model "provides a clear definition of the LD construct for adults in the community colleges" (p. 75). Mellard cautioned, however, that such procedures, including a definition, need to be tailored to individual postsecondary settings.

Determining Eligibility: The Challenge for Postsecondary Institutions

Agreeing on an institutional definition of learning disabilities is just the first step in determining if a student has a learning disability. Of greater concern are the diverse mechanisms by which institutions apply such a definition in determining eligibility for services (Kavale et al., 1991; Keogh, 1987; Mercer, 1987). Swanson (1991b, p. 242) cautioned that the NJCLD definition is not an operational definition "because it does not specify the operations or procedures by which the construct of learning disabilities can be recognized and measured." The selection and measurement of the parameters used to create an operational definition of learning disabilities must be determined by each postsecondary institution. An operational interpretation of the NJCLD definition at the postsecondary level involving four stages of investigation is discussed at length in Chapter 3.

At the elementary and secondary levels, the definitional controversy is reflected in the sizable growth in the number of children with learning disabilities receiving special education services. Current figures in the *Fourteenth Annual Report to Congress on the Implementation of the Education of the Handicapped Act* (1992) indicate that 50.5% of all students with disabilities have learning disabilities. Since the 1976–77 school year, the number of students with learning disabilities has grown by more than 170% (*Fourteenth Annual Report to Congress on the Implementation of the Education of the Handicapped Act*, 1992). This change in incidence may in part be attributed to the multitude of operational definitions used across the United States to determine eligibility for services under the IDEA (Chalfant, 1989a).

Although state definitions of learning disabilities are relatively consistent for grades K–12 (Frankenberger & Harper, 1987), guidelines for eligibility differ from state to state and frequently change based on current funding and legislation. Under such conditions, a child who meets the eligibility criteria for LD services in one state might not be eligible for services in a different state. This multitude of variations often results in misdiagnosis and overidentification (Algozzine & Ysseldyke, 1986; Shepard & Smith, 1983; Ysseldyke, Algozzine, Richey, & Graden, 1982). For postsecondary institutions, the impact of misdiagnosis on service delivery poses significant problems (Mellard & Deshler, 1984; Scott, 1990). As McGuire et al. (1990, p. 70) indicated, "If misdiagnosis occurs at the elementary and secondary levels, and that misdiagnosis constitutes the basis for eligibility for accommodations at the postsecondary level, then it is predictable that colleges and universities may have identified grossly disproportionate numbers of students who may not actually possess specific learning disabilities."

For the postsecondary service provider, regulations under the IDEA present two additional concerns. The IDEA mandates that children be reevaluated at least every 3 years (and more frequently if requested) to document the effectiveness of a student's current educational program and determine his or her future needs and continued eligibility for special education services. The regulations, however, do not specifically stipulate the components of assessment required to meet these objectives. Postsecondary institutions may not have access to current and comprehensive documentation if they rely on school-based diagnostic information to appropriately plan for students at the college level with no agreed-upon criteria for triennial evaluations. An ongoing dialogue between secondary and postsecondary personnel regarding data-based assessment information and reasonable, appropriate recommendations is critical to ensure a smooth transition to post–high school educational and training opportunities for students with learning disabilities. If the information required as proof of eligibility at the postsecondary level is not the same as what has been provided by elementary and secondary schools, then assessment frequently must be obtained elsewhere, often at the time, effort, and expense of the adult with a learning disability.

Assessment practices under the IDEA have questionable relevancy for postsecondary LD service providers. Of particular concern is the use of aptitude-performance discrepancy formulas to identify individuals with learning disabilities. Under the IDEA, a student diagnosed as having a learning disability must demonstrate a severe discrepancy between intellectual ability (aptitude) and academic achievement (performance) in order to be eligible for services. While there is much disagreement regarding the definition and measurement of this discrepancy, over 50% of the states have incorporated it into their eligibility criteria (Biller & White, 1989; Frankenberger & Harper, 1987; McNutt, 1986; Mercer, Hughes, & Mercer, 1985). In contrast, Section 504 does not specify guidelines for identifying students with learning disabilities or determining eligibility. As discussed in Chapter 3, the use of the aptitude-performance discrepancy model is not appropriate when diagnosing adults with learning disabilities or determining eligibility for services at the postsecondary level. Additional research has strongly advised against using this concept among adults (Gajar et al., 1989; Gregg & Hoy, 1990; Vogel 1987a).

These widely varying practices may also contribute to the frequent delay and possible denial of services for students with learning disabilities as they attempt to access services in adult agencies or postsecondary institutions (Biller & White, 1989). The IDEA now requires that all special education students be provided with "transition services." Transition services are defined as "a coordinated set of activities . . . that promotes movement from school to postschool activities including postsecondary education, vocational training, integrated employment . . . , continuing and adult education, adult services, independent living or community participation" (U.S. Department of Education, 1992, p. 44804 [§ 300.18 (a)]). The IDEA requires that a student's IEP must now include an annual transition plan beginning no later than age 16 (but earlier when appropriate). Without recent comprehensive assessment information, adequate transition plans for students with learning disabilities may not be developed appropriately. For the student going on to higher education, there may be insufficient information to determine appropriate academic adjustments or auxiliary aids necessary to ensure an "equal educational opportunity." On the other hand, secondary school personnel are often frustrated and confused by the myriad of eligibility and testing requirements frequently requested by postsecondary institutions (Anderson, 1992), which may differ from those used in secondary schools. Clearly there is confusion about the type of diagnostic information necessary to provide students with learning disabilities with a smooth transition into postsecondary institutions and other adult services and about who is responsible for providing that information.

Complexity of Adult Assessment

Another assessment challenge is the complexity of diagnosing adults with learning disabilities compared to children. Research conducted throughout the past decade leaves little doubt that learning disabilities persist into adulthood, yet, to date, little evidence has been presented regarding the effect of varying degrees and types of learning disabilities on the performance of adults in postsecondary settings. To complicate matters even further, the manifestations of a learning disability can be expected to change throughout the life span of an individual, influenced by different levels of development and life events (Learning Disabilities Association of America, 1990; National Joint Committee on Learning Disabilities, 1985; Ryan & Heikkila, 1988). For example, a child identified as having a language deficit in elementary school might be diagnosed as having a deficit in written expression in high school. A student with word-recognition problems in junior high school may be identified as having a deficit in reading comprehension in college. In addition, all adults experience many adjustment challenges throughout their lives. For some adults, these challenges might be significantly affected by their learning disability, which may have a negative impact on their ability to concentrate or learn. A diagnostician evaluating adults must have some background in adult development theory to be able to determine, for example, the extent to which a learning disability may be the cause of the learning difficulties of a single parent returning to college for retraining after losing a job and going through a divorce.

The complexities of assessment of adults can be better understood by considering the long-term effects of learning disabilities as documented in adult follow-up studies. In a classic study regarding the problems and concerns of young adults, Blalock (1981) reported that while the processing deficits of these adults appeared to be similar to those of children and adolescents with learning disabilities, they were often more subtle. Problems for this population were most frequently observed in the areas of metacognition and automaticity of skill integration and strongly affected learning and employment situations. In addition, the information and tasks adults were asked to learn and the situations in which they had to function were different from those of younger individuals.

In a comprehensive review of research on the adult status of individuals with learning disabilities, White (1992) concluded that the effects of learning disabilities were frequently not the same as in school-age children. While the majority of the adults in these studies still demonstrated or reported substantial deficits in basic academic areas, their learning disabilities more frequently caused difficulties in employment and social situations. Furthermore, Gerber et al. (1990) found that conditions worsened over time for many adults with learning disabilities. Roughly a quarter of the 133 respondents in their study reported increasing difficulties in adulthood on every survey item that included academic, information-processing, and behavioral characteristics. The significance of the results of these studies for diagnosticians working with adults is twofold. First, the young adults in White's review (1992) were in their 20s and 30s, while the mean age in the Gerber et al. study (1990) was 42.1, with an age range of 23 to 71 years. These data unequivocally document the persistence and pervasiveness of learning disabilities well into adulthood. Second, the Gerber et al. study provided self-reported comparisons of problems resulting from learning disabilities during school-age years (retrospectively) and in adult years. The adult participants were given the opportunity to determine which of their difficulties were currently more of a problem than in past years. Clearly, this research provides some initial evidence for the existence of an adult population with learning disabilities and distinct characteristics and support needs, a population that also has very unique diagnostic needs.

Traditionally, the diagnosis of children with learning disabilities includes the exclusion of other factors as the primary cause of learning difficulties. While this process is relatively easy to implement with young children, it is much more difficult to apply to adults (Cohen, 1984). Because of their developmental status, adults bring with them a much more extensive history of academic problems, compensatory strategies, physical constraints, and psychological concerns (Anderson & Brinckerhoff, 1989; Carlisle & Johnson, 1989;

Cohen, 1984). Identification of a learning disability as the primary cause of an adult's difficulties often depends on a diagnostician's ability to differentiate learning disabilities from other disabilities that could manifest themselves in academic underachievement, language deficits, emotional and social-interpersonal difficulties, nonverbal deficits, and functional limitations in an individual's life-style. Given the heterogeneous population and diverse symptomatology of adults with learning disabilities, evaluators must rule out, or consider the contribution of, sensory impairments, physical disabilities, below-average intelligence, lack of motivation, social-emotional concerns, neuropsychological conditions, lack of educational opportunities, and cultural or language differences as factors affecting an adult's current learning difficulties (D. J. Johnson, 1987b; National Joint Committee on Learning Disabilities, 1987; Vogel, 1989). Making a differential diagnosis regarding an adult with a potential learning disability requires an evaluator to gather extensive assessment information and to have considerable experience with the interpretation of such material.

Constraints of Instrumentation and Qualified Diagnosticians

The subtlety of adult manifestations of a learning disability and the heterogeneity of the population require careful scrutiny of areas to be evaluated and vigilance in the selection of appropriate instruments and procedures. However, a scarcity of standardized, reliable, and valid diagnostic measures for use with college students and adults contributes to the complexity of the assessment process (Cordoni, 1982; Gregg & Hoy, 1990; Mangrum & Strichart, 1988; National Joint Committee on Learning Disabilities, 1985; Vogel, 1987b; Woods, Sedlacek, & Boyer, 1990). Vogel (1985) aptly noted that most diagnostic tests used with this age group are also inappropriate in format, content, and level of difficulty. Research has shown that tests frequently used in the diagnosis of learning disabilities in children (Shepard & Smith, 1983), college students (Beirne-Smith & Deck, 1989; Hughes & Osgood-Smith, 1990; Ostertag & Baker, 1982), and adults (McCue & Goldstein, 1990) are technically inadequate, yet many diagnosticians continue to use them. Shepard and Smith (1983) concluded that many evaluators were unaware of the technical inadequacy of the instruments they used. Others tended to select these measures as the result of the traditional habits of a particular professional group even though more valid instruments were available.

A final concern rests in the dearth of competent and adequately prepared professionals to diagnose or work with adults with learning disabilities (Anderson & Brinckerhoff, 1989; Cordoni, 1982; National Joint Committee on Learning Disabilities, 1985, 1987; Vogel, 1982). Compounding this issue is the wide variety of educational levels and backgrounds of professionals administering LD assessments. In a survey of 35 postsecondary institutions, Carlton and Walkenshaw (1991) reported that the backgrounds of those participating in diagnosis varied significantly and included such fields as education, psychology, clinical psychology, counseling psychology, school psychology, neuropathology, rehabilitation counseling, speech-language pathology, special education, reading, and learning disabilities. The educational training of evaluators surveyed included 46% with doctoral degrees or working on a doctorate, 48% with master's degrees, and 6% at the bachelor's level. McGuire, Hall, Ramirez, and Cullen (1992) noted that the most frequent source of evaluations submitted to the University of Connecticut to validate learning disabilities consisted of school psychologists (64%), followed by private psychologists (29%), and others (7%) such as private educational consultants. D. J. Johnson (1987a) noted that scholars from the fields of medicine, linguistics, neuropsychology, and cognitive and developmental psychology also contribute to the assessment of individuals with learning disabilities.

With such a diverse range of professionals providing diagnostic assessment information, it is not surprising that service providers are concerned about inconsistent findings, confusing reports, and a lack of useful recommendations. Because of the heterogeneity of learning disabilities and the complexity of adult development, many professionals lack adequate training to diagnose adults with learning disabilities. Frequently, these professionals receive training with regard to adults or in the area of learning disabilities (Gregg & Hoy, 1990), but an adequate combination of the two rarely occurs. For the most part, diagnosticians evaluating adults with learning disabilities have little practical experience with this distinct population as a whole. This raises serious concerns about interpretation of diagnostic results as well as about application of those results to recommendations that bear relevance across the wide variety of settings in which these adults must function (e.g., formal education, job training, work, social situations, the community, and relationships). The Learning Disabilities Association of America (1990, p. 2a) further states that "the validity of the Specific Learning Disabilities diagnosis increases when the responsibility for making the judgment is placed with clinicians who hold advanced professional degrees in generally accepted fields and who have two or more years of clinical experience with the relevant age group of the Specific Learning Disabilities population." As a result of nonspecific training among professionals charged with the responsibility of adult assessment, many adults with learning disabilities are misdiagnosed, are provided with little or no guidance regarding appropriate recommendations, or fall through the proverbial cracks.

Multicultural LD Assessment: A Growing Concern

The lack of standardized tests and qualified diagnosticians is nowhere more evident than in the challenge of evaluating individuals with learning disabilities from diverse cultural and linguistic backgrounds. Linguistic and cultural barriers can hamper the administration of test instruments and confound the subsequent interpretation of findings. Researchers have found that cultural bias will inevitably occur and adversely affect the test performance of nonwhite students when the evaluation measures used depend heavily on an understanding of the values of the predominant culture and on proficiency in that language (McLoughlin & Lewis, 1990). Richard, Bloomer, Negron, and Lesser (1991) observed that a number of inappropriate instruments are currently being used to obtain standard scores on minority students. Salvia and Ysseldyke (1991) similarly indicated that there has been a tendency to systematically exclude nonwhite individuals from standardization samples, which further biases the norm samples. Salvia and Ysseldyke (1991) added that if nonwhites differ in acculturation and are excluded from the field testing of test items, the test scaling would be in error. Beyond these concerns regarding test construction, the identification of learning disabilities in minority groups is further complicated by the lack of a uniform definition of learning disabilities and the inappropriateness of its application to individuals from diverse cultural backgrounds. Olivarez, Palmer, and Guillemard (1992, p. 175) aptly pointed out that "a critical definitional marker of learning disabilities (LD) is the presence of a severe discrepancy between a student's general cognitive ability and achievement. An important assumption underlying this concept of discrepancy is that the predictive relationship between IQ and achievement measures is similar across students, regardless of ethnic or other demographic differences."

As discussed in Chapter 3, educational problems that are the result of learning disabilities may resemble problems that are related to diverse sociocultural backgrounds. It is often difficult for diagnosticians and LD service providers to differentiate learning disabilities from poor academic backgrounds or a lack of educational opportunities with the evaluation tools presently available. Junkala and Paul (1987) noted that identification of minority individuals with learning disabilities is further complicated because conjecture remains among some researchers as to whether or not learning disabilities occur universally in the population and are cross-cultural in nature. Given that by the year 2050, at least 47% of the population will have minority status in the United States (Davis, 1993), it is imperative that more research be conducted in this area. A growing body of literature has begun to address issues related to cultural diversity and assessment of children with disabilities (Fradd, Figueroa, & Correas, 1989; Olivarez, et al., 1992), but a paucity of research exists regarding the assessment of minority adults with learning disabilities.

Jarrow (1990) is one of the few authors who have explored this topic at the postsecondary level. She stated that "there seems to be little doubt in the professional community that the currently available testing instruments and batteries used to determine a learning disability in postsecondary education are largely inappropriate for minority students" (p. 15). She pointed out that very few tests have been developed and normed for use with individuals other than native speakers of standard English. Despite these problems with test construction, Jarrow (1990) concluded that there is no need to develop new or different tests to determine a learning disability in diverse populations; instead, what is needed is that tests be given by "enlightened evaluators" who can administer them in a nonstandardized fashion. Richard et al. (1991) concurred, noting that one approach that avoids the problems of invalid norms, inaccurate estimation of ability and skills, and a misunderstanding of cultural experiences is an evaluation strategy that integrates data from a variety of sources: observation, interview, diagnostic teaching, and direct assessment.

At the postsecondary level, diagnosticians and service providers need to ask students from culturally or linguistically diverse backgrounds in-depth questions about their ability to master skills in their native language, the extent to which their performance in English is at variance with their performance in their native language, and, most importantly, the types of compensatory strategies that have been helpful in working around their deficits. It is essential that practitioners utilize informal diagnostic procedures rather than relying exclusively on standardized measures that may have little generalization to non-white populations. Furthermore, diagnosticians who are sensitive to cultural and linguistic differences in students are able to tease out subtle language-based deficits that standardized test instruments may miss. By carefully observing the student's level of metacognitive awareness and his or her use of problem-solving strategies during testing, a more accurate picture of the student's true abilities can be established. On occasion it may be necessary for practitioners to alter or eliminate selective subtests, extend test administration time, or clarify questions for a student. Although these procedures greatly affect test reliability and validity, diagnosticians may find such creative approaches necessary for use with linguistically and culturally diverse students. As long as these deviations from the standardized testing protocol are explained to the student in advance and are well documented in the diagnostic report, all parties may benefit by having a more complete picture of a student's true potential for college success.

IDENTIFYING THE PURPOSES
OF LD ASSESSMENT

When providing or requesting an LD assessment, service providers and diagnosticians must give serious consideration to the purpose for which the assessment is being administered. Frequently, an initial assessment is sought to establish a diagnosis or verify a prior diagnosis of a learning disability. In this instance, an adult seeking assessment may have several objectives: (a) to determine if past and/

or present problems could be attributed to the existence of a specific learning disability; (b) to identify or eliminate other potential reasons for existing learning problems; or (c) to obtain a better understanding of his or her strengths, limitations, educational or employment potential, and severity of deficits (D. J. Johnson, 1987b; Vogel, 1989). For most adults, becoming aware of the manifestations of their disability is crucial to obtaining appropriate academic adjustments, auxiliary aids, or reasonable accommodations in an educational or employment setting.

In many postsecondary institutions or adult service agencies, documentation of a learning disability is required to determine eligibility for services. Rothstein (1986) addressed this issue of eligibility criteria and pointed out the problems that arise in determining whether a student actually has a learning disability. Although identification of a learning disability under the IDEA is not binding, Rothstein (1986, p. 236) suggested that such a determination would be likely to carry significant weight in justifying eligibility under Section 504. She further stated: "Individuals with a record of the disability as a result of public school identification or of an assessment done by qualified professionals should have little difficulty in providing the college or university with the documentation necessary to indicate that a handicap exists. This should entitle the student to nondiscriminatory treatment and some accommodation."

Although a previously diagnosed learning disability may fall within the Section 504 eligibility criterion of having a history of a disability, the type, quality, and recency of information contained in the documentation may be of questionable value in assisting service providers to determine appropriate postsecondary accommodations (Brinckerhoff et al., 1992; Gregg & Hoy, 1990; Scott, 1990; Vogel, 1985). As Brinckerhoff et al. (1992, p. 419) indicated, "There should always be a data-based connection between the student's learning strengths and weaknesses and his or her eligibility for *specific* types of accommodations." It is important that both diagnosticians and service providers recognize the individual nature of a learning disability and reflect this in the corroborating documentation rather than suggesting the same academic adjustments or auxiliary aids for all students with learning disabilities (D'Amico, 1989). Scott (1990) underscored the importance of this "match" by asserting that requests for support services and/or academic accommodations should be based on evidence of individual needs in addition to documentation of a learning disability.

Another important purpose of LD assessment is to assist students in developing a plan or program for pursuing realistic educational and career goals. Additionally, diagnostic data can provide the basis for identifying appropriate support services such as individualized instruction, remediation, or tutorial support in specific coursework (Vogel, 1987b). Such information also plays a key role in the LD service provider's ability to recommend specific instructional or testing accommodations, program modifications, adaptive equipment, or compensatory techniques. LD service providers are often asked to substantiate the validity of a request for a course substitution or waiver. Assessment data should be used as the basis for rendering such judgments. The practice of waiving course requirements or providing substitutions as a uniform policy for all students identified as having a learning disability does a disservice to students, who should have the opportunity to pursue specific courses with reasonable accommodations. Chapter 8 provides a detailed discussion of this topic. The next section addresses the current status of assessment procedures among postsecondary institutions.

THE ASSESSMENT PROCESS

Traditionally, assessment for students with learning disabilities has been viewed as a single evaluation in which students perform a set of formal tasks or tests, the results of which are used to make decisions about instructional strategies or program selection. This approach is too restricted and ignores many clues that are valuable in identifying the causes of a student's learning difficulties (Gregg & Hoy, 1990) as well as the modifications or accommodations necessary to assist students with learning disabilities to successfully adapt to educational, employment, or life situations. Salvia and Ysseldyke (1991) define assessment as a process of collecting information or data for the purposes of clarifying and verifying the existence of educational problems and making decisions about students. Clearly, a key element in the assessment of students with learning disabilities is that it is an ongoing *process*, a process that is essential to differentiate learning disabilities in college students from other handicapping conditions that can result in difficulties at the postsecondary level. Furthermore, if the ultimate goal is to help students to accommodate their learning disability in employment and daily-living settings, they must practice the skill of evaluating learning situations and incorporating, learning, or integrating new strategies. When it is viewed as an ongoing process, assessment can be placed on a continuum that can be modified and refined as the field changes or an institution or program grows and matures.

Providing LD Assessment: The Role of Postsecondary Institutions

In several recent position papers addressing the needs of adults with learning disabilities, the National Joint Committee on Learning Disabilities (1983, 1985) stated that postsecondary institutions must provide guidelines for the development of assessment procedures that will identify an individual's needs, including patterns of abilities and disabilities. Mangrum and Strichart (1988) recommended that programs for college students with learning disabilities make arrangements for diagnostic testing followed by the development of an individualized student plan. They also advised that an LD college program requires at least one psychoeducational diagnostician to compile the evaluation data used to identify the specific educational needs of these students. Levinson (1986) and T. Decker, Polloway, and Decker (1985) proposed that comprehensive postsecondary LD programs must include identification and assessment services. Others argue that it is the responsibility of the institution to provide diagnostic assessment to ensure quality control of eligibility as well as appropriate recommendations concerning programs and accommodations (Gregg & Hoy, 1990; Mellard & Deshler, 1984; Vogel, 1985, 1987a; Whyte et al., 1991).

However, Section 504 does not mandate the provision of diagnostic assessment by a college or university. Instead, the "burden of proof" is shifted to the student (Brinckerhoff et al., 1992). Heyward, Lawton, and Associates (1991b, p. 3) further stated: "A student requesting academic adjustments is responsible for providing documentation that clearly identifies the disability and provides sufficient information regarding the manifestations of the disability to permit the institution to make a determination as to whether the requested adjustments are appropriate."

In the past few years, the issue of whether or not to provide LD diagnostic assessments has become more than just a decision about program philosophy and service-delivery options. As the numbers of self-identified students with learning disabilities increase, service providers are faced with serious gaps in the type and quality of the documentation they receive (Gregg & Hoy, 1990; McGuire, Shaw, Bloomer, & Anderson, 1992), placing them in the middle of a major ethical, and potentially legal, dilemma. If an institution disputes the documentation provided by a student, it may have to pay for or provide a second or updated evaluation (D'Amico, 1989; Heyward, Lawton, & Associates, 1991b). In addition, institutions may risk possible litigation based on a student's documented history of a disability. On the other hand, LD service providers are obligated to uphold the academic integrity of the institution by ensuring that documentation provides sufficient information to support a student's request for specific modifications. Thus it is not surprising that many postsecondary institutions are wrestling with the dilemma of whether or not to provide diagnostic assessment services.

As postsecondary institutions define their role in the LD assessment process, three areas must be carefully examined: (a) the mission of the institution or program, (b) the institutional purpose for LD assessment, and (c) the availability of appropriate resources. As discussed in Chapter 6, an institution's mission must be considered as the foundation for the development of LD support services or programs. A research institution that offers strategy-based services by trained LD specialists might provide diagnostic assessment within the context of graduate training programs and diagnostic internships. In other settings that offer generic support services to all students, the availability of assessment services may not be as critical.

Determining the purpose of LD assessments depends on the function of assessment within the delivery of services to students with learning disabilities. If a diagnostic assessment is primarily used to determine eligibility for general support services, such as counseling, peer tutoring, auxiliary aids, and exam modifications, documentation that includes a disability label might be sufficient. In open-admissions institutions, however, where the incidence of at-risk students including those with learning disabilities is traditionally much higher, more extensive assessment procedures involving screening, identification, and documentation of specific accommodations might be necessary to serve this growing cohort (Vogel, 1985). Institutions that provide data-based services might implement elaborate assessment procedures including individual student plans.

The availability of campus resources is the final and often the most critical issue for postsecondary institutions considering the option of providing LD assessment services. As previously noted, the assessment of college students and adults with learning disabilities is complex and requires professionals who are explicitly trained to diagnose this population. Such procedures are best performed by a multidisciplinary team (Gregg & Hoy, 1990; Learning Disabilities Association of America, 1990; Mellard, 1990; National Joint Committee on Learning Disabilities, 1987), including personnel knowledgeable in areas such as special education, school psychology, speech and language, and psychology. This is often a feasible option only for those institutions with sufficient staff, faculty, or graduate training programs. Financial resources also strongly affect an institution's decision to incorporate this service component, since LD assessment is a very time-consuming, labor-intensive procedure, often involving several days of testing and extensive staff hours to write reports and review results with students. In these times of staff reductions and budget cutbacks, colleges and universities must determine if providing LD assessment is an efficient use of institutional resources (Oliker, 1991; Trueba, 1991; Woods et al., 1990).

LD Assessment on Campus: State of the Art

Information regarding the availability or function of LD diagnostic assessment services on college campuses is scarce. What little research has been done is primarily limited to general surveys or descriptions of LD assessment in a single institution or geographic area. In an overview of services offered to students with learning disabilities by the California Community College system over a five-year period, Ostertag, Pearson, and Baker (1986) reported that over 97% of the institutions offered diagnostic learning assessments. Beirne-Smith and Deck (1989) surveyed 108 contact persons at 4-year institutions regarding the types of services provided to students with learning disabilities during the 1985–86 academic year. When questioned about assessment procedures, 71% of the respondents reported the availability of academic assessment, 58% provided intellectual testing, 43% offered career or vocational assessment, and 40% provided psychological or personality testing. Over one-fourth of the responding institutions (29%) did not provide any type of assessment at all. Even less is known about the availability of assessment services to students with learning disabilities attending graduate and professional schools. Parks, Antonoff, Drake, Skiba, and Soberman (1987) surveyed 223 schools to determine the status of programs and services. Although some of the results appear to be conflicting, it was clear that only a minimal percentage (<25%) offered on-site diagnostic testing services.

To date, only one descriptive study has focused exclusively on diagnostic assessment practices and procedures for students with learning disabilities at the postsecondary level. Carlton and Walkenshaw (1991) surveyed thirty-five 2- and 4-year college programs that provide support services for college students with learning disabilities and include a diagnostic component. With respect to eligibility, all programs in this sample required similar documentation for students with a previous LD diagnosis, including a psychoeducational assessment and/or an IEP from the previous school. Few schools requested the administration of specific tests, but most had requirements for the recency of the evaluation information. The majority of respondents requested completion of the evaluation within the past 3 years. Carlton and Walkenshaw also reported that 50% of the schools appeared to be using a diagnostic team of two or more individuals, although a single person was making the diagnosis in 40% of the responding institutions. Survey results indicated confusion and inconsistencies regarding the assessment of both international students and those with emotional illnesses or disabilities.

In order to provide adequate support services for college students with learning disabilities, consistent, reliable, and comprehensive diagnostic assessment procedures are crucial for this population (Gregg & Hoy, 1990; Mellard & Deshler, 1984; Parks et al., 1987; Vogel, 1985; Woods et al., 1990). However, there are advantages and disadvantages to providing LD diagnostic assessment services on campus. Postsecondary institutions must carefully balance the availability of resources with the benefits to the institution and the students. In some instances, this may require selecting a less than optimal alternative until additional resources become available. In others, it may necessitate the reduction of existing services. A few colleges or universities may have the resources to develop and support comprehensive assessment services.

Although the evidence is sparse, several institutions have begun to seriously grapple with various aspects of providing LD diagnostic assessment. At the University of Georgia, an extensive review of documentation provided by applicants with learning disabilities since 1986 revealed that a significant percentage (53.6%) did not meet the university's eligibility criteria (Gregg & Hoy, 1990). As a result, the University of Georgia chose to take a "proactive stance," requiring students who requested modifications because of a learning disability to undergo a psychoeducational evaluation. Diagnostic information from outside evaluators is used to supplement the university's findings and often shortens the assessment process, but such documentation is not used as the primary basis for determining eligibility for services. As Gregg and Hoy pointed out, "While the initial development of a clinic operation is costly, the long-term maintenance of the evaluation component is minimal to a university when compared to what could happen if everyone who said he [or she] was learning disabled or who provided outside assessments requested services. Control of the assessment process provides accountability in an equitable and cost-efficient manner" (p. 33).

Through the McBurney Disability Resource Center, the University of Wisconsin–Madison provided a comprehensive educational assessment both to students with a previous LD diagnosis and to students with suspected learning disabilities in order to determine the nature of their academic difficulties and make appropriate recommendations (Trueba, 1991). Although the assessment services were widely used, the size of the center's staff did not grow to meet the demand. In the spring of 1990, since the majority of students requesting this service were identified as not having a learning disability (82.5%) and the time required for testing was lengthy, the center decided to limit the services to those who had a previous diagnosis and needed to update their documentation. Students seeking an initial diagnosis were referred to appropriate campus or community resources.

In an attempt to find a more permanent solution, the McBurney Center collaborated with the School of Education to develop a student assessment service that provides LD assessment for all students (C. Trueba, personal communication, December 2, 1992). Although the McBurney Center staff supports the decision to meet staffing considerations by reducing LD assessment services, they are attempting to respond to student needs by securing an institutional commitment to increase testing efforts. Since the cost of LD assessment can be very high for an institution in terms of the inevitable backlog of referrals, extensive staff hours for testing, and, ultimately, staff "burnout," the decision to provide such services must be carefully considered. As Trueba (1991, p. 6) stated: "Providing faculty and staff . . . with evidence of need as well as the reality of current resources . . . can be a compelling argument for a more integrated approach to providing a valuable and much requested educational service such as psycho-educational assessment."

In light of these issues, colleges and universities must develop assessment policies and procedures that are consistent with the institution's mission, services, and resources. The next section will provide a detailed discussion of elements in the assessment process, including referral procedures, screening, diagnostic testing (e.g., areas and methods of assessment), obtaining appropriate diagnostic testing, the diagnostic report, and interpreting and applying diagnostic assessment data.

COMPONENTS OF THE ASSESSMENT PROCESS

The level of assessment services available at an institution plays a significant role in the institution's response to the requirements of Section 504. Assessment services in postsecondary institutions can be viewed on a continuum, as shown in Figure 4.1, ranging from the least comprehensive to the most comprehensive. Some institutions provide general support services to all students; those who self-identify as having a learning disability receive requested accommodations on a case-by-case basis. Other institutions have developed policies regarding the appropriateness of LD documentation and provide assessment services to corroborate diagnoses and validate requests for accommodations. The assessment procedures on this continuum will vary from campus to campus and may change within a single institution over time as the result of staffing or funding alterations. For example, a private university with LD support services located within

STAGES IN THE ASSESSMENT PROCESS

STAGES IN THE ASSESSMENT PROCESS	Least Comprehensive					Most Comprehensive
Determination of Eligibility for LD Support Services Under Section 504	Based on student request for services	Based on any documentation of previous LD diagnosis	Based on previous documentation and supplementary testing	Based on previous documentation by qualified professionals	Diagnostic assessment provided by on-campus resources and supplemented with previous documentation	Comprehensive diagnostic assessment provided by LD program and supplemented with previous documentation
Determination of Initial LD Diagnosis	No testing provided	No testing provided	Prereferral screening provided	Prereferral screening and assistance obtaining assessment from appropriate outside sources provided	→	→
Referral to Outside Sources for Diagnostic Testing	Provided for students requesting initial LD diagnosis	Provided for students requesting initial LD diagnosis	Provided for students requesting initial LD diagnosis	Provided for students requesting initial LD diagnosis	Provided for students requesting initial LD diagnosis	Provided for students needing additional specialized assessments
Development and Implementation of Individual Student Service Plan	None provided	None provided	None provided	Provided by LD program or support services	Provided by LD program or support service	Provided by LD program

disabled student services might periodically convene an advisory group to review LD documentation and recommend appropriate accommodations. As this population becomes the largest category of students with disabilities on campus, the university might hire a full-time LD coordinator whose job responsibilities include providing diagnostic evaluations. Within a short period of time, the demand for LD assessment services can consume the majority of the coordinator's time and attention. If funds are not available to hire additional staff, the institution may be forced to eliminate or reduce the scope of the assessment services.

The following sections discuss a variety of considerations in five major components of LD assessment services: (a) referral procedures, (b) screening options, (c) diagnostic testing, (d) obtaining appropriate diagnostic testing, and (e) interpreting and applying diagnostic information.

REFERRAL PROCEDURES

One of the most important steps in the assessment process is the referral. Whether students self-identify or suspect that academic difficulties may be due to a learning disability, an institution must have some mechanism for helping students access the office or individual responsible for providing appropriate services. Heyward (1992, p. 208) reported that under Section 504, "while an institution is responsible for providing information to students regarding its duty to provide auxiliary aids and academic adjustments and regarding the persons to contact to receive such, it has no obligation to accommodate needs that have not been brought to its attention or to provide accommodations that have not been requested."

The regulations do not state the method by which such information must be provided; however, Heyward, Lawton, and Associates (1990) further advised that the chosen method, while up to the discretion of the institution, must be effective. It is no longer sufficient for institutions to merely indicate that services are available for students with learning disabilities. Proactive and systematic efforts must be made to educate students, faculty, and staff regarding the availability of these services as well as to clearly delineate the procedures for accessing them.

Referrals can originate from a variety of sources including the student, faculty, parents, and counselors (Beirne-Smith & Deck, 1989; Ostertag et al., 1986). Once a referral has been initiated, the service provider must either validate the learning disability and recommend appropriate accommodations or, in the case of a suspected learning disability, facilitate the process for pursuing an initial diagnosis. The exact procedures implemented at this stage will depend on the available assessment services (see Figure 4.1); however, certain basic concepts are often addressed through the initial contact. Of utmost importance is the issue of confidentiality. Many students are reluctant to disclose their learning disability and only seek institutional assistance after much deliberation. Therefore, it is critical for LD service providers to assure students that all information is confidential and will be kept in a secured fashion. Section 504 permits institutions to make inquiries subsequent to admission for the purpose of determining whether students might require accommodations (see § 104.42[b][4]). However, Heyward (1992, p. 191) noted that "information provided as a result of such inquiries must be kept confidential and the purposes for which it may be used are limited to the provision of accommodations." LD service providers should clearly explain procedures regarding the procurement and release of confidential information during the referral process. A signed release-of-information form should be obtained from each student.

At this point in the process, the issue of the recency of previous LD documentation often surfaces. Service providers concerned about fulfilling an institution's obligation to provide academic adjustments and accommodations for qualified students may question the validity of documentation that is more than 3 years old, the yardstick commonly accepted under the IDEA. Section 504 does not set any standard for the quantity and quality of documentary evidence that students with learning disabilities must provide to justify the need for services (Heyward, Lawton, & Associates, 1992a). A student must provide documentation that clearly identifies the existence of a learning disability and the need for the requested accommodation. In turn, the institution should review the documentation to determine whether it has sufficient data to support the student's request. Heyward, Lawton, and Associates (1992a, pp. 9, 10) concluded, "If it does not, it doesn't matter whether the documentation is three months or three years old. Conversely, if it does, the same should hold true."

In the best interests of both students and the institution, the LD service provider should provide a detailed explanation of the procedures, time lines, and outcomes that follow the initial referral. Students must be aware of their responsibilities—for example, providing previous records or evaluation reports, completing a detailed referral form, providing copies of transcripts, and following through on any subsequent appointments. Services provided by the institution (e.g., intake interview, screening, diagnostic testing, or referrals to outside practitioners) must be clarified as well. At this point, as Vogel (1985) indicated, students may have an underlying assumption that they have a learning disability by the mere fact that they have referred themselves or been referred to the appropriate office or individual on campus. In reality, this assumption must be verified, and the referral is only the first step in a potentially lengthy assessment process. Once students become aware of the time, effort, and commitment involved, they may choose not to pursue the assessment process and may opt for a different solution to their academic difficulties.

Clarifying the reason for referral is the next step in this process. Without a clear understanding of the presenting problems, the student and the LD service provider may not have sufficient information on which to base a decision regarding further action. In addition to a brief initial interview, it is helpful to have students provide their perceptions of their current difficulties by completing a referral information form to be used in the next stage of the process.

SCREENING OPTIONS

The screening phase of the assessment process serves two basic purposes. In some institutions this phase consists primarily of an intake interview and is considered the first step of the evaluation. The intake interview is used to develop a rapport with a student and to obtain detailed background information to assist the LD service provider or diagnostician choose appropriate tools, interpret results, and recommend services and accommodations. On other campuses, as the number of students with learning disabilities increases, a screening process is implemented as a "first sort" to determine eligibility for further diagnostic testing.

Several institutions that provide in-house testing developed screening procedures after examining their assessment "hit rate" or the percentage of students who were identified as having a learning disability after receiving diagnostic testing. Over a 4-year period, the University of Wisconsin–Madison identified only 17.5% (35) of the 200 students tested as having a learning disability (Trueba, 1991). The Ohio State University described their "hit rate" in recent years as only one-third of all students tested (Carlton & Knapke, 1991). As a result of similar findings, the University of Connecticut recently instituted a screening process that appeared to increase the accuracy of identifying students with suspected, yet unidentified learning disabilities. Over a 1-year period, 46% of the students referred to the LD program were advised to complete psychoeducational testing (McGuire, Shaw, et al., 1992). Of those evaluated, 54.5% were diagnosed as having a specific learning disability. After the implementation of a formal screening and interdisciplinary assessment process, the University of Massachusetts at Amherst's rate of accuracy in identifying students with learning disabilities increased from 20–25% to 64% (Gillespie-Silver, Vincent, Mercaitis, Baran, & Fldrych-Puzzo, 1992).

Whether students receive LD diagnostic evaluations on campus or are referred to outside professionals, many colleges and universities acknowledge the excessive cost and time commitment involved for both students and staff. In such cases, the function of a screening process is to systematically examine potential predictors of LD diagnosis (e.g., memory deficits, writing deficiencies, or organizational problems) and identify those students who are most likely to benefit from more extensive assessment services. Screening procedures can greatly enhance the accuracy of the assessment process, thus providing efficient use of existing resources.

Screening Procedures

Although procedures used in the screening process vary across institutions, some similarities do exist. The use of an interview appears to be the most common approach to screening (Carlton & Walkenshaw, 1991). Some institutions implement two interview levels. The first level, a prescreening interview, often occurs during the referral process and serves two purposes. First, it provides the opportunity for service providers and students to gather information relevant to the presenting problems, to document a history of past difficulties or attempts to seek assistance, and to obtain additional input (e.g., from instructors). Most frequently, prescreening information is collected through an oral interview, although in some instances—for example, at the University of Connecticut—students are also requested to complete a detailed questionnaire and study-skills inventory, and to compile a variety of data into a comprehensive packet (McGuire, Shaw, et al., 1992). Second, a prescreening interview allows service providers to determine whether a student's difficulties appear to be the result of a possible learning disability or whether other issues, such as poor study habits, difficulty living independently, or social or emotional concerns are interfering with academic progress.

The second interview is at a more in-depth level and is frequently called an intake interview. A review of the assessment process in a number of institutions reveals that the intake interview is used to review referral information or gather more information, through either formal or informal measures. At the University of Connecticut, for example, a service provider reviews the responses to a detailed questionnaire with a student and administers a series of subtests as an informal screening (McGuire, Shaw, et al., 1992). The University of Massachusetts uses an interdisciplinary team to conduct an extensive screening that includes both group and individual activities (Gillespie-Silver et al., 1992). This team is composed of professionals from the areas of audiology, speech and language, counseling and academic development, and neuropsychology.

The last stage in the screening process involves a review of all information gathered through the prescreening process and/or the intake interview in order to render a judgment about subsequent steps. Depending on the structure of the LD assessment services, such decisions are made by either a single individual or a team of professionals. Recommendations can then be made to refer the student to the next level of LD assessment services or to other services on campus (e.g., counseling services or an academic-skills center).

As a final note, some institutions, particularly those offering LD assessment on campus, include an additional interview level. This level is usually the first segment of the diagnostic evaluation and is conducted by the professionals providing the assessment. Referred to by such terms as *diagnostic intake* or *clinical intake interview*, this procedure actually documents information that is integrated into the diagnostic report and is not considered a screening process.

Methodology

The fact that limited information is available to describe the actual methods or tools used by various institutions during screening suggests that this process is in its infancy. While there are no clear answers, research is beginning to emerge regarding the experiences of several postsecondary institutions. The Program for Students with Learning Disabilities at the University of Alberta, Canada, reported initially trying a number of screening devices that were available on the market (Whyte et al., 1991). However, while it was initially time-consuming to develop their own intake interview schedule, this method provided much more valuable information for use in developing strategies with students. In a similar fashion, Carlton and Knapke (1991) conducted a study of intake questions on 101 screening interviews to determine which questions were good discriminators between those students who were ultimately diagnosed as having a learning disability and those who were referred for a variety of other learning problems. In the California Community College system, over 95% of the LD programs provide personal intake interviews (Ostertag et al., 1986). Currently, this intake interview is being distributed in a computerized format that is designed to increase the efficiency and accuracy with which information is collected and shared with both students and staff (Mellard, 1990).

In addition to or in conjuction with the personal interview, a number of institutions are using and developing intake questionnaires. Some questionnaires are designed to be completed by the service provider during an interview with a student. Others are completed independently by the student and are later reviewed in an interview with the service provider. Frequently, procedures at this stage also include an analysis of past records or previous documentation. Additional measures utilized during the screening process include standardized self-report instruments (Mellard, 1990), informal writing samples (Carlton & Walkenshaw, 1991), and screening "batteries" composed of both formal and informal tasks (McGuire, Shaw, et al., 1992). There is no one "best" method for gathering information. An institution's choice of methodology depends on staffing, resources, program philosophy, and knowledge of the needs of the specific population accessing such services.

Content and Sources of Screening Information

Regardless of the screening procedures implemented or the methodology used to gather information, there is ample evidence that a wide range of topics must be addressed during this process to elicit the critical information necessary to diagnose and meet the needs of adults with learning disabilities (Block et al., 1986; Gillespie-Silver et al., 1992; Mellard, 1990; Vogel, 1989; Whyte et al., 1991). Areas to be considered during the screening interview process should include:

- Current areas of difficulty
- Medical history
- Employment history
- Psychological history
- Processing abilities
- Interpersonal skills
- Educational history
- Family history
- Developmental history
- Academic strengths and weaknesses
- Study skills and work habits
- Personal issues

Information relevant to these areas may be obtained by direct questions, but it is more than likely that student responses will surface throughout a personal interview or review of a questionnaire. Additional areas that may be used to probe for further details during the screening process and a sample intake questionnaire, "The McBurney Resource Center Student Inventory" (Brinckerhoff, 1986), are included in Appendix C.

The primary source for obtaining background information is the student. Indeed, as Vogel (1989, b. 121) noted, "Some of the most valuable information is provided by the adults themselves during the intake interview, or from questionnaires, rating scales, and check lists that they fill out." While this may appear obvious, many service providers and diagnosticians fail to take advantage of this valuable resource, tending to rely instead on formal diagnostic measures that are often not appropriately designed to procure reliable information from adults with learning disabilities. A second source of background information consisting of other professionals who have interacted with the student can be used if time permits. These professionals may include campus faculty or staff, high school personnel, or other specialists who have evaluated or worked with the student (e.g., counselors, therapists, or psychologists). In certain cases, particularly where issues of family or developmental history are of concern, a parent or other relative may be able to provide additional information. LD service providers must be cognizant of the fact, however, that these students are adults and any attempt to communicate with other individuals must be done only with the students' written consent.

DIAGNOSTIC TESTING

Once a student has completed the referral and/or the screening processes, the LD service provider or a team of professionals must determine the next step in the assessment process, as illustrated in Figure 4.2. Students with previous LD documentation may be eligible for services on some campuses and a determination can be made regarding appropriate interventions. If at either the referral or screening stage a student is not eligible for services, he or she should be referred to other general campus supports. Institutions that do not provide in-house diagnostic services may request that students obtain an evaluation from outside professionals.

Areas of Assessment

Frequently further diagnostic testing is provided by an institution to either supplement previous LD documentation or establish an initial LD diagnosis in order to identify appropriate academic accommodations. Although the extent of the testing may vary depending on the type of services to be provided (e.g., remediation, learning

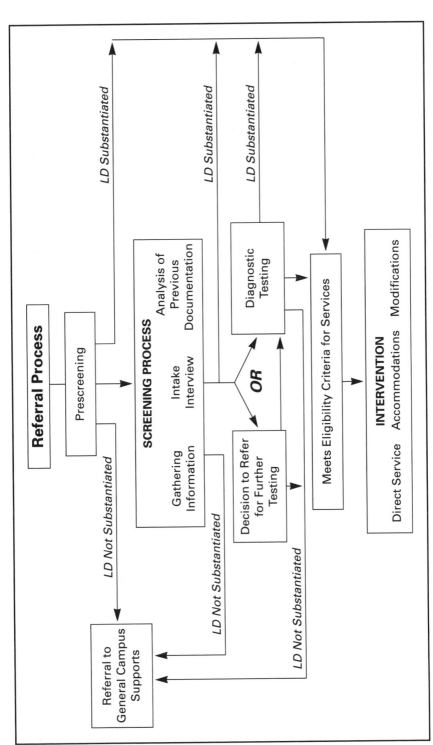

Figure 4.2. The assessment process for students with learning disabilities.

strategies, compensatory techniques, individual instruction, and content tutoring), certain areas of functioning should be addressed in any LD assessment. Furthermore, the NJCLD (National Joint Committee on Learning Disabilities, 1987) stressed the importance of evaluating a student's strengths as well as weaknesses when diagnosing and planning for individuals with learning disabilities.

An initial area of concern in postsecondary institutions is whether a student has the intellectual or cognitive ability to successfully perform college-level work. This is a growing issue, particularly in open-admissions institutions where the enrollment of students who are not "college-able" is increasing (Anderson, 1992). Assessment of college students should also include those areas of functioning that have been observed to be more of a problem for adults with learning disabilities (Vogel, 1985). Two of the most critical areas affecting students' ability to succeed in college are academic achievement and information processing. Vogel (1989) and Whyte et al. (1991) identified aspects of these areas that should typically be evaluated: receptive and expressive oral and written language, including phonemic, syntactic, and semantic abilities; word-attack skills and reading comprehension of single words and paragraphs read orally and silently, as well as reading rate; mathematical reasoning and computation; verbal and nonverbal concept formation; and auditory- and visual-processing abilities, including memory, sequencing, speed, perception, and discrimination. Additional concerns to be addressed are attention and motor skills, especially fine motor and coordination abilities. Finally, written expression, a skill that is vital to the success of most college students, is rarely adequately evaluated. Of particular importance to college success is the evaluation of a student's study skills and habits. Included should be measures of organizational skills, learning strategies, and application skills.

Recently, the social and emotional aspects of adults with learning disabilities have received increased attention. It is clear that psychosocial issues (discussed in Chapter 5) often have a significant impact on postsecondary performance. In a review of four follow-up studies, Bruck (1987) revealed that adults with learning disabilities were more likely to show adjustment problems than their normal peers and that social and emotional difficulties were widely distributed in this population. Likewise, Cohen (1984, p. 27) suggested that for college students with learning disabilities "it is very likely that psychological concerns and conflicts will also be present." Thus, it is important to consider the social and emotional development of students (e.g., social competence, communication skills, interpersonal relationships, and self-efficacy) during the LD assessment process.

LD assessments traditionally address the areas that have the most significant impact on a student's ability to be successful in a college environment; however, ultimately these individuals must leave their campuses and enter the world of work. As Satcher and Dooley-Dickey (1991, p. 50) indicate, "The impact of learning disabilities is not limited to academic functioning." Particularly for students in vocationally oriented programs, it is critical to address the career goals and interests of students with learning disabilities, especially as they are affected by individual strengths and weaknesses.

Methods of Evaluation

An LD diagnostic evaluation is a process that begins with the initial referral and continues throughout the entire assessment process, including interviews, testing, and evaluation of interventions. As D. J. Johnson (1987b, p. 12) emphasized, "Diagnosis is not simply a matter of administering a test battery." Assessment procedures will vary according to the referral needs of each student but should not be limited to academic areas or rely primarily on formal, standardized measures (National Joint Committee on Learning Disabilities, 1987; Vogel, 1989). Service providers and diagnosticians alike must integrate data obtained through a variety of methods and activities in order to understand the extent and scope of the difficulties experienced by adults with learning disabilities.

In a position paper addressing assessment and diagnostic issues confronting the field of learning disabilities, the NJCLD (National Joint Committee on Learning Disabilities, 1987) recognized the importance of collecting data from both academic and nonacademic sources, since the manifestations of a learning disability persist over the life span and vary based on a person's age and developmental stage and the demands of a particular task or setting (e.g., social, academic, or employment). They recommended that in addition to standardized testing, information should be gathered using methods such as interviews, direct observations, case histories, error analysis, curriculum-based assessment, and diagnostic teaching. Houck, Engelhard, and Geller (1989, p. 66) recommended the use of self-assessment instruments as a "quick means for focusing on important student attributes and identifying perceived areas of need." In some instances, when no other appropriate tools exist, professionals may have to devise their own informal tasks as well. Other informal methods suggested in the literature include record reviews (Brinckerhoff & Anderson, 1989; Hawks et al., 1990), task analysis, checklists, inventories, and rating scales (Whyte et al., 1991).

Testing Instruments

Literature regarding the assessment of college students and adults with learning disabilties revealed one indisputable finding: No single battery of standardized tests is consistently used to diagnose this population (Brinckerhoff, 1989; Carlton & Walkenshaw, 1991; Mangrum & Strichart, 1988). The lack of consensus among diagnosticians regarding which specific tests to use reflects the heterogeneity of adults with learning disabilities, the specific needs of various populations, the lack of available valid and reliable instruments, and the varied background and training of professionals administering diagnostic evaluations. For many practitioners, time and economic constraints may also contribute to the choice of particular measures.

Current research provides a more comprehensive overview of the types of instruments being used by postsecondary institutions to diagnose students with learning disabilities (Beirne-Smith & Deck, 1989; Carlton & Walkenshaw, 1991; Mangrum & Strichart, 1988; McGuire, Shaw, et al., 1992; Ostertag et al., 1986; Woods et al., 1990). The tests most frequently used to measure cognitive or intellectual ability are the *Wechsler Adult Intelligence Scale–Revised* (*WAIS-R*) (Wechsler, 1981), the *WAIS* (Wechsler, 1955), or the *Wechsler Intelligence Scale for Children–Revised* (Wechsler, 1974) in the case of high school documentation. At the postsecondary level, the *Woodcock-Johnson Psycho-Educational Battery–Revised* (*WJPEB-R*), Part I (Woodcock & Johnson, 1989), or the first edition (Woodcock & Johnson, 1977) are often used as cognitive ability measures.

Achievement or educational instruments are the next most widely reported assessment tools. The two most popular tests are the *WJPEB-R*, Part II (Woodcock & Johnson, 1989), or the first edition (Woodcock & Johnson, 1977) and the *Wide Range Achievement Test–Revised* (*WRAT-R*) (S. R. Jastak & Wilkinson, 1984) or the *WRAT* (J. E.

Jastak & Jastak, 1978). Other achievement measures include the *Woodcock Reading Mastery Tests–Revised* (Woodcock, 1987), the *Stanford Diagnostic Reading Test* (Karlsen, Madden, & Gardner, 1984), and the *Stanford Diagnostic Mathematics Test* (Beatty, Madden, Gardner, & Karlsen, 1984). Instruments reported to measure language and communication skills include the *Clinical Evaluation of Language Functions: Diagnostic Battery* (Semel-Mintz & Wiig, 1980) and the *Peabody Picture Vocabulary Test–Revised* (Dunn & Dunn, 1981).

Information-processing abilities are often addressed through subtests of previously mentioned instruments such as the *WAIS-R* and the *WJPEB-R*. Many practitioners opt to use a variety of different measures to evaluate information processing rather than a single instrument or battery. The area most frequently measured with a specific test is visual processing. In this instance, the *Bender Visual Motor Gestalt Test* (Bender, 1946) appears to be the instrument of preference.

In the interest of comprehensive yet time-efficient assessment, some institutions have developed a standard battery of tests that are administered to all students requesting LD evaluations and use a supplementary battery if further measures are warranted (Block et al., 1986; Whyte et al., 1991). Most institutions will refer to other campus or outside resources if more extensive testing is needed in such areas as speech and language, psychology, or neuropsychology. Additional standardized tests frequently used in the diagnosis of adults with learning disabilities are listed in Appendix D.

Caveats Regarding Instrumentation and Technical Standards

LD service providers and diagnosticians must be clearly aware of the specific limitations of available test instruments when diagnosing adults with learning disabilities and recommending accommodations based on test data. One of the most important decisions in selecting diagnostic instruments is the choice of reliable, valid standardized tests with appropriate norms. Evaluators are clearly at a disadvantage when diagnosing adults with learning disabilities since, as mentioned previously, there is a lack of technically adequate instruments available for this population.

Salvia and Ysseldyke (1991) indicated that normative data should be representative of the population to which comparisons are being made. Few currently available standardized instruments are normed on college students, let alone adults with learning disabilities. Reliability is the extent to which one can generalize the results from a particular set of conditions (e.g., a test or set of scores) to other occasions in three different ways (Salvia & Ysseldyke, 1991). First, would a student's scores be the same if another evaluator were to score the test? Second, would a student's demonstrated behavior be similar if it were evaluated at a later point in time? In other words, does the instrument measure behavior that is stable over time? Finally, if a student were tested with similar but different items, would the results be similar? With respect to test reliability, Salvia and Ysseldyke suggested that reliability coefficients approximating .90 are recommended as the minimum standard for tests used to make educational decisions for students. Validity is the extent to which a test measures what it purports to measure. According to Salvia and Ysseldyke (1991, p. 145), "Specifically, test validity concerns the appropriateness of the inferences that can be made on the basis of test results." In light of these issues, service providers must interpret standardized test scores with caution unless the technical aspects of the instrument are available and made clear either in the report or through supporting evidence.

Although many LD service providers are not diagnosticians, a logical approach may assist them with the interpretation of diagnostic data. First, the evaluation of any individual with a disability requires an understanding that the format of a test or the procedures used for evaluation may present potential problems in measuring performance and achievement. For example, D. J. Johnson (1987a, p. 143) states: "If reading comprehension is assessed by retelling a passage without regard to the subject's conceptualization, auditory receptive and expressive language, as well as decoding, the final assumptions may be inaccurate." Likewise, visual-processing difficulties may reduce the level of performance on a math test, particularly in a timed situation. Therefore, several measures in a particular area of learning may be necessary to accurately determine an individual's ability and whether processing deficits interfere with achievement (D. J. Johnson, 1987b).

Most tests evaluate multiple functions and usually require more skills than those they claim to measure. For example, a subtest such as Digit Span on the *WAIS-R*, which involves the repetition of a series of numbers in exact order, requires auditory perception, memory, attention, and articulation abilities (D. J. Johnson, 1987b). Thus test or subtest scores may need to be interpreted in light of a number of processes rather than primarily by what they purport to evaluate. Similarly, conclusions may be drawn from scores with little consideration as to the skills actually being measured or tests may be used to measure areas for which they were not designed (Carlton & Walkenshaw, 1991). In some instances, for example, inferences are made about a student's reading-comprehension ability based on subtests that measure word-attack skills. While there is a connection between the ability to decode words and reading-comprehension skills, such a conclusion cannot be substantiated without additional supporting evidence. The input, output, and integration required to complete a task must also be considered. For example, a spelling test might involve the identification of an incorrectly spelled word, thus requiring visual-verbal input with a recognition response, whereas a dictated spelling test would incorporate the conversion of an auditory-verbal input to a visual-motor response (D. J. Johnson, 1987a).

Another issue of concern to service providers is the global scores yielded by many standardized tests. Information obtained from such scores often does not indicate the appropriate remediation techniques or accommodations necessary to assist a student. Error analysis of specific subtests may be required in order to define specific difficulties. For example, many spelling tests do not differentiate among types of errors. Therefore, the use of a spell-check device as an academic accommodation might not be an appropriate or effective request if a student's spelling errors are linguistically based (e.g., errors in homonyms such as *piece* and *peace*) and would not be corrected by such a tool. Furthermore, tests rarely have sufficient items, particularly for adults, to indicate a person's level of rule acquisition (D. J. Johnson, 1987b). In some instances, when a test is designed with basal-ceiling levels, the performance of adults will be affected either because they quickly reach ceiling levels (Oliker, 1991) or because they have so many knowledge gaps that the items are insufficient to demonstrate their actual ability (Hughes & Osgood-Smith, 1990). If remediation is to be provided, additional informal procedures or criterion-referenced testing must be done to identify the specific tasks to be addressed. Likewise, the Learning Disabilities Association of America (1990) reiterated its position regarding the inappropriate use of composite scores in identifying adults with learning disabilities. Since an individual's learning disability "selectively interferes with one's abilities" (p. 2a), composite scores may not accurately reflect specific areas of strength or weakness. A depressed composite score in written language, for example, does not indicate by itself whether an individual's difficulty is with mechanics, spelling, word choice, syntax, or semantics. Thus it would be impossible to determine from such a score if a student could benefit from the use of a word processor or if additional strategies or remediation would be necessary.

The next section addresses factors involved in the process of referring students to other resources for diagnostic assessment.

OBTAINING APPROPRIATE DIAGNOSTIC TESTING

Referral Questions for Diagnosticians

When referrals are made to other campus resources or outside professionals, LD service providers can significantly increase the likelihood of obtaining useful diagnostic reports by helping the student to be a wise assessment consumer. Primarily this involves providing a list of guidelines regarding an institution's requirements for "appropriate documentation" such as those developed at the University of Connecticut (see Appendix E). Specific referral questions a student can present to a diagnostician, such as those illustrated in Figure 4.3, might enhance the quality of the final evaluation product. Finally, students and service providers should be encouraged to investigate the professional qualifications and background of diagnostic practitioners, including their past experience with college students with learning disabilities, their approach to assessment (i.e., areas of assessment, methods of evaluation, and typical test battery), and their report format.

The Diagnostic Report

The information presented in a diagnostic report can be overwhelming; however, careful examination can provide valuable information to assist the LD service provider in making decisions about

- Does the student have a learning disability?

  —What are the identifying characteristics?

- What abilities, strengths, or compensatory skills have been noted?

  —What are the implications of these strengths regarding the student's academic success?

  —What are the implications of these strengths regarding the student's vocational success?

- What functional weaknesses or limitations have been noted?

  —What are the implications of these limitations regarding the student's academic success?

  —What are the implications of these limitations regarding the student's vocational success?

- What support services are needed?

- Where can the student most effectively obtain these support services?

- What specific instructional strategies and accommodations does the student require?

- On what specific data or information are these recommendations based?

- Is any further assessment suggested?

- Is the student able to explain his or her strengths, weaknesses, and subsequent implications in plain language?

Figure 4.3. Referral questions to ask a diagnostician regarding college students with learning disabilities.

appropriate services. Although formats will vary, certain critical data should be included in any thorough evaluation. All reports should begin with demographic data about the student (e.g., birth date, age, or grade) as well as the dates of testing, the examiner's name, and his or her qualifications. McGuire, Hall, et al. (1992) noted in a review of LD documentation that only 57% of the reports provided any information about the student's age or grade at the time of initial diagnosis.

The following section should specifically address the presenting problems or reasons for referral. Without a clear framework in which to operate, neither the diagnostician nor the student will have a reference point for subsequent tasks or procedures. The referral questions outlined in Figure 4.3 may help to structure the assessment process and ensure that the information needed by the LD service provider will be addressed.

Adults frequently arrive at an evaluation with a long history of academic problems as well as possible social and emotional problems resulting from their learning difficulties. While it is not appropriate or feasible to include an individual's entire case history in a report, it is important for the diagnostician to spend some time exploring the relevance of the presenting problems to past experiences. This background information section should also refer to any additional data that were reviewed, such as student records or information gathered from the screening process.

Behavioral observations of the student are critical to the overall interpretation of the evaluation results and should be addressed in a separate section as well as being integrated into the report as appropriate. Direct observation of the way a student presents himself or herself, the student's manner of dress, and his or her verbal and nonverbal communication and interpersonal skills, as well as behavior during testing, provides significant information that is not easily obtained through standardized measures. Interestingly, McGuire, Hall, et al. (1992) reported that only 27.8% of the diagnostic reports they evaluated mentioned observations of the student during testing.

The next two sections of a diagnostic report pertain to standardized instruments. Service providers should request a list of the tests administered, including the full name of the test as well as the version used (e.g., revised or second edition). In this way, sufficient information will be available to permit the service provider to investigate the technical adequacies and specific content of tests that are unfamiliar. The subsequent section should provide the results of all tests administered, including data about both strengths and weaknesses. Some reports only reflect areas of deficit and the reader is left wondering if a particular test was ever administered or if the evaluator inadvertently or intentionally omitted results. Test results should be clearly expressed in scores that have the "highest degree of comparability across measures" (National Joint Committee on Learning Disabilities, 1987, p. 5). It is especially critical to have test performance represented by standard scores or percentiles rather than developmental scores (e.g., age or grade scores), which are meaningless for adults. This section should also include the results of any previous testing that is relevant to the presenting problems or the interpretation of current results. For example, comparing scores across periods of time may give some indication of other factors that have or had an impact on a student's performance (e.g., significant life events or changes, or emotional problems). Similarly, information such as medical or speech and language data that are not specifically addressed during the current assessment may play a significant part in the interpretation of the test results.

An analysis or interpretation of results is usually the heart of any diagnostic report. Both a narrative explanation and illustrative test scores should be available for review. With respect to the presentation of test results, McGuire, Hall, et al. (1992) indicated that 18.6% of the evaluation reports reviewed reported only scores, while 29.6% included scores and interpretation. An additional 49.3% included recommendations as well as scores and interpretation. To facilitate comprehension, test and subtest scores must clearly indicate what skills are being measured and how the measurement is obtained. This will provide the LD service practitioner with additonal information regarding a student's performance and achievement levels.

The summary of a diagnostic report should provide a brief composite of the entire assessment process. This is significant because it is often the section that professionals see first or will read if they do not have sufficient time to peruse the entire report. Therefore it is critical for the summary to specifically address the concerns raised in the section on reasons for referral. A determination must be made as to whether or not a learning disability is present if that was one of the presenting issues. Gregg and Hoy (1990) noted that the majority of psychological reports received by the University of Georgia did not contain a specific diagnostic-category summary statement for students with learning disabilities. Documentation that employs terminology such as "learning differences" or "atypical learning style" does little to clarify the diagnostic picture (Brinckerhoff, 1989) and does not provide enough documentation to determine eligibility for services under Section 504.

The final section of the diagnostic report and the most crucial for the LD service provider addresses recommendations. Information and data collected during the assessment process must be used to develop relevant procedures, goals, and objectives. Both strengths and weaknesses must be addressed in determining appropriate strategies to assist the student in becoming an efficient learner as well as successful in personal and career endeavors. In recommending support services, modifications, or accommodations, it is critical for a diagnostician to identify the areas that are affected by a student's learning disability and to back those conclusions up with hard diagnostic data (Anderson & Brinckerhoff, 1989). It is not enough for diagnosticians to simply list general areas of concern without also providing suggestions for specific techniques that would allow the student to be successful in a postsecondary setting.

As a final step in this process, the diagnostician and the student should schedule an appointment to review the results. Not only is it important for students to completely understand the report, but the evaluator or diagnostic team are the best people to answer any questions. In such a situation, many students are overwhelmed by the amount of information presented, and even though they should receive a copy of the report to take with them, they may have many questions after they leave. Students should be advised to either take notes or bring a tape recorder with them to the meeting. Putting the information into a visual format such as a profile chart or graphic representation may assist students in comprehending and remembering the diagnostic information (Brinckerhoff, 1989; Vogel, 1985).

In most instances, the purpose of an LD diagnostic assessment is to provide information for the student and the service provider regarding the individual's strengths and weaknesses in order to make appropriate recommendations. Therefore, the diagnostic report must be individualized, readable, and, above all, "student-friendly." Too often reports are filled with terminology and jargon understandable only to other professionals in the field. If students are to become self-advocates, they should be helped to articulate their learning strengths and weaknesses in understandable terms with the basis for such understanding emanating from reliable and valid reports (McGuire, Hall, et al., 1992).

Funding Sources

In settings that do not have the resources to administer diagnostic assessments, LD service providers must rely on other campus sources or outside professionals to provide diagnostic testing for students with learning disabilities. Subsequently, a question arises about who must bear the cost for testing to determine if an enrolled student has a learning disability. Rothstein (1986) reported that the answer is not available in the regulations or in current case law. However, she noted that "if psychological assessment is provided through the campus health program, then assessment of a student for learning disabilities should be part of the services available to the student" (p. 236). If such routine services are not available, the cost and burden of providing documentation rests solely with the student. When insufficient documentation is provided to substantiate a request for services, an institution has the right to seek more information from the student. Once a student has provided the necessary documentation, the institution "must assume full responsibility, including financial responsibility, for obtaining additional documentation" (Heyward, 1992, p. 207).

An institution's inability to provide assessment services for students who are seeking an initial LD diagnosis often becomes an ethical dilemma for LD service providers who are cognizant of the extreme expense involved in obtaining such documentation. Some institutions provide diagnostic evaluations at no additional charge (Carlton & Walkenshaw, 1991); however, many do operate on a fee basis, particularly if other campus services are providing the testing. One response to this financial dilemma is to develop a list of professionals in the community who are willing to work on a sliding scale. Another innovative and cost-effective method of securing evaluations is to recruit alumni who are willing to provide evaluations at a reduced cost (Brinckerhoff, 1989). Although some insurance companies may provide coverage for diagnostic testing under a student's family policy, these carriers typically request that such evaluations be performed by licensed psychologists, who may not be familiar with the needs of college students with learning disabilities. Several colleges, such as Brown and Brandeis universities, have been able to help students obtain coverage for LD assessment under student health coverage. In other instances, institutions have expanded a student's financial aid package to cover the cost of diagnostic evaluations. Additionally, pockets of funding have been set aside in some institutions to either partially or completely, cover the cost of a predetermined number of evaluations per year. This funding originates from a number of sources including faculty funds, minority student resources, student fees, and even soda machine profits. Finally, referrals can be made to Vocational Rehabilitation services for LD diagnostic assessments, even though the quality and expediency of services varies from state to state.

INTERPRETING AND APPLYING DIAGNOSTIC INFORMATION

Regardless of where an institution falls along the continuum of LD assessment services, many rely on previous documentation, either as evidence to support eligibility for services or as a basis for further assessment to enhance planning of appropriate services. LD service providers are often faced with the dilemma of integrating information from diagnostic reports, interviews, and informal tasks to determine accommodations and modifications for students with learning disabilities. It is important to consider the competencies and training backgrounds of postsecondary LD service providers who are responsible for rendering judgments on a case-by-case basis. Data reported by Norlander et al. (1990) from a survey of postsecondary LD service providers suggested that the ability to interpret standardized achievement tests was the most desired competency, followed by effective communication of evaluation results to students. Similarly, using evaluation data in diagnosing learning disabilities, interpreting criterion-referenced assessment, interpreting standardized tests of intelligence and information processing, utilizing informal assessment procedures, and evaluating the psychometric properties of assessment instruments were ranked at or above 4.53 on a 5-point Likert scale (5 = most desired). These results suggested that LD service providers recognize a need to improve their skills in using diagnostic testing data to determine appropriate services for students with learning disabilities. Likewise, Shaw, Cullen, and McGuire (1992) reported that the majority of service providers at the postsecondary level have educational backgrounds that include little training in diagnostic assessment, special education, or psychology.

Analyzing diagnostic reports is frequently the most expedient method for determining appropriate academic adjustments and modifications. A composite chart such as the student profile summary chart in Figure 4.4 can assist the LD service provider in integrating and organizing information. Abilities and limitations relative to a student's performance can be charted in a manner that is clear to the student rather than focusing on statistically significant strengths and weaknesses (Anderson & Brinckerhoff, 1989). For example, a student who reports having difficulty with reading comprehension on college-level texts may be recorded under limitations for achievement levels, yet standardized scores recorded in that column indicate that the student is reading well within expected levels. This type of discrepancy would clearly indicate that further investigation of a formal or informal nature is required to determine what, if anything, is contributing to the student's reading difficulty. Such probing is critical to the accommodation process, since it would be difficult to justify a request for extended time on a test because of a reading-comprehension problem if the student's reading scores were within the average ability range. Columns are labeled according to general assessment areas and may be adapted to meet the diagnostic criteria of a specific postsecondary institution. Information recorded on the chart should include both formal and informal data, such as standardized test scores, interview data, record review information, and observation data. A column for listing specific accommodations and recommendations is included to facilitate the interpretation of data. An LD service provider may complete the chart with or without input from a student. The exercise of compiling and interpreting diagnostic data in a visual format may serve as the basis for helping a student to understand his or her learning disability and to be able to effectively verbalize academic abilities, limitations, and related strategies. The student profile summary chart will serve as a permanent record for both the service provider and the student and will be of use throughout a student's academic career to make future recommendations for accommodations.

Since many LD service providers report that they do not have the ability to interpret standardized tests or informal assessment measures (Norlander et al., 1990), using diagnostic data to identify appropriate academic accommodations may be difficult at best. The student profile summary chart can assist the service provider in matching a student's individual needs with appropriate support services. Figure 4.5 provides a list of instructional accommodations and

STUDENT PROFILE

Student: _____
Reviewer: _____
Date: _____

IQ: FS ___ V ___ P ___

	Observations and Personal Characteristics	Academic Performance	Cognitive Abilities	Learning/Study Strategies	Achievement Levels	Accommodations and Recommendations
A B I L I T I E S						
L I M I T A T I O N S						

Figure 4.4. Student profile summary chart. From "Interpreting LD Diagnostic Reports for Appropriate Service Delivery" by P. L. Anderson and L. C. Brinckerhoff, 1989. In J. J. Vander Putten (Ed.), *Proceedings of the 1989 AHSSPPE National Conference* (pp. 91–100),

READING

- Extended time
- Reader
- Taped textbooks
- Oral exams
- Taped exams
- Separate location
- Alternate test format
- Other:

WRITING/ SPELLING

- Extended time
- Note taker
- Tape recorder
- Oral exams
- Computer with spellchecker
- Alternative demonstration of mastery
- Scribe
- Proofreader

LANGUAGE

- Extended time
- Note taker
- Tape recorder
- Oral exams
- Computer with spellchecker
- Alternate demonstration of mastery
- Scribe
- Proofreader
- Other:

MATH

- Extended time
- Use of calculator
- Talking calculator
- Separate location
- Alternate test format
- Other:

AUDITORY

- Tape recorder
- Note taker
- Visual clues
- Physical proximity
- Other:

VISUAL-PERCEPTUAL

- Tape recorder
- Taped textbooks
- Auditory cues
- Physical proximity
- Extended time
- Oral or taped exams
- Separate location
- Alternate test format
- Proofreader
- Other:

PROGRAM MODIFICATIONS

- Extended time to complete a program
- Adapting methods of instruction
- Course substitution
- Part-time rather than full-time study

Figure 4.5. Instructional and program modifications.

program modifications that might be appropriate for specific areas of limitation. This list is not comprehensive and may need to be modified depending upon the support services available on each campus. Not all students with learning disabilities will require all accommodations in any one area; therefore, care should be taken to match a student's specific needs with appropriate accommodations for the demands of each course or situation. Chapter 8 provides an in-depth discussion of academic adjustments and auxiliary aids.

CONCLUSION

The assessment and diagnosis of college students and adults with learning disabilities is an extremely complex process compounded by the lack of a comprehensive definition, variability in eligibility guidelines, and a paucity of qualified diagnosticians and technically adequate instruments. Although institutions are not required to provide an LD diagnostic assessment under Section 504, many colleges and universities are struggling with the development of some level of assessment services. This is a direct response to the significant increase in students with learning disabilities accessing college campuses. As more and more students request eligibility for services and academic accommodations, institutions must struggle with fulfilling their legal responsibilities under Section 504 with less available staff and funding. As a result, LD service providers are frequently required to review and interpret previous documentation, either for use as the primary source to verify eligibility or as a basis for further assessment to facilitate the provision of appropriate services. Service providers with minimal knowledge regarding learning disabilities or the assessment process can integrate and organize information from a variety of sources on a composite chart such as the student profile summary chart and use this information to assist students in determining appropriate academic adjustments and modifications.

CHAPTER 5

Psychosocial Characteristics and Issues of Adults with Learning Disabilities

Lynda Price

Susan is a college junior with severe auditory memory and discrimination problems, who has been working part-time at a fast-food restaurant for the last 2 years. She often complains about feeling "stuck and frustrated" in her low-paying job. She desperately wants a job with potential for more career growth when she graduates from college.

Her friend, Joan, wants to go to the local university and get an education degree to teach math and science to secondary students. She is afraid to explore the possibilities on campus; because of her poor spatial and directional skills, her mother has always helped her find her way around. Joan is also worried that she will never be able to support herself and live independently after high school graduation.

Phil is a high school senior with reading, writing, and spelling problems. He just received his high school diploma but has been rejected for admission to the electronics programs in the local private and public technical schools because he was unable to read some of the questions on the admission tests. He has recently been fighting with his girlfriend and even hit her a few times. He always tells her that he is sorry but explains that he is "just really stressed out."

Bob, who has problems with short-term memory and restlessness, was recently released from a treatment facility for chemical dependency. Bob is confused and anxious about his future despite the fact that the staff at the treatment center encouraged him to complete his general equivalency diploma. He has no idea what to do next with his life.

These four people have a number of characteristics in common. They are all adults with specific learning disabilities. These individuals with disabilities all have important psychosocial attributes that are having a significant impact on their daily lives. All four individuals need assistance with psychosocial issues and dealing with the ramifications of their learning disabilities if they are to fulfill their potential as adults.

When students have the relatively protected atmosphere of high school, they may try to get help for these pressing problems. Unfortunately, such assistance often is not available to adults with learning disabilities, due in part to the dearth of credible research, methodology, and professional expertise where the fields of psychology and learning disabilities come together. For instance, such important techniques as chemical dependency treatment or traditional psycho-therapeutic interventions for adults with learning disabilities have long been neglected areas in the literature (Fox & Forbing, 1991; Hayes & Sloat, 1988; Huestis & Ryland, 1986; Price, 1990). This lack of knowledge has led to misunderstandings about learning disabilities by many postsecondary practitioners, counselors, and therapists who see adults with learning disabilities in their offices every day but have little or no idea how to address the complex mix of psychological problems and disability-related issues they face. This vacuum of knowledge and expertise can have a serious impact on the clients they serve. The focus of this chapter is to address two important questions that influence service delivery in postsecondary education:

1. What are the psychosocial implications of learning disabilities?

2. How can they be effectively addressed in postsecondary academic and vocational settings?

THE IMPORTANCE OF PSYCHOSOCIAL ISSUES IN POSTSECONDARY EDUCATION

The psychosocial implications of learning disabilities and ways to address them are important for many audiences. They are vital concerns for practitioners in postsecondary education, for adults with learning disabilities, for their families, and for their friends. They are also being explored by numerous professionals in education who have indicated that there is a strong relationship between learning disabilities and social or psychological disabilities (Fox & Forbing, 1991; Gerber, 1991; Hall & Haws, 1989; Maag & Behrens, 1989a; Stevenson & Romney, 1984; Weinberg, McLean, Snider, & Nucklos, 1989; L. S. Wright & Stimmel, 1984). For example, it has been suggested that children with learning disabilities are more vulnerable to emotional disturbances (T. H. Bryan, 1989; Epstein, Cullinan, & Neiminen, 1984; Rourke, 1989; Silver, 1984; Weinberg et al., 1989). Additionally, there are a number of adults with learning disabilities who received psychological counseling as children and continued it in adulthood.

Lehtinen and Dumas (1976) reported that of the 90 adults they studied the vast majority (73%) had received psychological counseling sometime in their lives. As adults, 24% of this same sample were currently attending therapy sessions, and 11% had started therapy but later stopped. Although it is impossible to determine if this is a truly representative sample of all adults with learning disabilities, it does raise a disturbing trend that clearly needs further investigation.

As illustrated in the preceding brief case studies, adults with learning disabilities can bring all types of social and emotional baggage with them when they enter college. But frequently, their diverse psychosocial needs have not been successfully met in postsecondary settings. For instance, Ostertag (1986) described psychosocial services needed by students with learning disabilities that have not typically been provided by the California Community College system. These vital services include assistance for personal growth and development, learning style awareness, self-help groups, self-advocacy training, support for disability management, and family orientation and support.

This is ironic, since other service providers who work in postsecondary academic or vocational settings have emphasized that equal efforts must be focused on assistance for both academic and psychosocial concerns (Cohen, 1984; Hill Top Preparatory School, 1988; J. Johnson, Evelo, & Price, 1992; National Joint Committee on Learning Disabilities, 1987; Price, 1990; Scheiber & Talpers, 1987). Fisher (1985, p. 5) aptly summed up this philosophy when she said, "The college or university must recognize that the educational program component and the psychosocial ones are equally important and that regular individual and group counseling support academic achievement." Other authors (Bursuck, 1989; Cohen, 1984; Mangrum & Strichart, 1984; Neault, 1988; Ostertag, 1986; Scheiber & Talpers, 1987) have recommended that some type of psychosocial assistance be available to students with learning disabilities in addition to other postsecondary services. They stress that providing academic support without psychosocial assistance is not enough to meet individual student needs.

One critical misconception held by some professionals who counsel students with learning disabilities is that both positive and negative psychosocial issues and characteristics related to learning disabilities have been remediated or "fixed" in childhood. Many professionals now point out that specific cognitive deficits and their related psychosocial problems do not disappear with age, but often continue to have a significant impact on the lives of adults with learning disabilities in slightly different forms (Alley, Deshler, Clark, Schumaker, & Warner, 1983; J. H. Bryan, 1983; Cohen, 1985; Cruickshank, Morse, & Johns, 1980; Gerber, 1991; Maag & Behrens, 1989b; Margalit & Heiman, 1986; Renick & Harter, 1989; L. S. Wright & Stimmel, 1984).

DEFINITION OF PSYCHOSOCIAL ISSUES

Before discussing the types of psychosocial issues that can have such a significant impact on the daily lives of some adults in post-secondary settings, it is necessary to understand exactly what constitutes different psychosocial issues. Chapter 3 explored an operational definition of learning disabilities in adults. Figure 3.1 showed that adults could have different learning disabilities as their primary disabilities, with additional overlays of psychosocial issues. These psychosocial characteristics then become secondary components in each student's profile of individual strengths and weaknesses. To expand this concept further, a brief definition of the term *psychosocial* can give us important insights into the ramifications of learning disabilities on individuals as they try to reach their full potential in the many facets of adult life—work, home, school, relationships, leisure activities, and financial success. All of the material described in this chapter refers to adults who have learning disabilities as their primary disability with related, secondary psychosocial characteristics.

The term *psychosocial* neatly summarizes two integral areas of the lives of every individual with learning disabilities. Those areas are (a) the *psycho* part or psychological aspects (i.e., how one sees oneself or feels about oneself), and (b) the *social* part or social aspects (i.e., how one relates to others in one's everyday environment and communicates with others). For greater clarity, several psychosocial characteristics will be grouped into categories and their implications for counseling adults with learning disabilities discussed. We can examine psychosocial issues in greater depth in terms of: (a) negative self-concept, (b) lack of socialization skills, (c) dependency on others, (d) stress and anxiety, (e) various negative behaviors and feelings, and (f) depression and dependency. The following sections investigate each category in greater depth.

Self-Concept

Perhaps the one consistent counseling issue that repeatedly emerges regarding individuals with learning disabilities is the lack of a positive self-concept (Freils, 1969; Gerber, 1991; Maag & Behrens, 1989a; Morse, 1977; Rosenthal, 1973; Wilchesky & Minden, 1988). Geist and McGrath (1983), in their study of students with learning disabilities, observed a low self-image in these students. They often saw themselves negatively, despite numerous successes that they may have achieved throughout their lives (e.g., successful job interviews, making an "A" in a difficult college course, or winning an artistic or athletic competition). They also perpetuated a negative self-image because these feelings were known and comfortable to them. B. K. Smith (1986) expanded this characteristic further by explaining that problems seen in adulthood such as marriage or job failures, antisocial behavior, or suicide can be directly related to a lack of self-concept, self-confidence, and self-respect.

Perhaps some of the most poignant and thought-provoking literature currently available about the significant long-term effects of low self-esteem in the lives of adults with learning disabilities consists of the case studies by Gerber & Reiff (1991). Through extensive interviews with successful adults with learning disabilities, they illustrated how the hurdles of learning disabilities often leave adults angry, frustrated, and stressed out because they can't do certain tasks easily or efficiently. These negative feelings are often turned inward and reinforce feelings of low self-esteem, self-confidence, and self-respect. But interviews also showed that the reverse can be true. These negative feelings can be used to motivate individuals to try one more time or to look for new ways to jump the hurdles. This creativity and persistence can feed feelings of competence and self-respect. As Gerber (1991, p. 26) observed, "In a sense, the hard knocks of past experience offer a source of strength."

Ineffective Socialization Skills

A second psychosocial issue that repeatedly emerges in the literature on adults with learning disabilities is inappropriate or ineffective socialization skills (Alley et al., 1983; Cooper, 1986; Denckla, 1986; Epstein et al., 1984; Jackson, Enright, & Murdock, 1987; Renick &

Harter, 1989; Schumaker, Hazel, Sherman, & Sheldon, 1982). B. K. Smith (1986) emphasized the importance to adults of relationships and feelings of self-worth. He further stated that many adults with learning disabilities may have missed the opportunity to develop certain socialization skills. These include interpretation of social clues, a sensitivity to subtle signals from facial or body language, an awareness of vocal tonality, a realization of time, and the ability to interpret other people's moods. Cronin and Gerber (1982) stated that inappropriate socialization often manifests itself in adolescents with learning disabilities as inappropriate comments and use of social space, difficulty in anticipating the behavior of others, rigid behavior patterns, difficulty in generalizing from experiences, inflexibility, and a tendency toward impulsive decisions.

Unfortunately, socialization problems are often prevalent in children with learning disabilities and continue through adulthood. In a study by Pihl and McLarnon (1984), parents rated their children with learning disabilities more negatively in the area of sociability and social skills than parents of nonlearning-disabled children did. Alley et al. (1983) stated that the social deficits of some students with learning disabilities may have a significant influence on their lives after they leave high school. Kroll (1984) summarized a number of studies by concluding that socialization seems to be a problem area for many adults with learning disabilities. She stated that they may have difficulty making friends and establishing relationships.

Dependency Issues

Difficulties with socialization and a poor self-concept can exacerbate a third psychosocial attribute that may be seen in some individuals with learning disabilities. This attribute can be categorized as an overdependence on others—especially teachers, parents, or counselors. For instance, Kunkaitis (1986) observed that a learning disability often brings out a wide range of reactions from parents, ranging from overprotection and overcompensation to total detachment. These dynamics in the parent-child relationship can be strongly influenced by the child's poor self-image and isolation from peers. Such responses may also inhibit the child's natural maturation toward independence. As an adolescent, the individual with learning disabilities will often, in turn, transfer these "helpless" feelings from parents to others significant in his or her environment (i.e., a teacher, a trusted adviser, a sponsor, a significant adult, or a friend).

This shift in locus of control may reflect a pervasive difficulty with making decisions that affect one's daily life (Fisher, 1985; Hill Top Preparatory School, 1988; Jackson et al., 1987). For example, Geist and McGrath (1983) described their observations of some women with learning disabilities who have chosen marriage primarily to have a productive, nonacademically challenging role in society. The authors observed that these women often became wives who were very dependent upon their husbands for assistance in such daily tasks as personal or household finances.

Stress and Anxiety

A fourth area soon emerges from the other attributes that have been discussed. It concerns the impact of stress and anxiety on individuals with learning disabilities. It is not unusual for many adults with learning disabilities to exhibit signs of stress and anxiety (J. H. Bryan, 1983; Cohen, 1985; Gerber, 1991; Hall & Haws, 1989; Hayes & Sloat, 1988; Livingston, 1985; Payne, 1992; Rourke, 1989). For instance, Worcester (1982) observed that all of the college students with learning disabilities whom she studied exhibited both overt and covert symptoms of stress throughout her study. Freils (1969) reported the following signs of stress during all sessions with students with learning disabilities: physical mannerisms (i.e., tics, red eyes, bleeding fingernails), general physical health problems (i.e., long-term colds, coughs, stomach disorders), and conversations that repreatedly focused on stress or anxiety.

A few studies have described similar results in children with learning disabilities. For example, Silver (1984) studied the neuropsychiatric profiles of 60 children with learning disabilities (ages 8–14). Fifty-nine of these children exhibited symptoms of diagnosable psychiatric disorders, with 21 children showing symptoms of severe anxiety. Epstein et al. (1984) gave the Behavior Problem Checklist to 150 children with and without learning disabilities (ages 7–14). The Personality Problem dimension (i.e., anxiety and withdrawal) was the only factor that differentiated the children with learning disabilities from those who were not disabled. J. H. Bryan (1983) gave the Test Anxiety Scale to 60 children, 30 of whom had learning disabilities. The children who had learning disabilities, in this study, clearly showed more anxiety than the nondisabled children. Such consistently high levels of anxiety may be due, in part, to the stressful family climate that many adolescents and adults with learning disabilities clearly recall when they describe their childhood memories (Jackson et al., 1987; Margalit & Heiman, 1986; L. S. Wright & Stimmel, 1984).

Negative Behaviors and Feelings

All these attributes are, in turn, significantly influenced by a fifth psychosocial area that can be loosely categorized as overt negative behaviors and feelings. A number of authors report that students with learning disabilities can exhibit a wide variety of negative behaviors in different situations. For instance, Geist and McGrath (1983) described some of their students with learning disabilities as frustrated, angry, depressed, and dependent. They also asserted that some of these same individuals are withdrawn and may be emotionally disturbed. The authors theorized that, as children, people with learning disabilities may see society as hostile, demanding, and threatening. The result in adulthood may be neurotic defenses or maladaptive behaviors.

B. K. Smith (1986) reported that adults with learning disabilities themselves describe intense feelings of isolation, lack of competence in social relationships, and a pervasive sense of insecurity in certain situations. Freils (1969) discussed tests and interviews with adolescents with learning disabilities in which they reported intense feelings of hostility, rejection, and problems in achieving a healthy self-identity. The staff (Fisher, 1985, p. 3) summarized this psychosocial concern well with a description of students with learning disabilities in their facility as "shy, egocentric, inflexible, immature, and lacking in social skills. They may display poor impulse control, excessive frustration, anxiety, denial, projection, anger, depression, strong dependency needs or health problems because of the difficulty with an energy drain in coping in school and/or stressful social situations. They misunderstand and are misunderstood."

Because this misunderstanding is so crucial to grasping the ramifications of learning disabilities in adults, three additional psychosocial areas are now emerging from this fifth category for further exploration by professionals. These areas are depression, suicide, and chemical dependency in people with learning disabilities.

Depression, Suicide, and Chemical Dependency

Many professionals have started examining the specific incidence and impact of depression, suicide, and chemical dependency on adults with learning disabilities. Although this literature continues to grow, caution is advised because of inherent discrepancies and ambiguities found in the various studies (e.g., populations not clearly defined or research protocols unclear). Some studies are worth exploring, however, based on preliminary observations concerning adolescents and adults with learning disabilities.

Depression. One psychosocial issue that seems to be receiving more and more interest is the relationship between learning disabilities and depression. Numerous trends are reported in the literature. For example, some experts are examining the correlation between a diagnosis of attention deficit-hyperactivity disorder and signs of depression among both children and adults with learning disabilities (Weinberg, et al., 1989). Other authors describe studies that found more signs of clinical depression in females with learning disabilities than in males (Maag & Behrens, 1989a, 1989b). Incidence statistics for individuals with learning disabilities who appear depressed also vary in the literature. They range from 14% (Stevenson & Romney, 1984) to 21% (Maag & Behrens, 1989a), 22% (Silver, 1984), and 64% (Weinberg et al., 1989) of the total sample with learning disabilities analyzed in various studies. All of these authors conclude that depression is truly a prevalent condition among some individuals with learning disabilities.

Suicide and chemical dependency. Another related area that is receiving attention is that of suicide among individuals with learning disabilities. The literature clearly demonstrates that this population may be at great risk for either committing suicide or frequently thinking suicidal thoughts, perhaps due to the prevalence of depression or low self-concept discussed earlier in this chapter (T. H. Bryan, 1989; Hayes & Sloat, 1988; Livingston, 1985; Maag & Behrens, 1989b; Rourke, 1989). Some authors report a relationship between drug abuse and suicidal thoughts. They describe studies in which adults with learning disabilities frequently see themselves in more negative ways than their peers who do not have learning disabilities. The adults with learning disabilities more frequently report more delinquency, problems with drug abuse, and suicidal thoughts than their peers. (T. H. Bryan, 1989; Fox & Forbing, 1991; Hill Top Preparatory School, 1988; Stevenson & Romney, 1984; Weinberg et al., 1989; L. S. Wright & Stimmel, 1984).

Drug abuse may be a common theme for some students with learning disabilities, who may also be at risk for suicide or depression because of past treatment with therapeutic drugs, low academic achievement, low self-esteem, or a family history of alcohol or drug abuse (Bryan, 1989; Fox & Forbing, 1991; Hill Top Preparatory School, 1988; Stevenson & Romney, 1984; Weinberg et al., 1989; L. S. Wright & Stimmel, 1984).

Two other points must be kept in mind when examining psychosocial issues. First, it should be noted when addressing the psychosocial needs of adults with learning disabilities that one cannot generalize these psychosocial characteristics to all individuals. Neither the currently available research nor the authors' own experiences support such a broad generalization. It can be concluded, however, that many adults with learning disabilities may exhibit one or more of these characteristics over time.

Second, the previous material may seem depressing to the reader because it is so negatively skewed. This obviously does not represent the whole picture for the specific strengths and weaknesses of each unique adult with learning disabilities. This population frequently exhibits many positive psychosocial traits as well. In fact, some of the most creative, motivated adults with the best sense of humor may be adults with learning disabilities. Gerber and Reiff's case studies (1991) support these observations. For instance, one provocative theme that is repeatedly illustrated in Gerber's ethnographic research on adults with learning disabilities is how they have come to view their learning disabilities as assets—not hurdles—in everyday life. So it would be a tremendous disservice to students not to take into account their psychosocial strengths as well as their problems. Finally, there are problems associated with much of the research done on psychosocial needs.

LIMITATIONS IN THE CURRENT RESEARCH

Numerous testimonials and articles in professional journals describe in dramatic terms the various psychosocial issues just discussed. However, it is currently difficult, if not impossible, to determine the generalizability of both the qualitative and quantitative data that are currently available. Probably most of these data contain at least a grain of truth about the complexity and incidence of psychosocial issues in adults with learning disabilities. But given the state of the art of the current research base on both psychosocial issues and learning disabilities in adults in general, we must proceed with caution into this newly investigated territory. A number of important points must be kept in mind by the reader when examining this research.

First, not all studies follow standard quantitative research protocols (e.g., using a research design, random sampling from a representative population, rigorous comparisons of findings with a matched control group, and consistent definitions of learning disabilities and related terminology). Second, all studies seem to draw pertinent behavioral generalizations and significant conclusions about psychosocial issues, but it is difficult, if not impossible, to determine if these findings are applicable to all students with learning disabilities or all adults with different configurations of learning disabilities. Third, few studies report any type of replication. This again raises the critical question of the generalizability of the findings for individuals with learning disabilities with a wide variety of psychosocial issues, in a wide variety of settings.

Presently, numerous articles and books are being written as the area of psychosocial issues gains prominence in the fields of both special and vocational education. The resulting qualitative and quantitative data will continue to make a valuable contribution regarding the psychosocial ramifications of learning disabilities on adults. However, it must be emphasized that all research that focuses on the psychosocial characteristics of adults with learning disabilities must be viewed with caution.

THEORETICAL RATIONALE FOR PSYCHOSOCIAL SERVICE DELIVERY

Besides defining the psychosocial issues of adults with learning disabilities, it is equally important to develop a theoretical model upon which to base psychosocial service delivery at the postsecondary level. Integrating Abraham Maslow's model of self-actualization into postsecondary services for students with learning disabilities provides a theoretical rationale that is worth further examination.

Maslow, a leader in psychology, investigated the developmental phases of adults. In 1962, he explored a branch of psychology that he named "the psychology of being." This particular model postulated various stages of human development throughout the life span from childhood to late adulthood. It should be noted that Maslow created this model for individuals without disabilities, but it is equally applicable for individuals with disabilities. He postulated that the psychology of being was propelled by a developmental process he named "self-actualization" (Cormier & Cormier, 1991).

Maslow further theorized that all people go through various developmental stages that have certain characteristics in common. He then identified eight characteristics of individuals, both with and without disabilities, as they move through the self-actualization process (Cormier & Cormier, 1991, p. 262). These characteristics describe adults who are:

- Becoming fully functioning as mature individuals (e.g., self-identity, self-realization, and self-direction)
- Being responsible for their own behaviors and attitudes
- Realizing their own unique potential as human beings
- Having a strongly developed sense of integrity based on a defined personal value system
- Exhibiting high levels of personal creativity
- Being challenged rather than defeated by new events or information in daily life
- Having a sense of humor
- Showing high levels of motivation and persistence

To fully appreciate Maslow's model, another point must be emphasized. When considering this list of eight characteristics, it is easy to become overwhelmed and to be tempted to reject them outright. How can anyone, either with or without disabilities, achieve such lofty goals? But to view self-actualization in those limited terms totally negates Maslow's thesis. Instead, the overriding theme of the self-actualization model is growth, not perfection. Maslow believed that no one will every truly reach a state where all of these goals are simultaneously achieved. However, is it the *process* that is important. Maslow postulated that the central focus of adult development is the continual movement toward personal levels of integration, wholeness, and fulfillment in all experiences of life. And if this is true, what is a better rationale for services for adults with learning disabilities than to assist them on this journey?

It is also important to note that employers are now demanding psychosocial skills for their employees similar to both the skills necessary to succeed in college and those proposed in Maslow's model. For example, the SCANS Report (Secretary's Commission on Achieving Necessary Skills, 1991) for the U.S. Department of Labor recently identified five key competencies (resources, interpersonal, information, systems, and technology) that will be necessary to enter and keep employment in the workplace of the 21st century. The report has six subpoints, which address various psychosocial skills that are critical for employment and academic success for postsecondary students, both with and without disabilities. The skilled individual (a) participates as a member of a team; (b) teaches others new skills; (c) serves clients and customers or works to satisfy customer's (instructors') expectations; (d) exercises leadership; (e) negotiates or works toward agreements involving exchange of resources, resolving divergent interests; and (f) works with diversity.

Under these subpoints are an additional set of important personal qualities that employers and educators view as part of the foundation for this new work force. These qualities seem to repeat what Maslow in 1962 originally suggested were the characteristics of self-actualization. Examples are: responsibility, self-esteem, sociability, self-management, and integrity and honesty. The commission concluded that such basic skills as reading, writing, and mathematical computation will no longer be enough to qualify all individuals throughout America, with or without disabilities, for work by the year 2000. And yet these are the exact skills often emphasized by disability service providers to pass college courses. One sweeping ramification of the ADA may be that workplace accommodations throughout America will become an integrated and gradual process that continues throughout the life of adults with learning disabilities (Payne, 1992). Then postsecondary practitioners will literally have no choice. They must start making accommodations and addressing psychosocial issues, such as those delineated by the SCANS Report, while a student is still in college.

The Interpersonal section of the SCANS Report is especially relevant to psychosocial issues and to Maslow's characteristics of self-actualization. The SCANS material mirrors in many ways exactly what we are now trying to achieve in postsecondary education with a holistic service-delivery model. There are numerous ways for postsecondary practitioners to provide this assistance, but the most essential way is to ground any psychosocial technique or method in appropriate self-actualization goals. These goals, which clearly address the psychosocial issues previously described in this chapter, are developed by both the student with learning disabilities and the postsecondary service provider during the initial counseling sessions. Examples of appropriate session goals for self-actualization are (a) improving problem-solving abilities, (b) developing goal-setting skills, (c) developing effective communication skills, (d) fostering appropriate socialization, (e) working on assertiveness skills, (f) providing values clarification, (g) decreasing negative behaviors, (h) teaching self-monitoring and self-reinforcement, and (i) understanding individual strengths and weaknesses. It should be noted that understanding one's individual strengths and weaknesses is definitely a priority that must be accomplished as a foundation for all other goals. If this goal is not achieved, the rest are much harder, if not impossible, to implement for adults with learning disabilities.

Postsecondary practitioners must use goals that emphasize the ongoing process of adult psychological development and continually reinforce the student's responsibility. As a result, self-actualization goals have a number of similar qualities that are critical to successful postsecondary service delivery for students with learning disabilities. Self-actualization goals are purposely open-ended to allow for individual change as the student grows and changes. They actively involve the student in every aspect of service delivery, instead of allowing the student to be passive. They have a flexible time line to encompass all of the changes inherent in the complicated lives of adults, who often bring multiple commitments to postsecondary education, including part-time work, day care issues, limited finances, and responsibilities as either a part-time or full-time student. And, of special importance, the goals are evaluated periodically (usually every three to four sessions) by both the student and the practitioner to see if they are still appropriate or need adjustments as the student grows and matures in psychosocial skill development.

It must also be stressed, however, that if the practitioner is actively involved in working on these self-actualization goals with the student, the service provider will change as the student changes.

The role of the postsecondary practitioner evolves from a teacher or tutor who commands and leads to a "change agent" who guides and shares appropriate ideas, skills, values, and beliefs as an equal partner with the student with disabilities. The "process of being" will often take place for the professional while it is taking place for the student. This truly makes service provision in postsecondary settings more challenging and rewarding, because the professional starts to receive new insights and knowledge about his or her own belief system as well. It is not unusual for the practitioner to have many beliefs and values affirmed as the student grows, but also to have other ideas, beliefs, and values challenged and reevaluated as the student becomes self-actualized. There is no finer reward as a professional than to be a partner on such a journey of self-discovery and growth.

USING A TEAM APPROACH AND MAKING REFERRALS

All of the previous theories sound fine, but the question most post-secondary practitioners will ask is, How can I do all of this in my setting? The remainder of this chapter will provide practical hints, ideas, and suggestions about putting an effective psychosocial service-delivery model into practice in such diverse settings as a community college, a technical college, and a university. All of these techniques and ideas can be successful in postsecondary settings, but they are provided as a "smorgasbord," so that each postsecondary practitioner can choose and refine the mix of ideas and strategies that best fits local needs. Additional changes and adaptations according to each service provider's own expertise, values, and beliefs are also strongly encouraged.

Perhaps one of the most basic strategies used by practitioners in postsecondary settings is providing referrals and working in tandem with other professionals. However, very few professionals at the post-secondary level are trained to effectively provide services as part of a team of diverse professionals. Given the wide variety of academic, psychological, vocational, and human service expertise and knowledge possessed by service providers, a multidisciplinary team is crucial when addressing the psychosocial needs of individuals with learning disabilities. Consequently, the following material explores how to most effectively use a team approach in postsecondary settings.

In some situations, students with learning disabilities may display behaviors or attitudes that affect their ability to function with their peers or instructors in the classroom or in campus activities. Action must be taken by the postsecondary practitioner in these situations. Figure 5.1 outlines a process that postsecondary practitioners can use immediately to provide assistance to students who are experiencing significant emotional or personal difficulties. If a stu-

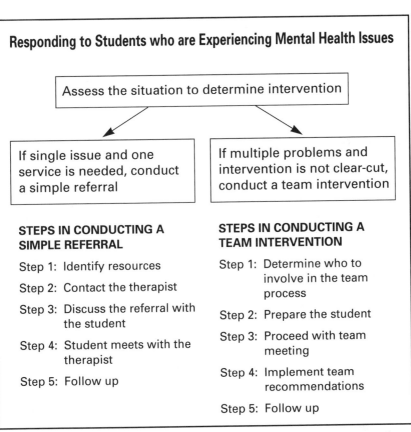

Figure 5.1. Steps in responding to students who are experiencing mental health issues. From *When Therapy Is Not Enough: How Learning Disability Specialists Can Work Effectively with Mental Health Professionals* by J. Johnson, S. Evelo, and L. Price, 1992. Minneapolis, MN: Project Extra. Manuscript submitted for publication. Reprinted with permission.

dent is struggling with one primary psychosocial issue (e.g., chemical use or sexual abuse) a referral to one specific individual or agency should be provided. For more information, use the steps for conducting a simple referral. However, a student may also be experiencing multifaceted difficulties. In that case, the treatment or intervention may not be so clear-cut and steps for a team intervention should be followed (J. Johnson et al., 1992). The interventions are summarized in Figure 5.1 and described more fully below:

Steps in Conducting a Simple Referral

Step 1. *Identify resources:* Postsecondary practitioners must have a working knowledge of a variety of campus and community resources such as the local Division of Rehabilitative Services, counselors, therapists, or mental health clinics. They can refer to those resources when conducting a simple referral or when coordinating a team evaluation. If possible, professionals should be identified in these agencies beforehand who are knowledgeable about the specific needs of adults with learning disabilities. However, because the literature about this population is still emerging, it may be necessary for LD service providers to furnish ongoing information, consultation, and guidance to sensitize therapists and other professionals about the multiple issues affecting adults with learning disabilities (Huestis & Ryland, 1986; Johnson et al., 1992; National Joint Committee on Learning Disabilities, 1987; Price, 1988; Price, 1990). It should also be stressed in both steps 1 and 2 that the following activities are conditional on receiving a consent to release information from the student.

Step 2. *Consult with professionals:* Postsecondary practitioners should contact and consult with a professional to discuss the reasons for considering the referral, especially in a crisis situation. This first contact helps the counselor or therapist to prepare for the arrival of the student. It is also helpful to ask the professional for other recommendations if she or he is unable or unwilling to provide the appropriate counseling needed.

Step 3. *Discuss the referral with the student:* After the post-secondary practitioner has assessed the situation and made the initial contact with the professional, the student must be prepared for the referral. The specific reasons for the referral should be reviewed with the student. The postsecondary practitioner should review his or her role at the college to provide reassurance that the student can continue to work on other areas affected by the student's learning disability. The initial appointment should then be made with the assistance of the postsecondary counselor, if needed.

Step 4. *The student meets with the therapist:* The postsecondary practitioner can help prepare the student for the upcoming session by rehearsing appropriate self-advocacy skills. The student must also be assured that continued support will be available in the postsecondary setting, as requested by the student.

Step 5. *Follow up:* At the beginning of their next meeting, the postsecondary practitioner should briefly follow up on the referral. This is an appropriate time to ask whether the student has attended the counseling appointment. It is also a good idea for the postsecondary practitioner to ask the referral source if further assistance is required from the postsecondary practitioner. The two professionals and the student may decide to coordinate joint meetings so that both academic and psychological issues can be addressed at the same time.

The second model is a team approach, based upon coordination of the relevant people involved in the student's life. The advantages of this model include identifying the student's primary needs, determining appropriate and acceptable treatments, developing a common set of goals, eliminating duplication of service, and providing continuous monitoring and evaluation that consider the total needs of the student. The steps in conducting a team intervention (J. Johnson et al., 1992) are described next.

Steps in Conducting a Referral for a Team Intervention

Step 1. *Determine who is involved in the team process:* The postsecondary practitioner should coordinate a team that includes members from various aspects of the student's life (school, home, and work). Possible team members could be a psychologist; an instructor; the student's division of rehabilitative services counselor; a nurse; parents, if appropriate; and the student. Goals for the initial team meeting could be to identify the individual needs of the student, determine problem areas, and decide what the next step should be.

Step 2. *Prepare the student:* The postsecondary practitioner should prepare the student for the team meeting by giving a brief explanation of the roles of the various team members and helping the student to express his or her own wishes and needs during the team meeting. Reviewing self-advocacy skills by role-playing situations that could be expected at the team meeting is also helpful.

Step 3. *Proceed with the team meeting:* The focus of this meeting is to address the complete needs of the student. The postsecondary practitioner usually functions as a facilitator for the group by encouraging interaction from all the members, documenting decisions, and taking notes describing a practical plan of action for the student and the team members. A holistic approach should be used to assess the physical, emotional, academic, and social issues that may be affecting the student's overall performance in the postsecondary setting. Each team member can describe specific strengths and weaknesses observed in the student's performance in different or similar settings. Then, all the team members together can determine what type of intervention is necessary and who will provide it. Usually, these joint recommendations involve specific services that will be provided to the student. Sometimes, the team determines that a referral to an individual therapist is appropriate. In that case it would be useful to invite the therapist to the next team meeting.

Step 4. *Implement the team recommendations:* After the team meeting, the student should participate in all of the recommended services suggested by the team. It is the responsibility of the team members who agreed to provide service to follow through with their commitments as soon as possible. The postsecondary practitioner should also solicit periodic feedback from the student and others, as needed.

Step 5. *Follow-up:* It is important that the postsecondary practitioner coordinate a follow-up team meeting to check on the student's progress and to assess whether the interventions have been successful. A major focus of the follow-up meeting is to examine whether the student is satisfied with the services previously suggested by the team. Team members can also determine whether there are additional needs to be addressed. This meeting will provide an opportunity for team members to communicate about strategies that are helpful in continuing to address the student's psychological and academic needs.

There are a few additional points that postsecondary practitioners must keep in mind when providing referrals or functioning as part of a team to deal with psychosocial issues. For example, when providing psychosocial assistance it is vital for postsecondary practitioners to continually find new resources or update referral information. Some practitioners keep this information handy at all times on their desks on index cards or a Roladex, or in a business card file. Because it is always at their fingertips, they can easily make changes, additions, or deletions. Referral information can be gathered from a wide variety of sources. Networking at local, regional, or national conferences, workshops, or symposia can serve as an invaluable source of information. Local and state governmental, educational, vocational, and human service agencies can be very useful resources of psychosocial assistance. Privately funded agencies, especially United Way, and private foundations are another good source for ideas and referrals. When all else fails, it is amazing what can be found by "walking" through the local White or Yellow Pages under categories like "mental health agencies" or "psychologists."

It must also be stressed that to fully utilize the benefits of any referral to an outside agency or professional, one must first lay the proper groundwork. This means preparing both the student and referral source beforehand, if time permits, for what will take place after the initial contact by the student or the postsecondary practitioner. This preparation can be summarized into who, what, where, when and why. The postsecondary practitioner should tell the student with learning disabilities *who* they are going to see, *what* will happen during the first session, *where* the student should go, *when* the first appointment will take place, and *why* the student is being referred to this particular resource. Similar information should also be provided to the contact at the referral agency. As a general rule of thumb, the postsecondary practitioner should always make at least one follow-up contact with the referral source to see if additional assistance is needed. This follow-up is a critical step in ensuring that such miscellaneous concerns as financial issues, conflicting services, and medication are dealt with as quickly and efficiently as possible.

ADDRESSING PSYCHOSOCIAL ISSUES WITH SUPPORT GROUPS

Another type of service delivery that can be extremely beneficial to postsecondary students with learning disabilities who are struggling to address psychosocial concerns is the use of group activities, especially supports groups (Aune & Ness, 1991; Cooper, 1986; Crimando, 1984; J. Johnson, 1989; Kunkaitis, 1986; Ostertag, 1986; Payne, 1992; Price, 1988a; Scheiber & Talpers, 1987). Support groups have been shown to be a successful way to address a wide variety of psychosocial issues (e.g., ineffective social skills, negative self-concept, or problems with communication) for students with learning disabilities (Cooper, 1986; J. Johnson, 1989; Kunkaitis, 1986; Neault, 1988; Price, 1988a; Scheiber & Talpers, 1987). Group activities, especially those used in a college setting, are excellent vehicles for reinforcing self-actualization goals (e.g., self-realization or understanding personal strengths and weaknesses). Support groups in postsecondary settings should have a flexible format that can work simultaneously on a wide spectrum of related issues by using different themes to focus the group activities (e.g., disability self-awareness, study skills, job readiness or job seeking). Most importantly, in this era of shrinking financial resources and increasing caseloads of students with disabilities in postsecondary education, they are also a cost-effective way to provide psychosocial assistance to small groups of students (J. Johnson, 1989; Price, 1988a).

Unfortunately, as many professionals have found in the past, successful support groups for students with disabilities can be challenging to establish and maintain in postsecondary settings. It may be difficult to get students to come to the first group session. Or many students may show up for the initial meeting, but then attendance may gradually fade away, until only two or three students remain. How can the postsecondary practitioner guard against these problems? The answer lies in establishing the proper groundwork for the group. This preparation can be categorized into eight steps that have been found over the years to maximize the success of group activities:

1. Determine the purpose of the group.

2. Decide who will facilitate the group.

3. Determine who will be the members of the group.

4. Decide how individuals will be recruited for group membership.

5. Decide when and where the group will meet.

6. Design what will actually take place during group sessions.

7. Build in allowances for the various learning styles of group participants.

8. Evaluate the group when it is finished.

Details on how to actually implement these steps in postsecondary academic or vocational settings is provided by J. Johnson (1989) and Price (1988a, 1988b). These three references provide many details for practitioners, including sample recruitment materials, support-group evaluation forms, examples of various activities that promote self-actualization skills, and specific ideas from community colleges and other postsecondary educational institutions that have implemented successful support groups in the past.

ADDRESSING PSYCHOSOCIAL ISSUES WITH INDIVIDUAL COUNSELING TECHNIQUES

Group activities are only part of the picture. Most counseling in postsecondary education is typically done in one-on-one interactions with students. The following material provides hints and strategies to maximize individual sessions that address psychosocial issues:

1. *Timing of sessions:* The actual time when sessions take place can be a critical factor. For example, some counselors use regularly scheduled appointments to provide consistency for students with learning disabilities. Other counselors agree to see students during a specific crisis in unscheduled sessions. These impromptu sessions may be especially meaningful to some students with learning disabilities because the practitioner can apply therapeutic ideas or techniques while the problem is actually taking place. However, it should also be emphasized to the student that making regular appointments and keeping them is the most advantageous use of both the counselor's and the student's time. No matter when the student sees the postsecondary practitioner, the focus must always be on a consistent check-in time for both the student and the practitioner.

2. *Focus on one behavior at a time:* It is also helpful for some students with learning disabilities (especially those with memory problems, sequencing problems, or difficulty transferring ideas from one situation to another) to look at only one behavior or episode at a time during sessions. If one primary goal is worked on per session, the student has more time to focus his or her energy and concentration on a particular problem and then process it fully. When the student thoroughly understands the problem or behavior, he or she can then move successfully on to other areas as needed.

3. *Summarize each session:* It is very important for the counselor to ask a student with learning disabilities, especially someone with difficulties in short-term memory, auditory memory, or sequencing, to verbally summarize each session. This

clarifies for both the student and counselor what the student has just learned. It also helps the student to see how ideas that he or she has just learned are related to previous knowledge. The counselor should then write down a clear, practical plan for change with discrete steps for the student to use after the session is finished. This written record again emphasizes for the student how diverse ideas discussed during the session are connected into a cohesive whole.

4. *Self-monitoring behaviors:* If adults with learning disabilities are indeed to become independent individuals, they must also learn to be responsible for their own self-defeating behaviors (interrupting others, standing too close to someone when talking to them, avoiding eye contact). It is vital that the counselor teach the student with learning disabilities to monitor his or her own behaviors as much as possible (Clary, 1984). This can be done in many different ways. The student with learning disabilities can be encouraged to count a certain behavior whenever it occurs during a specific length of time (e.g., hourly, daily, or weekly) and record it for the counselor. Or the student can keep a diary or a narrative log that is then analyzed during individual sessions. Some counselors teach students to develop self-questioning techniques. Others have them analyze their own behaviors after participating in informal role playing during group sessions. Another useful technique, if the institution has access to tape recorders or video cameras, is to record a student's typical behavior and then have the student review the audio- or videotapes for feedback.

5. *Relaxation activities:* Excessive frustration and stress can significantly influence and disrupt cognitive processing for individuals with learning disabilities who already have difficulties in retrieving, understanding, and retaining new knowledge. Many students come to the counselor's office already overburdened with a great deal of frustration, stress, and anxiety; therefore, relaxation techniques used at the beginning of one-on-one or group sessions are often beneficial. Once these barriers have been dealt with, the students are free to focus their full attention and energy on the goals of the session.

WORKING WITH RESISTANT STUDENTS

Some students may be referred to postsecondary service providers but will be less than cooperative. Some will not want to seek accommodations in the first place, because they are convinced that they do not have learning disabilities. And some are so ashamed or under so much stress that taking new risks by talking to a stranger or asking for assistance one more time are just too much to face. These scenarios, and many more, set up barriers that keep adults with learning disabilities from receiving the services that can literally turn their postsecondary education from failure to success. Consequently, it is imperative for all postsecondary service providers to know effective counseling techniques that will work with resistant students.

A student who is uncooperative with the postsecondary practitioner may lack skills or knowledge about learning disabilities and their daily ramifications. Helpful suggestions in this situation include (a) giving information about learning disabilities (e.g., handouts, films or articles), (b) giving specific skill training, and (c) using related techniques (e.g., peer tutoring, mentoring, or role modeling).

Students with learning disabilities may have pessimistic expectations resulting from a history of past failures, difficulty communicating with authority figures or service providers, or a low self-concept. In this situation, the following simple techniques can be instrumental in turning around negative attitudes: (a) acknowledging up front with the student that there may have been failures or problems in the past but emphasizing a focus on the here and now, (b) avoiding false optimism or a cheery denial of the student's perception of the problems ("Don't worry, it will be all right! I can help you"), (c) immediately discussing negative or anxious thoughts as they emerge, (d) affirming any progress made, and (e) providing consistent support.

Other beneficial counseling techniques that can be used to address resistant attitudes and behaviors include (a) starting with small steps, (b) using rehearsal or role playing to practice new behaviors and anticipate reactions from others, (c) altering the environment, if needed (e.g., using study skills in a quiet place), (d) changing the student's pattern and routine to avoid previous unsuccessful behaviors and attitudes, and (e) reinforcing any positive change immediately.

It is vital for the practitioner to follow the wise rule: *Always take care of yourself, as well as the student.* This is especially important when the service provider is averse to working with a particular student with a learning disability. The practitioner and the student are equal partners in the counseling process. All professionals—just like all students—occasionally find that they have trouble relating to or communicating with an individual student. In this case, it is important for them to implement the following steps: (a) acknowledge their feelings with their support system and discuss with another professional what options are available in this situation, (b) remember to keep asking themselves, Who is responsible for the change in this student's life? and (c) look at either referral or termination as options to consider.

CAVEATS FOR PRACTITIONERS IN POSTSECONDARY EDUCATION

It is unfortunate, but true, that it is the practitioner who is often neglected when the psychosocial needs of students with learning disabilities in postsecondary education are addressed. It would be naive at best, and untruthful at worst, to give the impression that providing all of the psychosocial assistance and guidance necessary for a wide variety of adults with a wide range of needs and assets is not a taxing job, and even an overwhelming one at times. The comprehensive rationale, techniques, and ideas discussed in detail in this chapter, while clearly beneficial to any student with learning disabilities, can be challenging and draining to implement on a daily basis. This is especially true when the practitioner is the only service provider who is responsible for students with learning disabilities in a particular postsecondary institution. Postsecondary practitioners must be aware of two important caveats at all times. They must be aware of the limits of their own professional expertise and, whenever possible, they should be protected and guided by their own professional code of ethics.

Limits of Professional Expertise

Previous sections in this chapter described in detail the benefits of making referrals and working as part of a team to provide the wide range of psychosocial assistance often needed by adults with learning disabilities in postsecondary settings. These important strategies are excellent ways to build on the knowledge and skills that many practitioners bring to postsecondary education.

For example, an LD specialist in a community college may have extensive training and experience in study skills and test taking, but little background in assertiveness training. This practitioner will benefit from working in tandem with a colleague who has more experience in personal counseling techniques. But when more serious psychological disorders emerge, such as chemical dependency, sexual abuse, or bimodal disorders, this same practitioner will need to totally rethink the service delivery provided for such students. At this crucial point, it is necessary for the postsecondary practitioner to ponder some probing questions and listen carefully to the answers.

- Am I prepared to deal with the ramifications of this student's psychological problem?

- Do I truly understand this disorder?

- Can I obtain enough training and knowledge to meet this student's immediate needs?

- Can I really provide effective assistance to this student in this particular situation?

- Do I feel that I can do the job as well as someone else?

If the answer to any of these questions is no, it is the ethical and moral responsibility of the postsecondary practitioner to refer the student *immediately* for additional assistance. In this situation, the referral techniques described earlier in this chapter will be the most beneficial in the long run to both the student and the practitioner.

Cormier and Cormier (1991) noted many complex psychological disorders that need immediate attention from neurologists, psychologists, and psychiatrists. Examples that demand further assistance include psychoactive-substance-use disorders, schizophrenia, delusional or paranoid disorders, psychotic disorders, mood disorders, anxiety disorders, impulse control disorders, and personality disorders. Unless the postsecondary practitioner has had extensive training in psychology and is licensed in this area, these problems are often out of the realm of his or her expertise. Also, these disorders are usually addressed in the intensive therapeutic environment of treatment centers, mental health facilities, and hospital inpatient or outpatient care. This is where the postsecondary practitioner can function well as part of the team intervention previously discussed.

Having a Personal Code of Ethics

Another safeguard that is usually unavailable to practitioners in postsecondary settings is the use of a professional code of ethics. A code of ethics is typically a list of detailed policies and procedures that provide direction for professionals during the counseling relationship.

It is ironic and disturbing that other professional disciplines have carefully and thoughtfully developed principles of professional conduct (i.e., codes of ethics) to guide individual members in their ongoing relationships with clients (Cormier & Cormier, 1991) but that no such document exists for LD specialists, who often see the largest population of students with disabilities in postsecondary settings. Such a well-defined code of ethics is a critical component in daily service delivery by postsecondary practitioners.

A code of ethics clearly and consistently delineates up front the expectations of both the professional and the student. It often provides guidance to the professional when a crisis or life-threatening situation develops, particularly when the practitioner faces an area where his or her expertise is limited. It is an extremely valuable tool for professionals to use when delineating the boundaries of their professional knowledge, and it often assists them to evaluate both themselves and their institutional services for specific student populations. An examination of the codes of ethical principles from such differing organizations as the American Psychological Association, the Association of Counselors and Family Therapists, and the American Association of Social Workers (Cormier & Cormier, 1991) illustrates common issues that practitioners in postsecondary settings encounter every day. Such isues as dual personal and professional relationships with students, emotional objectivity, prevalence of stereotypic attitudes, and appropriate uses of assessment certainly have relevance in effectively meeting the psychosocial needs of students with learning disabilities in postsecondary settings.

Whether the postsecondary practitioner is currently guided by a formal code of ethics or not, it is his or her responsibility to ask these probing questions and thoughtfully weigh the consequences of the answers:

- How do the issues of personal values, racial or cultural stereotypes, confidentiality, and dual relationships with students affect my daily counseling relationships with adults with learning disabilities?

- Is the primary focus of my postsecondary service delivery always on client-student welfare?

- Before I start the first session with each student do I spend time discussing the rights of both the client-student and the practitioner?

- Do I make appropriate referrals whenever necessary?

- Do I strive for emotional objectivity throughout my sessions with each student?

- Do I provide appropriate use of student assessment?

- Do I periodically evaluate my counseling sessions with client-students?

- Do I do periodic self-evaluation as a counselor-practitioner?

- Do I take advantage of my own counselor support systems (e.g., continuing education, staffings, or supervision)?

If the answer is no to one or more of these important questions, it is imperative for the postsecondary practitioner to get assistance as soon as possible by contacting colleagues, referral sources, or supervisors for guidance and information. It is also important to get additional training as soon as possible in the areas of concern. Obviously, this puts a heavy burden of responsibility on the practitioner, but it also protects him or her from unforeseen problems. It also ultimately greatly enriches the psychosocial service delivery provided to students with learning disabilities.

CONCLUSION

Much of this chapter has been devoted to an initial exploration of two questions:

1. What are the psychosocial implications of learning disabilities?

2. How can they be effectively addressed in postsecondary academic and vocational settings?

As the material throughout this chapter clearly illustrates, there are no simple answers to these questions.

We now know that some psychosocial characteristics, both positive and negative, have a lifelong impact on individuals with learning disabilities. For instance, the literature is starting to paint a disturbing portrait of many individuals with learning disabilities who exhibit negative psychosocial characteristics as they mature through adolescence and adulthood. It must be emphasized again that not all individuals with learning disabilities will fit these patterns. But if the postsecondary students described in this chapter are representative of students in your setting, they may choose lives for themselves that never allow them to show their full promise. The options they pick may include dropping out of school, erratic job histories, unemployment or chronic underemployment, criminal activity, unfulfilling marriages, dependent relationships with their spouses or family members, continued difficulties with mental or physical health, dysfunctional families, and suicide.

Who wants to leave a legacy like that for students with learning disabilities? The puzzle pieces in this chapter provide a rosier picture. Psychosocial issues can be effectively addressed in your postsecondary institution. You can function successfully as part of a team. You can provide a wide variety of powerful individual and group counseling activities. You can work together with students to influence the outcomes of their lives. You can grow, too, both professionally and personally, as the students with learning disabilities grow into full self-actualization. You can address both psychosocial needs and academic-skills development in postsecondary institutions. And when you do, everyone comes out a winner!

CHAPTER 6

Issues in Program Development

Since the organizational "positioning" of programs for students with learning disabilities bears heavily on issues such as funding, staffing, and visibility on campus, it behooves the LD coordinator or service provider to address the question of "affiliation" very carefully. Ideally, decision making should emanate from a structured, systematic process of weighing the benefits and limitations of program alliance across a variety of settings within an institution (e.g., disabled student services, learning centers, and campus departments). In reality, it is more likely that planning for serving the needs of students with learning disabilities occurs informally or evolves in response to the increasing demands from this growing cohort. Whether services are designed from scratch or broadened to include components specifically related to the nature of a disability, familiarity with the organizational structure of the institution is critical, since change is often the goal. In this chapter, the following areas are addressed: (a) administrative concerns in planning LD programs, (b) service-delivery issues, (c) considerations in garnering administrative support, and (d) approaches to program development.

ADMINISTRATIVE ISSUES: LAYING THE GROUNDWORK

Institutional Mission

An institution's mission must be considered as the foundation or underpinning for the development of LD programs. Bloland (1991, p. 28) wisely cautioned that we cannot "discuss the culture of higher education as if it were a single, monolithic entity. We have major research universities, community colleges, freestanding professional schools, denominational colleges, trade schools, and liberal arts colleges." A corresponding caveat applies when developing LD programs at the postsecondary level. No single model or approach will fit every institution, given the diversity that is a hallmark of the American system of higher education.

Consider the following examples of mission statements that portray qualitatively divergent environments. Hudson Valley Community College's mission is

> [To serve] its people and people from other areas in appropriate and diverse ways, striving always to improve their quality of life through education, training, and service at an affordable cost.
>
> . . . To offer an appropriate range of programs which serve the educational needs of a diverse population. (*Hudson Valley Community College Catalog*, 1991–92, p. 1)

The mission statement from the University of Georgia reflects the teaching, research, and service functions of large, publicly financed universities:

> To disseminate knowledge through teaching in the academic disciplines and fields of professional study that make universities distinctive; related to this purpose are programs and other opportunities for students' intellectual, professional, and personal development.
>
> To advance knowledge through research, scholarly inquiry, and the creative arts; related to both teaching and research is the observation and enhancement of the state's and the nation's intellectual, cultural, and environmental heritage.
>
> To provide service to the public through consultation, technical assistance, short-term instruction, training, and other opportunities for continued learning, growth, and development. (*The University of Georgia: Undergraduate Bulletin*, 1991–92, pp. 14–15)

Reed College is a 4-year, liberal arts, nonsectarian college that describes its mission as follows:

> Dedication to the highest standards of academic scholarship is central. . . . A well-structured curriculum, and small classes with motivated students and dedicated faculty provide the environment in which a student's quest for learning can be given broad rein. Students most likely to derive maximum benefit from a Reed education are individuals who possess a high degree of self-discipline and a genuine enthusiasm for academic work.
>
> Reed is first and foremost a teaching institution. Reed faculty are expected to commit themselves primarily to teaching, with scholarly and scientific research aimed at furthering this primary goal. Because it is a college rather than a university, students are assured

that their classes are being taught by professors rather than graduate students or teaching assistants. (*Reed College Catalog*, 1991–92, p. 7)

How an institution envisions its mission and places it in operation will have profound implications for many facets of campus life including support services. For example, in smaller, less academically competitive settings, the institutional mission may imply a commitment to a holistic education where teaching, learning, and student development are equally valued. In large, research-focused universities, functions may center more on research productivity and scholarly initiatives with less emphasis on the service aspect of student development.

In order to lay the groundwork for LD program development, there must be a "goodness of fit" between program goals and objectives and the institution's mission. To push for institutional change or improvement, which is often the case when advocating for the development of LD program services, without reflecting upon whether this change is consistent with the institutional mission, is to jeopardize one's credibility and long-term effectiveness. As an example, requesting LD program staff to address remediation of basic skills deficits in a highly academically competitive research setting could be construed as being dissonant with institutional purpose.

Understanding the Organizational Structure

Many colleges and universities have been formally serving students with disabilities as required under Section 504 since the early 1980s, in varying degrees and through divergent approaches. It has been suggested that 90% of the progress in service delivery for students with disabilities has occurred within the past 10 years (Jarrow, 1986). Given this history of service delivery for students with physical disabilities, it is more likely to be the exception rather than the rule to have the opportunity to create services for students with learning disabilities from the ground up. However, as the demand for LD services increases, existing support staff from the disability services office can be instrumental in shaping the development of these services. Collaborative planning with personnel from other campus student support services affords an opportunity to promote disability awareness and avoid duplication of services. However, sensitivity to "turf" issues and tact in working with veteran campus support staff are paramount.

In most instances, the organization of a postsecondary institution is clearly established, with divisions and units delineated according to the organizational chart. According to Sandeen (1989), higher education organizations are typically composed of divisions addressing academics, finances, student affairs, and development. Results of a recent nationwide survey of postsecondary disabled student service programs substantiated the location of the majority of these programs within the division of student affairs. Clark (1990) reported the following results based upon a response rate of 37% from 700 surveyed postsecondary institutions: 62% reported organizational location in student affairs, 20% were within academic affairs; 7% were in other college units, 4% were within departments, and the remaining 7% indicated divergent affiliations. In another study of 18 large state universities with comprehensive LD services, 69% of the 13 institutions that responded reported that LD services were located within the disabled student services unit (Woods et al., 1990). It appears, then, that the location of LD services predominantly rests under student affairs (with services located under academic affairs a distant second).

Whether LD services or programs have evolved from already-existing offices (e.g., disabled student services) or are developed through a comprehensive planning process, careful consideration needs to be paid to the *benefits and constraints* inherent in the student affairs and academic affairs models. Figure 6.1 illustrates a comparison between the two organizational approaches to housing the LD service function.

Under academic affairs, policy making often takes place within the purview of the unit. As more critical issues such as reasonable testing and curricular accommodations are raised by students with learning disabilities, postsecondary institutions can expect to be required to develop nondiscriminatory policies and procedures relating to the academic realm. Faculty may identify more strongly with a program within academic affairs, and there is the potential for establishing a rationale to have the LD program serve as a practicum site for areas such as special education, educational psychology, counseling, or clinical psychology. In a community college setting, linkages with 4-year institutions can result in cooperative agreements about field sites for clinical experiences. At the same time, limitations of the

Organizational Structure

Academic Affairs	Student Affairs
BENEFITS:	BENEFITS:
• The mission of the divison is academic matters; LD program goals and objectives may be congruent.	• The mission of the division is student support; this subsumes the traditional function of disabled student services.
• Access to key administrators (e.g., deans, vice president, or president in the case of small colleges) may be more feasible within the organizational hierarchy.	• Specific functions within the division are often related to the needs of students with learning disabilities (e.g., admissions, housing, registration, or orientation).
• Policies and procedures (e.g., foreign language substitutions) that affect students with learning disabilities are often generated by academic affairs.	• The potential exists for developing a centralized, comprehensive system of services using a center or cluster model (e.g., a campus learning center with computers, tutorial assistance, note takers, adaptive equipment, etc.).
• There are more opportunities for program research, given the emphasis on data and productivity.	• Retention is a major concern that relates to outcomes for students with learning disabilities.
• There is a possibility of developing a practicum site for graduate assistants and interns.	• Fiscal needs can be justified within the context of "student support services."
• Funding may be more predictable and secure, with options for work-study students.	• The position of the administrative staff is often 12-month.
• Faculty attitudes may be more supportive, given student affairs "perceived lack of status" (Bloland, 1991).	• There is campus-wide visibility by virtue of its student-based focus.

LIMITATIONS:

- Fiscal support may be problematic, given the "teaching" function of this division.
- Space allocation is a concern.
- The role and responsibilities of the LD services coordinator may be inconsistent with traditional faculty responsibilities.
- A 9-month contract is the traditional employment arrangement.
- Budget constraints exist in areas such as equipment and supplies since these are not perceived as integral to the academic function.
- If faculty status is to be allocated to the LD coordinator, obtaining such a position is extremely challenging.

LIMITATIONS:

- This area is vulnerable to budgetary cuts in eras of limited funds.
- Space allocation is a concern.
- The credibility of disabled student services' initiatives to promote reasonable accommodations may be devalued by some faculty concerned with lowering standards.
- Competencies of the staff may not include expertise in learning disabilities, thus requiring ongoing staff training dependent upon staff roles.
- Salary levels may be too low to attract well-qualified LD personnel.
- Participation in decision-making regarding academic policies may be limited.
- Depending upon the type of organizational structure, there may be more "hoops to jump through" regarding decision making.

Figure 6.1. Academic affairs or student affairs: pros and cons. *Note.* From J. M. McGuire (1992). Unpublished material. The University of Connecticut, A. J. Pappanikou Center on Special Education and Rehabilitation: A University Affiliated Program, Storrs. Reprinted with permission.

academic affairs model include lack of fiscal support and space, dissonance between the responsibilities of an LD service provider and those of faculty, and contractual arrangements that are usually not of 12-month duration.

The traditional mission and activities of the student affairs division are well suited to service delivery. If a constellation of support services is already in place, there is an opportunity to centralize them under a generic office such as a learning and academic support center. Given the student-focused nature of this division, visibility on campus may be easier to promote. On the other hand, the question of status should be considered, since it has been suggested that student affairs and its supporters are not seen by faculty as particularly important (Bloland, 1991). This has implications with respect to faculty attitudes and openness to change that are critical to ensuring equal opportunity for students with learning disabilities. Student affairs personnel may be particularly subject to the bureaucracy of a campus, and funding can become problematic in times of fiscal vulnerability. Barr and Fried (1981, p. 81) summed up the dichotomy succinctly: Academic affairs, with its cadre of faculty and student affairs, may "constitute two distinct subcultures on many campuses."

This is not to suggest a simplistic approach to deciding on the optimal position of LD programs on campus. But by understanding the culture of an institution and its impact on service delivery, the LD service provider can draw upon an awareness and knowledge of the unique character and climate of a setting in order to advocate effectively regarding programmatic concerns and divisional affiliation. Since the culture of an institution affects its decision-making process as well as its formal and informal organization, sensitivity on the part of LD program personnel has the potential to serve as a powerful tool in effecting change regardless of organizational placement.

Key Questions

In laying the groundwork for developing LD programs, additional points should be considered in juxtaposition with the institutional mission and organizational structure. Figure 6.2 outlines a series of questions that can promote a planned process for program development.

Areas such as admissions, eligibility criteria for services, and access to and assurances of reasonable accommodations all imply a

- Is there a clear, consise statement of philosophy or mission for LD services?

- Is there detailed information on procedures for accessing LD services?

- What role, if any, will staff from LD services assume in the admission process?

- What criteria will be used to determine student eligibility under Section 504?

- What documentation will be required from students seeking services?

- Will assessment and evaluation services be offered by the LD program?

- What procedures will be used to determine reasonable accommodations and how will accommodations be efficiently and effectively provided?

- How will policies and procedures relating to equal educational opportunity for students with learning disabilities (e.g., course substitutions) be developed?

- What range of services will be offered by the LD program (e.g., diagnostic assessment services, counseling, learning-strategies instruction, career or vocational guidance, or self-advocacy training)?

- How accessible to students with learning disabilities are generic services offered to nondisabled students?

- What mechanisms will exist for promoting faculty and staff awareness and knowledge regarding learning disabilities?

- How will program evaluation be conducted? For Whom? By whom?

Figure 6.2. Questions to be addressed in program development.

need for explicit procedures to be in place within the LD program unit. As campus awareness of LD services broadens, referrals to the program will increase, underscoring the importance of defining the scope of activities such as assessment. Because of the pivotal role played by faculty in the area of reasonable accommodations, planning should address their need for information and technical assistance with respect to classroom accommodations that promote access, yet do not compromise standards. Finally, systematically planning for program evaluation will ensure expedient data collection so that program and student outcomes can be monitored and serve as a basis for program planning and modification.

SERVICE DELIVERY ISSUES

Services or Programs: A Definitional Maze

Depending upon the institution, students with learning disabilities are assisted in their pursuit of postsecondary education through offices that are often described either as providers of services or providers of a program. On the surface, this may seem like semantic hairsplitting. In reality, this dichotomy can create confusion on the part of consumers, parents, and professionals seeking information, resulting in a lack of clarification that can be seen in a recent review of the literature on types of services available to college students with learning disabilities (R. Nelson & Lignugaris/Kraft, 1989). Only 14 of the 31 articles that were reviewed reported on surveys of *services* to support students in postsecondary settings; evaluations of specific *programs* were described in 6 articles. Guides such as *Peterson's* (Mangrum & Strichart, 1992) or *Lovejoy's* (Straughn, 1988) contain detailed information ranging from the size of the institution, number of staff, availability of diagnostic testing, and types and extent of support services offered. In order to eliminate ambiguity in terminology, a brief discussion of terms is warranted.

Comprehensive college LD *programs* are characterized by a planned process that includes the support of key campus administrators. There is often one person who spearheads the efforts to develop the program (Vogel, 1982); that individual typically has expertise in the area of learning disabilities. A program at the postsecondary level should be based upon the specific individual needs of students. Determination of needs should proceed from reliable and valid documentation that often is gathered through in-house assessment services. Programs are coordinated in a centralized location (Brinckerhoff, Shaw, McGuire, Norlander, & Anderson, 1988). A range of services is available, and a diagnostic-prescriptive approach is often used to select appropriate services tailored to match each student's unique needs. Mangrum and Strichart (1988) identified the following as components of postsecondary programs for students with learning disabilities: diagnostic testing, individual educational programs, academic and program advising, basic skills remediation, subject-area tutoring, specialized courses, auxiliary aids and services, and counseling. Although not every component will be offered on every campus, the critical aspects of LD programs are individualization, a basis in diagnostic data, and coordination by a professional with training in learning disabilities. In some instances, because of the specialized nature of services provided by trained staff, LD programs offer a limited number of "slots" for students with learning disabilities.

Services at the postsecondary level can be defined as those generic activities that are carried out to ensure equal educational opportunity for any student with a disability. Brinckerhoff (1991) outlined a variety of "minimal resources" that can ensure adequate support services in a climate of fiscal austerity that may preclude formal programs. Again, the critical distinction between programs and services centers upon the qualifications of the personnel and the availability of diagnostic services. Brinckerhoff stated that an LD service provider can have training in broader areas such as counseling or student affairs, rather than in learning disabilities and assessment.

Basic LD services typically might include taped textbooks, assistance in arranging testing accommodations, auxiliary aids such as tape recorders, readers, note takers, and provisions for making course substitutions. The operative word in a service approach is *generic*, meaning that the services are inclusive of and available to all students with disabilities.

Brinckerhoff (1991) described another type of service as "user-fee services," which are more like programs since they typically include diagnostic services, a trained LD specialist, individualized tutoring, and counseling. This level of support includes a fee that is usually assessed every semester. The legitimacy of charging a fee for specialized programs was discussed by Rothstein (1986), who pointed out that, to date, case law as well as the regulations do not seem to require special training programs. As long as a student with a learning disability can access generic support services at no cost, user-fee services are not deemed discriminatory because special training programs are above and beyond the Section 504 requirements for reasonable accommodations.

Rather than becoming bogged down in semantics, there is a value for every institution in clearly delineating its approach to ensuring equal access to students with learning disabilities. It is very possible for an office of disabled student services to assist students with learning disabilities in a programmatic way. Staff may be expanded to include a part-time or full-time LD specialist. Tutorial services can be developed to focus on areas that are typically a problem for students with learning disabilities, using a learning-strategies approach (Deshler et al., 1984) and emphasizing student independence and autonomy (Brinckerhoff et al., 1992). No one approach will fit the needs of every student. Support services may provide a suitable match for some, whereas a comprehensive, highly structured program may offer the intensive intervention required by others (Shaw et al., in press).

A "Developmental" Continuum of Service-Delivery Models

Fifteen years ago, only a handful of colleges and universities were addressing the needs of students with learning disabilities in a programmatic way (Vogel, 1982). Today, the picture has changed. McGuire and Shaw (1989) developed a continuum that highlights various types of support services. Administrators and service providers should carefully consider components of this model so that it conceptually fits with the overall institutional mission.

The notion of a continuum (see Figure 6.3) also captures the evolution of approaches for serving students, since increasing demands have often served as a catalyst for moving in the direction of increased program specialization. Although this raises the question of compliance with Section 504, there are institutions that even now maintain that no services exist (McGuire & Shaw, 1989). In some settings, services may be available on a hit-or-miss basis as represented by

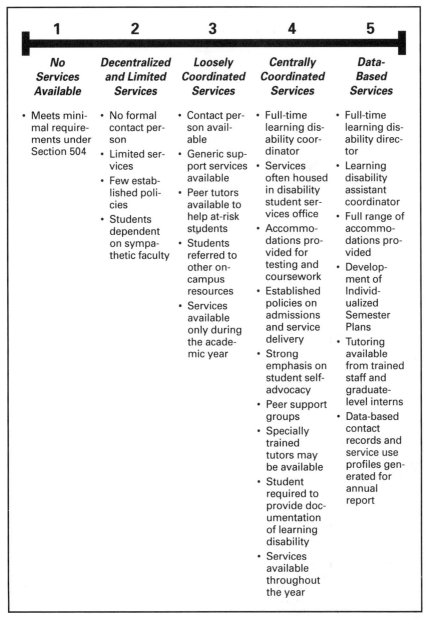

1	2	3	4	5
No Services Available	**Decentralized and Limited Services**	**Loosely Coordinated Services**	**Centrally Coordinated Services**	**Data-Based Services**
• Meets minimal requirements under Section 504	• No formal contact person • Limited services • Few established policies • Students dependent on sympathetic faculty	• Contact person available • Generic support services available • Peer tutors available to help at-risk students • Students referred to other on-campus resources • Services available only during the academic year	• Full-time learning disability coordinator • Services often housed in disability student services office • Accommodations provided for testing and coursework • Established policies on admissions and service delivery • Strong emphasis on student self-advocacy • Peer support groups • Specially trained tutors may be available • Student required to provide documentation of learning disability • Services available throughout the year	• Full-time learning disability director • Learning disability assistant coordinator • Full range of accommodations provided • Development of Individualized Semester Plans • Tutoring available from trained staff and graduate-level interns • Data-based contact records and service use profiles generated for annual report

Figure 6.3. Continuum of postsecondary LD support services. Adapted from *Resource Guide of Support Services for Student with Learning Disabilities in Connecticut Colleges and Universities*, ed. by J. M. McGuire and S. F. Shaw, 1989. Storrs: A. J. Pappanikou Center on Special Education and Rehabilitation: A University Affiliated Program, University of Connecticut. Reprinted with permission.

Level 2 on the continuum. As pressure for services increases in both scope and the number of students requesting them, an institution may move to centrally coordinated or data-based services. Regardless of where on this continuum an institution falls, the threshold question remains the same: Are qualified students with learning disabilities provided equal educational opportunities in a nondiscriminatory fashion through access to academic adjustments and auxiliary aids? An annual review based upon goals and the scope of the services offered should be conducted to address this question and conduct planning for future needs (McGuire et al., 1990). The next section discusses considerations to bear in mind concerning administrative support, whether program development occurs from the ground up or evolves from already-existing services.

GARNERING ADMINISTRATIVE SUPPORT

After the mission and organizational structure of the institution have been studied, it is important to find the best fit along the continuum of LD support services. As pointed out in the previous section, the process of finding the right niche for LD services can have long-term implications. In this section, the issue of garnering administrative support will be viewed from two vantage points: that of service providers who are initiating LD support services and that of veteran service providers who are trying to maintain services or perhaps develop new programming initiatives in response to escalating requests for services.

Initiating LD Support Services

A common mistake of many well-meaning campus support staff is to try to develop LD services overnight. This process takes at least 6 months of careful, comprehensive planning to become established. During the early stages, it is important to determine which key players on campus are most likely to support efforts for developing LD services. Similarly, the question of who is most likely to be resistant or threatened by the development of LD services should be posed early on. A campus-wide survey of an array of stakeholders should be conducted in order to determine what is currently being done on campus for students who are at risk, and by whom. Survey data can be helpful in identifying allies, determining the scope of services to be offered, and creating an interface between LD services and existing campus resources (e.g., the academic assistance center or counseling center).

After conducting campus fact-finding initiatives, the LD contact person should survey what other peer institutions are doing regionally and across the country. Many 2- and 4-year institutions have notable services for students with learning disabilities. (See Appendix F for a listing of LD contact persons in the United States and Canada through AHEAD.) LD specialists at peer institutions are valuable resources when discussing future plans and pinpointing roadblocks and triumphs. Telephone discussions, fax interchanges, and information sharing are very useful techniques for fact finding to build a rationale for establishing services on campus. If feasible, after the LD service provider conducts an informal telephone survey, he or she should target one or two institutions for a site visit. A half-day site visit with a veteran LD service coordinator can be very beneficial for the neophyte. These meetings can be further enhanced if a team of one or two key players from the visiting campus have the opportunity to meet with a variety of administrative staff, LD service personnel, and students. Such fact-finding meetings can focus on a variety of issues ranging from eligibility criteria to service-delivery options. It is often helpful for the newcomer to review and collect sample service-delivery forms that can be adapted for future use. Additional service-delivery forms and suggestions for standard operating procedures can be found in resource books by Dalke (1991), Gajar (1987), McGuire and Litt (1992), and Stewart (1989). In addition to site visits and telephone contacts, articles cited in the References at the end of this book contain a wealth of valuable information pertinent to creating services. The HEATH Resource Center in Washington, DC, is another valuable resource for gathering information on higher education and disability issues (1-800-54-HEATH). National conferences, such as the annual AHEAD conference and the annual Learning Disabilities Postsecondary Training Institute (sponsored by the University of Connecticut, Storrs) offer in-depth topical information and opportunities for future networking.

To ensure that the planning process becomes a collaborative effort and not the sole initiative of any one individual, it is best for planning efforts to emanate from a cross-section of campus constituencies. A task force or ad hoc committee can provide further direction and shape the newly emerging services. This group can often make more inroads with members of the administration than any one individual could. The committee may be tightly focused on LD issues or it may have the broader mission of addressing the needs of students with any disability. In either case, it should be composed of representatives from a cross-section of the entire campus community, including faculty, staff, deans, alumni, students, consulting psychologists, speech and language clinicians, and parents. These individuals can offer insights into developing a workable plan of action. Involving staff from the psychology department, special education department, or other campus disciplines may result in suggestions for hiring of future personnel and the development of intern training sites. Faculty, staff members, or alumni who have a family member with a learning disability or have learning disabilities themselves may be particularly supportive of these efforts. Members of the advisory group can serve as a "political action committee" that can strategize on how to approach the administration and financial planners on campus with a broad-based proposal that is likely to attract support. Using the CIPP model of program evaluation, McGuire, Harris, and Bieber (1989) offered the following format for developing a program proposal:

Context:

- What is the context in which the program will operate (e.g., within disabled student services or as part of an academic support center)?

- What needs (e.g., student requests for services) underlie program development?

- What resources already exist?

Input:

- What program services are needed to meet program goals?

- What are the personnel requirements for program implementation?

- What are the budgeting considerations?

- What are space and facility needs?

Process:

- What methods and activities will be implemented to put program goals and objectives into operation?

Product:

- What are the outcomes to be achieved through program implementation (e.g., student graduation or training of graduate students)?

The proposal should begin with a strong rationale for services and should emphasize that existing campus resources cannot effectively meet the needs of a growing number of students with learning disabilities. Data collected on service requests and numbers of campus students with learning disabilities make the case more convincing. Even the most resistant administrators will take note of the fact that in an age of declining enrollments, it is important to attract "otherwise qualified" students and to retain them. Therefore, the proposal can be strengthened by promoting LD services as a marketing tool to attract additional students. Coordinated efforts with the admissions office can help to sell these services to a broader high school audience. Arguing that LD support services are only another aspect of the institution's retention efforts can be a convincing idea. Finally, service providers can use the legal justifications for providing these services as a powerful rationale for a proposal. Avoiding costly litigation and addressing issues of institutional compliance with Section 504 and the ADA are additional motivators that catch the attention of administrators. Drafting a program proposal provides an opportunity to create a document tailored to attract seed money from corporate sponsors, internal grant sources, and alumni. One often-overlooked consideration is the potential impact that parents may have on helping to expand fledgling services. Parents are often very appreciative of efforts to ensure access through support services and may be willing to commit some of their own financial resources to get these services off the ground. If a fee is charged for specialized tutorial support, then the possibility of scholarship funds needs to be addressed during these early planning stages.

There are a variety of ways of presenting the proposal to the department head or dean who is the most likely to be responsible for overseeing the operations of the proposed LD support services. It may be useful to invite this individual to a meeting where the proposal can be showcased by several members of the planning or advisory team. This initial meeting should clearly stipulate the rationale for providing the services. Supporting testimony from faculty and students may also be appropriate. The proposal should include the overall goals and objectives for the program, the range of services to be offered, staffing considerations, operating expenses, suggestions for the location of the services, and a projected time line. An executive summary of the proposal could be used as an outline for the meeting. A more low-key approach is for the designated LD contact person to approach the dean or department head privately to discuss the proposal informally, while concurrently soliciting his or her support. The new LD service provider should be prepared to demonstrate to the dean of student affairs or academic affairs how the mission of the LD support services interfaces with the overall mission of the institution.

For the vast majority of service providers, the luxury of offering a comprehensive LD program is impossible due to funding limitations, inadequate space, or a lack of institutional commitment. Brincker-hoff (1991) pointed out that it is not easy to garner administrative support for new initiatives in these challenging fiscal times. Consequently, colleges and universities may want to develop a "core of generic support services" for students with learning disabilities and not attempt a comprehensive program until long-term institutional support is ensured. By starting small, LD service providers can take a systematic approach that will give them the opportunity to gradually gain the attention of campus administrators over the competing demands of other campus personnel. Another consideration for starting small was noted by Mangrum and Strichart (1988), who pointed out that not all students with learning disabilities need the support and services of a comprehensive program.

LD coordinators must realize that their ground-breaking efforts may not be received warmly by all constituencies on campus. Administrators may not be as receptive to the idea of providing educational opportunities to students with learning disabilities as they are to providing services for students with physical disabilities or vision or hearing impairments. Faculty members may be concerned that admitting students with learning disabilities will lower academic standards or require them to water down their curriculum. Some may fear that academic adjustments will infringe upon their academic freedom in the classroom. Mangrum and Strichart (1988) surveyed

LD college program directors and found that there generally was no change in a college's image as long as the population of students with learning disabilities did not exceed 10% of the base population. They also observed that many college administrators and faculty still think that "the learning disabled have insufficient intelligence to succeed in college" (p. 220). Consequently, one of the first priorities for LD service providers is to build awareness and to assure faculty and administrators that serving college students with learning disabilities does not devalue the professional stature of the institution. Convincing the faculty is probably one of the most challenging jobs an LD program director will face. Attending departmental faculty meetings, meeting with individual faculty members, and making presentations to heighten awareness can all help to win faculty support for the idea of LD services on campus. Follow-up meetings with key administrators and faculty will depend on a number of factors, including the amount of perceived backing behind the LD services office, the level of training and experience of the LD service provider in working with college students with learning disabilities, and available financial resources.

Once the proposal for establishing specialized LD support has been accepted by the administration, staffing needs must be addressed. Mangrum and Strichart (1988) noted that the person who served as the "initial catalyst" for the college LD program often becomes the first program director. This individual is formally charged with the responsibilities of establishing services and negotiating, on their own turf, with the campus support staff who have already been working with these students. These initial meetings often take place in the academic development center or learning assistance center. The meetings should be nonthreatening, and the LD service provider needs to be humble in proposing an expanded service model that may initially appear to be an infringement to the director of the campus peer-tutoring program or to an academic-skills counselor. It is possible for LD services to become a component of one of these generic campus support services offices or to expand the mission of these existing offices to serve students with learning disabilities. For example, at Boston College, LD services have been incorporated into the Academic Development Center in the college library. On this campus, LD services are viewed as one type of service among many that are readily available and visible to both students and faculty. Institutions with federally funded student services programs such as TRIO that are charged with serving first-generation college students, members of minority groups, or individuals with physical disabilities may consider adding an LD specialist to the staff who can work with students who have learning disabilities.

Once the LD support services are well defined and funded, it is time to market services to the campus community. Brinckerhoff (1991) offered several suggestions for publicizing LD services and for enhancing program visibility. Dalke (1991) presented a variety of suggestions for disabled student service coordinators on ways to develop program literature and materials, offering specific ideas for developing a program brochure and an informational videotape, as well as suggestions on marketing program information to potential students and the general public. Dalke (1991) noted that people do not become informed overnight and that "it will take time to disseminate information about the services, but perhaps more importantly, it will take time to help everyone become more aware and appreciative of the unique needs of students with disabilities as they pursue their careers in higher education" (p. 77).

The guidelines and suggestions presented in this section should lay the foundation for establishing a well-defined set of core services for students with learning disabilities. By keeping the first-year plan manageable in scope, service providers can be responsive to the changing needs of the administration, faculty, and staff and, most importantly, of the students they serve. The following section will address many of the administrative challenges that veteran LD service providers may face as they seek to ensure program viability and stability.

Veterans: How to Maintain and Enhance LD Support Services

One of the best ways to ensure the future security of LD services is to make them an indispensable and *visible* entity on campus. This can be achieved in several ways. Service providers need to keep deans and other college administrators informed about the activities of the office. These individuals should receive annual updates about the services being offered, including demographic information, retention figures, and other related data that will help to underscore the impact of these services on campus. An executive summary of the annual report should also be distributed to other campus resource personnel and deans. College administrators should be invited to sponsored events and workshops that focus on the LD office's activities. Memos from faculty and letters of appreciation from parents, students, and alumni are also useful in expanding awareness. The role of the LD support services office can also be promoted by holding volunteer or faculty awards receptions each spring. These annual gatherings afford an opportunity to spotlight faculty, staff, or volunteers who have been supportive of college students with learning disabilities. Administrative superiors and college deans should be on hand for these events. Such small-scale, low-cost publicity efforts should be covered by campus reporters who can heighten awareness through the campus newspaper. By letting key administrative players know about services throughout the year, and not just at the beginning of the next funding cycle, the attitudinal support base can be strengthened. A newsletter with a special column featuring LD issues could be sent to all faculty, staff, and students who have contact with the LD student services office. Private consultants, community contact persons such as rehabilitation counselors, Learning Disabilities Association of America parent groups, and local high school teachers could receive invitations to an "LD Open House" at the beginning of each semester. If the college admissions office sponsors information workshops for regional high school personnel including guidance counselors, the LD program director can be a part of the agenda, highlighting services offered to students with learning disabilities. Middlesex County College in Edison, New Jersey, sponsors a high school guidance counselors' breakfast each year to enhance the awareness of high school personnel about a variety of postsecondary LD issues. Another successful technique for expanding outreach efforts is to establish an LD speakers' bureau on campus. This group might be composed of three or four college students who are willing to talk with high school students, speak at college fairs, and give talks to departmental faculty (Brinckerhoff, 1991).

Second- or 3rd-year veterans should contact the chairs of less supportive departments on campus in the spirit of building bridges. It may be useful for the program director, rather than a member of the staff, to personally meet with the department chair to discuss mutual concerns about the LD support services on campus. A successful student with a learning disability from within the department may be a powerful contributor at such meetings. Faculty development efforts can expand in areas that are often more complex and sensitive, such as the appropriateness of course substitutions or policies regarding withdrawal from a course beyond the standard deadline without penalty. Other key departments on campus, including athletics or minority affairs, may be prepared to "join forces" with the LD support services office, once the office is respected and accepted as a critical campus resource.

LD service providers must monitor the rate of expansion of services in subsequent years to prevent an erosion in the level of personal service available to students who are already being served. Providing personal service means appreciating faculty who drop in unexpectedly to see the office, unflinchingly repeating information to parents of prospective students over the telephone, and knowing when to drop current work for a student who needs immediate attention. These actions convey the message that even though the LD support services office may be expanding in the number of students being served, personal contact has not been sacrificed. A related concern as services expand is support staff burnout. Professional stress can be minimized by ensuring reasonable schedules for daily appointments, providing meetings for staff on a weekly basis, and supplying opportunities for ongoing professional training. As the staff expands to address the changing needs of students, the LD service provider may seek to share some job duties with staff so that they can assume control of some aspect of the LD support services office. This might involve cofacilitating a peer support group, or conducting interviews with all prospective students and their parents.

It is important to note that heightened campus awareness and a professional image are not enough to guarantee future services. Supplemental funds must be sought out by LD service providers so that services can be maintained and expanded where needed. When it is not possible to achieve a strong internal institutional commitment to funding, it may be possible to raise funds through additional user fees. Some LD support services offices are now charging additional fees for summer orientation programs, specialized tutorial support, or diagnostic testing. Even in these times of fiscal restraint, opportunities exist to secure additional funding through fund-raising activities or by soliciting the support of alumni or parents of students with disabilities. For example, the University of Wisconsin–Madison was able to fund a tape-recording studio in the Disabilities Resource Center solely through the contributions of alumni. The 25th and 50th class reunions are looking for "pet projects" to support and disability services are often a good prospect. Service providers need to keep in mind that potential donors are much more likely to donate to a cause that is supported by a track record of success, rather than to a trial balloon. The adage that "people give money to people" bears careful thought. By personalizing the services that are offered, service providers give potential donors an opportunity to view firsthand, or through the eyes of their son or daughter, the effect that these supports can have on their child's academic progress and self-esteem.

DEVELOPING A SUMMER TRANSITION PROGRAM

Another approach to increasing revenues for program services is to develop a summer orientation program. Transition programs attract the interest and attention of prospective students with learning disabilities, thereby increasing the numbers of students who visit the campus and ultimately apply for admission. In an age of declining enrollments and a shrinking market of traditional college-age students, this benefit alone could help garner additional administrative support. Another advantage of a summer transition program is the opportunity it provides for members to gather both formal and informal data on new students. Observational data obtained from new students can be very useful to service providers in planning future services for these students.

According to Dalke and Schmitt (1987), transition programs should accomplish the following:

- Provide students with an educational experience similar to what is expected in higher education.
- Assist students in obtaining a clear picture of their strengths and weaknesses and needs as they relate to the demands of the post-secondary environment.
- Provide opportunities for students to explore and address issues related to the emotional factors involved in losing a familiar support system of family, friends, and teachers.
- Provide students opportunities to practice self-advocacy skills.
- Familiarize students with the physical environment of the campus and community.

- Identify and explain campus and community organizations, agencies, and related support services that are available to students.
- Provide instruction to students in areas such as study skills, time management, notetaking, and test-taking strategies, and library usage.
- Provide direct instruction to students in academic areas such as reading comprehension, written language, and basic math skills.
- Provide staff with formal and informal student performance data.

The activities planned to meet these goals will vary from campus to campus depending on the availability of financial resources, qualified staff, and the location of the institution. Dalke (1991) noted that ideally the program should occur during the summer prior to the semester that students enter as first-year students. In order for the program to achieve the breadth and scope of its goals, it should last between 4 weeks and 2 months. Finally, although the summer is the logical time for service providers to offer such a program, the summer months are not a prized time for students with learning disabilities to attend still more school. Some may be looking for freedom after high school graduation or a special vacation with friends before setting off for college. Others may depend upon summer employment to generate funds to finance their education. With these factors in mind, marketing efforts must be assertive and address both the desires of parents to boost their son's or daughter's scholastic achievement before college and the student's desire to enjoy the summer.

Many direct service providers underestimate the amount of advance planning time it takes to develop, publicize, and implement a summer orientation program for students with learning disabilities. Planning should begin at least 6 months in advance. Initially, the LD service provider must assess the amount of administrative support that the institution is willing to provide. Drawing up a brief proposal concerning the program to share with unit directors and deans is a good starting point. The proposal should include a rationale for the services, expected duration, range of services to be offered, staffing and space considerations, and projected income and expenses. The LD service provider may need to "sell" this transition program idea to the administration (Brinckerhoff & Eaton, 1991). It is important to anchor the purpose of the program within the overall mission of the college or university. Service providers may need to assure the administration that this outreach effort will not devalue the academic stature of the institution and will ultimately provide many benefits, such as improving the retention of students with learning disabilities, generating additional tuition income, and enhancing institutional recognition. These preliminary planning sessions should take place in early fall so that dates can be set and publications and mailings can occur in a timely manner.

At Boston University, one technique that proved effective for garnering administrative and faculty support was the development of a pilot program. The first Summer Transition Program (STP) ran for 6 weeks during the traditional second summer session, but enrollment was limited to only eight students. This approach had several distinct advantages. A small group permits greater flexibility in altering services in response to changing and unanticipated needs. Also, convincing adjunct campus staff (e.g., residential life, food services, and library services staff) to provide support the first time through is easier if the numbers are manageable. Similarly, up-front publication costs can be kept to a minimum when only a small number of slots are to be filled. Future marketing efforts can build upon these preliminary efforts so that target audiences can be more clearly defined and feeder networks established. Some of the best referral sources for the STP were private psychologists or college consultants, the most competitive public high schools in the area, and private preparatory schools that specialize in working with bright students who may be at risk for success in college.

Start-up funds for summer program efforts may be sought from a variety of sources, both on and off campus. If the administration is supportive of the idea but unable to provide monetary backing, corporate underwriting or private foundations are another possibility. Foundations are often interested in providing seed money for efforts such as this that have a good potential for becoming self-supporting in a short period of time. Service providers should also explore the possibility of securing scholarship funds for students, since these programs are often staff-intensive, which necessitates additional tuition charges. Fees typically range from a few hundred dollars for state-funded programs to over $5,000 for the highly specialized 7-week program at Landmark College in Putney, Vermont. Regardless of the cost, marketing considerations should focus on what makes the orientation program unique.

Some campuses direct themselves exclusively to an LD audience, while others cater to any high school student who is at risk. Some programs are exclusively designed for students who will be attending the sponsoring institution and others are open to students who will be attending any postsecondary institution. For example, the STP at Boston University is open to any high school graduate with a documented learning disability who is "otherwise qualified" for admission to Boston University or any other competitive institution. The SmartStart orientation program at New York University is more typical of other summer programs and is exclusively for students with learning disabilities who will be matriculating at NYU in the fall (duChossois & Brinckerhoff, 1992).

Admission criteria for most LD college orientation programs at competitive 4-year colleges require average-to-superior intellectual potential, a formalized diagnosis of a learning disability, no primary emotional or behavioral problems, a high school diploma or general equivalency diploma, and a high level of motivation to succeed. Supporting documentation typically includes a high school transcript, a copy of the high school IEP, if applicable, and a current psychoeducational evaluation that clearly indicates the diagnosis of a learning disability. Personal interviews and brief essays are another way to determine the level of maturity and motivation that potential participants may have for attending the program. Especially during the first year or two of such transition programs, service providers need to be very careful in selecting appropriate candidates. Enrolling a student with mild mental retardation, or one who has a history of psychiatric distress, may quickly dilute the targeted purpose of the program, which is solely for students with *learning disabilities*, not just students who have problems with learning. Some parents overlook this point as they desperately seek summer options for their son or daughter after high school graduation.

Determining Transition Program Content

The content of summer orientation programs varies from campus to campus. Nearly all summer programs include a strong emphasis on refining study skills, enhancing academic performance, and addressing psychosocial issues. Training may be conducted either on a one-to-one basis or in small groups. The University of Wisconsin–Whitewater, Southern Illinois University, Boston University, New York University, and Landmark College are a few of the postsecondary institutions that have well-defined orientation programs for students with learning disabilities. The goals of these programs are to make students more aware of their strengths and weaknesses and to teach them how to compensate for their learning disability, manage time more effectively, enhance interpersonal and self-advocacy skills, and familiarize themselves with campus and community resources. Some programs are offered for course credit, others offer credit toward graduation, and some are noncredit-bearing. The 5-week program at the University of Wisconsin–Whitewater emphasizes the following components: affective support, a diagnostic evaluation, academic reinforcement and instruction, strategy training, awareness of support services available on campus, and general campus awareness. Other institutions may also provide specific instruction on researching and writing a term paper, using adaptive computer equipment, learning anxiety-reduction techniques, exploring career goals, or developing public-speaking skills. Several of the programs surveyed also include a special workshop for parents on how to let go and how to respond from a distance to the continuing support needs a son or daughter may have.

In addition to the core curriculum elements previously cited, the STP at Boston University has three primary components: (a) a mainstreamed four-credit content course, (b) a learning-strategies seminar, and (c) a series of three topical workshops. For a complete listing of the essential components of the STP, refer to Figure 6.4.

As mentioned previously, academic expectations and competition increase significantly as students move from high school to college. Nowhere does this become more apparent than when students enroll in a fully mainstreamed credit-bearing content course. In the realities of a real classroom with a bona fide college professor, these students are often surprised and frightened by the rigors of college-level coursework. Students enrolled in the STP select one of three possible courses from those offered to the general student population. Class size is typically about 25 students, including approximately 8 students affiliated with the LD support services office. These students are expected to meet the same standards as any other student in the course. One unforeseen benefit of this totally mainstreamed approach is that the classes become a logical testing ground for STP students to try out their developing self-advocacy skills by meeting with professors to discuss their learning disabilities, asking for testing accommodations, seeking out note-taking assistance, or using taped textbooks.

- *Four-credit content course in one of the following:*
  General Psychology 101
  Social Sciences 101
  The Astronomical Universe 102

- *Learning-strategies seminar to reinforce lecture content*
  Active textbook reading
  Note taking and mapping
  Time management
  Using adaptive technology
  Test preparation and test taking
  Writing a research paper

- *Specific instruction in University of Kansas learning strategies*
  I-PLAN, a procedure for teaching self-advocacy skills
  MULTIPASS, a textbook reading-comprehension strategy
  PIRATES, a test preparation and test-taking strategy

- *Topical workshops on critical survival skills*
  Library resources tour
  Microcomputer instruction workshops including:
      Word processing with a Macintosh
      Developing a data base
      Graphics instruction
      Creating HyperCard stacks
  Self-advocacy seminars including:
      "LD 101 Lecture: Describing LD in Plain Language"
      "Rights under Section 504 and Negotiating
      Accommodations"
  Role playing with group leaders
  Reviewing LD diagnostic testing and developing a
      personal profile
  Exploring psychosocial concerns
      Residence life issues
      Weekly planned social events and outings
      Outward Bound experience in New Hampshire

- *Parents' workshop*

Figure 6.4.   The Summer Transition Program at Boston University: Program components.

The second academic component of the STP is a learning-strategies seminar that focuses on training students to learn how to improve their ability to study more effectively and efficiently. The learning-strategies approach is directly taught with content material from one of the four-credit courses. Similar approaches using Supplemental Instruction (Martin & Arendale, 1992) have been used with significant results in large, core college subjects, such as Psychology 101 and U.S. history. Some of the learning strategies presented were developed for adolescents at the Learning Disabilities Training Institute at the University of Kansas and modified for use with college students. Byron and Owen (1990) discussed the utility of this approach for teaching college students to apply metacognitive strategies across content areas. They noted that using a learning-strategies course in a linked relationship to a general college course is an effective way to introduce learning strategies to students with learning disabilities. The linked model of instruction provides a way to help students improve their performance while simultaneously acquiring learning skills. A required textbook, *College Learning and Study Skills* (Longman & Atkinson, 1991), is integral to the STP learning seminars. Additional training in self-advocacy is provided by using components of the I-PLAN strategy (Van Reusen, Bos, & Deshler, 1987). A reading-comprehension strategy (MULTIPASS) (Schumaker, Deshler, Alley, Warner, & Denton, 1982) and a test-taking strategy (PIRATES) (Hughes, Schumaker, Deshler, & Mercer, 1988) are also included in some of the learning seminars in the STP. Plans are under way to fully incorporate this component into next summer's program (Goldhammer & Brinckerhoff, 1993).

The third component is a series of workshops on using the Macintosh computer. All students, regardless of their skill level, are given the opportunity to use a computer. The instructor individualizes the program for the students and encourages them to use the computer as a tool for completing assignments in their content course, developing their own personal data base, and making graphics. A library tour and other less structured activities on and off campus give students a greater sense of community awareness. It is also essential to make students aware of other support services or offices available on campus, such as financial aid, parking services, student health services, career planning and placement, and tutorial services. Representatives from some of these support services offices are also invited to welcome the students in the program and to answer questions.

Support services provided during the summer should assist students in evaluating both their educational and psychosocial needs. As noted in the previous chapter, the key to academic success in college often rests on psychosocial adjustment. One option for facilitating this adjustment is to hire peer support leaders who can participate in an "icebreaker" panel discussion the first night of the program. Peer support leaders are often juniors, seniors, or graduate students with learning disabilities who can help new students by modeling active student participation and independent decision making in all facets of the college program. The student leaders often have an interest in human service professions and find this summer work experience valuable for building up their résumés. The increase in credibility that comes from employing successful young adults with learning disabilities to model appropriate college behavior as opposed to hiring a staff member to handle crisis situations cannot be underscored enough. However, professional staff may be used for conducting mock interview sessions with faculty members, leading small-group discussions on college adjustment, or role playing on how to ask for accommodations from faculty. Videotapes such as *Learning Disabilities: Coping in College* (Wright State University, 1985) and *Understanding Learning Disabilities in Higher Education: A Georgetown University Perspective* (Georgetown University, 1991) can provide students with an opportunity to articulate their own strengths and weaknesses (Brinckerhoff, in press). In addition to workshops and guided discussion groups, the program should provide ample opportunity for a variety of prearranged social activities such as swimming, picnics, sporting events, and day trips to vacation spots. Dalke (1991) pointed out that social activities provide students with yet another setting where they can make new friends and begin to build a support network.

Evaluation of the Transition Program

Chapter 9 presents a comprehensive overview of methods for conducting an evaluation of services provided. However, a few points that may be unique to a summer orientation program warrant mentioning here. The relatively brief duration of these programs gives service providers an ideal opportunity to gather formal and informal observational data on this "captive" student group. This information can be used to evaluate the effectiveness of the services offered in order to plan for students' service needs in the fall and to improve the overall content of the program for future years. Dalke (1991) emphasized that any transition program should include a mechanism for recording and summarizing student data. McGuire et al. (1990) stated that until college personnel systematically identify the interventions that facilitate positive outcomes for college students with learning disabilities, we will continually ask ourselves whether we are not simply stringing together services that have limited potential for fostering success among this group.

Before the transition program is completed, it is essential to collect a variety of outcome data from participants. One of the most comprehensive follow-up surveys of a summer orientation program was conducted at the University of Wisconsin–Whitewater by Dalke (1986). Her study indicated that first-year students attending the summer program and receiving services through the LD support services office (ASSIST) had significantly higher first-semester grade-point averages than first-year students with learning disabilities who did not attend the program. Dalke (1986) also found that students in the orientation program indicated that communication with professors was easier and they were more aware of the limitations caused by their disability. The transition from home to college was easier, and they were able to establish friendships before the beginning of the fall term.

Ideally, the transition to college for students with learning disabilities should begin years before enrollment, but realistically it often does not begin in earnest until late in the junior year of high school. Through summer programs, veteran service providers can help to bridge this transition by providing the necessary training in social and academic skills before college. The philosophy of a summer orientation program should not be one of holding hands or raising false expectations, but instead one of building awareness and empowerment so that students with learning disabilities can begin the fall term confident that they are equipped with a variety of strategies and techniques that will foster college success.

CHALLENGES IN SERVICE DELIVERY

Service providers who are just entering the field as well as veterans can profit from considering the research on effective interventions at the secondary level (Schumaker, Deshler, Alley, & Warner, 1983) as they make decisions about tutorial interventions at the postsecondary level. Students with learning disabilities are often characterized by difficulties in some aspect of information processing (Swanson, 1987). To compensate for these deficits, instruction in "learning how to learn" and to monitor one's approach to the learning task offers an alternative to the traditional content-tutoring model. Rather than tutoring to "remediate, placate and suffocate students while intending to be supportive and empathetic" (Ellis, 1990, p. 61), the goal should be to foster the development of academic self-sufficiency. Some students with basic skills deficiencies may require remedial courses, but the LD service provider is in a position to investigate the availability of such remediation through other campus services (e.g., the academic skills center) rather than trying to be all things to all students.

Institutions must offer services to all students with learning disabilities regardless of their status as full- or part-time students. A recent survey by the 11th U.S. Circuit Court of Appeals affirmed the responsibility of an institution to provide auxiliary aids without consideration of a student's enrollment in a regular program (Heyward, Lawton, & Associates, 1991c). The implications of this ruling for settings that offer flexible class scheduling, such as evening and weekend courses, are significant since provisions for reasonable accommodations cannot be constrained by the parameter of traditional "office hours."

Finally, it is important for service providers to create linkages on campus with personnel in other support offices so that fragmentation of services and lack of coordination can be avoided. Albert and Fairweather (1990) used a case study methodology to examine the array of services offered and methods of service delivery in a large, public research university. In addition to the Office of Disabled Students within the general administrative organization, a comprehensive LD program was available through academic affairs within departments such as special education, educational psychology or counseling. Feedback gathered from students pinpointed the confusion that can emerge because of differences in functions between offices offering assistance. Lack of communication and coordination among service providers (e.g., disabled student services, financial aid, and the LD program) resulted in uncertainty by students with learning disabilities as to where they should seek assistance. The authors concluded that a horizontal organizational structure can contribute to unclear administrative roles and lines of authority as well as to ambiguity regarding the locus for accessing services.

CONCLUSION

In their essay addressing the political nature of student affairs, Mamarchev and Williamson (1991, p. 77) sounded a vibrant chord: "No matter how competent you are, no matter how much you believe in yourself, no matter how much integrity you may have, if you do not understand the politics of your institution, you will not last." Extrapolating from this, it is reasonable to conclude that regardless of the locus of LD programs, an overriding goal of every LD coordinator must be to "network" and monitor the political pulse on campus. Despite the legal foundations underpinning institutional responsibilities to students with learning disabilities, diminishing resources underscore the critical importance of developing LD programs that complement, rather than duplicate, other campus initiatives.

CHAPTER 7

Issues in Staffing and Personnel Development

Too previous chapter delineated a range of service-delivery models and personnel necessary to meet the needs of students with learning disabilities. Ideally, each institution should consider its population and mission, determine an appropriate service-delivery model, and then identify the appropriate departments and personnel with the skills to fulfill the necessary roles. Unfortunately, it rarely happens that way in reality. Typically, one individual sees the need, attempts to rally institutional support, and often is designated as the service provider. The role of this visionary, who may come from the faculty, disabled student services, or the learning center, is instrumental in establishing the organizational base for future services. The background and training of this individual may be special education, counseling, social work, psychology, or higher education, among others. His or her previous experience and knowledge base will ultimately determine the perspective and configuration that the services will assume.

This chapter will attempt to address a variety of questions related to staffing and personnel development. How does an institution staff a program of support services? What kind of training will administrators, direct service personnel, and faculty need? What mechanisms and approaches to personnel development can be implemented? What are the first steps that need to be taken? And once the program is fully implemented, what types of ongoing professional development will be necessary?

STAFFING NEEDS

As previously noted, the support services model an institution establishes will dictate both the type and number of personnel to be hired. Five different service-delivery models with related philosophy and staffing implications are outlined in Table 7.1. Although few institutions rigidly apply just one model, most can be described as applying one approach in the majority of cases.

Remedial services, which are most typical at public community colleges, focus on basic skills instruction. Personnel are typically teachers, particularly special education or Title I instructors, who are

TABLE 7.1. Staffing Implications of Service-Delivery Models

Model	Philosophy	Staffing Requirements
Remedial	Teach students basic skills, typically in reading, math, and language, to allow them to compete in regular college courses	Personnel who are skilled teachers able to implement remedial instruction *with adults*
Compensatory	Enable students to succeed in school through the use of technological and media resources	Personnel who have knowledge of a range of resources that they can match to student needs
Content Tutoring	Help students to succeed in college by providing supportive tutoring in subjects affected by the disability	Personnel who are skilled teachers in specific content areas
Learning Strategies	Teach students learning skills such as memory strategies, time management, study skills, note taking, and outlining, so that they can eventually function more independently in college	Personnel who can identify the impact of student weaknesses on specific intructional situations and teach the application of effective strategies to overcome these weaknesses
Comprehensive	Provide approaches and services to ameliorate the diverse academic, social, and emotional needs of students with learning disabilities	An array of personnel from different disciplines and with varying degrees of training who can do diagnosis, instruction, and counseling

experienced in teaching reading, math, and writing skills to older students. Personnel using this approach are effective, particularly in open-admissions settings, if students can be brought up to a competitive level with their peers. The concern is that many students with learning disabilities have been receiving remedial instruction for years, often with limited results.

Compensatory services that feature the provision of accommodations may require fewer personnel with less formal training, but these personnel should have extensive knowledge of technological resources, such as computers, tape recorders, and adaptive equipment. While this approach is less costly in terms of personnel, it relies on the availability of a large array of increasingly expensive adaptive technology.

Support services that feature a content-tutoring model may require personnel who have specific subject-matter expertise, but they may have relatively little knowledge of learning disabilities. On the other hand, students who receive only content tutoring and not strategy-based instruction may need extensive support throughout their school career, which will require extensive staffing. In addition, personnel with only content knowledge may have difficulty understanding students' learning disabilities and therefore may be of little help in changing faculty attitudes and behaviors toward these students.

Programs that implement the learning-strategies approach, which has gained increasing validity in recent years (Ellis, 1990), will require a well-trained, highly skilled staff who understand learning disabilities and can implement instruction in strategies across content areas. The positive aspect of this approach from a staffing perspective is that effective learning-strategies programs foster independence, allowing staff to reduce time commitments to individual students as they learn to apply strategies on their own.

Comprehensive models may involve personnel who can implement a number of the approaches described above. In addition, they typically include the availability of diagnostic testing (e.g., psycho-educational evaluation) and make a huge personnel investment in the time of highly trained diagnosticians and school psychologists.

Comprehensive support programs also attempt to address the psychosocial issues that have proved to be critical stumbling blocks to success for students with learning disabilities (Ness & Price, 1990). Such efforts often require a range of personnel from peer counselors to highly skilled mental health professionals, including psychologists and psychiatrists who may or may not be located within the disabled student services office.

Given the issues described above, it is critical for each support program to identify the institutional mission and philosophical orientation for support services. Only then can appropriate personnel be hired and trained. Following are specific recommendations for an institution to follow in identifying staffing needs.

First, no one department or office can provide *all* the services needed by students with learning disabilities. Personnel from that one department or agency cannot be expected to possess the wide diversity of skills necessary to meet student needs. Some of the remedial, compensatory, academic, social, mental health, or vocational needs of students can be met by personnel in other offices, both on and off campus. Cooperative agreements can help to overcome professional turf issues while limiting the responsibility and narrowing the focus of LD support personnel. Academic departments such as special education, counseling, psychology, reading, and school psychology can provide interns or practicum students to do diagnostic testing, instruction, or counseling. Institutions that do not have these professional training programs can seek out neighboring colleges that do. These linkages between institutions can be mutually beneficial by providing field experience sites for one and service delivery for the other.

The decision regarding an institution's approach to service delivery should be driven by the needs of the student population served and research on effective postsecondary programming. Service models should not be established based on the skills, training, or style of initial personnel or the professional bias of an administrator. Since the field of postsecondary learning disabilities is relatively new, professionals will individually and collectively need to consider current research and evaluate what they do. This will encourage each institution's programmatic efforts to evolve over time.

Any academic department can provide content tutors for students experiencing difficulty in that subject. The obvious advantage of this approach is that such tutors are content-area experts. However, they probably lack knowledge about learning disabilities and the alternative instructional approaches necessary for success with some students with learning disabilities. Offices in the student affairs area such as the counseling center, disabled student services, and the learning center may provide the specific tutoring services necessary to overcome the learning problems of some or all students with learning disabilities. Other campus agencies including the job placement office, cooperative education office, writing or computer labs, and library can provide students with skills and information that LD personnel do not possess. In each case, specific arrangements should be developed and some training of these generic support personnel may be needed regarding methods of serving students with learning disabilities. In all these cases, collaboration between offices and agencies is the key to meeting student needs.

Personnel should be hired who can diminish the impact of the disability by training students for independence. Teaching self-advocacy, writing skills, and learning strategies will allow students to succeed in college with diminishing support over time. If an institution is using such an approach, it is best to use personnel up front as early in the student's college career as possible. This can be done by giving extra hours of support to first-year students or implementing an extensive orientation and training program for new students. Teaching students the skills necessary to become independent learners early in their college careers could allow them to reduce their need for services in subsequent semesters (Brinckerhoff et al., 1992) and prepare them to function more independently in the adult world.

The passage of the ADA and implementation of Section 504 of the Rehabilitation Act have encouraged many professional schools to move from preparing personnel to work with children with disabilities to teaching them to work with individuals with disabilities across the age span. Identifying staff such as special educators, counselors, and psychologists who have training and experience with adults with learning disabilities is now a distinct possibility. For example, graduate programs at New York University, The Ohio State University, the University of Connecticut, and the University of Oregon, among others, prepare personnel to work with adults with disabilities. One such person can then be used as a trainer to provide staff development for personnel throughout an institution, applying any of the approaches described later in this chapter.

Regardless of the backgrounds of the personnel hired to serve students with learning disabilities, ongoing staff development is necessary. This can take a variety of forms that will be described later in this chapter. First, we will review the specific training needs of a variety of postsecondary personnel relevant to services for students with learning disabilities.

PERSONNEL DEVELOPMENT NEEDS

Personnel development needs stem from three distinct concerns:

1. Until recently, relatively few people have received the necessary preservice training to work with adults with learning disabilities.

2. The multifaceted needs of adult students with learning disabilities include instruction, accommodations, and counseling across a broad range of subjects and disability severity.

3. The changing nature of the field requires practitioners to constantly upgrade skills to deal effectively with information from current research.

Training Needs of Service Providers

The only comprehensive survey of training needs in this field was recently completed by Norlander et al. (1990). They collected data from 299 postsecondary LD administrators and direct service personnel regarding both professional competencies and training needs. Table 7.2 indicates the results that were considered according to the needs of direct service personnel and support services administrators.

The competencies that were found to be most critical for direct service personnel included assessment skills, cognitive interventions, and instructional skills and techniques. The ability to interpret standardized tests of academic achievement received the highest possible ranking on *every* survey. The three most critical personnel training needs were in the same areas:

1. Administering and interpreting criterion-referenced tests

2. Providing instruction in learning strategies

3. Use of technology

The competencies that were most important to administrative personnel, not surprisingly, were in the area of management and leadership skills. In addition, specific items rated highly were the ability to interpret standardized tests of academic achievement (which also received the highest possible rank on every survey from administrators, as it had from direct service personnel); knowledge of the effect of both academic demands and study skills; familiarity with other campus support services; the ability to maintain rapport with college students with learning disabilities, faculty, and administration; and the ability to facilitate curricular modifications including

TABLE 7.2. Perceived Training Needs

Item Number	Competencies	LD Specialist Difference Present/Desired	Administrator Difference Present/Desired
ASSESSMENT SKILLS			
1.	To be able to evaluate the psychometric properties and usefulness of assessment instruments	1.14	
2.	To be able to use evaluation data in diagnosing learning disabilities	1.22	
4.	To interpret standardized tests of intelligence	1.13	
6.	To interpret standardized tests of academic achievement	1.21	2.00
7.	To be able to administer criterion-referenced assessments of academic abilities	1.31	
8.	To be able to interpret criterion-referenced assessments	1.16	
9.	To administer standardized tests of information processing	1.09	
10.	To interpret standardized tests of information processing	1.12	
11.	To utilize diagnostic-prescriptive teaching techniques and other informal assessment procedures	1.17	
AFFECTIVE INTERVENTIONS			
18.	To be able to identify appropriate intervention strategies to effectively address lack of social competence as a concomitant problem and ameliorate inappropriate social relations	1.01	

COGNITIVE INTERVENTIONS

23. Is knowledgeable in the areas of information processing, memory, and intelligence   1.12

24. Is knowledgeable in the areas of learning strategies, self-monitoring (metacognition), and problem solving   1.15

INSTRUCTIONAL SKILLS and TECHNIQUES

25. To be able to determine student needs and the interventions to meet those needs   1.02

26. To be competent in the use of supportive technology (word processors, computers, texts on tape, etc.)   1.21

29. To be able to effectively provide direct instruction in learning strategies (Paired Associate Learning, Rehearsal, etc.)   1.42

30. To be able to utilize diagnostic prescriptive teaching to plan effective instruction   1.11

MANAGEMENT-LEADERSHIP SKILLS

48. To be able to write competitive grant applications   1.12

52. To be knowledgeable about high school special education programs and personnel   1.01

Note. Competencies receiving a difference in score of > 1.00 are reported. Ratings range from 1 to 5 with 1 = no skill and 5 = very high skill level. No differences above 1.00 were reported for the following competency areas: counseling and consultation skills and research skills.

From "Competencies Needed by College Personnel Serving Students with Learning Disabilities: Issues in Preparing and Hiring" by K. A. Norlander and S. F. Shaw, 1988, pp. 254–255. In D. Knapke and C. Lendman (Eds.), *Proceedings of the 1988 AHSSPPE Conference* (pp. 248–263). Columbus, OH: Association on Handicapped Student Service Programs in Postsecondary Education. Reprinted with permission.

waivers and exam modifications. The only items identified by administrators as personnel training needs were:

1. Test interpretation
2. Writing of competitive grants
3. Knowledge about high school special education programs and personnel

The scores for the latter two items confirm the importance of accessing external resources in these difficult economic times and the concern with helping students to make an effective transition from high school to a postsecondary institution with appropriate support services.

It is clear from these data that both administrative and direct service personnel require a broad range of competencies. It is unlikely that any person hired will have all the necessary skills. Interpretation of diagnostic data to determine both eligibility and necessary interventions is a critical training need for everyone. In addition, direct service personnel need instructional skills and administrators require management training.

Faculty Training Needs

There is a long history of research on perceptions of faculty toward college students with disabilities (Fonosch & Schwab, 1981; Newman, 1976; M. L. Walker, 1980). Only recently has the literature included studies on faculty attitudes toward, knowledge about, and willingness to accommodate college students with learning disabilities (Aksamit, Morris, & Leuenberger, 1987; Matthews, Anderson, & Skolnick, 1987; J. R. Nelson, Dodd, & Smith, 1990).

As has been documented with regular classroom teachers in public schools, college faculty have generally negative expectations of students labeled as learning disabled (Minner & Prater, 1984). However, research by J. R. Nelson et al. (1990) and Matthews et al. (1987) indicates that faculty are generally willing to make accommodations for students with learning disabilities as long as academic standards are maintained.

The most encouraging data come from research undertaken at the University of Nebraska (Aksamit et al., 1987; Morris, Leuenberger, & Aksamit, 1987) that demonstrated that knowledge about learning disabilities, previous interactions with students who have learning disabilities, and *effective in-service training over time* were significantly related to faculty knowledge, attitudes, and expectations. These studies indicate that faculty training needs include:

1. Determining who has a learning disability

2. Understanding procedures for identification and referral

3. Understanding federal laws (Section 504, the ADA) that apply to students and adults in postsecondary settings

4. Understanding faculty's responsibility to provide accommodations to students

5. Understanding the responsibilities of the student to the faculty and institution

6. Identifying the availability and type of support services on campus

7. Understanding student "rights" versus academic freedom and maintaining academic standards

8. Determining what constitutes appropriate and reasonable accommodations

9. Understanding how to provide accommodations and modifications

10. Providing effective instructional strategies for students with learning disabilities and all students

11. Understanding the importance of independence and self-advocacy for students with learning disabilities

12. Providing examples and case studies of accommodations, modifications, and effective instructional techniques implemented by faculty

Training Needs of Higher Education Administrators

Higher education administrators from academic affairs (e.g., vice presidents, deans, and department chairs) and student affairs personnel from the residential life office, the office of the dean of students, admissions, and support services typically have no training and little contact with students who have learning disabilities. They do, however, develop and implement institutional policies and procedures that often directly affect these students. Equally important, resources for personnel and programs that serve students with learning disabilities are allocated by these campus administrators.

A number of initiatives to provide information and technical assistance to higher education administrators regarding services for students with learning disabilities (Anderson & McGuire, 1991; Brinckerhoff, Shaw, & McGuire, 1989; Hartman, personal communication, December 16, 1991; J. K. Walker, Shaw, & McGuire, 1992) have resulted in identification of the following generic training needs among such personnel:

1. Understanding institutional obligations under Section 504

2. Developing policies and procedures regarding services for students with learning disabilities

3. Identifying program development models and support service-delivery models

4. Establishing policies for identifying and assessing students with learning disabilities

5. Developing a staff training program for faculty awareness and delineating staff responsibilities

6. Identifying admission policies and procedures

7. Implementing data collection and program evaluation initiatives

The number of different personnel classifications at each institution also has an impact on services for students with learning disabilities. Most of these groups require a range of training to help them meet the needs of the growing cohort of college students. The following section will describe approaches to personnel development that can enable each institution to prepare personnel who can effectively fulfill their responsibilities to students with learning disabilities.

APPROACHES TO PERSONNEL DEVELOPMENT

It is clear that rounding up a large number of staff or faculty for a mandatory in-service training session on "Everything you need to know about college students with learning disabilities" is not a very productive approach (Michaels, 1986). It is critical to begin with a thorough understanding of the many constituencies at an institution of higher education who may need training on this topic. Each group should receive a different sequence and level of training depending on its entering knowledge and degree of involvement with students with learning disabilities. Personnel development activities should be multifaceted to reach and motivate individuals with different levels of interest in and commitment to these students.

The NJCLD, in its position paper on in-service programs (National Joint Committee on Learning Disabilities, 1988a), made recommendations that include the following:

- A needs assessment should be conducted prior to beginning a personnel development program.

- Trainers must have competence in the content and the ability to complete the stated objectives of the in-service program.

- Administrative personnel should support effective in-service programs through (a) personal participation; (b) providing incentives and/or release time for participating professionals; (c) encouraging constituent involvement in planning, implementing, and evaluating the program; and (d) providing fiscal support.

Needs assessments are typically implemented through surveys or questionnaires that assess knowledge (definitions, characteristics, laws), attitudes toward disability, instructional methodologies, and willingness to make reasonable modifications (Marchant, 1990; Morris et al., 1987). A powerful, though unwelcome, needs assessment can come from feedback by the Office of Civil Rights (OCR) resulting from an investigation of a complaint. At some colleges, consumers (students or their parents) have specified concerns about the institution's ability or willingness to meet the needs of students with learning disabilities. As these students have developed their self-advocacy skills, increasing numbers of peer support and disability rights groups have made their concerns known to college officials.

One of the most effective ways for an institution to determine its current ability to serve students with learning disabilities is through an on-site evaluation (Brinckerhoff et al., 1989). A consultant can review college documents (e.g., catalogs, policy statements, and admission information); talk with administrators, faculty, staff, and students; and visit campus support services. An exit interview with college officials and a written report specifying strengths and weaknesses have proved to be effective tools in identifying needs and planning staff development activities (Brinckerhoff & Anderson, 1989). Evaluation data from site visits conducted through the Northeast Technical Assistance Center for Learning Disability College Programming demonstrated that 86% of recipients rated their value as very good to excellent.

The following sections describe an array of personnel development alternatives for direct service personnel, higher education administrators, and personnel and faculty in student affairs and related areas. Although a needs assessment will determine the specific scope and sequence of training for an individual institution, a general sequence of events is apparent. Typically, it is necessary to first address the needs of direct service personnel who work with students on a regular basis. Then higher education administrators should receive the training necessary to understand the rights of students with learning disabilities and support the development of appropriate policies and procedures. Finally, student affairs personnel and faculty require training regarding their roles with these students. Attempts to work with faculty before effective support services and appropriate policies are in place can create more problems than solutions.

Direct Service Personnel

Direct service personnel, whether part-time or full-time, are hired with some degree of skill and commitment to working with students who have learning disabilities. At the onset, they need training regarding the program's mission and service-delivery model and its particular procedures, forms, and data collection requirements. In addition, they need an orientation to the institution, campus, and facility. This initial staff development can best be provided in several days of training prior to the start of service delivery at the beginning of the academic year. Major topics for this training could include:

- Program philosophy, policies, and procedures
- The roles and responsibilities of direct service personnel
- Assessment and instructional and counseling strategies

Trainers for this in-service program might include program administrators, experienced direct service personnel, college faculty (e.g., faculty in special education, counseling, or school psychology), and other campus support services personnel (e.g., personnel from the counseling center or learning center).

Over time, direct service personnel will need additional training regarding new materials and approaches, current research, and, ideally, a broadening of competence across different domains. This latter area can often be dealt with through a peer-teaching approach. A special educator can share instructional methodology, a school psychologist can provide information on test interpretation, or a counselor can share approaches for developing self-advocacy skills. This training should occur through regularly scheduled weekly or monthly staff meetings. These sessions can also provide opportunities for problem solving with respect to difficult cases, for reviewing and revising program policies and procedures, and for learning about other campus or community services.

The development, adaptation, or use of a training manual to give to direct service personnel would be a very productive supplement to the training program. These materials typically contain specification of institutional policies and procedures regarding students with learning disabilities, assessment procedures, academic and social intervention strategies, instructional resources, and program forms. A number of manuals, guides, training programs, and videotapes have been developed by exemplary projects across the country, and are described in Appendix M.

Higher Education Administrators

It is most important for college administrators to understand and be supportive of service-delivery efforts for students with learning disabilities. In addition to fiscal issues, college administrators must deal with litigation and related concerns about program modifications and instructional accommodations. As noted previously, a site visit by an expert outside consultant has often been effective in encouraging higher education administrators to adjust policies and procedures to meet the needs of students with learning disabilities (Brinckerhoff et al., 1989). The consultant can do formal training on such topics as legal requirements under Section 504, alternative service-delivery models or policies, and procedures for meeting the needs of students with learning disabilities, and can implement a needs assessment and present recommendations.

A concerned administrator or the coordinator of the direct service program can also make presentations to executive councils or deans' meetings. Individual discussions with key college officials are an effective initial approach to reinforcing the reason, mission, and legal base for services to students with learning disabilities. Ongoing collaboration with the dean of students, dean of academic affairs, admissions director, and Section 504 coordinator provides important opportunities to share information needed by those officials to effectively serve this population. Relevant articles from the *Chronicle of Higher Education*, court cases, OCR rulings from newsletters (e.g., AHEAD's *Disability Accommodation Digest* or the University of Connecticut's *Postsecondary LD Network News*), or journal articles and brief handouts from conferences shared with college administrators can be very effective in keeping them aware of their responsibilities to this group. An excellent vehicle for informing the college of the effectiveness and utility of services is an annual report with a concise executive summary that is disseminated to campus administrators.

Student Affairs and Related Personnel

Any campus has many offices that play important roles in retention and quality of life for students with learning disabilities. Student affairs departments including the dean's office, the housing and residential life office, counseling and learning centers, and the placement office are particularly important. Other offices such as admissions, the library, and cooperative education are also in need of knowledge about and sensitivity to this population. Meetings with the head of each office would be helpful but a presentation at fall orientation or at a staff meeting would be better. Identifying a particular contact person in each office who will facilitate opportunities for a number of staff development activities is another productive approach.

Faculty

Often consultants are called in to encourage faculty to be more supportive in providing reasonable accommodations for students with learning disabilities. Unfortunately, this approach has too often tended to be the first staff development activity. This may set up expectations for faculty before the organization, as a whole, is ready to be supportive. It is therefore suggested that faculty training occur only after the elements described above have been implemented.

Morris et al. (1987) have noted that multiple in-service contacts over time are necessary to provide sufficient information about learning disabilities to improve faculty knowledge and attitudes. Tomlan, Farrell, and Geis (1990) have developed a sequenced model for the delivery of faculty in-service training beginning with large-group training; followed by staff development for individual departments, divisions, or committees; and ending with individual meetings with faculty who have students with learning disabilities in class.

Staff development for faculty can be implemented in a variety of ways. Typically, only smaller institutions can succeed with mandatory training sessions for faculty. In some community colleges course credit or continuing education units have proved effective in encouraging participation (Aune & Ness, 1991a).

Information on learning disabilities can also be included in training sessions on effective instruction, dealing with diversity, or legal issues. Most departments and schools have regularly scheduled meetings where staff development activities can be planned. An advantage to this approach is that accommodations and modifications particular to specific disciplines can be discussed.

Staff development for faculty can occur in a number of ways other than presentations. A meeting with a student to review diagnostic data and plan instruction or accommodations is an ideal time to invite a faculty adviser or course instructors. In this way, faculty have the opportunity to develop an understanding of what a learning disability is, how it affects learning, and what kinds of instruction ameliorate the disability's interference. Not so incidentally, when these meetings are data-based and professional, the perception of LD service-delivery efforts is greatly enhanced.

Teaching students with learning disabilities to be self-advocates, with particular emphasis on explaining the disability and needed accommodations in plain language, will improve faculty understanding and acceptance. At some institutions, student panels at "disability awareness day" programs have proved very effective in reaching faculty and staff. In a similar vein, the newspaper or other campus media are vehicles for pieces by or about students with learning disabilities and information on disability rights or services. Finally, a somewhat devious but nonetheless effective strategy is to identify "friends" (i.e., administrators, faculty, or staff who have a learning disability or have loved ones with this disability) who can formally or informally advocate for services for students with learning disabilities.

CONCLUSION

The field of postsecondary programming for students with learning disabilities is relatively young. We lack definitive research regarding the efficacy of various service-delivery models or instructional approaches. Few personnel-preparation programs, whether in education, counseling, psychology, or higher education, provide professionals trained to work with this population. It is, therefore, incumbent upon each institution to carefully consider its mission, resources, and service-delivery philosophy in order to select the appropriate administrative and direct service personnel. Then a comprehensive, multifaceted, ongoing personnel development program must be implemented for *all* college staff as well as service-delivery personnel. Only with this kind of training effort will the institution be able to keep up with the rapidly developing field of postsecondary programming for students with learning disabilities.

CHAPTER 8

Issues in Determining Academic Adjustments at the Postsecondary Level

Ohne of the greatest challenges for postsecondary LD service providers centers upon the day-to-day implementation of the constructs included in Subpart E of Section 504, "Postsecondary Education." Legal precedents covered in Chapter 2 can guide institutions in their efforts to ensure equal educational opportunity for students with learning disabilities. There remain, however, a number of issues that fall into gray areas and that require sound problem-solving approaches based upon weighing the obligation to ensure equal educational access in a nondiscriminatory fashion with the "otherwise qualified" criterion and the need to avoid substantially altering technical standards. The intent of this chapter is to provide specific examples of academic adjustments in two broad categories: (a) programmatic and policy-related modifications and (b) instructional modifications. Figure 8.1 provides an overview of the areas that are discussed in detail, considered in light of the legal mandates established under Section 504 and the ADA. Policies, procedures, and suggestions for assisting faculty in their efforts to accommodate students are also included.

ADMINISTRATIVE CONSIDERATIONS IN PROGRAM MODIFICATIONS

Academic adjustments may be instructional or programmatic in nature. Program modifications are often premised upon policy statements or guidelines, which implies that LD service providers can play a critical role by keeping abreast of current challenges in the field and serving as campus change agents. In light of emerging case law and findings of the OCR that offer interpretation of Section 504 as it relates to students with learning disabilities, postsecondary institutions are in a position to proactively develop policies and procedures to ensure equal educational opportunity. It is imperative that LD service providers develop collaborative approaches in working with key administrative personnel such as provosts, vice presidents, legal counsels, or directors of admissions. Establishing disability-related policies requires time and input from a variety of campus constituencies; for example, administrative decisions may involve a process of review by academic committees or the faculty senate. It behooves the LD

PROGRAM MODIFICATIONS

- Alternative admission requirements
- Priority registration
- Special financial aid arrangements
- Special housing requests
- Substituting one course for another (e.g., foreign language or math)
- Part-time rather than full-time study

INSTRUCTIONAL MODIFICATIONS

- Taped textbooks
- Readers
- Note-taking modifications:
  Carbonless paper
  Note takers
  Tape recorder
  Laptop computer
- Testing modifications:
  Extended time
  Separate locations
  Different format
  Reader
  Oral exam (or taped answers to be transcribed later)
  Use of a word processor or typewriter
  Use of aids during the exam (calculator, dictionary, spell-checker, etc.)
  Alternative demonstration of mastery
- Auxiliary aids and equipment
- Adapting or modifying methods of instruction

Figure 8.1. Possible academic adjustments for students with learning disabilities.

service provider to understand the mechanisms for instituting campus academic policies and to remain informed about national developments regarding legal challenges based upon Section 504 and the ADA as well as about practices emerging on other campuses.

As postsecondary institutions move forward in establishing policies and procedures, several cautions articulated by Scott (1990) should remain paramount in the process. She noted that in some instances, "individuals within postsecondary education will respond to federal regulations with minimal levels of compliance accomplished in the most expedient way possible. The spirit of the law in Section 504, however, mandates that professionals in higher education apply informed judgment in admitting, accommodating, and educating students with learning disabilities" (p. 404).

With these provisos in mind, several areas are examined with respect to their potential for proactively establishing policies and procedures that relate to program access and academic adjustments.

Alternative Admission Procedures

Section 504 states that institutions "may not make preadmission inquiry as to whether an applicant for admission is a handicapped person" unless the institution "is taking remedial action to correct the effects of past discrimination . . . or . . . is taking voluntary action to overcome the effects of conditions that resulted in limited participation" (Section 104.42 [b][4] and 104.42 [c][1][2]). In those instances, preadmission inquiry can occur as long as the institution communicates the reason for the inquiry and assures the applicant that the information is being requested on a voluntary basis and will be kept confidential, and that refusal to provide the information will not result in adverse treatment.

Some colleges and universities have developed special procedures to ensure that students with learning disabilities can voluntarily self-identify and have an opportunity to provide supplementary evidence (e.g., psychoeducational assessment or IEPs) to assist in determining whether they are "otherwise qualified." Examples from several admission applications that include a voluntary self-disclosure statement or optional checkoff box are included in Appendix G.

Mangrum and Strichart (1988) described a variety of admission policies and raised concerns about the validity of standard policies, which often use data such as rank in class, scores on tests such as the Scholastic Aptitude Test (SAT) or the American College Test (ACT), and high school grade-point average, with no consideration of the "otherwise qualified" criterion. Some postsecondary institutions have developed cooperative admission procedures that are based not only on standard criteria but also on voluntarily submitted supplementary information that further supports an applicant's potential.

Figure 8.2 illustrates the procedure in use at the University of Connecticut. Upon voluntary self-disclosure, the applicant is sent a letter (see Appendix H) by the admissions office encouraging him or her to voluntarily submit documentation for consideration in the admission process. A copy of the letter is forwarded to the University of Connecticut Program for College Students with Learning Disabilities (UPLD) for the purpose of record keeping. If documentation such as psychoeducational testing and an IEP are provided by an applicant, the Learning Disability Admissions Review Committee, consisting of an admissions counselor, the Director of the UPLD, and additional staff, reviews it to glean information about the nature of the student's high school coursework, the impact of the specific learning disability on the student's academic performance (e.g., on foreign language grades), compensatory strategies used by the applicant, and motivation. If an applicant chooses not to provide supplementary documentation, the application is processed according to the standard admission procedure.

Since the criteria typically used to determine eligibility for admission may be discriminatory for applicants with learning disabilities (Scott, 1990), some sort of revision in policy and procedures may be warranted and, in fact, required. For example, a case-by-case analysis of a student's high school transcript in conjunction with psychoeducational test results may suggest a need to factor out the student's grade in a subject that taps into the specific learning disability. In this situation, the question of whether an applicant is qualified may be answered by weighing his or her performance in all other courses based upon a recalculated GPA to glean insight into the student's potential for being a college student in that particular institution.

Research conducted by the Educational Testing Service (Centra, 1986; Ragosta, 1986; Ragosta & Nemceff, 1982) on the nonstandard version of the SAT scores of students with learning disabilities indicates that they typically score lower than their peers. Similar lower results for students with "motor" disabilities that included learning

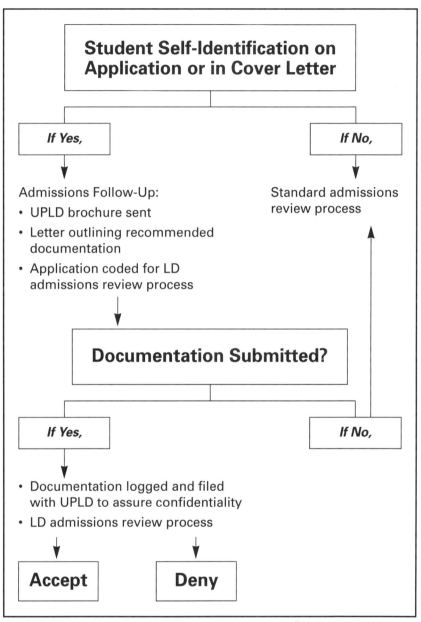

Figure 8.2. University of Connecticut admissions application process for students with learning disabilities. From *University of Connecticut Admissions Application Process for Students with Learning Disabilities* by J. M. McGuire, 1991. Presentation at Admissions Annual Open House. Storrs: A. J. Pappanikou Center on Special Education and Rehabilitation: A University Affiliated Program, University of Connecticut. (UPLD = University of Connecticut Program for College Students with Learning Disabilities.) Reprinted with permission.

disabilities were also found in research on the American College Testing Program (Laing & Farmer, 1984). These facts may bear examination in instances where the student's SAT or ACT scores are weak but academic performance as indicated on the transcript is competitive for that institution. Placing less weight on the learning-disabled applicant's standardized test scores may constitute a form of "academic adjustment" to ensure nondiscriminatory treatment. If the applicant was identified in the junior or senior year, that fact may be important and may support a need to determine any subsequent differential effect that services and/or accommodations may have had on the student's GPA. Some institutions require a personal interview, which can provide an opportunity to observe less tangible qualities such as the ability to self-advocate, goal-directedness, and motivation, as well as evidence of special talents in art, music, or other specialty areas. The underlying consideration in the admission process should be to look beyond a purely mathematical profile reflected in numerical data in order to ensure that a student's abilities as well as weaknesses are weighed in a nondiscriminatory fashion in the decision-making process.

LD service providers should consider establishing a data base to gather longitudinal data on the characteristics of successful students with learning disabilities (e.g., high school rank, SAT or ACT scores, achievement test scores, motivation and study skills, GPA, and degree completion). This information can be used to develop a profile of "typical students with learning disabilities" who have already been determined to be "otherwise qualified" as this criterion relates to eligibility for admission. Although these approaches are only a beginning, they may serve as incentives for campus personnel to examine admission procedures and to enhance access for students with learning disabilities. Similarly, existing policies regarding recruitment efforts may need to be examined in light of shifting demographics and expanded efforts at attracting qualified minority students and international students with disabilities.

Access to Services

It may not be sufficient for an institution to simply describe the services available to students with learning disabilities in its catalog or brochures. In a case that involved a student suspended from

Oklahoma State University, the state district court ruled in favor of the plaintiff based upon several factors, including the absence of any clearly defined university procedures for accessing services (McCarthy, 1992). Although this case has been appealed to the Oklahoma Supreme Court, it establishes a rationale for college and university publications to include a detailed description of LD services *and* the procedures students should follow to access those services. This will eliminate any confusion about the process.

In a broader context, institutions should be encouraged to incorporate a statement of commitment to individuals with all disabilities that demonstrates compliance not only with the letter of the law but also with its spirit. An example of such a statement from the University of Connecticut (1992–93) is included in Appendix I. This is published in the university's general catalog in the general information section.

Students should have ready access to information about LD services; these services can be described in publications such as the student handbook and in promotional materials disseminated through campus publicity initiatives. A mailing to incoming first-year students and transfer students is an effective vehicle for alerting them to the array of support services offered. The LD services coordinator may want to negotiate a place on the agenda for orientation for new students, in-service activities for residential life staff, and administrative workshops for new faculty. Sponsorship of an open house at the support services center adds an informal and personal element while showcasing the facility and any assistive technology that may be housed there.

Upon a student's self-identification and request for services and accommodations, the institution can require documentation to verify the specific learning disability. According to Heyward, Lawton, and Associates (1991b), this documentation must provide sufficient information to assist the institution in making a judgment as to what constitutes an appropriate academic adjustment. Delineating the nature of acceptable documentation creates serious professional dilemmas for LD service providers since there are no uniform administrative regulations or policies to guide the field. Areas that are problematic include recency of the documentation, selection of technically adequate testing instruments, extent of the testing, credentials of the evaluators, and reasonableness of the recommendations for adjustments.

Chapter 4 provided a detailed examination of a myriad of considerations in the assessment of adult students with learning disabilities.

Rothstein (1986) also pointed out that problems often arise in determining whether a student actually does have a specific learning disability. Although identification in public schools under the IDEA is not a binding determination of learning disabilities, Rothstein speculated that such a determination most likely would carry considerable weight in justifying eligibility under Section 504. While this designation may fall within the parameter of "having a history of such impairment," the relevance of diagnostic data varies according to their recency. Information gathered at the elementary school level is of questionable value in determining appropriate postsecondary accommodations (Brinckerhoff et al., 1992). Given the dilemma that often faces service providers as they use documentation to validate eligibility for services and the provision of appropriate academic adjustments such as course substitutions, it would not be unlikely to expect litigation in this area. Until precedent is established as to what constitutes adequate documentation, LD service providers should carefully weigh their legal obligation to ensure equal educational opportunity without substantially altering technical standards or creating unfair advantage for the student with the specific learning disability by randomly offering extensive accommodations that are not data-based.

Finally, in light of findings described in Chapter 2 regarding the University of Alabama, colleges and universities must ensure equal access to services and academic adjustments to students who are enrolled in nondegree programs or those who have not yet matriculated. This requirement may have particular implications for community colleges, especially as it relates to extending the hours of a disability support services office or making provisions to accommodate students in evening classes who may require adjustments in testing.

Academic Adjustments in Course Examinations

Legal precedent exists to support the importance of a clear, unequivocal policy regarding the rights of students with learning disabilities to "reasonable accommodations." Both *Wynne v. Tufts University School of Medicine* (1992) and *Campbell A. Dinsmore v. Charles C. Pugh and the Regents of the University of California*

(1989), which were described in Chapter 2, include commentary about Section 504 regulations, which state: "In its course examinations or other procedures for evaluating students' academic achievement in its program, a recipient to which this subpart applies . . . shall provide such methods for evaluating the achievement of students who have a handicap that impairs sensory, manual, or speaking skills as will best ensure that the results of the evaluation represents [sic] the student's achievement in the course, rather than reflecting the student's impaired sensory, manual, or speaking skills (except where such skills are the factors that the test purports to measure)" (104a 44 [c]).

As a result of the litigation in *Campbell A. Dinsmore v. Charles C. Pugh and the Regents of the University of California*, the University of California at Berkeley developed a model to accommodate the needs of students with disabilities. Integral to the model is an Academic Accommodations Policy Board that has three functions: "(a) advising the Provost for Undergraduate Affairs about policies and procedures related to the provision of academic accommodations for students with disabilities; b) developing mechanisms for increasing faculty understanding of disabilities and their accommodation in an academic setting; and c) assisting the Provost in resolving any disagreements that might arise concerning particular academic accommodations" (University of California at Berkeley, 1990, Academic Senate Policy).

Appendix J contains a detailed explanation of the model including its members and a time frame for resolving disagreements about a specific accommodation and its appropriateness. The board is composed of seven members, including three faculty members who are knowledgeable in the field of disabilities, three professional staff members from the Disabled Students' Program (DSP), and the campus Section 504 coordinator. It should be noted that the DSP staff member who determined the accommodation in question for a particular student does not participate in the board's review of the case.

If an instructor has questions concerning the appropriateness of an accommodation that has been recommended by a DSP staff member, the professor is advised to contact the DSP office immediately. If the instructor disagrees with the recommended accommodation, he or she is advised to then seek review by contacting the Section 504 coordinator within five days of being notified of the accommodation. Under this policy, the instructor is obligated to provide the accommodation "until it is either set aside or modified by the Campus 504 Coordinator or the Vice Chancellor for Undergraduate Affairs." The coordinator attempts to resolve the matter on an informal basis; however, if such effort is unsuccessful, he or she will refer the instructor to the Academic Accommodations Policy Board, which then reviews the matter and advises the vice chancellor for undergraduate affairs of the final decision. Every effort is made to resolve disagreements as expeditiously as possible, generally within five working days. It should be emphasized that the University of California at Berkeley has clearly stated that it is the responsibility of all department chairs and deans to inform instructional staff concerning Section 504 and university policy regarding nondiscrimination on the basis of a disability.

Given the heterogeneous nature of the college population with learning disabilities, requests for testing accommodations must be addressed on an individual basis. To provide blanket accommodations to all students is a disservice both to students whose strengths may mitigate against a need for accommodations in specific courses and to faculty who are pivotal in ensuring access while maintaining technical standards. There should always be a data-based connection between students' strengths and weaknesses and their eligibility for *specific* types of accommodations. Developing a policy board similar to the Academic Accommodations Policy Board at the University of California at Berkeley may be an approach worthy of adaptation as a mechanism for resolving disagreements over what is appropriate.

Course Substitutions

In her examination of how the Section 504 construct of "otherwise qualified" is applied to students with learning disabilities, Scott (1990) raised provocative questions regarding the challenge of balancing a student's rights to equal educational opportunities with the provision that a qualified student must meet the academic and technical standards deemed essential to a program. Academic adjustments such as substitution of specific courses required for the completion of degree requirements are suggested in Section 504 (104.44 [a]). For students with language-based learning disabilities and math disabilities (dyscalculia), a requirement for foreign language or mathematics courses can create a barrier to educational access. Policies and procedures for addressing a student's need for course substitutions are typically not in place. In addition, rigid course requirements can also deny educational access to other disability groups, including students with hearing impairments and speech or language disorders.

The first discussion of difficulty in foreign language learning was by Dinklage (1971), who described the problems of a small number of students at Harvard University. As more students with language-based learning disabilities have pursued higher education, the question of reasonable accommodations as defined by course substitution or waiver policies has become more visible and controversial.

Ganschow, Myer, and Roeger (1989) conducted a national survey of 478 four-year institutions to learn more about policies and procedures for foreign language waivers and substitutions. The response rate of 35%, although low, is probably reflective of the state of the art, since only 25% of the respondents indicated that written policies were in place. It may be that other institutions did not reply because of limited or no experience in dealing with this policy issue. Based upon survey results, it is reasonable to conclude that the majority of institutions favored substitutions rather than waivers. Documentation that substantiates the relationship between a student's learning disability and foreign language learning was required by 80% of the respondents. A variety of acceptable substitutions were identified, including courses in foreign culture or civilization (81%), foreign literature courses taught in English (64%), computer courses (25%), and sign language courses (25%).

Although the issue of substitutions in the area of mathematics has not been systematically investigated at the college level, there is ample evidence that some students with learning disabilities experience problems in mathematical reasoning and problem solving (Cawley, 1985; Fleischner & O'Loughlin, 1985). In light of this, it is reasonable to speculate that institutions are facing instances where the nature of the student's learning disability and curricular requirements must be examined within the construct of a range of academic adjustments. Figure 8.3 illustrates a variety of options that should be considered in ensuring equal access to courses in foreign languages and mathematics.

Depending upon the nature of a student's learning disability, adjustments such as the use of auxiliary aids, including calculators, and flexible guidelines regarding courses for substitution may afford the student an opportunity to demonstrate mastery in alternative ways. Students should not have to demonstrate a history of failure,

Administrative Academic Adjustments

- Pass-fail option vs. letter grade
- Late drop–withdrawal option without penalty
- Transfer credits from another institution
- Audit without fee with enrollment in next semester
- Campus policy regarding substitution-waiver

Programmatic Academic Adjustments

- Testing accommodations (e.g., oral tests vs. written in foreign language; no penalty for spelling errors in translations; use of calculator in math; more frequent quizzes over smaller units of content)
- Flexible policy regarding equivalent course substitutions (e.g., courses relating to foreign culture; computer courses; computer programming courses; sign language)
- Enrollment in language courses (e.g., Chinese, Swahili) using a logographic (e.g., character) rather than orthographic system; enrollment in logic course or research methods rather than conventional math courses
- Independent study with language or math professor
- Credit by arrangement while enrolled in a semester abroad

Figure 8.3. Range of administrative and programmatic adjustments relating to foreign language or math requirements.

however, before applying for a substitution option. Clearly, if the documentation verifies that there are serious deficits in information-processing abilities related to course mastery (e.g., auditory short-term memory, or simultaneous or sequential processing), then a policy regarding substitution should be accessed. A "fail first" philosophy not only has an impact on overall academic status but also is damaging to self-esteem and motivation.

Regardless of whether an institution decides to adopt a substitution or waiver approach, it should have a policy and procedures for students to follow. It is critical that each case be reviewed on its own merits and verified by objective documentation about the effect of the specific learning disability on the ability to learn in the content area in question. To institute a blanket policy for *all* students with learning disabilities is to deny them the opportunity for a foreign language or math experience that they may wish to pursue and in which they may be successful with reasonable accommodations and instructional adaptations (Javorsky, Sparks, & Ganschow, 1992). Appendix K contains an example of a policy and procedures for substitutions in the areas of foreign language and mathematics that was recently developed at the University of Connecticut (McGuire, 1992).

Additional Considerations

It is predictable that issues relating to administrative policies and procedures will take on a more complex hue, since there are so many gray areas open to interpretation. Defining the essential components of a program or course of study is analogous to defining essential job functions as stipulated in the ADA. Scott (1990) has outlined a set of guidelines as a framework for dealing with issues of compliance with Section 504. She indicated that the essential components of a program or course, reasonable accommodations in methods of instruction, auxiliary aids and alternative testing formats, and student variables must all be considered. A list of questions can be used to shape guidelines and policy development; Scott (1990, pp. 403–404) suggested that these might be included:

- Can the student with a learning disability meet all the essential program requirements when he or she is given reasonable accommodations?

- Will the accommodations provided pose any risk to personal or public safety?

- Are the proposed accommodations stipulated in writing in advance, and do they reflect the purpose of a program or course?

- What skills or competencies will be needed for graduation, licensure, or certification?

- Which program elements are negotiable and which are not?

Other areas that may require policy making on the part of campus administrators could include (a) eligibility for financial aid regardless of student status (full-time versus part-time), (b) adjustment of scholastic standards that require students to carry a minimum course load in order to be eligible for the dean's list (i.e., earning a GPA that meets criteria for the dean's list but not being granted such recognition because of carrying a reduced course load), and (c) determination of what constitutes valid and reliable documentation to verify eligibility for services based upon a specific learning disability.

Additional programmatic and policy considerations that may require administrative review address other sections in the regulations for Section 504 including housing, financial assistance, and treatment of students in general. Some students with learning disabilities exhibit significant deficits in sustaining attention, with extreme distractibility and difficulty in focusing. Adjustments in access to dormitory arrangements such as providing a single room or a "quiet" dorm may constitute a reasonable accommodation. Also, as students with learning disabilities extend their course of study over a longer time period, institutions can expect requests to address this need through modified financial aid packages that cover one or two additional semesters. Questions regarding the criteria used to determine eligibility for financial aid packages may require verification that factors such as high school grades and SAT scores are not being used in a discriminatory fashion for students with learning disabilities.

Policies regarding grading (e.g., placing a foreign language course on a pass-fail basis), priority registration, and withdrawal from a course without penalty following the standard withdrawal period may evolve in response to increasing requests for equal access from students with learning disabilities. As LD service providers and postsecondary institutions grapple with these issues, several caveats regarding policy decisions that have been identified by Chalfant (1989b) should be considered. He cautioned that policy decisions "should not be the result of public pressure, the arguments of a small group of persuasive professionals, . . . political expediency, or premature changes in service delivery systems. . . . There is too much at stake to make radical and revolutionary policy changes without first considering the evidence supporting each policy alternative" (p. 398).

The next section will extend the discussion of determining academic adjustments to the areas of service delivery and classroom instruction.

SERVICE-DELIVERY OPTIONS AND CONSIDERATIONS

The previous section discussed how implementing clear administrative policies and procedures regarding academic adjustments can benefit all parties involved. This section will present several practical suggestions for service providers that will enhance service delivery by providing students with an array of academic adjustments and technological aids that adhere to the spirit of Section 504 and the ADA. Since equitable policies and access to academic adjustments are not the only factors that affect student success, it is also important to examine the classroom environment and methods of instruction. This chapter will conclude with suggestions for tutors and faculty on ways to enhance their instruction in the classroom using a learning-strategies approach. When LD service coordinators can couple appropriate academic adjustments with quality-based instruction, a powerful combination is created that promotes student learning and achievement at the postsecondary level.

Several postsecondary institutions have developed standard accommodation policy statements regarding service for students with disabilities. These statements usually are general in nature, address the needs of all students with disabilities, and are primarily designed to be used by administrative personnel. An example of a nondiscrimination policy from Boston University, shown in Appendix L, is specifically designed to be used with college students. It is an "action plan" that should be shared with students at the beginning of the semester so that they can understand the process involved in securing an accommodation. A comprehensive nondiscrimination policy statement developed by the University of Wisconsin System is referenced under "Other Resources" in Appendix M. This statement includes procedures for providing accommodations across a variety of areas and is suitable for use by 2- or 4-year institutions.

Vogel (1990) stated that certain academic adjustments, commonly referred to as accommodations, are mandated under Section 504, especially in regard to the provision of alternative testing-and-evaluation methods for measuring student mastery, unless such an alternative would result in a modification of course objectives. To expand upon this point further, the purpose of providing academic adjustments to students with learning disabilities is to ensure that they have "equivalent access" that allows them the opportunity to obtain the same result or reach the same level of achievement as their nondisabled peers. The intent of Section 504 is clearly not to lessen or otherwise compromise the standards or academic integrity of the curriculum or program of study. Stewart (1989) noted: "Although Section 504 guarantees that students who are identified as having learning disabilities may be afforded accommodations if requested, it does not guarantee that the student will be successful at the institution. Sometimes students with learning disabilities make poor choices in curriculum, in time management, in study methods, and in other areas of their lives. Should they make poor choices, they, like other students, will need to deal with the consequences" (p. 10).

Therefore, it is often incumbent on LD service providers to walk the fine line that balances the academic freedom of faculty members and the mission of the institution along with the rights of students with disabilities. It is important for service providers to keep in mind that even though students have a documented disability, it should not be assumed that they are eligible for or will derive benefit from all the accommodations that they may have requested. It is not unusual for a student to request an extensive array of accommodations only because he or she was advised by a parent or a high school guidance counselor to accept whatever the institution has to offer. The need for academic adjustments will depend upon the nature and severity of the student's disability, the student's compensatory skills, and his or her level of independence. It is important that LD service providers do not inadvertently grant accommodation requests premised on stereotypes or generalizations about a particular type of disability, but instead render these decisions on the unique needs of the individual and the documentation provided. A case-by-case approach that evaluates each accommodation request for its effectiveness in minimizing disability-related factors and its fairness with respect to the other students in the class must be carefully considered.

Mooney and Bashir (1992) developed a checklist for helping college students with learning disabilities determine their own academic adjustments, based on the students' knowledge of their particular learning strengths and weaknesses. This self-directed selection process includes an easy-to-use three-column checklist. Such an approach empowers students to become informed decision makers about their own disability and the types of academic adjustments and learning strategies that will help them succeed. The checklist could be used during a summer orientation program or at the end of the semester to reevaluate which academic adjustments and auxiliary aids were appropriate and which were not effective. Over time, students may be able to generate their own "accommodation profile," which will be helpful in determining exactly which accommodations will ultimately be useful in the world of work.

PROVIDING ACADEMIC ADJUSTMENTS, TECHNOLOGICAL AIDS, AND SUPPORT SERVICES

The first section highlighted program modifications as examples of academic adjustments. Another form of academic adjustment consists of instructional adjustments or modifications, which may include access to taped textbooks, readers, note-taking modifications, testing modifications, use of technological aids, and adaptation of methods of instruction in the classroom. Instructional modifications, which were summarized in Figure 8.1, often constitute the ongoing requests that service providers face on a day-to-day basis.

Each of these targeted areas is briefly discussed in light of the legal mandates established under Section 504 and the ADA. For assistance in implementing these services, readers are encouraged to consult Appendix M for a variety of available books, articles, media, technological aids, and other useful materials that discuss the fine points of service delivery.

Tape-Recorded Textbooks

Dalke (1991) noted that for many students with disabilities, textbooks on tape can be effective aids in their coursework. There are two national resources available to service providers for securing taped materials for college students with learning disabilities. The largest repository of tape-recorded textbooks is Recording for the Blind (RFB) in Princeton, New Jersey. RFB is a national, nonprofit, voluntary organization that provides recorded educational books free on loan to individuals who cannot read printed materials because of a visual, physical, or perceptual disability. Currently, over 51% of its users are individuals with learning disabilities. RFB has over 78,000 books on tape and over 3,000 new titles are added every year to the collection. In order to access this service, students must have detailed documentation of their disability, attested to by a certifying authority, which clearly indicates the nature of the disability and how it affects reading. A disability statement must be signed by an individual who either is certified medically, such as a neurologist, or is a specialist such as a neuropsychologist, special education counselor, or LD specialist. A one-time application fee of $37.50 must accompany the application. If a textbook is not available from RFB, it can be tape-recorded with advance notice at one of their 28 recording studios located throughout the country. Materials are available on loan for up to one year, and longer if an extension is requested. Book requests may be made in writing, by telephone, or by fax. RFB's toll-free number is 800-221-4792.

In order to have a text recorded, RFB must be provided with two copies of the book or manual, at least six weeks in advance of the date it is needed. RFB acknowledges receipt of the books and advises the requester on the projected time lines for processing the order. Typically, RFB will mail chapter installments to the requester as they are completed. Since RFB requires considerable lead time to process a new request for a tape-recorded book, LD service providers should help students to place their book orders early. Textbooks should be ordered as soon as students register for their courses. In cases where students are accessing taped texts, priority registration can assure advanced planning, since students are guaranteed access to a specific course, section, and professor. Some colleges and universities are now requiring their faculty to select their textbook materials a semester ahead and submit their book requests to the department chair or the college bookstore so that students with disabilities are able to arrange for taping if necessary.

The recorded tapes must be played on a special tape recorder that is capable of playing four-track cassettes at $^{15}/_{16}$ inch per second at variable speeds. The cassette tapes used in the recorders are no different from standard cassettes; it is the equipment that is unique. Compact four-track recorders, similar in appearance to a Sony Walkman, may be purchased directly from RFB for a cost of approximately $170. The American Printing House for the Blind, in Louisville, Kentucky (phone 502-895-2405), also has standard desktop recorders with two-speed operation and rechargeable AC-DC power sources, which are available for purchase. Some students may prefer to try out a tape recorder on loan to determine if they derive a benefit from tape-recorded materials. Applications for the loan of a tape recorder are available from most local public libraries or from the Library of Congress, in Washington, DC (phone 202-287-5100).

The Library of Congress is also a source for over 45,000 books and 70 magazines. The books in the collection consist of recreational and informational reading and do not include standard textbook materials. In order for individuals with disabilities to borrow materials, they need to provide documentation of their disability by a certified doctor of medicine or a doctor of osteopathy. Since many medical doctors are not familiar with the educational ramifications of having a learning disability, they are encouraged to consult with colleagues in the fields of psychology or special education. Mangrum and Strichart (1988) noted that it is important that LD service providers have some means of recording materials through their own resources to supplement the services of RFB and the Library of Congress.

Unfortunately, it is not unusual for professors to make last-minute decisions about textbook selections or to assign volumes of handouts that require prompt attention. Most campuses have established a cadre of support staff or volunteers who can attend to these last-minute taping requests. One of the best ways to attract volunteers is to solicit the expertise of retired faculty who may welcome the opportunity to read current materials in their discipline. For additional information on how to establish a volunteer reader-taper service on campus, readers are encouraged to consult the *Volunteer Reader/Taping Service Handbook* (Lendman, 1991).

Readers

If taped textbooks are not readily available, LD service providers may choose to use readers. These individuals are available to read printed materials to students or to record materials for future listening. On some campuses, they are available to read examinations to students who prefer not to use a tape recorder. However, this procedure should be used judiciously since well-meaning readers have been known to inadvertently provide the test taker with additional clues or to clarify information beyond the professor's intent. It is also important to encourage students to use accommodations that lead to their increasing independence and self-sufficiency.

Note-Taking Modifications

Many college students with learning disabilities need alternative ways to take notes because of auditory processing problems, illegible handwriting, or short-term memory deficits that make note taking difficult. Note-taking assistance is viewed as a reasonable academic adjustment under Section 504 and therefore needs to be provided to individuals with documented disabilities. There are a variety of alternative ways to provide this assistance. Volunteer note takers who are presently enrolled in the course and who are committed to learning the material are often the most popular resource for students with learning disabilities. Students with learning disabilities should be encouraged to talk with the professor early in the semester about their note-taking needs. While some professors are comfortable sharing their own personal lecture notes, others are ready to recommend or to help recruit a note taker by making an announcement in class. At Boston University, students are encouraged to find their own note takers either by informally interviewing prospective note takers in the classroom or by using a resource file of volunteers that is kept in the disability services office. Some students with learning disabilities may choose to remain anonymous. If this is the case, the LD service provider may need to hire a note taker in the class who is willing to drop off a copy of the notes after each class at a central location, such as disability services. Requests for anonymous note takers are more common in graduate and professional programs where students with learning disabilities may be reluctant to be identified.

Note takers may find it advantageous to use carbonless paper. The note taker can make a duplicate set of notes on the pressure-sensitive paper and give these notes to the student immediately, without having to access a copy machine. On most campuses, it is the responsibility of the student who is receiving the notes to purchase the special pressure-sensitive paper from the bookstore. Paper and binders can be ordered directly from the Rochester Institute of Technology Bookstore in Rochester, New York (phone 716-475-2504). Regardless of the technique used, note takers must be dependable, be familiar with the subject matter, and have legible handwriting. Dalke (1991) emphasized the importance of providing note takers with special training to be sure that they are well qualified for the job. Mangrum and Strichart (1988) stressed that when note takers are provided or lectures are taped, students with learning disabilities should still be required to attend class and take their own notes. The very act of taking notes forces students to pay attention and to be an active participant in the classroom. Furthermore, it demonstrates their motivation and commitment to learn.

Many students with learning disabilities prefer to tape-record lectures with the thought that they will listen to the tapes at a later time. Dalke (1991) aptly pointed out that LD service providers should exercise caution when suggesting to students that they tape-record all their lectures. For example, if a student has twelve 50-minute class sessions a week, it is highly unlikely that he or she will have an additional 10 hours of study time per week to listen to the lectures again. Recordings of lecture notes should be listened to immediately after class for clarification purposes and not depended upon as a fruitful exam preparation technique. It may be more beneficial for students to selectively tape-record lectures. The counter on the tape recorder allows students to use taped notes as a backup at places where the lecture material becomes too dense or is presented too rapidly. Students should jot down the counter number in the margin of their notes for easy reference. The pause button should be used during breaks and general class discussions. Instead of recording an entire 50-minute lecture, students can return to 10–15 minutes of tape-recorded high points and problem areas from the lecture to help augment their notes and guide their future studying.

Service providers may need to remind students to ask professors, as a courtesy, for permission to tape-record the lecture. Most professors are comfortable with being recorded, but for some it may be intrusive. In such situations it is important that students not be confrontational, but inform the professor of the learning disability that affects their note-taking abilities. They should listen to the professor's objections about being recorded and offer to discuss the situation privately after class. Many colleges have a standard agreement form that can be signed by both parties to indicate that the tapes are for a student's personal use and will be erased at the conclusion of the course (Appendix N).

Laptop computers are becoming more and more popular as note-taking aids for students with learning disabilities. There are multiple benefits to having a student take his or her own notes. A student who has been trained to become an effective note taker has mastered a skill that is applicable to a variety of settings. Keyboarding knowledge is a useful survival skill for most college students; for students with learning disabilities, it is essential. Laptop computers need no longer be viewed as an intrusion in the classroom. The latest models operate quietly, and because of rechargeable batteries, an outlet is not essential. The benefit of being able to spell-check notes and print a clean copy has immediate appeal for students with poor handwriting and those who have difficulty writing rapidly. In the last few years, state vocational rehabilitation agencies have become more receptive to the idea of purchasing such equipment, since it can be viewed as integral to the student's career objective as a journalist, businessperson, or educator.

Testing Modifications

Scheiber and Talpers (1987) noted that college students with learning disabilities may have difficulty reading and/or understanding questions, writing under pressure, organizing thoughts, or remembering the mechanics of spelling, punctuation, and syntax. Stewart (1989) indicated that one of the most helpful accommodations to college students with learning disabilities is allowing them extra time on tests. The standard allocation is time and one-half. It may be appropriate to double the time in some isolated situations where the student is using technological aids, or when the student's rate of processing is extremely slow. This general policy should serve as a guide to both the faculty member who may be inclined to give only an extra 5 minutes and the good-natured professor who allows the student to take an examination home for the weekend, while the rest of the class has just 50 minutes. Other academic adjustments may involve changes in the test format, such as permitting a student to take an oral exam rather than a written one, having the exam material on tape, permitting a student to dictate his or her answers into a tape recorder for later transcription, or permitting a student to write directly on the test as opposed to filling in a computer-scored answer sheet. For a comprehensive overview of ways to provide testing accommodations to students with disabilities, readers are encouraged to consult, *Testing Accommodations for Students with Disabilities* (King & Jarrow, 1990).

Service providers must not overlook the possibility of having a student take an exam in a quiet room. Sometimes allowing a student to read out loud, work in a distraction-free setting, or take frequent stretch breaks can make a tremendous difference. A more delicate issue to address with faculty concerns student use of computers, calculators, and spell-checkers during the exam. Many professors feel that such technological aids give students with disabilities an unfair advantage. Yet experience has shown that these auxiliary aids help students with disabilities to compete equally with their nondisabled peers. Calculators with both a visual and audio output are especially helpful to students with mathematical disabilities that result in the reversing of letters and numbers, or for students with severe memory deficits who will never be able to memorize the multiplication tables. Word processors can be used in a private room by students who have difficulty in spelling, writing, or organizing their thoughts on paper.

The area that often generates the most resistance from faculty concerns alternative test formats. A survey of over 100 faculty members from a large northwestern university was recently conducted to determine faculty willingness to provide accommodations to students with learning disabilities (J. R. Nelson et al., 1990). The results indicated that only 53% of the respondents would allow a student to take an alternative form of an exam, whereas 85% indicated that they would permit additional time to complete exams. This discrepancy is understandable, since many faculty believe that once a test format has been substantially changed, the internal validity of the test instrument has also been altered. Suggesting that a professor modify a test format must be viewed as a last resort. However, it may be appropriate to recommend such changes if the recommendations are premised on recent documentation concerning the learning disability and if the student's previous test-taking history indicates that a change in format is warranted. If it appears that the exam discriminates on the basis of the student's disability, rather than measuring his or her knowledge of the course content, then changes in the testing format should be considered.

A variety of alternative testing procedures may be implemented by LD service providers, depending on the number of students to be accommodated. On many campuses, students with disabilities are expected to take responsibility for informing faculty of their testing needs, and to arrange for testing space in the disability services office or the academic development center. This is the perfect opportunity for students to use their self-advocacy skills. Students should arrange to discuss testing accommodations during the professor's regular office hours and not try to describe their disability and accommodation needs just before or after class. The Office for Disability Services at The Ohio State University has developed a set of procedures for obtaining testing accommodations that clearly spells out the procedures to be implemented (see Appendix O). By actively involving the professor in the completion of an alternative testing form, the student can learn the fine art of negotiating (see Appendix P). This form can be used to describe how the disability affects the student's mastery of course objectives, and what types of accommodations would be suitable. Policy statements like this help to clarify procedures for program staff, students, and instructors.

LD service providers often begin to feel overwhelmed by the numbers of students who request alternative testing procedures. At one large midwestern university, an LD service coordinator was faced with making arrangements for over 40 final examinations during a 3-day period. On such campuses, where quiet space is at a premium, scheduling testing space, keeping track of exams in transit between faculty and the disability services office, and ensuring that the proper academic adjustments are provided as specified in a contract can be a monumental task. Consequently, many LD service providers now consider that providing these accommodations should be a shared responsibility among student, faculty, and service providers. At the University of Connecticut, students may take examinations in the department under the supervision of the faculty or a teaching assistant, or they may arrange to take their examinations in the college library. The examination is delivered to a central location and arrangements are made in advance for a quiet testing location and coordination of the test pickup. At The Ohio State University, confidentiality has been assured in the disability services office by returning examinations in tamperproof envelopes. At the University of Wisconsin–Madison, the LD coordinator became overwhelmed with the number of alternative testing requests. Recently the office developed a new policy that requires students to make arrangements with faculty to take the exam with them if the only accommodations are additional time and a quiet room. Since over two-thirds of all alternative testing requests involve these two types of accommodations, the workload of the disability services office has been greatly reduced. The remaining students are encouraged to take their examinations at the testing and evaluation center on campus. Regardless of which approach is used, the adapted system should guarantee that tests are handled in a secure and confidential manner. Concerned service providers sometimes need to remind themselves that with the provision of appropriate academic adjustments goes the same opportunity for success *or* failure that characterizes all students.

Negotiating Academic Adjustments

Matthews et al. (1987) surveyed faculty at a small public university in Pennsylvania and found that, if asked, faculty would almost always accommodate students with documented learning disabilities "but not to the extent of lowering certain course standards involving instruction, assignments, and academic policy" (p. 49). In addition, they would not assign extra-credit projects exclusively to students with learning disabilities, overlook misspellings or incorrect grammar, or permit a substitution for a required course. They also would not give students copies of their lecture notes. Mangrum and Strichart (1988) stated that it was not unusual for college faculty to initially resist the idea of having students take exams in alternative ways. The major concern among faculty is that academic adjustments would give the student with a learning disability an unfair advantage over the other students in the class. LD service providers may need to reassure faculty that this will not be the case. Hartman and Redden (1985) found that equity is enhanced when alternative testing procedures are agreed upon at the beginning of the semester. It should be pointed out that if the institution considers the proposed accommodation or auxiliary aid desired by the student to be excessive or beyond what is deemed necessary to promote equal access, it only needs to provide the most basic accommodation necessary to do the job (Brinckerhoff et al., 1992). For example, if a student with a learning disability wants verbatim class notes from a lecture, but it is determined by the LD service provider that an equivalent level of access could be achieved with a tape recorder or by a student note taker, the less costly accommodation may be provided. This process is often a delicate balancing act of determining what is effective (Heyward, Lawton, & Associates, 1991c). If the institution makes a good-faith effort to provide an effective accommodation, it does not have to provide the most costly or comprehensive accommodation requested by the student. However, the institution must also be prepared to defend its actions based on the documentation provided by the student.

Attaining an accommodation in college is a two-way street (Scott, 1991). It is the responsibility of the institution to provide the accommodation and the responsibility of the student to make a timely request. Scott suggested that there is a need to delineate the parameters of "reasonableness." If the source of the academic difficulty is not disability-related, the student is not entitled to the accommodation. The LD service provider, the student, and the faculty member should work closely together to discuss the types of accommodations that may be necessary in a particular course. King and Jarrow (1990) stated that the final determination of the accommodation should be made by disability services staff and should not be open to reinterpretation by the faculty member. King and Jarrow also affirmed that "whether or not an accommodation is to be made is not negotiable. How an accommodation is to be made is negotiable" (p. 8). The appropriateness of the accommodation request should be based on the LD service provider's knowledge of the student's disability, the impact that the disability has on performance, and the effect that the auxiliary aids may have on the student's test-taking ability.

It is the faculty member's role to ensure that the proposed accommodations do not have the effect of "watering down" the curriculum or substantially altering standards. For example, a student with a documented learning disability may request that the professor replace the midterm exam, which consists of multiple-choice questions, fill-ins, and a written essay, with an oral examination. If the professor feels that replacing the entire exam with one that has a different format does not permit a fair evaluation of the student's knowledge of the course material, then a substitution of only the sections of the exam that have a direct impact on the disability may be appropriate. It is the job of the LD service provider to assist students in this negotiation process with the faculty, realizing that the fine art of compromise is an imperfect science. On occasion, the agreed-upon accommodations do not work out in the student's best interests. Under such circumstances, it is imperative that the LD service provider assist the student in renegotiating for accommodations that will fill his or her needs more effectively. This trial-and-error process can be unsettling to faculty at first, but if a collaborative team approach is used from the outset, the knowledge and attitudes among all constituencies can be enhanced. Adapting the ways in which content material is evaluated will undoubtedly help faculty get a more realistic picture of the performance level of students with learning disabilities, but that is only a partial solution. In order to be fully effective, faculty must also be willing to adapt or modify their methods of presenting course material.

Assistive Technology and Computers

Students with learning disabilities frequently find that computers offer them opportunities to compensate for their processing problems by using a multisensory approach that can build on their strengths. For these students in particular, computers are often the great equalizer that permits them to compete equitably with their nondisabled peers. Section 504 stipulates that auxiliary aids must be permitted in the classroom when they are required to ensure full participation by students with disabilities. Section 508 of the Rehabilitation Act of 1986 (P.L. 99-506) requires electronic equipment bought or leased with government funds to be usable by persons with disabilities. Stewart (1989) stated that this legislation was designed to help reduce discrimination in hiring workers with disabilities resulting from a lack of adaptive equipment. Although Section 508 does not directly affect colleges, this legislation has a spillover effect that will put pressure on the highly competitive computer industry. Consequently, any student who may be professionally involved in a public service job, education, or any of a myriad of fields that depend on federal funding can be relatively secure knowing that electronic equipment at the job site must be accessible.

Kolich (1985) found that word processing accounts for the heaviest use of computers among all college-age students, including students with learning disabilities. Word processing is a survival skill that allows these students to write and edit papers not only for assignments but also for examinations, class notes, and research projects. The most beneficial word-processing programs by far for students with learning disabilities are spell-check programs. Some of the most effective programs will flag words with common letter reversals and words that sound alike but are spelled differently. Raskin and Scott (1993) noted that when they are not preoccupied with the "mechanical" aspects of writing, students with learning disabilities are free to focus on the "meaning" of their written communication. This is particularly important for students who have developed a fear of translating their thoughts to text as a result of making frequent errors and of having those errors pointed out to them over a period of many years (p. 308). Once students realize that they can "generate" language and correct errors effortlessly later, their anxiety is reduced and they become liberated by the word processor. Collins (1990) conducted extensive research in the impact of word processing on college writers with learning disabilities at the University of Minnesota. He found that word processing contributed to a heightened sense of self-esteem and accomplishment in these students.

Some students with learning disabilities find that computers with synthesized speech give them the additional feedback they need on their writing. A new program called SoundProof enables students with learning disabilities to hear words in a high-quality synthesized speech as they are simultaneously visually highlighted on the screen (HumanWare, 1992). This program allows text to be read back a letter, word, line, sentence, paragraph, or "screen" at a time. Raskin and Scott (1993) note that in most cases, the speed, pitch, and tone of voice of these programs can accommodate the individual preferences of the user. Depending on the software employed, the quality of the voice output will vary considerably, ranging from a very human-sounding voice to a more mechnical, artificial-sounding one. In any case, this additional auditory feedback can alert students of contextual errors in the document. Raskin and Scott add that "if students use a speech synthesizer to listen to—as well as read—each word, they are often in a better position to select the correct word when using the spell-check mode" (p. 251).With a portable headset, students can use these programs in a lab without bothering others.

Students with written language problems will find an array of technological options available to them. Proofreading programs that not only can scan documents for errors in spelling but can also signal errors in punctuation, grammar, and word usage are gaining recognition. Some students with learning disabilities have found it helpful to change the size of the text and the background color to improve visual clarity. For students who have severe problems with written expression but strong verbal abilities, a voice-recognition system such as DragonDictate may be helpful. Instead of entering words on a keyboard, the user speaks into a headset microphone. This system permits the user to dictate about 40–70 words per minute depending on the speed of the particular computer in which the system is installed.

The more the program is used, the greater the accuracy of the computer in determining what the user is saying (Raskin & Scott, 1993). After several hours of training, the computer will "learn" to recognize many of the unique speech patterns and word pronunciations of the user. DragonDictate comes equipped with an 80,000-word dictionary, and 5,000 vocabulary "slots" are available for new words added by the user (DragonSystems, 1991). The cost of DragonDictate is approximately $9,000. Additional technological resources and software are included in Appendix M.

Schell (1988) noted several of the distinct advantages of word processing for students with disabilities:

- It is a fair accommodation, since all students theoretically have access to computers.

- It is a marketable skill.

- It helps develop the concept of writing as a process.

- It is a multisensory activity and the student can benefit from visual, tactile, and kinesthetic input.

- It helps to develop automaticity in language production that may very well generalize to reading.

- It provides practice in reading skills because of the opportunity for frequent rewrites and rereadings.

- It can be a confidence booster, since papers tend to look more professional.

As a result of these benefits, many college programs for students with learning disabilities provide microcomputers specifically for student use. Mangrum and Strichart (1988) noted that by having access to computers in their college program, as well as access to specialists who can provide them with on-the-spot assistance, these students will continue to profit from this significant technological advance. One purpose of establishing a computer lab within the LD support services office is to help encourage students with disabilities to take advantage of computers. Brinckerhoff (1991) observed that in the comfort of the support services office, students can be introduced to computers with different types of adaptive equipment (e.g., speech synthesizers or redundant functioning systems) and to a variety of software without feeling threatened or pressured. After students become comfortable with computers and word-processing equipment, they should be encouraged to use equipment in the computer center or writing lab on campus. Stewart (1989) aptly pointed out that although microcomputers are not a panacea for every educational problem that may be encountered on a college campus, their potential has only begun to be explored and utilized. LD service providers may need to further assist students with learning disabilities in using some of these academic adjustments and auxiliary aids in their coursework.

Reading Machines

Reading machines have optical scanners that can turn printed materials into synthetic audio text. These machines can also make cassette recordings from written material and they are usually compatible with word-processing programs. One of the most popular machines is the Kurzweil Reading Machine (KRM). This portable optical scanning system can scan any document up to 11 × 14 inches. Words or lines of print can be repeated, spelled out, or marked for preference. Punctuation and capitalization can be announced, if desired. Direct audio recordings can be made from the control panel using standard peripherals (Mangrum & Strichart, 1988). The original KRM Series 400 desktop systems cost over $19,000. The latest portable readers, such as The Reading Edge, weigh less than 20 pounds, have all the capabilities of the earlier models, and cost approximately $5,500 (Xerox Imaging Systems, 1992). Scheiber and Talpers (1987) believe that the KRM is particularly useful for students with learning disabilities who have good listening and comprehension skills but are weak in decoding and spelling. For some students, this may provide the freedom to read classroom materials immediately, or to take examinations independently without needing a reader.

ADAPTING OR MODIFYING METHODS OF INSTRUCTION

Before faculty can consider how they can effectively teach students with learning disabilities, it is important that they *understand* how these students learn. Researchers have shown that students with learning disabilities frequently attribute their academic successes to external factors that are beyond their control (e.g., "luck" or "an easy test"). Academic failures are perceived to be due to lack of ability (e.g., "I'm stupid" or "I'm not really trying"). A poignant example of this self-perception of inadequacy occurred during a site visit to a highly selective women's college. One of the student leaders of the LD support group indicated in all seriousness that she "must have been admitted to the institution because of a computer error"! This response is typical. These students often do not view themselves as having effective control over their academic destinies. As a result, they may become "passive learners" who exhibit a sense of "learned helplessness" (Wang & Palinscar, 1989; Wong, 1987). That sense of helplessness can be seen in college students who think that no matter what they do, they will not be able to achieve success. This lowered sense of self-esteem, coupled with a lack of strategies, often sets the student up for a self-fulfilling prophecy. One of the most effective ways of helping students with learning disabilities to overcome these misconceptions is to teach them cognitive and metacognitive learning skills that empower them (Wade & Reynolds, 1989). In this section, the learning-strategies approach will be discussed as it affects tutorial instruction and classroom teaching.

Research has shown that students with learning disabilities, in comparison to their nondisabled peers, are often deficient in the deployment of attention and memory strategies and in the use of various metacognitive skills such as planning, monitoring, regulating, and scheduling (Brown & Palinscar, 1982; Wang & Palinscar, 1989; Wong, 1991; Wong & Jones, 1992). Wang and Palinscar (1989) noted that students need to know when and where to seek assistance for learning and problem solving, not just for the moment, but for future tasks as well. They observed that many students do not acquire these skills on their own and can therefore benefit a great deal from specific methods of learning effectively. Policastro (1993) elaborated on this point, stating: "This is a critical break-through for college students with learning disabilities who traditionally have been perceived as 'passive learners.' This allows the student to be viewed, and subsequently to view herself or himself, as a self-instructive learner" (p. 157). Once students take on an active role in their learning process by learning how to manage their metacognitive skills, not just for the task at hand, but for future tasks as well, they will be well positioned for meeting the challenges of a postsecondary curriculum.

Seidenberg (1986) pointed out that the major practical implications of the research on LD secondary and postsecondary students were that many students with learning disabilities exhibit skill deficits in reading-related study strategies (e.g., comprehension monitoring, summarizing, outlining, or scanning). She maintained that these students can be supported in a regular academic curriculum by teaching them specific learning strategies or metacognitive skills. One of the expanding roles of LD service providers is to provide content tutors and faculty with information about the merits of learning-strategies instruction so that they can incorporate these techniques into their teaching on a daily basis.

For nearly a decade, researchers at the University of Kansas (Deshler et al., 1984) have studied the benefits of a learning-strategies approach for teaching adolescents with learning disabilities versus a more traditional content-focused approach. The content approach is characterized by teaching students isolated academic facts and information that will prepare them for an upcoming test. Subject matter or content tutoring may act as a short-term Band-Aid, but it does not provide strategic learning and problem-solving skills that will transfer across the curriculum (Shaw et al., 1991). The learning-strategies approach is based on the assumption that students with learning disabilities are strategy-deficient, unable to spontaneously tap the strategies they need. With an emphasis on "learning how to learn," the goal of the learning-strategies model is to increase performance by teaching students how to acquire, organize, store, and retrieve information (Deshler et al., 1984). Learning strategies are defined as "techniques, principles, or rules which enable a student to learn to solve problems and complete tasks independently. In short, learning strategy instruction focuses on both how to learn and how to effectively use what has been learned" (Lenz, Schumaker, Deshler, & Beals, 1984). Bursuck and Jayanthi (1993) emphasize that a learning-strategies approach is "much more comprehensive than most study skills programs in that in addition to learning how to perform particular skills, students also learn why and when to use these skills as well as how to monitor their implementation" (p. 179). In the learning-strategies approach, the accent is on independent skill application as well as acquisition.

A variety of learning strategies for elementary and secondary school students have been developed over the last decade by the Kansas University Institute of Research in Learning Disabilities (KU-IRLD) (Lenz, Alley, & Schumaker, 1987). Research has shown that students with learning disabilities who use learning strategies can experience academic success and independence while developing a more positive self-image (Carlson, 1985). Generalizable skills such as outlining and note taking, memory techniques, test-taking techniques, study methods, and word processing are all basic learning strategies that can be incorporated into the regular college curriculum. Because of the success of the Kansas Strategic Intervention Model with low-achieving adolescents, a few researchers have begun to apply the model to college-age students with learning disabilities (Denton, Seybert, & Franklin, 1991; Knight, 1991). Goldhammer and Brinckerhoff (1993) used the PIRATES test-taking strategy (Hughes et al., 1988) with six high school graduates enrolled in a summer orientation program. Students were specifically taught, in accordance with the KU-IRLD curriculum, how to take multiple-choice and essay tests and how to budget time more effectively during exams. Results from this preliminary study were encouraging. All six students who elected to participate in the study improved their grades between the midterm exam and the final exam as compared to classmates who did not use the strategy.

Seidenberg (1986) stressed the importance of teaching college students with learning disabilities to use learning strategies spontaneously. She developed a list of suggestions for instructors to give students when presenting strategy material:

1. *What the strategy is*: Teachers should describe critical, known features of the strategy or provide a definition of it.

2. *Why the strategy should be learned*: Teachers should tell students why they are learning about the strategy. This is necessary in order to move from teacher control to student control of learning.

3. *How to use the strategy*: Teachers should break down the strategy or reenact a task analysis for students, explaining each component of the strategy as clearly as possible and showing the logical relationships among the various components.

4. *When and where the strategy is to be used*: Teachers need to describe appropriate circumstances for using the strategy. They

may also describe inappropriate uses of the strategy by modeling rule applications for both a good and a poor summary.

5. *How to evaluate use of the strategy*: Teachers should show students how to evaluate their successful or unsuccessful use of the strategy, including suggestions for fix-up strategies to resolve any problems.

If tutors are not going to use a "pure" strategy-based approach, it is important that they adhere to some general instructional practices for teaching students with learning disabilities that have been shown to be effective with high school and college students. Cowen, Bursuck, and Rose (1989) developed the following list of effective, instructionally sound practices for college students with learning disabilities that are based on solid curricular design:

1. Instructional goals are based on assessment information.

2. Instructional goals are based on learner's needs. The learner helps decide goals.

3. Instructional activities are consistent with goals.

4. Teacher provides explicit explanation of the steps necessary to perform academic tasks.

5. Instruction is introduced in small segments and at a slow pace.

6. Teacher provides guided practice with sufficient examples and review until mastery is reached.

7. Teacher provides positive and corrective feedback during the learning process.

8. Teacher addresses the adult's affective needs during instruction. The teacher is aware of potential emotional or psychological blocks to learning and provides genuine encouragement.

9. Instruction includes a self-monitoring component. Learner should be an integral part of lesson evaluation. (Bursuck & Jayanthi, 1993, p. 187)

Stewart (1989) developed several useful handouts on effective instructional techniques that can be used for in-service training of faculty and tutors. Handout 3.6 is a list of important characteristics of instructors who teach students with learning disabilities. Handout 3.7 is a list of techniques that faculty can use to facilitate the learning of *all* students in the classroom, while handout 3.8 is more specific to the needs of students with learning disabilities in the college classroom (see Appendix Q). The Association on Higher Education and Disability distributes a brochure entitled "College Students with Learning Disabilities," which includes a section with specific teaching suggestions for faculty and staff (Association on Higher Education and Disability, 1991). This brochure is an excellent resource to use in faculty workshops on the topic. Additional resource materials for faculty and staff training are listed in Appendix M. Mooney (1992) noted that faculty can do a variety of things to support students with learning disabilities in the classroom. Specifically, they can help the student by (a) developing accommodations or academic adjustments, (b) modifying their instruction, (c) promoting better access to faculty, (d) communicating effectively, and (e) serving as a referral source to other campus agencies that can facilitate self-advocacy.

Vogel (1990) provided numerous suggestions on ways that faculty can help students both inside and outside the classroom. For example, a creative adjustment for a student with a visual-spatial deficit might permit the student to use a large-print copy of the examination with fewer questions on each page and more space for answers. If more time is needed for completing class assignments, they can be done on a computer or completed in installments over time. One very effective way of modifying instruction is for faculty to teach students mnemonics and graphic organizers (e.g., flowcharts and time lines) in conjunction with the content material. Faculty can also facilitate students' organizational and study skills by developing a user-friendly course syllabus that clearly spells out goals, objectives, reading assignments, and examination dates (Mooney, 1992). An example of the essential components of a course syllabus is provided in Appendix R. Access to faculty can be improved if the faculty have phone machines to record student messages. Office hours may also need to be staggered during the week to provide students with more opportunities for faculty contact. Access to faculty can be broached if faculty members make a brief statement at the first class that they are happy to meet with students during office hours to discuss any special needs. At several institutions, including Barnard College in New York and Ball State University, Muncie, Indiana, faculty invite students to share disability-related information by including a brief statement on all course syllabi. A typical statement may read: "If you need course adaptations or accommodations because of a documented disability, or if you have emergency medical information to share, please make an appointment during my office hours."

Finally, faculty or teaching assistants who are on the front lines should be prepared to broach the subject of a suspected disability with students and to help them by referring them to the LD support services office or counseling center. O'Hearn (1989, p. 11) noted that college composition teachers are often in the best position "to hear the silent cries of the learning disabled" and to discuss the possibility of referring them to be evaluated for a possible learning disability.

If college students with learning disabilities are going to compete equitably in college, it is essential that professors believe in their right to be in college and believe that they can achieve with reasonable academic adjustments. LD service providers need to assure faculty that they play a critical role in helping students with learning disabilities succeed in college. Marchant (1990) stated: "The success of a college student with a learning disability depends on the match between the student and the instructor. The success of the instructor/ student match includes consideration for the teacher's instructional methods, as well as the teacher's attitude toward students with learning disabilities and the adaptations they require" (p. 106). Once faculty understand what learning disabilities are and what the true potential of these students can be, they will be more receptive to providing academic adjustments that will permit them to fully access their course and the curriculum.

Unfortunately, many college faculty members are not optimistic about the academic abilities of students with learning disabilities or about their ability to work with them (Vogel, 1985). Dean Harriet Sheridan, former director of the Center for the Advancement of College Teaching at Brown University, wisely noted that many college faculty members are unaware of the presence of students with learning disabilities, including dyslexia, on their campus and consequently are unaware of what they can do to help these students thrive in their studies. Sheridan (1990) observed, "If faculty teach well, if they identify what they are going to say, where they are going with what they have said, use multisensory approaches, and explain difficult terms, . . . all students will profit, not simply dyslexic students. And if the attention to dyslexic students leads to a heightened consciousness of the importance of skillful teaching, then the presence of these students on our campuses will have made a significant contribution to the improvement of higher education" (p. 19).

CONCLUSION

Providing academic adjustments to students with learning disabilities at the postsecondary level is a complex process that depends on the proactive efforts of administrators, support staff, faculty, and the students themselves. Campus policy makers need to establish procedures that legitimize the requests for accommodation that students with disabilities depend on. LD service providers need to develop and maintain a broad array of service-delivery options and technological aids that students with disabilities can access. And faculty must acknowledge that students with learning disabilities can and do learn differently and must be willing to explore alternative ways of determining a student's proficiency with course materials without lowering standards. Ultimately, the key players in this process are students with learning disabilities, who must be ready to demonstrate their willingness to take risks, to realistically assess their strengths and limitations, and to select academic adjustments that will allow them to effectively compensate for their disability.

CHAPTER 9

Determining Program Effectiveness

Decision making and accountability are considerations that should underscore systematic approaches to determining the effectiveness of college support services for students with learning disabilities. In periods of challenging economic conditions, when competition for funding becomes heightened, documentation about student use and the impact of special programs is critical to make the case for their continued operation.

This chapter will address the following areas:

- The need for conducting program evaluation in light of current research

- A model for program evaluation

- An example of an evaluation plan for a learning disability program

- Challenges in conducting program evaluation research

THE IMPETUS FOR MEASURING PROGRAM EFFECTIVENESS

Now that nearly two decades have passed since the enactment of P.L. 94-142 (the Education for All Handicapped Children Act) in 1975, policy makers as well as administrators are raising questions that move the focus of special education evaluation at the K–12 levels beyond compliance with P.L. 94-142 procedural requirements and on to the efficacy of special education interventions (Field & Hill, 1988). There is a growing national interest in determining the adult status of students with learning disabilities who received special education in elementary and secondary settings. Independent living skills, job placement and history, socioeconomic status, and the use of leisure and recreational time by adults have been explored with the intent of gleaning information to guide educational practice for children with learning disabilities (D. J. Johnson & Blalock, 1987; Minskoff, Sautter, Hoffman, & Hawks, 1987; White et al., 1982). In her comprehensive review of the literature on adult outcomes, J. O. Smith (1988) reported that higher education has become more accessible to adults with learning disabilities. However, she pointed out what can be an overwhelming task for consumers: locating a suitable postsecondary program that matches student needs.

In spite of Section 504's assurance of equal access, follow-up studies of special education students after high school graduation (Hasazi, Gordon, & Roe, 1985; McGuire, Archambault, Gillung, & Strauch, 1989; Mithaug, Horiuchi, & Fanning, 1985; Shapiro & Lentz, 1991) have substantiated underutilization of postsecondary education. A pattern of underemployment for students with learning disabilities has also been emerging. Results from the National Longitudinal Transition Study of Special Education Students (Valdés, Williamson, & Wagner, 1990) indicated that only 23% of students with learning disabilities in the sample were earning $5 or more per hour according to parent interviews. The average hourly wage was reported to be $4 per hour, below the minimum wage. Only 17.4% of the former special education students were employed full-time in competitive work. The authors also reported that only 15.6% of the former students had taken any postsecondary course in the past year, with the percentage slightly higher for high school exiters who were out of school for 1 to 2 years.

Extending the focus of follow-up studies to college graduates or college students who are academically dismissed or fail to complete degree requirements yields even sparser information about the effectiveness of postsecondary interventions on adult outcomes. The fact that there is little empirical evidence regarding the effectiveness of LD support services at the postsecondary level is a reflection of several variables. Because college access for students with learning disabilities is a relatively recent phenomenon, service delivery did not evolve and grow until the 1980s. Mangrum and Strichart (1988) reported that factors such as pressure from advocacy groups, declining student enrollment, and realization of the viability of college as an attainable goal have all contributed to the expansion of college LD programs. Thus, it has been only in the past decade that matriculation of students with learning disabilities has resulted in college campuses addressing their needs in order to comply with regulations under Section 504.

R. Nelson and Lignugaris/Kraft (1989) suggested that the dearth of information about postsecondary programmatic interventions may reflect the divergent approaches to service delivery at this level. Based upon their analysis of 31 articles, the authors identified a wide range of interventions. Some schools emphasized basic-skills remediation while others provided course-content tutoring and reasonable accommodations. These differences may reflect variations in the missions of postsecondary institutions, ranging from preparation for the general equivalency diploma to academic training in numerous fields of specialization. Given this diversity in programmatic approaches, evaluation studies must be designed within the context of each program's specific goals and objectives, which could create problems in generalizability of findings.

In a recent nationwide survey of coordinators of services for college students with learning disabilities conducted by Bursuck et al. (1989), only 10% of the respondents (the response rate was 58.6%) were able to report on the graduation rates of these students. For the few respondents who were able to report on this variable, the average graduation rate was 30%. The authors rightfully expressed their concern regarding the absence of data collection in this area as well as a need for follow-up studies of students' subsequent vocational and life adjustment.

Adelman and Vogel (1990) conducted a follow-up study of students who participated in a comprehensive support program at a small private liberal arts college in the Midwest. Questionnaires were mailed to 89 former students, and those who did not respond by mail were contacted by telephone. Of the 89 subjects, 36 (40.4%) earned an undergraduate degree; 31 of those graduates completed the questionnaire. Twenty of the 89 students were required to withdraw from college because of academic failure. The authors reported that the impact of the graduates' learning disability continued into their work experience, although most reported the ongoing effectiveness of compensatory strategies such as spending extra time on the job or asking for help.

In another study, Vogel and Adelman (1990) examined various factors to determine their relationship to graduation status among college students with learning disabilities ($n = 110$) and a stratified randomly selected sample of nondisabled peers ($n = 153$). The sample with learning disabilities had participated for at least one semester between 1980 and 1988 in a highly structured support program that included subject-matter tutoring, remediation of basic skills deficits, assistance in accessing appropriate accommodations, and instruction in individualized compensatory strategies. College performance of the two groups was compared and results indicated that grade-point averages for the LD sample were significantly lower than those of their peers at the end of each year of study as well as upon college exit. On the other hand, the authors reported a nonsignificant difference in the graduation rate between the two groups as well as a nearly identical failure rate. They speculated that the similarity in graduation rates was evidence of program effectiveness, since the LD sample was not equivalent to the non-LD group as indicated by lower college entrance examination scores and poorer high school performance. Given the dearth of comparative data from other postsecondary settings, Vogel and Adelman encouraged the development of research in program effectiveness in order to determine whether any generalized patterns might exist that could result in important recommendations for high school personnel as well as for students with learning disabilities in their transition to college.

The importance of conducting program evaluation activities was discussed in an article by McGuire, Harris, and Bieber (1989) that described two grant-funded pilot programs for students with learning disabilities, one at a 2-year community college and one at a 4-year, very selective public university. Data were gathered over the 2-year grant period to document the retention and academic performance of students with learning disabilities who received support services. In both settings, the students' mean grade-point averages were above the minimum 2.0 standard for satisfactory academic status. Retention rates were 82% at the 2-year school and 92% at the university. The authors reported that data from this evaluation study were used to lobby successfully with the state legislature, which subsequently appropriated funding for an additional LD support program.

It is clear that postsecondary LD service providers can profit from emulating the movement in special education evaluation at the public school level from compliance reviews to outcome measures. Both areas are relevant at the college level. As students with learning disabilities become more aware of protections assured them under Section 504, objective evidence of institutional compliance will be critical, as illustrated in recent court cases (*Campbell A. Dinsmore v. Charles C. Pugh and the Regents of the University of California*, 1989; *Wynne v. Tufts University School of Medicine*, 1992) that centered upon statutory obligations including provision of academic adjustments. Furthermore, data on outcomes and anecdotal reports of adults with learning disabilities who have pursued higher education have the potential to assist service providers in effectively addressing their needs through programmatic decision making.

AN APPROACH TO POSTSECONDARY LD PROGRAM EVALUATION

The CIPP Model

Although there are a myriad of evaluation models, Borich and Nance (1987) pointed out that the process-outcome method has frequently been used in educational settings. The CIPP model—context, input, process, and product evaluation—was developed by Stufflebeam et al. (1971) as a tool to assist in decision making. Stufflebeam (1988) offered a simple yet provocative evaluation purpose that is particularly relevant to the emerging area of postsecondary LD service delivery: "The most important purpose of program evaluation is not to prove but to improve" (p. 117). Stufflebeam et al. (1971) defined educational evaluation as "the process of delineating, obtaining, and providing useful information for judging decision alternatives" (p. 40).

Table 9.1 illustrates an adaptation of the CIPP model to postsecondary LD programs. This should be considered as a dynamic model since its application will vary depending upon each program's stage of development. For example, in settings where comprehensive LD programs are well established, the focus may center upon the process and product components of the model. If initiatives are under way to establish an LD program, the initial evaluation questions may include context and input variables. Regardless of the "age" of LD services, some component of the model can readily be implemented, whether for making decisions, improving services, or establishing mechanisms to document compliance.

Selecting the Evaluator

Another consideration in designing a program evaluation centers around who should actually conduct it. Clearly, the director or coordinator of the LD program will be more knowledgeable about its

TABLE 9.1. Application of the CIPP Model to Postsecondary LD Programs

	Purpose	*Method*
Context Evaluation	To determine whether the goals and objectives of the LD program are pertinent to the needs of students to be served as well as to the institution	Use of needs assessments, surveys, diagnostic data, institutional documents
Input Evaluation	To identify the services or approaches needed to assist students to meet program goals; to assess already existing campus resources (e.g., career counseling, mental health services, disabled student services) to determine whether they can be adapted to assist students with learning disabilities	Review of the literature to determine effective interventions for students with learning disabilities; site visits to other institutions with exemplary LD programs; institutional "inventories" of other student services; consideration of staffing, space, and budgetary needs
Process Evaluation	To determine the extent to which LD program services are implemented, as well as the efficiency of service delivery; to gather data for use in modifying the program; to monitor student participation in LD services; to account for program expenditures (e.g., tutoring, equipment); to determine student satisfaction regarding LD services	Establishment of a systematic data-collection procedure and time line; identification of LD program staff roles and responsibilities for data collection; review of program records and documents (e.g., logs, contact hours); establishment of an advisory group including students, faculty, and appropriate administrative staff; conducting of interviews with and questionnaires for student consumers as well as campus personnel (e.g., faculty)

(continued)

TABLE 9.1. *Continued*

	Purpose	Method
Product Evaluation	To determine the effects or outcomes of LD program services; to relate program outcomes to program objectives and procedures; to render judgments about program outcomes (both positive and negative) for the purpose of modifying the program to become more cost-effective and to better serve the needs of students with learning disabilities	Student pretest/posttest performance (e.g., self-efficacy surveys, *Learning and Study Strategies Inventory* [Weinstein, Palmer, & Schulte, 1987]); grade-point average data gathered over time; retention-graduation data; case studies of program participants; follow-up surveys of program graduates; experimental research designs including students with learning disabilities who received services and control groups (e.g., non-LD peers or documented students with learning disabilities who elected not to participate in LD services)

goals, objectives, and methods. Having an *internal* evaluator brings the benefit of an understanding of the nuances of the institutional setting, its politics, and its climate, but can also raise questions about objectivity. Use of an outside or *external* evaluator offers the benefit of an objective, neutral perspective. Selection of an evaluator may be related to the role of the evaluation. Scriven (cited in Worthen & Sanders, 1987, p. 34) differentiated evaluation roles as follows:

1. *Formative,* which is intended to help planners and/or staff to improve the program

2. *Summative,* which is conducted to determine the extent to which the program has been effective

Formative evaluation is conducted throughout a program's operation, whereas summative evaluation is typically undertaken at the end of a program. Worthen and Sanders (1987) noted that the audiences for these roles differ: Program personnel constitute the "users" of formative evaluation information; potential consumers, policy and financial decision makers, and program staff would be interested in summative findings. They also recommended that *both* types of evaluation are essential. This is particularly true in the field of postsecondary LD programming, since many colleges have only recently implemented support services or are in the process of considering the development of more comprehensive service-delivery approaches. This formative-summative distinction was addressed by Stufflebeam (1988), who concluded that the CIPP model can be tailored to both functions. The evaluator should design and conduct activities for the purpose of planning, implementing, and refining programs as well as for rendering conclusions about the program's merit and worth. Decision making and accountability are not mutually exclusive in the CIPP model.

It is reasonable to suggest that, at the very least, LD program coordinators should assume a proactive role on their campus in articulating a commitment to planning, conducting, and sharing program evaluation information. In reality, hiring an external evaluator may be a luxury, but this should not preclude ongoing, systematic data collection by internal program staff.

Planning for Evaluation

Whether the focus of evaluation is formative or summative, several general steps should be followed for conducting the evaluation. Herman, Morris, and Fitz-Gibbon (1987, pp. 27–41) outlined these stages as follows:

1. Establish the boundaries of the evaluation. This should include identification of program activities that will be assessed as well as the responsibilities of the program's staff in the data-collection process.

2. Determine appropriate methods of evaluation. Specification of program goals and objectives and the means or activities by which these goals will be met should be clarified at this stage.

3. Collect and analyze data to determine program implementation and progress in attaining outcomes.

4. Report findings and suggest changes.

Stufflebeam (1988) advised evaluators to approach the task as a process, not a product. This means that evaluation goals and procedures should be clearly spelled out prior to implementation of evaluation activities, but that flexibility must exist in reviewing the process, revising it, and putting it into operation.

Figure 9.1 provides a summary of steps that could be followed in the design and implementation of a postsecondary LD program evaluation as well as specific questions that should be considered in the process. This sort of preplanning is important in setting priorities and weighing which aspects of a program warrant evaluation in light of limited resources (Madaus, Airasian, & Kellaghan, 1980).

AN ILLUSTRATION OF PROGRAM EVALUATION: THE UNIVERSITY OF CONNECTICUT

As pointed out by R. Nelson and Lignugaris/Kraft (1989), there is no one approach to LD service delivery at the postsecondary level, nor are there yet data to substantiate the efficacy of one model over another. The following example illustrates one institution's method for conducting ongoing activities to assist in decision making and to document accountability and compliance. The University of Connecticut Program for College Students with Learning Disabilities has been in existence since 1984. A comprehensive program evaluation plan has been developed with formative evaluations conducted regularly. Various components of the evaluation plan illustrate that flexibility is a key in "individualizing" evaluation activities to meet institutional and setting needs.

Goals and Objectives

With an overall goal of promoting student independence and success within the context of a very competitive academic environment, 10 program objectives have been articulated and are illustrated in Figure 9.2. These objectives focus upon various program functions that

Steps	*Considerations*
1. Consider the audience.	*College administrators?* *Potential consumers (e.g., incoming freshmen, transfer students, nontraditional students)?* *Faculty?* *Program staff?* *Legislators?* *Research community?* *Governing boards?*
2. Determine the purposes of the evaluation.	*Justify program needs (e.g., staff, space equipment)?* *Monitor student achievement?* *Document compliance with Section 504?* *Monitor cost-effectiveness?* *Analyze use and effectiveness of program services?* *Assist in developing institutional policy (e.g., course-substitution policies)?*
3. Focus the evaluation.	*Context?* *Product?* *Input?* *Formative?* *Process?* *Summative?*
4. Determine appropriate methods of evaluation.	*Quantitative?* *Qualitative?*
5. Collect and analyze data.	*Time line established?* *Data collection instruments and procedures identified?* *Staff responsible for data collection identified?* *Data collection monitoring plan in place?* *Plan for organizing, coding, storing, and retrieving data?* *Data-analysis procedures identified?*
6. Report and utilize data.	*Format for reporting and communicating results (e.g., formal written reports, memos, presentations)?* *Plan in place for generating report?* *Follow-up activities planned?*

Figure 9.1. A step-by-step approach to questions to be asked. *Note.* From J. M. McGuire (1992). Unpublished material. The University of Connecticut, A. J. Pappanikou Center on Special Education and Rehabilitation: A University Affiliated Program, Storrs. Reprinted with permission.

1. To work cooperatively with admissions for first-year students and transfers to determine "otherwise qualified" students with learning disabilities who voluntarily self-identify at the time of application

2. To serve as a referral source for unidentified full-time university students with learning difficulties

3. To provide diagnostic evaluations for unidentified students with learning difficulties to determine eligibility for services through UPLD

4. To provide diagnostic evaluations for the purpose of planning individualized support services for previously diagnosed and documented students with learning disabilities seeking support services from UPLD

5. To provide a continuum of services designed to increase independence and success for students with learning disabilities

6. To promote awareness among university faculty, staff, and administration of learning disabilities, types of reasonable accommodations and academic adjustments, and the function of UPLD as a student support service

7. To serve as a training site for graduate students seeking to expand their competencies in administration, direct services, and research in programming for college students with learning disabilities

8. To conduct a program of research and evaluation based upon services offered through UPLD

9. To disseminate information regarding UPLD to appropriate campus personnel and other professionals (e.g., high school guidance counselors)

10. To conduct outreach activities at the local, state, and national levels to promote awareness of postsecondary opportunities for persons with learning disabilities

Figure 9.2. University of Connecticut Program for College Students with Learning Disabilities (UPLD) program objectives. *Note.* From J. M. McGuire (1990). Unpublished material. The University of Connecticut, A. J. Pappanikou Center on Special Education and Rehabilitation: A University Affiliated Program, Storrs. Reprinted with permission.

are conducted on a day-to-day basis by the staff, which includes the director, the assistant to the director, and graduate assistants. The program model, as portrayed in Figure 9.3, is student-centered, which promotes interaction among a number of existing campus resources; it operates on the assumption that it is unrealistic and inefficient in this setting for the LD staff to be "all things to all students." If a student with a learning disability requires individual counseling, a referral may be made to the campus department of counseling services or mental health services office. This "interactive" model requires ongoing interactions among campus personnel (e.g., participation in staff meetings) and is reflected in objectives 6 and 10 in Figure 9.2. With respect to the goal of promoting student independence, a three-stage continuum of services (see Figure 9.4) serves as the foundation for assisting students to master learning strategies and study and self-advocacy skills. Throughout their enrollment at the university, students are actively involved in decision making regarding their specific needs and are encouraged to work toward the goal of increasing self-sufficiency.

Evaluation Plan and Methods

In designing the evaluation plan, the emphasis has been predominantly upon the process or means by which services are implemented to meet program objectives. Product or outcome evaluations (e.g., retention and graduation rates) are also conducted at the end of each semester. A longitudinal data base is in place so that follow-up research on adult outcomes and employment data can be implemented at a later date.

In order to assure timely, comprehensive data collection, it is critical to identify staff responsibilities as well as a time line for gathering information. This relates to staff selection and ongoing staff development as discussed in Chapter 7. When tasks are laid out before the academic year begins, there is less opportunity for any misunderstanding about who is responsible for each activity. Table 9.2 presents an example of an evaluation plan that specifies the focus of the evaluation (program services and program outcomes) and the method, staff, and time line for data collection.

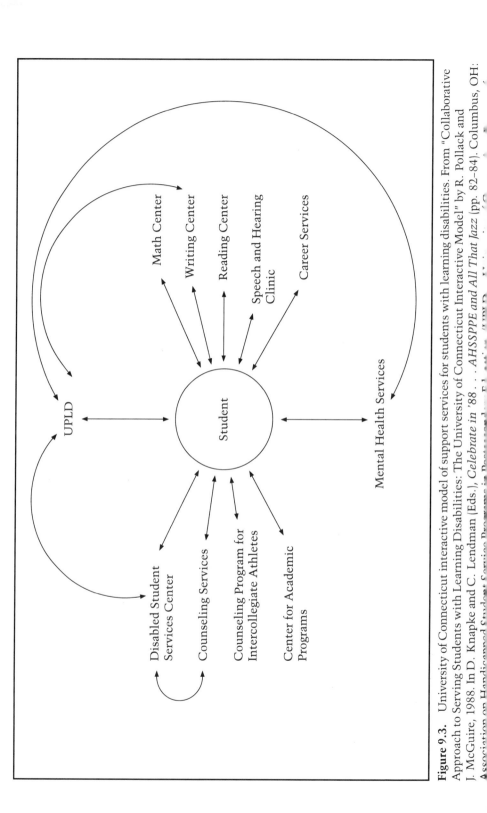

Figure 9.3. University of Connecticut interactive model of support services for students with learning disabilities. From "Collaborative Approach to Serving Students with Learning Disabilities: The University of Connecticut Interactive Model" by R. Pollack and J. McGuire, 1988. In D. Knapke and C. Lendman (Eds.), *Celebrate in '88 . . . AHSSPPE and All That Jazz* (pp. 82–84). Columbus, OH: Association on Handicapped Student Service Programs in Postsecondary Education (AHSSPPE). University of Connecticut Program

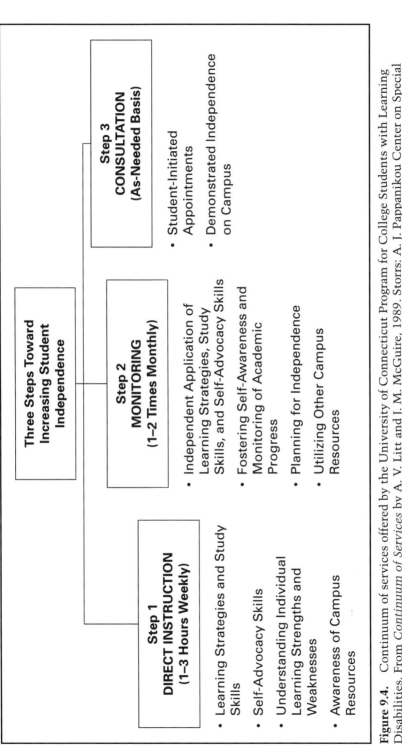

Figure 9.4. Continuum of services offered by the University of Connecticut Program for College Students with Learning Disabilities. From *Continuum of Services* by A. V. Litt and J. M. McGuire, 1989. Storrs: A. J. Pappanikou Center on Special Education and Rehabilitation: A University Affiliated Program, University of Connecticut. Reprinted with permission.

TABLE 9.2. Comprehensive Evaluation Implementation Plan

Focus of Evaluation	Method of Data Collection	Person(s) Responsible	Date of Data Collection
PROGRAM SERVICES	PROGRAM RECORDS		
Admissions reviews of self-identified first-year and transfer applicants	Admissions summary sheet; minutes of committee review meetings	Director/staff	May
Referral services	Referral log; intake interview and screening summary; referral follow-up sheet	Director; referral coordinator	January; May
Diagnostic services	Psychoeducational evaluation reports	Director	January; May
Continuum of direct student services	Learning specialist monthly summary sheets; semester summary reports; individual student semester goals	Assistant to director	Monthly; January; May
Faculty, staff, and administration awareness activities	Faculty contact log; departmental contact log; information dissemination log	Director; assistant to director; staff	December; May
Personnel training	Learning session logs; staff seminar evaluation form; monthly meeting summary; pre- and postcompetency surveys	Assistant to director	Monthly; May

Program component/outcome	Method/data source	Responsible person	Timing
Outreach activities	High school contact sheet; summary sheet for professional presentations	Director	May

PROGRAM OUTCOMES

Program outcome	Method/data source	Responsible person	Timing
Academic performance (GPA)	Transcripts; comparative institutional data	Graduate assistant	January; June
Retention and graduation	Transcripts; comparative institutional data (source: *Annual University Fact Book*); exit interviews	Graduate assistant; director	January; June
Student independence	Project records; interviews	Assistant to director	April
Student's self-perceptions of learning strategies and study skills	Pre- and postadministration of *LASSI* (Weinstein, Palmer, & Schulte, 1987)	Assistant to director	Upon program entry and progression to consultation
Attitudes of students, staff, faculty, and administration	Questionnaires/surveys	Director; assistant to director	April; annually
Personnel development	Pre- and postcompetency survey; staff seminar evaluations; job placement	Director; assistant to director	September; May; ongoing

Note. From J. M. McGuire (1990). Unpublished material. The University of Connecticut, A. J. Pappanikou Center on Special Education and Rehabilitation: A University Affiliated Program, Storrs. Reprinted with permission.

Evaluation Results

An example of product evaluation data is provided in Figure 9.5 to illustrate student success as defined by retention and graduation. As a method of collecting data, exit interviews were conducted. Two areas of difficulty emerged as themes among students who were dismissed ($n = 6$): (a) underpreparedness among transfer students to compete in a student population that is academically very competitive and (b) difficulty sustaining the motivation and effort that appear to be critical variables in student outcomes. Students who transferred ($n = 5$) were satisfactory academically (i.e., they had a grade-point average of 2.0 or greater) but found there was a lack of balance in their lives because of what they reported to be inordinate amounts of study time at the sacrifice of participation in campus social life. Students who withdrew ($n = 8$) did so for personal reasons (e.g., health problems) or, in the case of several students with traumatic brain injury, because of the stress of reentry into the competitive university environment. As the number of students who exit the university increases, longitudinal follow-up studies will constitute a valuable method of gleaning both quantitative and qualitative information about transition to employment, workplace accommodations, and adult adjustment.

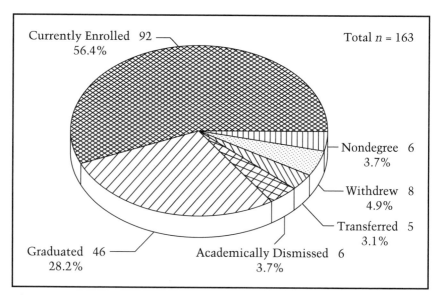

Figure 9.5. Student status/outcome data.

CHALLENGES IN EVALUATING PROGRAMS

The advice of Stufflebeam (1988, p. 140) about the critical role evaluation plays in program improvement should not be taken lightly:

> We cannot make our programs better unless we know where they are weak and strong and unless we become aware of better means. We cannot be sure that our goals are worthy unless we can match them to the needs of the people they are intended to serve. We cannot plan effectively if we are unaware of options and their relative merits; and we cannot convince our constituents that we have done good work and deserve continued support unless we can show them evidence that we have done what we promised and produced beneficial results.

At the same time, assurances that students' rights to equal educational opportunity are guaranteed must not be tied to outcome data regarding their retention and graduation. Section 504 guarantees equal opportunities, not unfair advantage, equal results, or equal achievement for persons with disabilities. Postsecondary LD service providers must cautiously distinguish between the need to comply with statutory regulations requiring reasonable accommodations and academic adjustments, and the desire to provide effective, comprehensive "programs." Evaluation of the services provided for students with learning disabilities is critical in documenting institutional compliance, but evaluation of how successful programs are in helping students achieve postsecondary goals is a different question.

If the principles of scientific research are to serve as guidelines for conducting program evaluations, methodological problems must be addressed. D. T. Campbell and Stanley (1966) and Cook and Campbell (1979) discussed a number of threats caused by external variables that can jeopardize the validity of conclusions drawn from outcomes. Factors such as subject maturation and the impact of history (i.e., "specific events occurring between the first and second measurement," D. T. Campbell & Stanley, 1966, p. 5) are particularly relevant in interpreting outcomes relating to college students with learning disabilities. The question of whether their success or lack of success in achieving goals is related to program intervention is complex and cannot be considered without careful research design.

In addition, identification of control groups may be a problem. If access to program services is determined by student self-identification, there may be a bias factor, since it is reasonable to assume that students with learning disabilities who choose to receive services and reasonable accommodations may possess characteristics (e.g., motivation, self-discipline, and persistence) that distinguish them from those students who remain anonymous. Random assignment of self-identified LD students to an experimental or control group is not feasible since withholding services is neither legal nor ethical. Random selection of a control group of nondisabled peers must address the question of group equivalency. To match students with learning disabilities with a control group drawn from the college undergraduate population, variables such as aptitude, high school performance, and achievement scores must be considered.

CONCLUSION

Postsecondary service providers are in the unique position of having some precedent to guide them in preparing to respond to consumers and administrators, and to legislative and advocacy groups' queries about the impact of services for college students with learning disabilities. It is not unreasonable to speculate that pressure will be forthcoming to document both compliance with Section 504 and effectiveness and cost of services in much the same manner as has occurred for special education programs mandated by P.L. 94-142. As George, George, and Grosenick (1990) so aptly described for elementary and secondary levels, service providers should expect a call for a more comprehensive approach to evaluation to "determine whether programs are designed on the basis of sound theoretical principles, operate competently . . . and impact positively on those students who are receiving services" (p. 24). The adage "forewarned is forearmed" is profoundly appropriate.

CHAPTER 10

Future Directions in Postsecondary Learning Disability Programming and Service Delivery

The field of postsecondary learning disabilities is still in its adolescence. As noted previously, 90% of the growth in service delivery has occurred in the last 15 years. We are now getting to the point where students with learning disabilities can expect to receive some kind of support service at most postsecondary institutions. The question remains whether service delivery at the postsecondary level will face the same haphazard development as exists at the elementary and secondary levels. A review of special education practice in the public schools demonstrates that unproved, experimental, and inappropriate interventions were implemented over extended periods of time long after research had challenged their validity (Alley et al., 1983; Hammill, 1972). Interventions among elementary students with learning disabilities have included visual-motor training, megavitamin therapy, patterning, and overuse of stimulant medication (Rooney, 1991). At the secondary level, approaches used with young children were often inappropriately adopted for high school students. Content tutoring, which has been identified as an inappropriate intervention for secondary school students for years, is still the approach that typifies LD resource rooms (Carlson, 1985). Can LD personnel at the postsecondary level avoid these pedagogical pitfalls and quickly move to effective service delivery based on current research and policy? The previous chapters in this book presented state-of-the-art information for postsecondary practitioners. This chapter will identify some of the opportunities for growth and change that need to be addressed in the future. The following areas will be discussed:

- How to foster the successful outcomes that the students we work with have the potential to achieve

- Developing personnel standards for postsecondary LD practitioners

- Proactive development of effective policies and procedures

- The need for field-based research

- Integration of students with learning disabilities into the postsecondary community

- How to be an effective change agent

FOSTERING SUCCESSFUL OUTCOMES

Historically, services for students with learning disabilities have focused on relatively short-term goals. In the early grades the priorities are to help the student catch up with peers or return to the regular classroom. At the secondary level the focus is typically on support in academic subjects so that the student can graduate. In spite of a national focus on transition since the mid 1980s and recent amendments to P.L. 94-142 requiring transition plans, secondary programs for students with mild disabilities still focus almost solely on academics (Lynch & Beare, 1990). In a review of studies of post–high school adjustment for individuals with learning disabilities, White (1992) assessed the results of current efforts. He noted that learning disabilities "frequently cause problems in the vocational and social domains, as evidenced by the adults' high unemployment rates, underemployment, and general lack of satisfaction with their personal and vocational lives. . . . the number of adults with LD who have been able to achieve the level of independence and self-sufficiency necessary to 'take their place in society' is disappointingly low" (pp. 454–455).

What are postsecondary institutions doing to reverse this alarming trend? A few individual studies of small LD support programs have documented successful outcomes (Herzog & Falk, 1991; Posthill & Roffman, 1991; Vogel & Adelman, 1992). There is concern, however, regarding the current direction taken by most postsecondary services for students with learning disabilities. In a large national study, data were collected from 510 postsecondary LD support service personnel (Shaw, et al., 1992). Independence-oriented practices were identified, including time management skills, note taking, study skills, listening skills, memory strategies, organizational skills, metacognitive strategies, communication skills, self-advocacy skills, and social-interpersonal skills. Those interventions were contrasted to the use of dependence-oriented practices such as correcting and proofreading students' papers, providing readers, and content tutoring. Surprisingly, practitioners who provided the most interventions associated with student independence also exhibited the highest rates of interventions associated with student dependence.

The authors concluded that as practitioners in the field of student support services at the postsecondary level expand services to students with learning disabilities, they fail to discriminate between services that foster student autonomy and those that do not. These findings suggest that those who are troubled by the manner in which services for students with learning disabilities are evolving at colleges and universities across the country may, indeed, have just cause for concern.

Given that more services do not necessarily equal appropriate services, those responsible for developing programs to serve students with learning disabilities at the postsecondary level would be well advised to reflect on the program's philosophy, mission, and priorities when determining service-delivery options. Likewise, given the growing evidence for a strong relationship between student autonomy and success in employment and other critical life endeavors, those who offer comprehensive programs for students with learning disabilities at the postsecondary level may wish to evaluate the extent to which their programs rely on services that undermine student autonomy and self-determination (Brinckerhoff et al., 1992; Reiff, Gerber, & Ginsberg, 1992). For example, practitioners who provide taped textbooks or note takers for students with learning disabilities should always consider implementing an instructional strategy that is more likely to foster independence.

DEVELOPING PROFESSIONAL STANDARDS

Personnel serving students with learning disabilities through high school graduation are all certified special educators, but that is not the case at the postsecondary level. In 1987, Shaw, Norlander, and McGuire noted that personnel providing services at the college level came from counseling, higher education administration, rehabilitation counseling, social work, psychology, and speech and language backgrounds. Of the 510 postsecondary LD professionals cited in the data collected more than 5 years later (Shaw et al., 1992), only 27% were from the field of special education. Other groups of professionals responding to the survey came from counseling (20%), elementary or secondary education (8%), rehabilitation (8%), and higher education (6%). Smaller percentages of these professionals came from clinical psychology, school psychology, social work, speech and language, and vocational education backgrounds. Another 16% indicated that they did not fit any of the above classifications. It is also interesting to note that in spite of the maturity of this group (65% are over age 40), fewer than half have been working with postsecondary students with learning disabilities for more than 5 years.

The data seem to indicate two trends: (a) the field is still developing and (b) professionals from a variety of disciplines and positions are being selected to implement and supervise these services. The fact that personnel being hired or given responsibility for postsecondary LD positions came from a broad range of backgrounds raises some questions. Are these professionals specifically trained for these positions? Do the higher education administrators doing the hiring know what the job descriptions should be or what qualifications are necessary in selecting a candidate to fulfill the job descriptions? The answer to both questions is likely to be no. The only data available to support these conclusions are found in a preliminary study by Norlander, Shaw, and McGuire (1990); they indicated that both direct service and administrative personnel saw significant limitations in the skill levels necessary for their current job.

Chapter 7 provided a comprehensive discussion of staffing and personnel development. What is important for the field in terms of future development is commitment to move ahead in defining personnel standards. Groups such as AHEAD or the NJCLD should assume a leadership role in examining the need to consider certification or the development of professional standards for personnel working with students with learning disabilities at the postsecondary level. The Council for Exceptional Children, for example, has adopted a standard called the CEC Common Core of Knowledge and Skills Essential for All Beginning Special Education Teachers (W. Swan & Sirvis, 1992). This document, which establishes minimum standards for entry into the special education profession, could be a model for a similar attempt at the postsecondary level. The executive director of AHEAD (J. Jarrow, personal communication, August 4, 1992) has indicated that plans for this are in process. Until we have recognized professional standards, postsecondary institutions will continue to hire personnel who may lack the skills necessary to develop state-of-the-art services that can afford students with learning disabilities equal access and the opportunity to pursue personal goals for higher education.

PROACTIVE OR REACTIVE SERVICE DELIVERY

Recent research conducted by Gillung, Spears, Campbell, and Rucker (1992, p. 89) noted that "it is evident from the importance given to laws and regulations that administrators of special education programs view their role as implementors of procedures." They noted that the IDEA is very prescriptive and requires detailed implementation to protect their school districts from legal action. Section 504 of the Rehabilitation Act, as noted in Chapter 2, was not developed by or for higher education and was not intended to provide a model of effective service delivery.

Unfortunately, some postsecondary personnel seem to inappropriately view their role as no more than implementers of procedures in the same way that public school administrators do. This was clearly illustrated at a recent national meeting involving postsecondary practitioners serving students with learning disabilities. There was a constant refrain from participants seeking clarification on Section 504 and recent court decisions and their implications for service delivery. Similarly, Bursuck et al. (1989) found that the majority of the respondents to their national survey saw Section 504 access as their primary service goal.

The issue is not *whether* institutions of higher education should strive to be in compliance with the law by providing equal access for students with learning disabilities. It is important for practitioners to document an institution's commitment to equal opportunity. The concern, however, is that it is now time for professionals in this field to identify "best practices" so that service delivery can be improved based upon current research. Rather than operating from a reactive base to ongoing court cases (some of which may be confusing or even lead to poor educational outcomes), professionals need to be proactive in establishing the parameters of effective service delivery. This is particularly important since courts and judges are generally reluctant to meddle in areas where professionals have rendered informed positions or recommendations. It is, therefore, essential for postsecondary practitioners to work with their professional organizations in order to develop position papers and policy statements based on the best in current knowledge, understanding, and expertise. Among the questions that need to be addressed in this manner are:

- Who is a student with a learning disability?
- What constitutes appropriate documentation?
- Who is "otherwise qualified"?
- What are appropriate accommodations?

These questions should not wait for a judge in some district court or an official from the Office of Civil Rights, neither of whom are likely to have expertise in postsecondary learning disabilities, to answer them.

KNOWLEDGE BASE

Although the previous section encouraged postsecondary practitioners to identify "best practices," it is necessary to acknowledge the very limited data base upon which we are attempting to stand. There is a tremendous need for field-based research regarding postsecondary services for students with learning disabilities. Unfortunately, this field seems to have fallen in a crack between funding sources. The U.S. Office of Special Education and Rehabilitative Services (OSERS) focuses its efforts on elementary and secondary schools, not colleges. OSERS' small postsecondary education division has been wholly concerned with transition to employment for the last several years. The rehabilitation services division has a community integration emphasis in addition to its focus on employment. There seems to be little room for funding research in postsecondary education, particularly for students with mild disabilities.

Another concern is the very limited number of researchers in positions to pursue this area of inquiry. Postsecondary practitioners usually are affiliated with student affairs rather than the academic unit of the institution. Typically, neither their role description nor the reward system foster the implementation of research. College professors, who have a stake in research and publication, are often restrained by ties to teacher certification programs and public school supervision.

A result of these factors is that relatively little research is published in this field. The editors of the *Journal of Postsecondary Edu-*

cation and Disability have noted their concern about the dearth of manuscripts and the importance of such research (McGuire & Shaw, 1992). Given the relative youth of this field of study, most of the research has dealt with basic areas such as the characteristics of students in selected LD support services and program evaluation (including outcomes) of individual college programs. Studies are now needed that determine effectiveness, not from a global program level, but in terms of specific interventions. Which interventions yield better skills, higher grade-point averages, and greater graduation or employment rates? How do taping lectures, using carbon paper, or employing note takers compare as effective accommodations in classroom settings?

To answer any research questions with confidence, we will need to stringently employ effective research methodology that addresses these concerns:

- Describing students with learning disabilities in a way that allows replication of the study

- Using samples of students across several institutions or service-delivery models

- Using a control or, at least, a contrast group

- Providing enough time in implementing the intervention to give it a reasonable opportunity to be mastered

- Delaying final data collection until long enough after the intervention has ended to assess use, maintenance, and generalization

Service providers who are not themselves conducting research may want to contact researchers in their institution. The offer of a readily available sample of students and important research questions in a developing field with many outlets for publication could be very enticing.

INTEGRATION INTO THE POSTSECONDARY COMMUNITY

The issue of where to educate students with disabilities in relation to their nondisabled peers has been debated for almost 50 years.

During the last decade, concepts such as mainstreaming, least restrictive environment, inclusion, and normalization have become critical to professionals and advocates alike. Public schools are now attempting to serve most students with learning disabilities in regular classrooms. As this change evolves, professionals serving students with learning disabilities in the public schools find themselves moving from a pullout direct service model to a collaborative inclusionary model. At this point it is not certain what the configuration of public school service delivery will be, but postsecondary practitioners need to take note of a changing educational climate.

Postsecondary students with learning disabilities will have already experienced a significant degree of integrated service delivery. Postsecondary practitioners will, therefore, increasingly face questions such as the following:

- Do students need to be labeled as having a learning disability to assure eligibility for services?

- Are support services to be provided for all students with learning problems or only for students with documented disabilities?

- How closely should support personnel work with faculty in providing services for students?

- Do institutional policies and practices foster the acceptance and integration of students with learning disabilities into all aspects of campus life?

- Do support services have a focus on teaching self-advocacy skills and learning strategies that develop successful independent learners?

- Does the institution have a philosophy and a process to wean a student from reliance on support services?

- Do support service personnel work collaboratively with the office of career planning and placement to encourage all appropriate employment options for students with learning disabilities?

In addition to concerns regarding the integration of students with learning disabilities, institutions of higher education are beginning to experience growing numbers of nondisabled students with "hidden" learning difficulties. These students may be at risk for learning failure because of drug exposure, family crises, educational deprivation, language problems, and many other reasons. Open-enrollment community colleges are, in many cases, already challenged by huge numbers of these students with significant learning needs. Practitioners need to develop approaches for dealing with this large at risk group while ensuring equal access under the law for the smaller group of students with documented learning disabilities who may or may not have similar learning needs. Approaches that have had some success in the public schools, such as teacher assistance teams (Chalfant & Pysh, 1989), peer tutoring (Harper, Maheady, & Sacca, 1988), team teaching (K. Decker et al., 1992), use of technology (Mirenda & Iacono, 1990), cooperative learning (Slavin, 1991), and collaborative consultation (Idol, Paolucci-Whitcomb, & Nevin, 1986), may need to be adapted for and evaluated in postsecondary settings.

BECOMING A CHANGE AGENT

There is little doubt that massive change will occur in the field of postsecondary learning disabilities in the years to come. This leads to two provocative questions:

1. Will the change be helpful or harmful to students with learning disabilities?

2. Will postsecondary LD practitioners foster effective change or be victims of haphazard or ill-conceived change?

Postsecondary LD practitioners need to seek out roles as change agents. This position is not new to those who have already accepted students with learning disabilities at their institutions, developed services for these students, or improved service delivery in spite of diminishing resources. It seems appropriate to end this chapter with suggestions for becoming an effective change agent that have been adapted from the public schools (Champlin, 1987):

1. Be data-driven; purge ineffective practices by heeding current educational research.

2. Be goal-driven; focus on your institution's mission and the student outcomes you seek so that every decision works to foster those ends.

3. Be committed to change, always correcting and adjusting. The ability to adjust allows you to take risks.

4. Do not accept personal or organizational mediocrity.

5. Train staff in every skill you ask them to perform.

6. Make the entire institutional community your ally by working with them and giving them reason to support you.

7. Win over your staff by creating a strong sense of need, ownership, and commitment.

8. Never lose sight of the goal.

Department of Education, Office for Civil Rights, Regional Civil Rights Offices

Region I

Connecticut, Maine, Massachusetts, New Hampshire,
  Rhode Island, Vermont
  Regional Civil Rights Director
  Office for Civil Rights, Region I
  U.S. Department of Education
  John W. McCormack Post Office and Courthouse Building,
    Room 222
  Boston, MA 02109-4557
  (617) 223-9662   (617) 223-9695 (TDD)

Region II

New Jersey, New York, Puerto Rico, Virgin Islands
  Regional Civil Rights Director
  Office for Civil Rights, Region II
  U.S. Department of Education
  26 Federal Plaza, Room 33-130, 33rd Floor
  New York, NY 10278-0082
  (212) 264-4633   (212) 264-9464 (TDD)

Region III

Delaware, District of Columbia, Maryland, Pennsylvania,
Virginia, West Virginia
Regional Civil Rights Director
Office for Civil Rights, Region III
U.S. Department of Education
3535 Market Street, Room 6300
P.O. Box 13716
Philadelphia, PA 19104-3326
(215) 596-6772   (215) 596-6794 (TDD)

Region IV

Alabama, Florida, Georgia, Kentucky, Mississippi,
North Carolina, South Carolina, Tennessee
Regional Civil Rights Director
Office for Civil Rights, Region IV
U.S. Department of Education
Mail to: P.O. Box 2048
101 Marietta Street, Tower, 27th Floor, Suite 2702
Atlanta, GA 30301-2048
(404) 331-2954   (404) 331-7236 (TDD)

Region V

Illinois, Indiana, Minnesota, Michigan, Ohio, Wisconsin
Regional Civil Rights Director
Office for Civil Rights, Region V
U.S. Department of Education
401 South State Street, 7th Floor, Room 700C
Chicago, IL 60605-1202
(312) 886-3456   (312) 353-2540 (TDD)

Region VI

Arkansas, Louisiana, New Mexico, Oklahoma, Texas
Regional Civil Rights Director
Office for Civil Rights, Region VI
U.S. Department of Education
1200 Main Tower Building, Suite 2260
Dallas, TX 75202-9998
(214) 767-3936   (214) 767-3639 (TDD)

Region VII

Iowa, Kansas, Missouri, Nebraska
Regional Civil Rights Director
Office for Civil Rights, Region VII
U.S. Department of Education
10220 North Executive Hills Boulevard, 8th Floor
P.O. Box 901381
Kansas City, MO 64153-1381
(816) 891-8026   (816) 374-6461 (TDD)

Region VIII

Colorado, Montana, North Dakota, South Dakota, Utah,
  Wyoming
Regional Civil Rights Director
Office for Civil Rights, Region VIII
U.S. Department of Education
Federal Office Building
1244 Speer Boulevard, Suite 310
Denver, CO 80294-3582
(303) 844-5695   (303) 844-3417 (TDD)

Region IX

*Arizona, California, Hawaii, Nevada, Guam, Trust Territory of
the Pacific Islands, American Samoa*
Regional Civil Rights Director
Office for Civil Rights, Region IX
U.S. Department of Education
Old Federal Building
50 United Nations Plaza, Room 239
San Francisco, CA 94102-4102
(415) 556-7000   (415) 556-6806 (TDD)

Region X

Alaska, Idaho, Oregon, Washington
U.S. Department of Education
Office for Civil Rights, Region X
Henry M. Jackson Federal Building
915 Second Avenue, Room 3310
Seattle, WA 98174-1099
(206) 220-7900   (206) 220-7907 (TDD)

National Headquarters

U.S. Department of Education
Office for Civil Rights
330 C Street, SW
Washington, DC 20202
(202) 732-1213   (202) 732-1663 (TDD)

APPENDIX B

Resources on Diagnosing Adults with Learning Disabilities

ASSESSMENT OF ADULTS

Gregg, N., Hoy, C., King, M., Moreland, C., & Jagota, M. (1992). The MMPI-2 profile of adults with learning disabilities at a university and rehabilitation setting. *Journal of Learning Disabilities, 25*, 386–395.

Hartlage, L. C. (1985). Identifying and understanding the learning disabled adult. In D. P. Swiercinsky (Ed.), *Testing adults: A reference guide for special psychodiagnostic assessments* (pp. 179–187). Kansas City: Test Corporation of America.

Kaufman, A. S. (1990). *Assessing adolescent and adult intelligence.* Boston: Allyn & Bacon.

McCue, M. (1989). The role of assessment in the vocational rehabilitation of adults with specific learning disabilities. *Rehabilitation Counseling Bulletin, 33*, 18–37.

Newill, R., Goyette, C., & Fogarty, T. (1984). Diagnosis and assessment of the adult with specific learning disabilities. *Journal of Rehabilitation, 50*, 34–39.

Nightingale, D., Yudd, R., Anderson, S., & Barnow, B. (1991). *The learning disabled in employment and training programs* (Research and Evaluation Report Series 91-E, Contract No. 99-9-0421-75-081-01). Washington, DC: Department of Labor, Employment and Training Administration; Office of Strategic Planning and Policy Development.

DIAGNOSTIC ASSESSMENT

DeBello, T. C. (1990). Comparison of eleven major learning styles models: Variables, appropriate populations, validity of instrumentation, and the research behind them. *Reading, Writing, and Learning Disabilities, 6,* 203–222.

Finlan, T. G. (1992). Do state methods of quantifying a severe discrepancy result in fewer students with learning disabilities? *Learning Disability Quarterly, 15,* 129–134.

Forness, S. R., & Kavale, K. A. (1991). Social skills deficits as primary learning disabilities: A note on problems with ICLD diagnostic criteria. *Learning Disabilities Research & Practice, 6,* 44–49.

Guidubaldi, J., Perry, J. D., & Walker, M. (1989). Assessment strategies for students with disabilities. *Journal of Counseling and Development, 68,* 160–165.

Kamphaus, R. W., Frick, P. J., & Lahey, B. B. (1991). Methodological issues and learning disabilities diagnosis in clinical populations. *Journal of Learning Disabilities, 24,* 613–618.

Lewis, R. B. (1989). Educational assessment of learning disabilities: A new generation of achievement measures. *Learning Disabilities, 1,* 49–55.

Mather, N., & Healey, W. C. (1989). Deposing aptitude-achievement discrepancy as the imperial criterion for learning disabilities. *Learning Disabilities, 1,* 40–48.

Morris, M., & Leuenberger, J. (1990). A report of cognitive, academic, and linguistic profiles for college students with and without learning disabilities. *Journal of Learning Disabilities, 23,* 355–360, 385.

Perreira, D. (1989). Study skills assessment for students with learning disabilities. In *Proceedings of the 1989 AHSSPPE conference* (pp. 112–118). Columbus, OH: Association on Handicapped Student Service Programs in Postsecondary Education.

Ross, R. P. (1990). Consistency among school psychologists in evaluating discrepancy scores: A preliminary study. *Learning Disability Quarterly, 13,* 209–219.

Voeller, K. (1991). Social-emotional learning disabilities. *Psychiatric Annals, 21,* 735–741.

Wiener, J. (1986). Alternatives in the assessment of the learning disabled adolescent: A learning strategies approach. *Learning Disabilities Focus, 1,* 97–107.

FOREIGN LANGUAGE

Faigel, H. C. (1990, Fall). The relationship between the Modern Language Aptitude Test (MLAT) and speech and language examinations in college students with learning disabilities. *Latest Developments*, 6–9.

Gajar, A. H. (1987). Foreign language learning disabilities: The identification of predictive and diagnostic variables. *Journal of Learning Disabilities, 20,* 327–330.

Ganschow, L., & Sparks, R. (1991, Spring). Foreign language learning difficulties and use of the Modern Language Aptitude Test: A response to Faigel. *Latest Developments*, 1–4.

Ganschow, L., Sparks, R., & Sudman, J. (1990). A case for collaboration in the diagnosis and remediation of students with language learning disabilities. *Learning Disabilities, 1,* 85–93.

Goodman, J. F., Freed, B., & McMannus, W. J. (1988). The measurement of foreign language learning disabilities in college students. *Journal of Learning Disabilities, 21,* 429–430.

Sparks, R., Ganschow, L., & Javorsky, J. (1992). Diagnosing and accommodating the foreign language learning difficulties of college students with learning disabilities. *Learning Disabilities Research & Practice, 7,* 150–160.

Sparks, R., Ganschow, L., & Pohlman, J. (1989). Linguistic coding deficits in foreign language learners. *Annals of Dyslexia, 39,* 171–195.

GENERAL

Anastasi, A. (1988). *Psychological testing*. New York: Macmillan.

Bracken, B. A. (1988). Ten psychometric reasons why similar tests produce dissimilar results. *Journal of School Psychology, 26,* 155–166.

Sattler, J. M. (1988). *Assessment of children*. San Diego: Jerome M. Sattler.

Silver, L. B. (Ed.). (1989). *The assessment of learning disabilities: Preschool through adulthood*. Austin: PRO-ED.

Sternberg, R. J. (1992). Ability tests, measurements and markets. *Journal of Educational Psychology, 84,* 134–140.

Wallace, G., & Larsen, S. C. (1978). *Educational assessment of learning problems: Testing for teaching*. Boston: Allyn & Bacon.

NEUROPSYCHOLOGY

Lezak, M. D. (1983). *Neuropsychological assessment* (2nd ed.). New York: Oxford University Press.

McCue, M., Shelly, C., & Goldstein, G. (1986). Intellectual, academic and neuropsychological performance levels in learning disabled adults. *Journal of Learning Disabilities, 19*, 233–236.

McCue, M., Shelly, C., Goldstein, G., & Katz-Garris, L. (1984). Neuropsychological aspects of learning disability in young adults. *The International Journal of Clinical Neuropsychology, 6*, 229–233.

Pennington, B. F. (1991). *Diagnosing learning disorders: A neuropsychological framework*. New York: Guilford Press.

Rothstein, A., Benjamin, L., Crosby, M., & Eisenstadt, K. (1988). *Learning disorders: An integration of neuropsychological and psychoanalytic consideration*. Madison, CT: International University Press.

Rourke, B. P. (1985). *Neuropsychology of learning disabilities*. New York: Guilford Press.

NONVERBAL LEARNING DISABILITIES

Denckla, M. (1991). Academic and extracurricular aspects of nonverbal learning disabilities. *Psychiatric Annals, 21*, 717–724.

Rourke, B. P. (1988). The syndrome of nonverbal learning disabilities: Developmental manifestations in neurological disease, disorder, and dysfunction. *The Clinical Neuropsychologist, 2*, 293–330.

SCREENING

Perreira, D. C. (1989). Informal assessment of the learning disabled: Making the assessment count. In *support services for LD students in postsecondary education: A compendium of readings* (Vol. 2, pp. 85–92). Columbus, OH: Association on Handicapped Student Service Programs in Postsecondary Education.

TESTING INSTRUMENTS

Costenbader, V. K., & Perry, C. (1990). The Woodcock-Johnson Psycho-educational Battery–Revised [test review]. *Journal of Psychoeducational Assessment, 8*, 180–184.

Cuenin, L. H. (1990). Use of the Woodcock-Johnson Psycho-Educational Battery with learning disabled adults. *Learning Disabilities Focus, 5,* 119–123.

Dalke, C. (1988). Woodcock-Johnson Psycho-Educational Test Battery profiles: A comparative study of college freshmen with and without learning disabilities. *Journal of Learning Disabilities, 21,* 567–570.

Harris, K. R., & Reid, R. (1991). A critical review of the Slosson Intelligence Test. *Learning Disabilities Research & Practice, 6,* 188–191.

Hoy, C., & Gregg, N. (1986). The usefulness of the Woodcock-Johnson Psycho-Educational Battery cognitive cluster scores for learning disabled college students. *Journal of Learning Disabilities, 19,* 489–491.

Kramer, J. J., & Conoley, J. C. (Eds.). (1992). *The eleventh mental measurements yearbook.* Lincoln, NE: The University of Nebraska Press.

Leonard, F. C. (1991). Using Wechsler data to predict success for learning disabled college students. *Learning Disabilities Research & Practice, 6,* 17–24.

Mather, N. (1989). Comparison of the new and existing Woodcock-Johnson writing tests to other writing measures. *LD Focus, 4,* 84–95.

Mather, N. (1991). *Instructional guide to the Woodcock-Johnson Psycho-Educational Battery–Revised.* Brandon, VT: Clinical Psychology Publishing Co.

Mather, N., & Jaffe, L. E. (1992). *The Woodcock-Johnson Psycho-Educational Battery–Revised: Recommendations and reports.* Brandon, VT: Clinical Psychology Publishing Co.

Mental measurements yearbook. (annual). Lincoln: Buros Institute of Mental Measurements, Univesity of Nebraska.

Sandoval, J., Sassenrath, J., & Penaloza, M. (1988). Similarity of WISC-R and WAIS-R scores at age 16. *Psychology in the Schools, 25,* 373–379.

Slate, J. R., Frost, J., & Cross, B. (1990, Summer). Comparability of WISC-R and WAIS-R scores for a sample of college students with learning disabilities. *Learning Disability Quarterly, 13,* 205–208.

Slate, J. R., Frost, J., & Cross, B. (1991). WAIS-R stability for college students with learning disabilities. *Learning Disability Quarterly, 14,* 2–6.

Taymans, J. M. (1991). The use of the Self-Directed Search and the Self-Directed Search Form E with people with learning disabilities. *Learning Disabilities Research & Practice, 6,* 54.

Tests in print 3. (1983). Lincoln: Buros Institute of Mental Measurements, University of Nebraska.

WRITING ASSESSMENT

Duques, S. L. (1989). Grammatical deficiencies in writing: An investigation of learning disabled college students. *Reading and Writing: An Interdisciplinary Journal, 1,* 309–325.

Gajar, A. H., & Harriman, N. (1987). Identifying data based procedures for written expression disabilities at the university level. *Education, 107,* 252–258.

Gregg, N., & Hoy, C. (1990). Referencing: The cohesive use of pronouns in the written narrative of college underprepared writers, nondisabled writers, and writers with learning disabilities. *Journal of Learning Disabilities, 23,* 557–563.

Leuenberger, J., & Morris, M. (1990). Analysis of spelling errors by learning disabled and normal college students. *Learning Disabilities Focus, 5,* 103–118.

O'Hearn, C. O. (1989). Recognizing the LD college writer. *College English, 51,* 294–304.

Weiner, E. S. (1980). Diagnostic evaluation of writing skills. *Journal of Learning Disabilities, 13,* 41–53.

Information to be Addressed During the Screening Process

ADDITIONAL AREAS TO BE ADDRESSED

I. Current Areas of Difficulty

A. Reason for referral

B. Presenting problems

C. Perceived strengths and weaknesses (academic, personal, social, emotional, vocational)

II. Educational History

A. Postsecondary

1. Transcript—current classes and status
2. Grade-point average—probation, dismissal
3. Major
4. Receiving help from instructors or other campus services
5. Nonacademic activities (sports, fraternity-sorority, clubs)

    B. Elementary and secondary school

       1. Favorite and least-liked subjects

       2. Previous difficulties—extra help, special classes, LD diagnosis, retention

       3. Grades, transcript, class rank

       4. Absences—number per year, length

       5. Type of curriculum (college preparatory, vocational)

       6. SAT or ACT performance

    C. Number of schools attended

III. Medical History

    A. Auditory and visual acuity (hearing aid, glasses)

    B. Last physical examination

    C. Significant illnesses (seizures, ear infections, fevers, asthma, allergies)

    D. Injuries or surgery (head trauma, surgical complications)

    E. Recurring difficulties (headaches, eyestrain, dizziness, difficulty sleeping)

    F. Coordination (gross and fine motor)

    G. Alcohol and/or drug use (medication, nonprescription drugs, frequency, amount)

IV. Family History

    A. Family of origin (parents, siblings)

       1. Occupation

       2. Education (level, learning difficulties)

       3. Relationship to family members

       4. Family response to learning problems, level of support

    B. Current family (spouse and children)

       1. Occupation

       2. Education (level, learning difficulties)

       3. Relationship to family members

       4. Family response to learning problems, level of support

    C. Cultural background, second-language abilities

V. Employment History

A. Types of employment (volunteer or paid positions, full-time or part-time)

B. Difficulties with employment (unable to find a job, fired, not promoted)

C. Career goals, areas of interest

D. Vocational rehabilitation

VI. Developmental History

A. Birth history (premature, medical complications before, during, or after birth)

B. Acquisition of language and motor skills

C. Illnesses, difficulties during infancy or childhood

D. Activity level (present level versus level as a child)

VII. Psychological History

A. History of emotional illness

B. Participation in counseling or therapy

C. Self-perceptions of personality, attitudes, issues of locus of control

D. Others' perceptions of personality, attitudes

VIII. Academic Strengths and Weaknesses

A. Samples of current academic work (papers, notes, handwriting)

B. Reading
   1. Speed, rate (silent versus oral)
   2. Comprehension (literal versus figurative)
   3. Vocabulary
   4. Phonetic and decoding skills (sounding out unfamiliar words)
   5. Types of materials read (magazines, texts, newspapers, novels)

C. Writing
   1. Spelling
   2. Grammar
   3. Mechanics (punctuation, capitalization)
   4. Handwriting
   5. Sentence structure
   6. Proofreading abilities
   7. Word substitutions or omissions
   8. Development of content, organization of ideas
   9. Types of writing (note-taking skills, letters, messages, term papers, research papers, in-class writing versus homework)

D. Mathematics
   1. Types of courses (algebra, geometry, statistics, accounting)
   2. Types of errors (calculations, spacing, careless errors, confusing signs and symbols)
   3. Mathematical reasoning
   4. Comprehension of lectures
   5. Ability to do homework
   6. Difficulties with tests

E. Foreign language difficulties

F. Oral expression
   1. Finding the "right" word
   2. Difficulty expressing thoughts or feelings

IX. Processing Abilities

A. Visual (reading graphs, maps, charts)

B. Auditory (lectures, phone conversations)

C. Spatial (driving, sports, following written or oral directions)

D. Memory (visual, auditory, long-term, short-term, difficulty with specific types of information such as numbers, names, dates, technical terms)

E. Organization (with respect to school, personal life, work space)

F. Sequencing (planning, goal setting, prioritizing)

X. Study Skills and Work Habits

A. Learning-style preferences (visual, auditory, kinesthetic)

B. Studying
  1. Hours per day, length of time at one sitting
  2. Strategies, specific techniques (ability to adapt to different situations as needed)
  3. Ability to integrate information from a variety of sources
  4. Physical environment (silence versus studying with television or radio, lighting, library versus bedroom)
  5. Attention span, frustration level
  6. Motivation

C. Note taking
  1. Method or style of organization (outline, columns, mapping)
  2. Ability to identify pertinent information as opposed to recording every word
  3. Ability to keep up with lecture

D. Test taking
  1. Difficulties in studying for and taking different types of exams (essay, multiple-choice, take-home)
  2. Strategies for studying and test taking
  3. Anxiety or pressure and stress in an exam situation

E. Time management and organization
  1. Using a daily and semester calendar
  2. Budgeting time for completing studying and long-term assignments

  3. Remembering and promptly keeping appointments

  4. Staying on task

F. Attitude toward learning and formal education

XI. Interpersonal Skills

A. Verbal communication (self-expression, starting conversations)

B. Nonverbal communication (reading body language and facial expressions, understanding sarcasm and humor)

C. Social skills

D. Self-advocacy, independence

E. Relationships

  1. Establishing and maintaining friendships and relationships

  2. Difficulty meeting new people

  3. Working with others

  4. Dealing with authority figures

  5. Ability to accept criticism, defensiveness

XII. Personal Issues

A. Self-esteem, self-confidence

B. Special interests, hobbies

C. Life goals

McBURNEY RESOURCE CENTER
STUDENT INVENTORY

Name _____ Current Grade _____ Date _____

DIRECTIONS: Place + next to items that are easiest for you to do.
Place - next to items that are the most difficult for you to do.

A. GATHERING INFORMATION

____ College-level textbooks
____ Course lectures
____ Group discussion
____ Audiovisual materials
____ Audio tapes
____ Concrete experience
(e.g., by doing something)
____ Observation of others
____ Asking questions
____ Role playing
____ Other:_____

B. LEARNING ENVIRONMENT

____ Working independently
____ Working with a peer tutor
____ Participating in a small group/classroom
____ Participating in a large group/classroom
____ Listening to audio tapes
____ Other:_____
____ Other:_____

C. ASSIGNMENTS

____ Worksheets
____ Short papers (2-3 pages)
____ Term papers (10-20 pages)
____ Demo/lab projects
____ Art/media projects
____ Oral reports
____ Group discussions
____ Word problems/math
____ Map/charts/graphs
____ Internships/practicums
____ Other:_____

D. TEST FORMATS

____ Short answer
____ Essay
____ Multiple-choice
____ True-false
____ Matching
____ Computation/math
____ Oral examinations
____ Other:_____

DIRECTIONS: Check (✔) the areas that give you the most trouble

____ Going to class on time
____ Going to class prepared (e.g., taking pens, paper, etc.)
____ Becoming motivated to start work
____ Budgeting time
____ Sticking with an assignment until completion
____ Following oral directions
____ Following written directions
____ Organizing ideas and information
____ Drawing conclusions, making inferences
____ Understanding abstract concepts
____ Finding the "right word" to describe something orally
____ Expressing ideas precisely in writing
____ Writing legibly

____ Reading comprehension
____ Reading rate
____ Sounding out unfamiliar words
____ Mathematical reasoning and word problems
____ Mathematical computation
____ Remembering specific course vocabulary
____ Test-taking anxiety
____ Lack of self-confidence
____ Making new friends
____ Understanding humor and sarcasm
____ Making "small talk"

(Please Turn Over)

DIRECTIONS: CHECK THE AREAS IN WHICH YOU WOULD LIKE SUPPORT

____ General information on learning disabilities

____ An assessment of basic skills

____ Counseling services

____ Tutorial instruction

a) ____ Notetaking in lectures

b) ____ Outlining a textbook

c) ____ Writing a term paper

d) ____ Spelling

e) ____ Basic grammar skills (e.g., punctuation, sentence construction, etc.)

f) ____ Basic math skills

g) ____ Basic reading skills

h) ____ Test taking skills

I) ____ Locating information in the library

j) ____ Special tutorial help in _____

_____

k) ____ Other: _____

_____

_____

_____

DIRECTIONS: DESCRIBE YOUR MOTIVATION

_____

_____

_____

_____

_____

_____

DIRECTIONS: DESCRIBE YOUR ACADEMIC STRENGTHS

_____

_____

_____

_____

_____

_____

_____

Tests Frequently Used for Diagnosing Adults with Learning Disabilities

	Test	Publisher
INTELLIGENCE AND GENERAL ABILITY	*Detroit Tests of Learning Aptitude-Adult (DTLA)*	PRO-ED, Austin, TX
	Halsted-Reitan Neuropsychological Battery for Adults	Assessment Resources, Odessa, FL
	Kaufman-Brief Intelligence Test (KBIT)	American Guidance Service, Circle Pines, MN
	Modern Language Aptitude Test (MLAT)	The Psychological Corporation, San Antonio, TX
	Peabody Picture Vocabulary Test–Revised (PPVT-R)	American Guidance Service, Circle Pines, MN
	Raven Standard Progressive Matrices (Standard Kit)	The Psychological Corporation, San Antonio, TX
	Slosson Intelligence Test (SIT)	Slosson Education Publications, East Aurora, NY
	Stanford-Binet Intelligence Test, 4th ed.	Riverside Publishing Company, Chicago, IL

(continued)

	Test	Publisher
INTELLIGENCE AND GENERAL ABILITY (*continued*)	*Test of Non-Verbal Intelligence-2* (*TONI*)	PRO-ED, Austin, TX
	Wechsler Adult Intelligence Scale–Revised (*WAIS-R*)	The Psychological Corporation, San Antonio, TX
	Woodcock-Johnson Psycho-Educational Battery–Revised Tests of Cognitive Ability	DLM Teaching Resources, Allen, TX
INFORMATION-PROCESSING SKILLS	*Bender Visual Motor Gestalt Test*	American Guidance Service, Circle Pines, MN
	Benton Visual Retention Test–Revised	The Psychological Corporation, San Antonio, TX
	Bloomer Learning Test (*BLT*)	Brador Publications, Scotland, CT
	Detroit Tests of Learning Aptitude–Adult (*DTLA*)	PRO-ED, Austin, TX
	Goldman-Fristoe-Woodcock Auditory Skills Test Battery	American Guidance Service, Circle Pines, MN
	Goldman-Fristoe-Woodcock Test of Auditory Discrimination	American Guidance Service, Circle Pines, MN
	Lindamood Auditory Conceptualization Test–Revised (*LACT*)	Teaching Resources Corporation, Hingham, MA
	Test of Visual Motor Integration (*VMI*)	PRO-ED, Austin, TX
	Wechsler Memory Scales	The Psychological Corporation, San Antonio, TX
	Woodcock-Johnson Psycho-Educational Battery–Revised Tests of Cognitive Ability	DLM Teaching Resources, Allen, TX
LEARNING STYLES AND STUDY SKILLS	*Canfield Learning Style Inventory* (*LSI*)	Western Psychological Services, Los Angeles, CA
	The Center for Innovative Teaching Experiences Learning Style Instrument (*C.I.T.E.*)	Wichita Public Schools, Staff Development Center, Wichita, KS

(*continued*)

Test	Publisher
LEARNING STYLES AND STUDY SKILLS (*continued*)		
Kolb Learning Styles Inventory	McBer and Company, Boston, MA
Learning and Study Strategies Inventory (LASSI)	H & H Publishing Co., Clearwater, FL
Learning Style Inventory	Price Systems, Lawrence, KS
Productivity Environmental Preference Survey (PEP)	Price Systems, Lawrence, KS
ACADEMIC ACHIEVE-MENT		
Adult Basic Learning Examination (ABLE)	The Psychological Corporation, San Antonio, TX
Brigance Diagnostic Inventory of Essential Skills	Curriculum Associates, North Billerica, MA
Gallistel/Ellis Test of Coding Skills (G/E)	Montage Press, Hamden, CT
Gates-MacGinite Reading Test: Survey F	Houghton Mifflin, Boston, MA
Gray Oral Reading Tests–Revised (GORT-R)	PRO-ED, Austin, TX
Kaufman Test of Educational Achievement (K-TEA)	American Guidance Service, Circle Pines, MN
Nelson-Denny Reading Skills Test	Riverside Publishing Company, Chicago, IL
Orleans-Hanna Algebra Prognosis Test	The Psychological Corporation, San Antonio, TX
Peabody Individual Achievement Test–Revised (PIAT-R)	American Guidance Service, Circle Pines, MN
Reading Skills Diagnostic Test III (RSDT)	Brador Publications, Scotland, CT
Scholastic Abilities Test for Adults (SATA)	PRO-ED, Austin, TX
Stanford Diagnostic Math Test (SDMT)	The Psychological Corporation, San Antonio, TX
Stanford Diagnostic Reading Test (SDRT)	The Psychological Corporation, San Antonio, TX
Stanford Test of Academic Skills (TASK)	The Psychological Corporation, San Antonio, TX

(*continued*)

	Test	Publisher
ACADEMIC ACHIEVE-MENT (*continued*)	*Test of Mathematical Abilities* (*TOMA*)	PRO-ED, Austin, TX
	Test of Reading Comprehension (*TORC*)	PRO-ED, Austin, TX
	Test of Written Language–2 (*TOWL-2*)	PRO-ED, Austin, TX
	Test of Written Spelling–2 (*TWS-2*)	PRO-ED, Austin, TX
	Tests of Adult Basic Education (*TABE*)	CBT/McGraw-Hill, Monterey, CA
	Wide Range Achievement Test–Revised Edition (*WRAT-R*)	Jastak Associates, Wilmington, DE
	Woodcock-Johnson Psycho-Educational Battery—Tests of Achievement–Revised	DLM Teaching Resources, Allen, TX
	Woodcock Reading Mastery Test–Revised	American Guidance Service, Circle Pines, MN
LANGUAGE	*Bateria Woodcock de Psico-Educativa en Español* (*Spanish*)	DLM Teaching Resources, Allen, TX
	Bilingual Syntax Measure II	The Psychological Corporation, San Antonio, TX
	Clinical Evaluation of Language Functions—Diagnostic Battery (*CELF*)	The Psychological Corporation, San Antonio, TX
	English Language Skills Assessment in Reading Context (*ELSA*)	Newbury House Publishers, Rowley, MA
	Test of Adolescent Language–2 (*TOAL-2*)	PRO-ED, Austin, TX
	Test of Written Language–2 (*TOWL-2*)	PRO-ED, Austin, TX
	Woodcock Language Proficiency Battery	DLM Teaching Resources, Allen, TX

(*continued*)

Test	Publisher
SOCIAL AND BEHAVIORAL SKILLS AND ATTITUDES		
Coopersmith Self-Esteem Inventory	Consulting Psychologists Press, Palo Alto, CA
Fundamental Interpersonal Relations Orientation– Behavior (FRIO-B)	Consulting Psychologists Press, Palo Alto, CA
Janis and Field Feeling of Inadequacy Scale–Revised Version (for students with learning disabilities)	Lynda Price/Terry Collins, Project Extra, General College, University of MN, 140 Appleby Hall, 128 Pleasant St., SE, Minneapolis, MN 55455
Nowicki-Strickland Locus of Control–Adult Form	Emory University, Atlanta, GA
Piers-Harris Self-Concept Scale	Western Psychological Services, Los Angeles, CA
Scales of Independent Behavior	DLM Teaching Resources, Allen, TX
Tennessee Self-Concept Scale–Revised (TSCS)	Western Psychological Services, Los Angeles, CA
Test of Interpersonal Competency for Employment (TICE)	James Stanfield & Company, Santa Monica, CA
VOCATIONAL INTERESTS AND APTITUDES		
Aptitude Tests for Occupations (ATO)	PRO-ED, Austin, TX
Career Development Inventory (CDI) (School Form)	Science Research Associates, Chicago, IL
Career Maturity Inventory (CMI)	CBT/McGraw Hill, Monterey, CA
Career Occupational Preference System (COPS)	EDITS, San Diego, CA
Career Orientation Placement and Evaluation Survey (COPES)	EDITS, San Diego, CA
Differential Aptitude Test (DAT)	The Psychological Corporation, San Antonio, TX
Holland Self-Directed Search	Consulting Psychologists Press, Palo Alto, CA

(*continued*)

	Test	*Publisher*
VOCATIONAL INTERESTS AND APTITUDES (*continued*)	*Interest Determination, Exploration, and Assessment System* (*IDEAS*)	National Computer Systems, Minneapolis, MN
	Kuder Preference Record– Vocational (*Kuder-C*) and (*Kuder-E*)	Science Research Associates, Chicago, IL
	Occupational Aptitude Survey and Interest Schedule (*OASIS*)	PRO-ED, Austin, TX
	Strong-Campbell Interest Inventory	Stanford University Press, Stanford, CA
	Wide Range Interest-Opinion Test (*WRIOT*)	Jastak Associates, Wilmington, DE

APPENDIX E

Guidelines for Documentation of a Specific Learning Disability

THE UNIVERSITY OF CONNECTICUT PROGRAM FOR COLLEGE STUDENTS WITH LEARNING DISABILITIES (UPLD)

Students who are seeking support services from the University of Connecticut Program for College Students with Learning Disabilities (UPLD) on the basis of a diagnosed specific learning disability are required to submit documentation to verify eligibility under Section 504 of the Rehabilitation Act of 1973.

The following guidelines are provided in the interest of assuring that evaluation reports are appropriate to document eligibility. The Director of UPLD is available to consult with diagnosticians regarding any of these guidelines.

1. Testing *must* be comprehensive. It is not acceptable to administer only one test for the purpose of diagnosis. Minimally, domains to be addressed must include (but not be limited to):

a. *Aptitude.* The Wechsler Adult Intelligence Scale–Revised (WAIS-R) with subtest scores is the preferred instrument. The Woodcock-Johnson Psycho-Educational Battery–Revised: Tests of Cognitive Ability or the Stanford-Binet Intelligence Scale: Fourth Edition are acceptable.

b. *Achievement.* Current levels of functioning in reading, mathematics and written language are required. Acceptable instruments include the Woodcock-Johnson Psycho-educational Battery–Revised: Tests of Achievement; Stanford Test of Academic Skills (TASK); Scholastic Abilities Test for Adults; or specific achievement tests such as the Test of Written Language–2 (TOWL-2), Woodcock Reading Mastery Tests–Revised, or the Stanford Diagnostic Mathematics Test. The Wide Range Achievement Test–Revised is NOT a comprehensive measure of achievement and therefore is not suitable.

c. *Information Processing.* Specific areas of information processing (e.g., short and long term memory; sequential memory; auditory and visual perception/processing; processing speed) must be assessed. Use of subtests from the WAIS-R or the Woodcock-Johnson Tests of Cognitive Ability is acceptable.

This is not intended to be an exhaustive list or to restrict assessment in other pertinent and helpful areas such as vocational interests and aptitudes.

2. Testing must be *current.* In most cases, this means within the past three years. Since assessment constitutes the basis for determining reasonable accommodations, it is in a student's best interest to provide recent and appropriate documentation to serve as the basis for decision-making about a student's needs for accommodations in a college environment which is academically very competitive.

3. There must be *clear* and *specific* evidence and identification of a learning disability. Individual "learning styles" and "learning differences" in and of themselves do not constitute a learning disability.

4. *Test scores/data* should be included. This is important since certain University policies and procedures (e.g., petitioning for permission to substitute courses) require actual data to substantiate eligibility.

5. Professionals conducting assessment and rendering diagnoses of specific learning disabilities must be qualified to do so. Trained and certified and/or licensed psychologists, learning disabilities specialists, and educational therapists are typically involved in the process of assessment. Experience in working with an adult population is *essential.*

6. Evaluators should be able to demonstrate that the selection of assessment instruments is based upon their suitability (i.e., reliability and validity) for use with an adult population.

7. Diagnostic reports must include the names and titles of the evaluators as well as the date(s) of testing.

All documentation is confidential and should be submitted to:

Joan M. McGuire, Ph.D.
Director, University of Connecticut Program for
College Students with Learning Disabilities (UPLD)
A. J. Pappanikou Center on Special Education and
Rehabilitation: A University Affiliated Program
U-64, 249 Glenbrook Road
Storrs, CT 06269-2064

(McGuire, J. M., Anderson, P. L., & Shaw, S. F., 1992)

APPENDIX F

Regional Learning Disability Contact Persons in the United States and Canada

The following individuals are members of the Association on Higher Education and Disability (AHEAD) and have generously offered to serve as contact persons for our readers.

UNITED STATES

Northeast Region

Nancy Oliker
University of Vermont
Special Student Services
A-170 Living/Learning Center
Burlington, VT 05405-0384
802-545-4602

Patricia Gillespie-Silver
University of Massachusetts at Amherst
Disabled Student Services
321 Berkshire House
Amherst, MA 01003
413-545-4602

Southern Region

Cessie Sanchez
Palo Alto College
Special Populations
1400 West Villaret
San Antonio, TX 78224-2499
512-921-5287

Arlene Stewart
University of North Carolina–Raleigh
P.O. Box 26053
Raleigh, NC 27611
913-715-0543

Midwest Region

Lydia Block
Counseling and LD
The Ohio State University
150 Pomerene Hall
1760 Neil Avenue
Columbus, OH 43210-1297
614-292-3307

Cathy Trueba
McBurney Disability Resource Center
905 University Avenue
University of Wisconsin–Madison
Madison, WI 53715-1005
608-263-5177

Susan Vogel
Department of Educational Psychology
Counseling and Special Education
Northern Illinois University
DeKalb, IL 60115
815-753-8420

Western Region

M. Kay Runyan
Learning Disabilities
University of California at Berkeley
230 Golden Bear Circle
Berkeley, CA 94720
415-566-4819

Molly Sandperl
Disabilities Resource Center
Stanford University
123 Meyer Library
Stanford, CA 94305-3094
415-723-1039

CANADA

Ann Kerby
Advancement and Academic Support
Concordia University
7141 Sherbrooke Street, Ad. 121
Montreal, PQ H4B 1R6 Canada
514-848-3501

Isabel Shessel
Special Needs
Seneca College
1750 Finch Avenue, East
North York, ON M2J 2X5 Canada
416-491-5050

Marc Wilchesky
Coordinator, LD Program, Counseling and Development Ctr.
York University
4700 Keele St.
North York, ON M3J 1P3 Canada
416-736-5297

APPENDIX G

Application Forms with Optional Checkoff Boxes

CLARK UNIVERSITY

Services for Students with Disabilities

Clark University provides special services to students with physical and learning disabilities. If you have a disability and wish to volunteer information, please check the appropriate box(es). The information you share will be kept confidential and will serve to help us prepare services and auxiliary aids if and as needed. Please note that Clark offers support services, not a comprehensive special needs program.

I have a   ☐ Vision Impairment   ☐ Hearing Impairment

☐ Mobility Impairment   ☐ Learning Disability

☐ Other (please explain) _____

BOSTON UNIVERSITY

Boston University encourages qualified students with disabilites to apply for admission. You may voluntarily request information about available services by writing to the Disability Services Office. *Your inquiry will be confidential and will not determine your eligibility for admission.* To assist us, you mav check the appropriate box:

☐ Blind/visually impaired   ☐ Deaf/hard-of-hearing

☐ Learning disabilities   ☐ Mobility impaired

UNIVERSITY OF CONNECTICUT

Students with Disabilities

The University of Connecticut encourages students with disabilites to apply for admission.

If you desire, you may voluntarily provide additional information which will be treated as confidential and have no negative effect on your eligibility for admission.

The Admissions Office will be happy to send you information about services available. To obtain such information, please check the appropriate box.

☐ Visual Impairments ☐ Hearing Impairments

☐ Mobility Impairments ☐ Learning Disabilities

APPENDIX H

Follow-Up Letter to Prospective Applicants

Dear SALUTATION:

Thank you for applying to The University of Connecticut. In your application, you identified yourself as a student who has a learning disability.

To ensure that the information in your application accurately reflects your academic ability and potential to succeed at the University, we suggest that you voluntarily submit further information. It is your choice to submit this information which will be used solely to determine the University's ability to meet your special needs. All information will be kept confidential, and your decision to withhold it will not subject you to adverse treatment. **The following information should be submitted to: The University of Connecticut Program for College Students with Learning Disabilities, Special Education Center, U-64, 249 Glenbrook Road, Storrs, CT, 06269-2064, Attention: Dr. Joan M. McGuire, Director (203-486-0178).**

(1) Results of a complete psychoeducational evaluation, which should at a minimum include:

  a. The Wechsler Intelligence Scale (WAIS-R or WISC-R), including subscale scores. Results should be less than three years old and the test must be administered by a certified school psychologist or a licensed psychologist;

  b. standardized achievement testing;

  RECOMMENDED ACHIEVEMENT TESTS:

    Woodcock-Johnson Psycho-educational Battery
    Stanford Achievement Test or the upper level of this
      test: TASK
    California Achievement Test
    Metropolitan Achievement Test
    Iowa Test of Basic Skills
    SPA Achievement Series

(2) a sample of your written work;

(3) a letter from a school psychologist, learning disabilities teacher, or guidance counselor to verify any waiver (e.g. foreign language) granted in high school;

(4) a copy of your current or most recent Individualized Education Program (IEP), Annual Review data, and/or other placement team data (these data should be available if you have previously received special education services); and

(5) any additional data, including diagnostic, medical, or educational reports which are available.

Upon receipt of this information, your application for admission to The University of Connecticut will be reviewed and a decision on your admission request will be made. If none of the information is received by The University of Connecticut Program for College Students with Learning Disabilities (UPLD) within six weeks from the date of this letter, it will be assumed that you have decided not to voluntarily submit the requested data and your application for admission will be considered under the standard admission procedure.

If you have already made arrangements to forward this material prior to receiving this letter, please disregard this request.

Sincerely,

Assistant to the
Director of Admissions

BU:cms

cc: Dr. Joan McGuire
       U-64

APPENDIX I

Sample Nondiscrimination Statement, University of Connecticut

The University of Connecticut Policy Regarding People with Disabilities

The University of Connecticut is committed to achieving equal educational opportunity and full participation for persons with disabilities. It is the University's policy that no qualified person be excluded from participating in any University program or activity, be denied the benefits of any University program or activity, or otherwise be subjected to discrimination with regard to any University program or activity. This policy derives from the University's commitment to non-discrimination for all persons in employment, access to facilities, student programs, activities, and services.

A person with a disability must be ensured the same access to programs, opportunities, and activities at the University as all others. Existing barriers, whether physical, programmatic, or attitudinal, must be removed. There must be ongoing vigilance to ensure that new barriers are not erected.

The University's efforts to accommodate people with disabilities must be measured against the goal of full participation and integration. Services and programs to promote these benefits for people with disabilities shall complement and support, but not duplicate, the University's regular services and programs.

Achieving full participation and integration of people with disabilities requires the cooperative efforts of all of the University's departments, offices, and personnel. To this end, the University will continue to strive to achieve excellence in its services and to assure that its services are delivered equitably and efficiently to all of its members.

Adopted June, 1989

APPENDIX J

Academic Accommodations Policy Statement, University of California at Berkeley

PLAN FOR ACCOMMODATING THE ACADEMIC NEEDS OF STUDENTS WITH DISABILITIES

This plan describes the roles of various units and individuals at the University of California at Berkeley in ensuring that students with disabilities receive appropriate accommodations in their instructional activities, as mandated by Federal and State law and by University policy. The fundamental principles of nondiscrimination and accommodation in academic programs were set forth in the implementing regulations for Section 504 of the Federal Rehabilitation Act of 1973 (which were published in the May 4, 1977, *Federal Register*, p. 22684); these regulations provide that:

> No qualified handicapped student shall, on the basis of handicap, be excluded from participation in, be denied the benefits of, or otherwise be subjected to discrimination under any . . . postsecondary education program or activity . . . [84.43 (a)]

[An institution] . . . shall make such modifications to its academic requirements as are necessary to ensure that such requirements do not discriminate or have the effect of discriminating, on the basis of handicap, against a qualified handicapped applicant or student. . . . Modifications may include changes in the length of time permitted for the completion of degree requirements, substitution of specific courses required for the completion of degree requirements, and adaptation of the manner in which specific courses are conducted. [84.44 (a)]

University of California policies are presented in the University of California Guidelines Applying to Nondiscrimination on the Basis of Handicap, which appear as Section 20 in Part B of the University's Policies Applying to Campus Activities, Organizations, and Students.

Academic Accommodations Policy Board. At Berkeley, the Administration and the Academic Senate have created an Academic Accommodations Policy Board. The Board has three primary functions: (a) advising the Vice Chancellor for Undergraduate Affairs about policies and procedures related to the provision of academic accommodations for students with disabilities; (b) developing mechanisms for increasing faculty understanding of disabilities and their accommodation in an academic setting; and (c) assisting the Vice Chancellor in resolving any disagreements that might arise concerning particular academic accommodations. The Policy Board is comprised of seven members:

- Three faculty members who are knowledgeable in the area of learning and disabilities (nominated by the Senate Committee on Committees). One of these will serve as the Board's chair.

- Three professional staff members of the Disabled Students' Program who are also knowledgeable in these areas (appointed by the Vice Chancellor for Undergraduate Affairs). The staff member who determined an accommodation for a particular student will not participate in the Board's review of that accommodation; he or she will be replaced by another staff member appointed by the Vice Chancellor for Undergraduate Affairs.

- The campus 504 Compliance Coordinator for Student Access to Programs, who has responsibility for ensuring that the policies and procedures the campus developed comply with Federal, State, and University requirements.

Vice Chancellor for Undergraduate Affairs. The Vice Chancellor for Undergraduate Affairs, a member of the faculty, is the senior administrative officer responsible for campus policies and services affecting students with disabilities. With the advice of the Academic Accommodations Policy Board, the Vice Chancellor ensures that these policies and services are both educationally sound and responsive to the needs of students with disabilities.

If there is disagreement over the appropriateness of a particular academic accommodation, the Vice Chancellor (in consultation with the Academic Accommodations Policy Board and the Assistant Chancellor for Legal Affairs) makes a final determination in the matter. In the rare instance when an instructor refuses to comply with the Vice Chancellor's decision, the Vice Chancellor and the Provost who oversees the instructor's school or college are jointly responsible for ensuring that the accommodation is provided in a timely manner and that appropriate administrative sanctions are pursued in accordance with established policy and procedures. (The University's Faculty Code of Conduct, presented in Section 015 of the *Academic Personnel Manual*, defines as unacceptable conduct "knowing violation of the University policy, including the pertinent guidelines, applying to nondiscrimination against students on the basis of handicap.")

Campus 504 Compliance Coordinator for Student Access to Programs. The Campus 504 Compliance Coordinator, who is a member of the Vice Chancellor for Undergraduate Affairs' staff, serves as a resource to the Vice Chancellor, other members of the Administration, and faculty members in meeting their obligation to provide appropriate academic accommodations to students with disabilities. The 504 Coordinator advises them about the requirements of Federal law and University policy and works to resolve informally any disagreements about accommodations for students with disabilities. As described above, the 504 Coordinator serves as a member of the Academic Accommodations Policy Board and has responsibility, in consultation with the Assistant Chancellor–Legal Affairs, for ensuring that the policies and procedures the campus develops comply with Federal, State, and University requirements. The 504 Coordinator also serves as a resource to students with disabilities who believe that they are not receiving appropriate accommodations or that they are being treated in a discriminatory manner. The 504 Coordinator may be reached at 641-6727.

Disability Specialists. Several professional staff members of the Disabled Students' Program are responsible for evaluating the documentation concerning a student's disability (which has been submitted by a physician, psychologist, learning disability specialist, or comparable professional), estimating the disability's effect on the student's participation in academic activities, and advising the student concerning appropriate learning strategies. These Disability Specialists also determine the nature of accommodations in instruction and testing that might be required for a student, consistent with policies developed by the Academic Accommodations Policy Board and approved by the Vice Chancellor for Undergraduate Affairs. The Disability Specialists explain the nature and purpose of the accommodations to the student and to the student's instructors at the beginning of each semester so that they may be implemented in a timely manner.

Instructors. Senate and non-Senate faculty (including Graduate Student Instructors) are responsible for conducting classes and administering examinations, as described in the By-Laws of the Academic Senate. They should be mindful, in developing tests or other procedures for evaluating students' academic achievement, that both Federal regulation and University policy require that:

> . . . methods should be provided for evaluating the achievement of students who have a handicap that impairs sensory, manual, or speaking skills as will best ensure that the results of the evaluation represents the student's achievement in the course, rather than reflecting the student's impaired sensory, manual, or speaking skills (except where such skills are the factors that the test purports to measure).

If an instructor has questions about an accommodation that a Disability Specialist has determined is appropriate for a particular student, he or she should contact the Disability Specialist promptly. If the instructor disagrees with the accommodation, he or she should seek its review by contacting the Campus 504 Coordinator (at

642-6727) within five days of being notified about it by the Disability Specialist or the student. The instructor should provide the accommodation until it is either set aside or modified by the 504 Coordinator or the Vice Chancellor for Undergraduate Affairs. The 504 Coordinator will attempt to resolve the disagreement informally; if this effort does not succeed, the 504 Coordinator will refer the instructor to the Academic Accommodations Policy Board, which will review the matter and advise the Vice Chancellor for Undergraduate Affairs, whose decision will be final.

Department Chairs and Deans. The administrative heads of departments and schools are responsible for ensuring that the instructional staff of their units understand the Berkeley Campus's full commitment to implementing Federal law and University policy assuring nondiscrimination for students on the basis of handicap. If an instructor fails to provide an academic accommodation that a Disability Specialist has determined is appropriate for a student, the instructor's Department Chair (or Dean), in consultation with the Campus 504 Compliance Coordinator, will ensure that the accommodation is provided in a timely manner until the matter has been reviewed by the Academic Accommodations Policy Board and a final decision reached by the Vice Chancellor for Undergraduate Affairs.

Time Frame for Resolving Disagreements. In situations where there is disagreement concerning the appropriateness of a particular accommodation, every effort should be made to resolve the disagreement as expeditiously as possible. In general, each phase of the review process (informal resolution by the Campus 504 Coordinator, review by the Academic Accommodations Policy Board, and final determination by the Vice Chancellor for Undergraduate Affairs) should be completed within five working days. As described above, the accommodation should be provided by the instructor until it is either set aside or modified by the Campus 504 Coordinator or the Vice Chancellor for Undergraduate Affairs.

Editor's Note: This policy statement is under revision in light of the ADA and will be available in the Fall 1993 in final form.

APPENDIX K

Course Substitution Policy Statement, University of Connecticut

POLICY AND PROCEDURES REGARDING MODIFICATIONS OF THE UNIVERSITY'S QUANTITATIVE (Q) OR FOREIGN LANGUAGE REQUIREMENT FOR STUDENTS WITH DOCUMENTED LEARNING DISABILITIES

Policy

The University of Connecticut offers comprehensive support services for students with documented learning disabilities through the University of Connecticut Program for College Students with Learning Disabilities (UPLD) which is located in the A. J. Pappanikou Center on Special Education and Rehabilitation: A University Affiliated Program, School of Education. It is the goal of UPLD to help students learn skills and strategies and develop the confidence to use them to be successful within the bounds of typical University policies and requirements. Sometimes, however, if the documented disability precludes learning in the quantitative or foreign language area, the University will permit the substitution of specific courses in order to best serve a student. Because these requirements are often important parts of a program, each case must be carefully considered on an individual basis before a decision is made by the appropriate Dean.

Procedures

The following procedures must be followed if a student with a documented learning disability is seeking a modification of the University's Q or Foreign Language requirement:

1. The petition process should begin as soon as there is strong objective evidence (e.g., previous documented difficulties) that the student will be unable to fulfill the requirement.

2. The student must provide the University Program for College Students with Learning Disabilities (UPLD) with *current*, relevant and comprehensive documentation and assessment data from a team of certified professionals. This documentation must substantiate both the specific learning disability and its specific impact upon the student's ability in the area of mathematics or foreign language learning.

3. A complete case history is required to document the student's history of problems in quantitative or foreign language learning from high school until the date of the petition. This case history should include:

   a. a personal statement by the student indicating the reasons for the request including prior experiences with the subject matter; and

   b. the names of courses and grades, as well as letters from high school personnel and/or college faculty attesting to the student's efforts and diligence in attempting to master the subject matter.

Upon completion of these steps, the documentation and the supporting evidence from the case history are reviewed by a team from the A. J. Pappanikou Center on Special Education and Rehabilitation including the Director of the University Program for College Students with Learning Disabilities (UPLD), a diagnostic evaluator and additional members such as faculty and staff with expertise in learning disabilities. A decision regarding the validity of a student's petition is rendered within one (1) month of the team's receipt of the entire file. The decision and recommendation of the team are then forwarded to the Dean of the student's college or school with a copy sent to the student. The student will be notified in a timely fashion of the final decision rendered by the Dean of his/her college or school. Any student who receives an exemption is expected to fulfill the University's Q or Foreign Language requirements according to the guidelines for selecting alternative courses.

GUIDELINES FOR ALTERNATIVE COURSES

When a course substitution is granted, the following guidelines exist with respect to meeting University requirements. To fulfill the Q-requirement, two alternative courses must be chosen from Groups VI, VII, and VIII. To fulfill the Foreign Language requirement, an equivalent number of courses must be chosen from Column A (Literature) of Group IV, and/or from Group V. The following are examples from extensive course offerings which can be substituted.

Group IV: Literature Category

CLAS 103	Classical Mythology
ENGL 113	Renaissance and Modern Western Literature
FREN 270W	Major Works of French Literature in Translation
GERM 240W	German Literature in Translation
ITAL 244	Main Currents of Italian Literature After the Renaissance
RUSS 232W	Masterpieces of 19th Century Russian Literature in Translation
SPAN 281	Great Works of Spanish Literature from its Origins to the Golden Age

Group V: Non-Western/Latin American Category

ANTH 100	Other Peoples' Worlds: Asia, Africa, the Americas
ANTH 222	Indians of South America
HIST 106	The Roots of Traditional Asia
LAMS 190W	Perspectives on Latin America
PHIL 264	Classical Chinese Philosophy and Culture
SOCI 226	Modern Africa

Group VI: Philosophical or Ethical Analysis

LING 101	Language and Mind
PHIL 102	Philosophy and Logic
PHIL 104	Philosophy and Social Ethics
SCI 240	The Nature of Scientific Thought

Group VII: Social Scientific and Comparative Analysis

ANTH 106	Introduction to Anthropology
GEOG 200	Economic Geography
LING 102	Language and Environment
POLS 173	Introduction to American Political Processes
SOCI 125	Race, Class, and Gender

Group VIII: Science and Technology

ANSC 160	The Science of Food
BIOL 110	Introduction to Botany
GEOG 205	Introduction to Physical Geography
GEOL 111	The Age of the Dinosaurs
MARN 170	Introduction to Oceanography
NUSC 165	Fundamentals of Nutrition
PHYS 155Q	Introductory Astronomy

Policy Issues Relating to Accommodations for Students with Learning Disabilities: A Step-by-Step Approach, Boston University

- Documentation of the learning disability must be on file with the Learning Disabilities Support Services (LDSS) office before an accommodation will be recommended.

- Documentation required is typically a psycho-educational evaluation. Evaluations should include information on the student's intellectual functioning, processing abilities, and achievement. Actual subtest scores and grade/age equivalent scores may be included in the documentation. Ideally, testing should have been administered within the last three years.

- In order for accommodations to be provided, documentation must clearly state that a learning disability exists. Terminology such as "learning difference" or "learning problem" does not constitute an LD.

- Students are encouraged to self-identify that they have a learning disability with their professors at the beginning of the semester. They should make this initial contact during office hours and be prepared to discuss strengths, weaknesses and the types of accommodations that may be necessary. The LDSS staff is available to both faculty and students to assist them in developing reasonable accommodations.

- If students choose not to inform their instructors that they have a learning disability, but subsequently change their minds during the course of the semester, then such changes in accommodations should be made at least *two* weeks in advance.

- Some students with documented learning disabilities may prefer to have LDSS staff write a letter of support regarding a particular accommodation request. Accommodations will be recommended by LDSS staff after carefully reviewing the diagnostic evaluation and the student's previous scholastic performance. A 1–2 page screening summary letter should not be construed as an endorsement of an accommodation request.

- The types of accommodations provided to students with learning disabilities may vary depending on the nature of the learning disability and the course content. For example, a student may benefit from an oral exam in one subject area, but not in another. A student's past scholastic record of success with one accommodation over another is often the best predictor of success. It is not unusual for there to be an initial trial-and-error period of finding the best way to evaluate a student's ability to demonstrate mastery of course material.

- It is the responsibility of the student and the faculty member to find a suitable location for administering the exam in accordance with the suggested accommodations made by the LDSS staff. If this is a hardship to the faculty member, then the LDSS office should be given timely notification so alternative arrangements can be made.

APPENDIX M

Postsecondary Learning Disability Resources for Professional Development

HIGHER EDUCATION AND DISABILITY INFORMATION RESOURCES

Apple Office of Special Education Programs
20525 Mariana Avenue
Cupertino, CA 95014
408-973-6484

Association on Higher Education and Disability (AHEAD)
P.O. Box 21192
Columbus, OH 43221-0192
614-488-4972 (Voice/TDD)
614-488-1174

Council for Exceptional Children (CEC)
1920 Association Drive
Reston, VA 22091-1589
703-620-3660

Council for Learning Disabilities (CLD)
P.O. Box 40303
Overland Park, KS 66204
913-492-8755

Department of Justice (DOJ)
Office on the Americans with Disabilities Act
Civil Rights Division
P.O. Box 66118
Washington, DC 20035-6118
202-514-0301
202-514-0381 (TDD)

Disabled Students Programs and Services
California Community Colleges Chancellor's Office
1107 Ninth Street
Sacramento, CA 95814

Equal Employment Opportunity Commission (EEOC)
1801 L Street, NW
Washington, DC 20507
202-663-4900
800-800-3302 (TDD)

HEATH Resource Center
One Dupont Circle, Suite 800
Washington, DC 20036-1193
202-939-9320
800-54-HEATH (Voice/TDD)

IBM National Support Center for Persons with Disabilities
4111 Northside Parkway
Atlanta, GA 30327
800-426-2133

Learning Disabilities Association of America (LDA)
4156 Library Road
Pittsburg, PA 15234
412-341-1515 or 341-8077

Learning Disabilities Association of Canada
323 Chapel Street, Suite 200
Ottawa, Ontario
CANADA K1N7Z2
613-238-5721
235-5391 (Fax)

Library of Congress
National Library Service for the Blind and
  Physically Handicapped
1291 Taylor Street, NW
Washington, DC 20542
800-424-8567
202-707-5100

National Center for Learning Disabilities
  (NCLD)
99 Park Avenue
New York, NY 10016
212-687-7211

National Network of LD Adults (NNLDA)
808 North 82nd Street
Scottsdale, AZ 85257

Orton Dyslexia Soceity (ODS)
Chester Building, Suite 382
8600 LaSalle Road
Baltimore, MD 21204-6020
301-296-0232
800-ABCD-123

President's Committee on Employment of
  People with Disabilities
1111 20th Street, NW, Suite 600
Washington, DC 20036
202-653-5010
202-653-5050 (TDD)

Recording for the Blind
20 Roszel Road
Princeton, NJ 08540
609-452-0606
800-221-4792

FACULTY IN-SERVICE RESOURCES

Dispelling the Myths: College Students and Learning Disabilities

K. Garnett & S. LaPorta, 1984
Hunter College of the City University of New York
695 Park Avenue
New York, NY 10021
212-772-4888

This booklet explains what learning disabilities are and what faculty members can do to help students with learning disabilities succeed in higher education. Chapters cover an understanding of learning disabiliites, the college-level student, learning issues, writing, math, foreign language, and faculty assistance; references and resources are included.

Faculty Guidebook—Working with Students with Learning Disabilities at New River Community College

HEATH Resource Center
One Dupont Circle, Suite 800
Washington, DC 20036-1193

This guidebook was created by the Center for the Learning Disabled, Learning Achievement Program, New River Community College (Dublin, VA). The main body of the guidebook is a compilation of brief articles written by various faculty members of New River Community College. Among others, topics addressed include suggestions for teaching general academic subjects, options for instruction in the social sciences, strategies and suggestions for mathematics and data-processing teachers, secretarial and related subjects, drafting technologies, and electrical-electonic technologies.

A Guide for Delivering Faculty Inservice on the Learning Disabled College Student

> J. Geis, M. Morris, & J. Leuenberger, Univerity of Nebraska-Lincoln, January 1989. OSERS #158—Public Domain Document

> This handbook is designed to serve as a guide for the preparation and implementation of faculty in-service training sessions in a postsecondary setting.

A Guide for Delivering Faculty Inservice on the Learning Disabled College Student

> HEATH Resource Center
> One Dupont Circle, Suite 800
> Washington, DC 20036-1193

> Produced by the LD-Talents Project at the University of Nebraska (Lincoln, NE), the guide focuses on providing faculty in-service programs and training on working with students with learning disabilities.

AHEAD Inservice Education Kit (1988)

> AHEAD
> P.O. Box 21192
> Columbus, OH 43221-0192

> This is a complete faculty awareness presentation that includes a cassette tape, handouts, and documentation regarding the inclusion of students with disabilities in campus life as well as suggested simulation exercises. A brochure, "College Students with Learning Disabilities" may also be ordered in quantity from AHEAD.

Keymakers II: A Staff Development Program for Postsecondary Educators (2 manuals and videotape)

> A. Grasso-Ryan
> MACLD
> 1821 University Avenue, Suite 494N
> Saint Paul, MN 55104
> 612-646-6136

Developed by the Minnesota Association for Children and Adults with Learning Disabilities, 1989, this resource has three parts:

LEADERS' MANUAL. Keymakers II was designed to inform the instructor of the unique characteristics and needs of students with learning disabilities.

PARTICIPANTS' MANUAL. A working manual to assist technical college educators in developing a working understanding of students with learning disabilities.

VIDEO: *Keymakers II* (see description in section on videotapes).

Learning Disabilities Program: Inservice Manual

M. Palek, D. Williams, & T. Walsh, 1988
South Seattle Community College
6000 16th Avenue SW
Seattle, WA 98106

A manual for an in-service program for faculty and administration regarding services for students with learning disabilities. Case studies are presented. Areas covered in the manual include assessment, program accommodation, counseling, peer support, learning assistance, technological aids, testing and minority students.

Opening Doors: A Faculty Guide to Assisting Learning Disabled College Students

J. S. Kuperstein, J. Olsen, N. Poppel, & M. Weir (1988)
Central Regional Connections
New Jersey State Department of Education
Joan Ikle CRC
Middlesex County College
155 Mill Road
P.O. Box 3050
Edison, NJ 08818-3050
908-548-6000

This booklet provides data, faculty questions and answers, suggestions regarding strategies and media and adaptive equipment, and support services available for students with learning disabilities. A resource index is included.

The Postsecondary Learning Disabilites Primer:
A Training Manual for Service Providers

WCU Bookstore
Western Carolina University
Cullowhee, NC 28723
704-227-7346

Developed by A. C. Stewart, The Learning Disabilities Training Project, Western Carolina University, 1989, this training manual provides narrative versions of workshops and handout materials for these areas: (a) transition from high school to postsecondary education; (b) institutional considerations in LD policy and programming, (c) academic concerns and accommodations, (d) social skills, academic advising, and counseling issues and concerns, (e) faculty and staff training; and (f) career choices and job skills.

Reasonable Accommodations: A Faculty Guide to Teaching
College Students with Disabilities (2nd printing)

Professional Staff Congress/City University of New York
25 West 43rd Street
New York, NY 10036

This handbook provides faculty with practical information and suggestions to help them meet the needs of students with disabilities in their classrooms.

College Students with Learning Disabilities: A Handbook

S. A. Vogel, 1993, 4th ed.
LDA Bookstore
4156 Library Road
Pittsburg, PA 15234
412-341-1515

This booklet is a useful resource to use with faculty, administrators, staff, or students. Specific suggestions are offered for students and faculty. This latest edition also includes a section for graduate and professional school students.

Understanding Learning Disabilities: Guide for Faculty

Office of Student Affairs
237 Leavey Center
Georgetown University
Washington, DC 20057
202-687-6985

This is an informational handbook from Georgetown University on the nature of learning disabilities in higher education and policies regarding students with learning disabilities. In addition to chapters such as "Zig Zag Lightning in the Brain: Introduction to Learning Disabilities" and "The Faulty Radio: Learning Disabilities at Competitive Universities Explained," additional chapters provide information on the symptoms of learning disabilities, a checklist to screen for learning disabilities, ways to advise and teach students with learning disabilities, accommodations, and policy in accordance with Section 504 of the Rehabilitation Act of 1973. Support services are discussed.

The University of Michigan Learning Disabilities Handbook for Students, Faculty, and Administration

E. Singer, University of Michigan, August 1991
The Services for Students with Disabilities Office
625 Haven Hall
Ann Arbor, MI 48109-1045
313-763-3000

A handbook written by a student with a learning disability that provides information on understanding learning disabilities, preparation strategies, stress management, improving time management and study skills, and using college resources. There is a processing and mailing charge.

CONTENT-SPECIFIC FACULTY RESOURCES

A Guide for Teaching Remedial Mathematics to Students with Learning Disabilities

J. Corn, 1988
Queensborough Community College
Department of Mathematics and Computer Science
222-05 56th Avenue and Springfield Boulevard
Bayside, NY 11364-1497
718-631-6364

This is a guide for topics in arithmetic and algebra as well as for remediation of specific difficulties. The materials are intended to focus attention on potential weaknesses of LD students and to offer suggestions for presentation.

Math and the Learning Disabled Student: A Practical Guide for Accommodations

Paul Nolting, 1991
Academic Success Press, Inc.
P.O. Box 2567
Pompano Beach, FL 33072
305-785-2034

This book is written for counselors and mathematics instructors, but it would also be a useful reference for diagnosticians and direct service providers. Learning disabilities are defined, reasons for mathematics learning problems are explained, information on learning and testing accommodations are provided, and case studies of students with learning disabilities are reviewed. Recommendations for accommodations are provided for individuals in the following areas: visual processing speed and visual processing, short-term memory and auditory processing, fluid reasoning, and long-term retrieval. This is an excellent resource to assist professionals in identifiying specific accommodations for students with learning disabilities who have difficulty with mathematics.

TRAINING OF SERVICE PERSONNEL

Independent Strategies for Efficient Study

Karen J. Rooney
Educational Enterprises
2115 Willowick Lane
Richmond, VA 23233
801-273-1760

This is a guide that teaches organizational strategies to improve performance. The strategies are simple, concrete, and flexible so that the ultimate outcome is a generalization of skills. The strategies are appropriate for elementary, secondary, and college students because they are organizational and developmental in scope.

Learning Specialist Training Manual

J. M. McGuire & A. V. Litt, The Univerity of Connecticut
Program for Students with Learning Disabilities
(UPLD), rev., 1992
A. J. Pappanikou Center on Special Education and
Rehabilitation
University of Connecticut, 249 Glenbrook Road, Box U-64
Storrs, CT 06269-2064

This manual provides training information developed for learning specialists in UPLD. It focuses on the following five areas: philosophy, policy, and procedures; roles and responsibilities; sample forms; resources; and strategies.

The Postsecondary Student with Learning Disabilities:
Issues in Identification and Integration

P. S. Tomlan
PST Educational Consultants
8241 West Walker Drive
Littleton, CO 80123

This course is designed for personnel preparation and is available to service providers working with persons with learning disabilities. It is a 30-contact-hour course for formal instruction with accompanying criteria; the content is carefully structured and sequenced.

Service Operations Manual

HEATH Resource Center
One Dupont Circle, Suite 800
Washington, DC 20036-1193

This manual was developed by the Northern Illinois Postsecondary Education Project, Northern Illinois University (De Kalb, IL). The manual describes a system for delivering services to students with learning disabilities at community colleges. The seven key components of this technical assistance project are legal foundations, needs assessment, technical assistance plans, transition plans, in-service training in awareness of learning disabilities, recommendations for service coordinators in staff development, and continuation of services.

Six Training Manuals from the Technical Assistance for Postsecondary Education (T.A.P.E.) Project

HEATH Resource Center
One Dupont Circle, Suite 800
Washington, DC 20036-1193

Produced by Northern Illinois University (De Kalb, IL), the manuals are designed to train community college personnel who work with individuals with learning disabilities. The topics of the manuals include specific intervention strategies, reading and written language, mathematics, counseling, and service networking.

TRAINING OF VOLUNTEER AND PEER TUTORS

Assisting College Students with Learning Disabilities:
A Tutor's Manual

P. Adelman & D. Olufs, AHEAD, 2nd printing, 1990
Item No. 1300
AHEAD
P.O. Box 21192
Columbus, OH 43221-0192

This manual is for service providers and tutors who work with college-level students with learning disabilities. The manual is divided into two sections: Section I includes information on learning disabilities with specific guidelines for developing tutoring programs in major academic areas, and Section II presents a case study of a student with a learning disability.

Handbook for Volunteer Tutors

HEATH Resource Center
One Dupont Circle, Suite 800
Washington, DC 20036-1193

This handbook was developed by Project SUCCESS, Richland College (Dallas, TX). It is filled with tips for both students and tutors, as well as materials to increase awareness and understanding of learning disabilities.

Peer Mentoring: A Support Group Model for Students with Disabilities (1992)

Cricket Park
AHEAD
P.O. Box 21192
Columbus, OH 43221-0192
614-488-4972

This manual contains an application of a support group model based on building trust and confidence between first-year students and older students to improve retention and development of interpersonal skills.

Volunteer Reader/Taping Service Handbook

Christy Lendman, University of Wisconsin-Stout for the Association on Handicapped Student Service Programs in Postsecondary Education, copyright AHEAD, 1991
To order, contact:
Item No. 1250
AHEAD
P.O. Box 21192
Columbus, OH 43221-0192

The Reader/Taping Service is a program designed to record textbooks onto tape for students whose disabilities limit the reading of print material. The objective of this training manual is to describe how a volunteer Reader/Taping Service can be implemented. The manual includes legal obligations, procedures and forms for access to Recording for the Blind and training of individual readers.

VIDEOTAPES

College: A Viable Option

HEATH Resource Center
One Dupont Circle, Suite 800
Washington, DC 20036-1193

This 20-minute videotape is produced by the University Bound LD Students Transition Project of the Univesity of Utah, Disabled Student Services (Salt Lake City, UT); it discusses what a learning disability is, learning strategies, and compensatory techniques.

Degrees of Success: Conversations with College Students with Learning Disabilities (1992)

Georgeann duChossois
The Access to Learning Program
New York University
566 La Guardia Place, #701
New York, NY 10012
212-998-4980

This videotape focuses on the experiences of college students with learning disabilities as described by students themselves. The students have diverse backgrounds, attend various types of colleges, and have had different experiences coping with their learning disabilities. The video is accompanied by a packet containing suggested questions for discussion and other resource information.

Effective Teaching for Dyslexic/All College Students

Center for the Advancement of College Teaching
Box 1867
Brown University
Providence, RI 02912
401-863-1141

Dr. Harriet Sheridan, who was Professor of English and director of the Center for Advancement of College Teaching at Brown University, states that the purpose of the videotape is to expand the knowledge of dyslexia to secondary and postsecondary institutions. Interviews are conducted with professors in four subject areas: math, German, English, and history. They discuss their individual approaches, which exemplify good teaching techniques. Dr. Sheridan describes the elements of good teaching and focuses on organization as central to the class syllabus, lectures, and class discussions. A descriptive guide is available.

How Difficult Can This Be?

PBS Video
1320 Braddock Place
Alexandria, VA 22314-1698
703-739-5380

This video is a presentation of the The F.A.T. City Learning Disability Workshop. Richard Lavoie demonstrates through simulation activities the frustration, anger, and tension children with learning disabilities encounter in the classroom. Areas of learning disabilities that are simulated include processing difficulties, visual perception, motivation, attention, behavior, visual-motor coordination, oral expression, reading and decoding, and auditory processing. A guide is available to assist with issues concerning learning disabilities and suggestions for group exercises and discussions.

Instructional Strategies for Learning Disabled Community College Students

Dr. Dolores Perin
CASE Institute for Research and Development in
  Occupational Education
City University of New York Graduate School
25 West 43rd Street, Room #620
New York, NY 10036
212-642-2937

Instructional Strategies for Learning Disabled Community College Students (1989) is a comprehensive training package that consists of a viewing guide and eight sets of videotaped vignettes on two tapes. The purpose is to stimulate discussion among instructors, tutors, and other community college faculty and staff to enhance instruction for students with learning disabilities. The viewing guide provides an overview of learning disabilities and issues relevant to the college population, a description of the purpose of the vignettes and suggestions for use of the material, background information, descriptions, and suggested questions for use in staff development activities. A bibliography is also included.

Keymakers II: Technical College Instruction of Students with Learning Disabilities

Kathy Heikkila, Executive Director
MACLD
1821 University Avenue, Suite 494N
Saint Paul, MN 55104
612-646-6136

This is the video component to the Keymakers *II* manuals. It specifically addresses the unique needs of students with learning disabilities at the vocational and technical college level. A balance of information is provided from a variety of sources: consumers, parent advocates, technical college faculty, and rehabilitation personnel. Ideas are shared on how to expand traditional curricular materials by changing the format. This joint project by the

Minnesota Association for Children and Adults with Learning Disabilities and the Minnesota Board of Vocational-Technical Education is a must for rehabilitation personnel. In addition, a companion participant guide and staff development leader's manual are available at additional cost.

Learning Disabilities: Coping in College (1985)

Handicap Student Services
Wright State University
Dayton, OH 45435-0001
513-873-2141

This video is a very useful resource for presenting a realistic overview of college life through the eyes of students with learning disabilities. Faculty and support staff will find the video useful in trying to understand the unique learning needs of these students.

Reader/Taping Service Videotape

Item No. 1251
AHEAD
P.O. Box 21192
Columbus, OH 43221-0192
614-488-4972

This videotape is a companion to Lendman's *Volunteer Reader/ Taping Service Handbook*, produced by the University of Wisconsin-Stout.

Understanding Learning Disabilities in Higher Education:
A Georgetown University Perspective (1991)

Office of Student Affairs
237 Leavey Center
Georgetown University
Washington, DC 20057
202-687-6985

This video, written and produced at Georgetown University, presents the experiences of an accomplished faculty member with dyslexia and those of a student needing assessment to determine if a learning disability exists. The video describes the assistance the university provides to faculty and students regarding policies and procedures and role of advocacy in working with students with learning disabilities.

TECHNOLOGICAL AIDS FOR COLLEGE STUDENTS

Portable Spell-Checker and Thesaurus

> Franklin Learning Resources
> 122 Burrs Road
> Mt. Holly, NJ 08060
> 800-525-9673

Portable four-track tape recorders

> Handi-Cassette
> American Printing House for the Blind, Inc.
> 1839 Frankfort Avenue
> P.O. Box 6085
> Louisville, KY
> 502-895-2405

> Recording for the Blind, Inc.
> 20 Roszel Road
> Princeton, NJ 08540
> 609-452-0606
> 800-221-4792

Talking Calculator

> Sharp Talking Calculator EL-640
> Sharp Electronics Corporation
> Sharp Plaza
> 20600 South Alameda Street
> Carson, CA 90810
> 213-637-9488

Adaptive Listening Devices

> Easy Listener
> Phonic Ear, Inc.
> 3880 Cypress Drive
> Petaluma, CA 94954
> 800-772-3374

Optical Character Recognition

Xerox/Kurzweil
Kurzweil Personal Reader
Kurzweil Computer Products
9 Centennial Drive
Peabody, MA 01960
800-343-0311

Proofreading Software

Grammatik IV
Reference Software
330 Townsend Street, Suite 123
San Francisco, CA 94107
415-541-0222

Correct Grammar
Writing Tools Group
1 Harbor Drive, Suite 111
Sausalito, CA 94965
415-332-8692

Speech Recognition

DragonDictate
Dragon Systems, Inc.
320 Nevada Street
Newton, MA 02160
617-965-5200

Speech Synthesizer

DECtalk Products
Digital Equipment Corporation
Digital Drive MK102-1/K06
Merrimack, NH 03054
603-884-4047

OTHER RESOURCES

Access to Education for the Disabled: A Guide to Compliance with Section 504 of the Rehabilitation Act of 1973 (1992)

Salome Heyward
McFarland & Company, Inc.
P.O. Box 611
Jefferson, NC 28640
919-246-4460

This book focuses on pertinent parts of the Rehabilitation Act of 1973 and analyzes how to put them into effect. Hypothetical situations based on actual cases show how the act has been interpreted by the courts and the Department of Education's Office of Civil Rights.

Accommodating Students with Specific Learning Disabilities in Post-Secondary Education: A Position Paper

CAPED
Debra Schinn, LD Specialist
5858 Wilshire Boulvard
Los Angeles, CA 90036
213-935-9980

This is a comprehensive paper that covers a broad range of methods of accommodations and suggestions for class modifications.

AHEAD Annotated Bibliography of Information Sources

Anne Augustine, Editor, 1990 revision
Item No. 1450
AHEAD
P.O. Box 21192
Columbus, OH 43221-0192
614-488-4972

This contains descriptions and contact information on more than 300 books, journals, associations, and products that may be of use to the postsecondary service provider to students with disabilities. Available as a loose-leaf manual or on disk (Macintosh HyperCard Version 2.0).

Facilitating an Academic Support Group for Students with Learning Disabilities: A Manual for Professionals (1989)

J. Johnson
AHEAD
P.O. Box 21192
Columbus, OH 43221-0192
614-488-4972 (Voice/TDD)

This manual outlines a practical approach for addressing a variety of issues that students with learning disabilities confront in a postsecondary setting. It is written for professionals who are in the process of designing a group curriculum to meet the needs of this population or redesigning existing group structures. The suggestions assist professionals in faciliting an academic support group for students with learning disabilities by outlining sessions and describing specific activities to develop specific study strategies and interpersonal skills.

Policy and Guidelines Applying to Nondiscrimination on the Basis of Disability (1988)

The University of Wisconsin System
1220 Linden Drive
1856 Van Hise Hall
Madison, WI 53706
608-262-2321

This is a comprehensive policy statement and listing of guidelines from the university's Board of Regents for compliance under Section 504 for students with disabilities in higher education. A revision is planned for Fall, 1993 that will include considerations under the ADA.

NEWSLETTERS

Information from HEATH

> National Clearinghouse on Postsecondary Education for
> Individuals with Disabilities
> One Dupont Circle, NW, Suite 800
> Washington, DC 20036-1193
> 800-544-3284

> The HEATH Resource Center publishes a newsletter, *Information from HEATH*, twice a year. Fact sheets and other information are available free by request.

Postsecondary LD Network News

> *Postsecondary LD Network News*
> A. J. Pappanikou Center on Special Education and Rehabilitation
> University of Connecticut
> U-64
> 249 Glenbrook Road
> Storrs, CT 06269-2064

> The *Postsecondary LD Network News* is published three times per year by the Postsecondary LD Unit of the A. J. Pappanikou Center on Special Education and Rehabilitation at the University of Connecticut. The newsletter is available on a subscription basis. The cost is $20 per year for individuals and $30 for a school or agency.

PERIODICALS ON TECHNOLOGY

Closing the Gap

> P.O. Box 68
> Henderson, MN 56044
> 612-248-3294

> (6 issues/$26 per year)

ConnSense Bulletin

University of Connecticut, U-64
Storrs, CT 06269-2064
203-486-0171

(3 issues/$15 per year)

STUDENT-FOCUSED MATERIALS

*A Study of Job Clubs for Two-Year College Students with
Learning Disabilities*

HEATH Resource Center
One Dupont Circle, Suite 800
Washington, DC 20036-1193
800-544-3284

This report was created by the "Using Job Clubs to Assist in
Transition to Work for Postsecondary Students with Disabilities"
Project, The Ohio State University (Columbus, OH). The report
describes the results of a study of how job clubs help 2-year college
students with learning disabilities improve their job-seeking skills
and work-world savvy in preparation for making a successful transition from school to work.

Study Skills and Learning Strategies for Transition

HEATH Resource Center
One Dupont Circle, Suite 800
Washington, DC 20036-1193
800-544-3284

This curriculum guide, produced by the University Bound LD
Students Transition Project of the University of Utah, Disabled
Student Services (Salt Lake City, UT), provides students with
learning disabilities with the skills and strategies they will need to
increase their level of success with the high school curriculum; to
graduate with their senior class; to meet entrance requirements for
the postgraduate school, college, or university of their choice; and
to be successful in the higher education environment.

TAP into Success with Transitional Assistance for Postsecondary Students

HEATH Resource Center
One Dupont Circle, Suite 800
Washington, DC 20036-1193
800-544-3284

Produced by the TAPS Project at Amarillo College (Amarillo, TX), this handbook is designed to help students with learning disabilities make the transition into college or employment.

APPENDIX N

Tape-Recording Agreement Form, Ball State University

Ball State University Tape-Recorded Lecture Policy Agreement

Students with disabilities who are unable to take or read notes have the right to tape record class lectures for their personal study only.* Lectures taped for this purpose may not be shared with other people without the consent of the lecturer. Tape-recorded lectures may not be used in any way against the faculty member, other lecturers, or students whose classroom comments are taped as a part of the class activity. Information contained in the tape-recorded lecture is protected under federal copyright laws and may not be published or quoted without the express consent of the lecturer and without giving proper identity and credit to the lecturer.

Pledge: I have read and understand the above policy on tape-recorded lectures at Ball State University, and I pledge to abide by the above policy with regard to any lectures I tape while enrolled as a student at Ball State University.

_____
Student signature

_____
Date

_____
Witness

*84.44 of Section 504 of the Rehabilitation Act of 1973 (P.L. 93-112, amended P.L. 93-516)

Procedures for Obtaining Exam Testing Assistance, Ohio State University

PROCEDURES FOR OBTAINING EXAM TESTING ASSISTANCE

Exam taking assistance is available through this Office in conjunction with your instructor(s). Please provide and comply with the following information as soon as you are aware of your testing needs. ALL EXAMS must be scheduled in our office at least 5 days in advance of the examination:

Meet with your professor to discuss your disability & exam arrangements. Find out what type of exams you will have (multiple choice, essay, short answer). If your instructor can provide you with the proper accommodations you need for your disability for your exams, you can take the exams in their office or in the classroom under their supervision. If they can't, then you may take the exams through our office with your instructor's cooperation. The following procedures must be followed in order to take your exams at ODS.

1. Schedule Date, Time Length and Type of Accommodation of exam at ODS.

   All exams are to be scheduled at the same time as your regular class is scheduled to take it. Exceptions are only when you have back-to-back classes or if you have an evening class or exam. If you have an evening class or exam some professors will allow you to take the exam the following day or give it to you before or after class. If you have a conflict check with your instructor before scheduling your exams to see when he/she will allow you to take it. (Math exams 050 to 150 are to be scheduled the day after your class takes it at night. A letter from our office must be on file each OTR at the Math office to allow you to take your Math exams at our office.)

2. It is necessary to notify ODS staff when scheduling exams of special accommodations that are required for each exam (i.e., reader, scribe, computer, distraction-free space or double time). If ODS staff is not aware of these needs at that time, these accommodations will not be made available at the time of your taking the exam. For example, space for double time will not be available if not scheduled originally. You must schedule in advance a reader or scribe if needed and inform us if the reader/scribe will need any special background. (ODS will schedule and contact the volunteer making all the necessary arrangements).

3. If special adaptive equipment is needed (e.g., CCTV, large print, taped exams, slide projector, special lighting or a computer) in order for you to take your exam. You must let us know in advance at the time you schedule your exams.

4. An Exam Proctoring Checklist must be completed by your course instructors and be on file in our office for every exam you take at ODS. A Midterm permanent checklist completed by your <u>course instructors</u> can be kept on file by ODS if the conditions for all your midterm exams are the same. A separate <u>Final Exam Proctoring Checklist</u> must be completed and on file in our office for each final exam that you are taking during finals week in our office.

5. For each course you must have a Proctoring Checklist Form filled out completely and <u>signed</u> by your instructor before any scheduling of exams will be done in our office. <u>Exception</u>: Students enrolled in Math courses 050, 075, 104, 130, 131, 148, and 150 will have a proctoring checklist form provided for them by the Math Dept. only if they have filled out a VERIFICATION LETTER REQUEST FORM for their specific Math course.

6. DELIVERY and RETURN arrangements is the STUDENT'S responsibility when taking exams at ODS. Exams can be handled in one of the following ways.

DELIVERY	RETURN
STUDENT	STUDENT
INSTRUCTOR	INSTRUCTOR
DEPARTMENT DESIGNEE	DEPARTMENT DESIGNEE
NOT BY CAMPUS MAIL	ODS (within 24 hours only)

Remember ODS <u>does not</u> pick up your exams or coordinate your exams arrangements!

<u>CHANGES/CANCELLATIONS OF EXAMS</u>: If a change in arrangements is necessary, please notify us as soon as possible. If you cancel an exam and want to reschedule for the next day or later, ODS must have written or verbal permission from your instructor. If you schedule volunteer assistance and fail to notify us of cancellations twice within a quarter, you will lose your privilege of volunteer assistance for the remainder of the quarter.

Each student is responsible for understanding and complying with the above procedures. If you have any questions or concerns regarding the above procedures please contact us before scheduling your exams.

APPENDIX P

Alternative Testing Request Form, Ohio State University

OSU DISABILITY SERVICES MIDTERM PROCTORING CHECKLIST

Please fill out all sections. See reverse side for instructions.

Section A: Course Information

1. Student's Name:_____ Qtr./Yr.:_____

   Instructor's Name:_____ Course: _____

   Instructor's office: _____ Tel. Ext.:_____

   Information provided by:_____ Instructor:_____
   (signature)

Section B: Exam Information
Please fill out all information. Failure to do so will result in delays.

2. **Is this proctor sheet permanent for all midterms this quarter?** (circle) Yes No
3. Dates of:

   Midterms ____ ____ ____ Quizzes _____
             1   2   3
4. Class meets on (circle) M T W R F at _____ (time)
5. Time (hrs./mins.) allowed for exams in classroom for:

   Midterms __:__ Quizzes __:__

Section C: Proctoring Conditions
All midterms and quizzes will be administered using standard proctoring conditions unless otherwise specified.

6. Must take exam at same time as regular class ____ (7:30 am–5:30 pm, Monday-Friday only.)
7. May take exam close to regular class time (same day) ____
8. Check only those items that apply:

   ____ No scrap paper ____ Notes allowed

   ____ No Calculator   ____ OPEN book allowed

   ____ No Dictionary   ____ Formula sheet allowed
9. ____ Student may keep exam _____
   (signature)

Special Instructions _____
_____

Section D: Exam / Quiz Delivery and Return

10. **Method of Delivery to ODS:**   **Method of Return:**
    DO NOT MAIL EXAMS

    ____ Student (in sealed envelope) ____ Student returns to: _____
    (address)

    ____ Instructor

    ____ Dept. Designee   ____ Instructor/Dept. designee to pickup

    ____ Faxed to 292-4190   ____ ODS returns to: _____
    (address)
    *see back

ODS Use Only
Date Exam Received: ____ Int:_____
Date Exam Taken: _____ Time Started:_____ Time Ended: _____
Blue Sheets: _____ Stf Int:_____ Stf Int:_____
EGR#3/Final proct sheet

PROCTORING CONSIDERATIONS

Each student is to meet with his/her professor to discuss his/her disability and exam arrangements. Student is then responsible for returning completed proctor sheet to ODS and scheduling his/her own exams.

INSTRUCTIONS

Section A: Course Information

1. Please fill out all of the requested information. This helps ODS know who to contact in case of a problem.

Section B: Exam Information

2. Circling "yes" at the top of Section B indicates that for the quarter all midterms/quizzes for this course for this student are to be proctored in the same manner. Any changes are to be made in writing prior to the specified midterm/quiz in question. If not marked, a new proctor sheet will need to be made out for each midterm/quiz taken.
3. List test dates of all midterms and quizzes. If currently unknown, **we will need a written statement advising of dates and times before scheduling.**
4. Mark the day and time that the class regularly meets.
5. Indicate the length of time allowed for exams and quizzes in the classroom.
   Our office has determined the appropriate accommodations and amount of extended time for each student. Standard extended time in most cases means *time and a half* (e.g. 1 hr. = 1 hr. 30 mins.). In special cases students may be eligible for *double time*. ODS cannot proctor untimed exams.

Section C: Proctoring Conditions

6. Checking this space indicates that the exam should be proctored at the same time as the regular class. ODS can only fullfill this request between the hours of 7:30 am and 5:30 pm Monday through Friday (space permitting).
7. Checking this space indicates that the exam may be proctored on the same day of original exam at the nearest available time.
8. Exams will be administered under standard proctoring conditions. If instructor wishes to change those conditions s/he may do so by checking those appropriate items in number 8.
9. No student will be allowed to keep exam materials unless authorized by a signature in this section.

Section D: Method of Exam/Quiz Delivery and Return

10. Indicate the method of delivery and return. Midterms and quizzes may be delivered and returned in any combination of the following:

Delivery:	**Return:**
Student (in sealed envelope)	Student (in sealed envelope)
Instructor	Instructor
Department Designee	Department Designee
Faxed to 292-4190	ODS (within 24 hours)

To ensure that exams/quizzes reach the ODS office prior to exam/quiz date/time, in addition to maintaining security, instructors are **NOT TO MAIL** exams through campus mail. Students bringing their own exams must bring them is a sealed envelope. Exams leaving the ODS office are sealed in another envelope and are signed out by the person picking up/returning the exam.

*Exams faxed to ODS at 292-4190 must be accompanied with a cover sheet providing name of student taking the exam and the number of pages in the exam.

Any questions, comments, or special requests about exam accommodations should be directed to Jim Baker, Coordinator, ODS Academic Support Services at 292-3307.

Effective Instructional Handouts, Western Carolina State University

HANDOUT 3.6: IMPORTANT INSTRUCTOR CHARACTERISTICS

Helps students distinguish what is important from what is not

Helps students stay interested in learning

Tailors the presentation to the student's level of development

Tries to reach all the different kinds of students in the course

Works to keep students attentive

Keeps students aware of the course goals

Helps students bring prior learning to bear on new material

Presents the subject matter clearly

Provides the right amount of structure: Neither too much nor too little

Guides students in their study

Provides helpful feedback

Helps students apply what they have learned to new situations

Helps students retain what they have learned

Is approachable

Respects students

Understands students

Keeps students challenged

Knows the subject well enough

Emphasizes what is important in the field

HANDOUT 3.7: FACULTY INTERVENTIONS

Outline on the board ahead of time.

Hand out complete outlines.

Put key words on the board.

Give the student a note-taking device.

Be redundant in noting major causes ("The third cause of the Civil War is . . .")

Beware of conceptual density, of cramming in too much.

Give time for questions in class.

Allow various methods of output.

Word questions carefully.

Avoid negative questions.

Mutiple-part questions should be in outline form.

Underline key words.

Use clear, simple questions.

Draw lines between multiple-choice questions.

Use a syllabus and stick to it.

Give hints on how to study.

Let the student know the focus of the course; include sample questions and answers.

Talk about your discipline.

Be clear in writing questions.

Talk with students, especially if they recieve low grades.

HANDOUT 3.8: FACULTY INSTRUCTIONAL TECHNIQUES AND PROCEDURES

Type all handout material for class.

Leave space between lines for notes on handouts.

Make sure that clear directions are given orally and in writing.

Use manuscript rather than cursive writing on chalkboards.

Stand away from windows when lecturing.

Close doors to classrooms.

Invite students with learning disabilities to sit near the front of the room.

Isolate critical reading materials for special projects in the library so that they are readily available.

Give time in class for feedback and questions.

Stick to dates given in the syllabus.

When a student asks a question that you just answered, avoid expressing annoyance.

When a student does not get the information the first time, repeat it distinctly or ask if he or she needs it in a different form.

Organize your lecture so that comments follow in a logical sequence.

Avoid going off on tangents from the lecture outline.

Allow extended deadlines for projects or let students with learning disabilities start early.

Encourage students to use proofreaders for written assignments.

Allow students to tape lectures.

Allow essay rather than multiple-choice exams.

Provide alternatives to computer-scored answer sheets.

Allow alternative testing options.

APPENDIX R

User-Friendly Course Syllabus, Boston College

MINIMUM REQUIREMENTS FOR USER-FRIENDLY SYLLABUS

TITLE AND NO. OF COURSE   TIME

PROFESSOR'S NAME

    Office location

    Office hours

    Phone #

REQUIRED TEXTS

    Supplemental Tests

PURPOSE OF THE COURSE

    A short paragraph giving a broad overview of the content to be covered, value of the course to the major, etc. If the course meets requirements for professional licensure, indicate which ones. Identify prerequisites.

COURSE OBJECTIVES

The course objectives should be stated in terms of learner outcomes.

COURSE REQUIREMENTS

Requirements should be clearly identified with the specifics of format, length, etc. Time schedule for handing in drafts and final projects should be provided.

GRADING POLICY

The criteria for judging the quality of each requirement along with point values should be assigned.

STANDARD FORMAT FOR EACH TOPIC

DATE	TOPIC	REQUIRED READING	GENERAL PURPOSE OF LECTURE

(STUDY QUESTIONS can be included for each topic in order to reinforce reading.)

(Mooney, 1992)

References

Aase, S., & Price, L. (1987). Building the bridge: LD adolescents' and adults' transition from secondary to postsecondary settings. In D. Knapke & C. Lendman (Eds.), *Capitalizing on the future* (pp. 126–149). Columbus, OH: Association on Handicapped Student Service Programs in Postsecondary Education.

ADA Requirements Handbook. (1991). Washington, DC: U.S. Department of Justice.

Adelman, P. B., & Vogel, S. A. (1990). College graduates with learning disabilities: Employment attainment and career patterns. *Learning Disability Quarterly, 13*, 154–166.

Aksamit, D., Morris, M., & Leuenberger, J. (1987). Preparation of student services professionals and faculty for serving learning disabled college students. *Journal of College Student Personnel, 28*, 53–59.

Albert, J. J., & Fairweather, J. S. (1990). Effective organization of postsecondary services for students with disabilities. *Journal of College Student Development, 31*, 445–453.

Algozzine, B., & Ysseldyke, J. E. (1986). The future of the LD field: Screening and diagnosis. *Journal of Learning Disabilities, 19*, 394–398.

Alley, G. R., Deshler, D. D., Clark, F. L., Schumaker, J. B., & Warner, M. M. (1983). Learning disabilities in adolescent and young adult populations: Research implications (Part II). *Focus on Exceptional Children, 15*(9), 1–14.

American Psychiatric Association. (1987). *Diagnostic and statistical manual of mental disorders* (3rd ed.). Washington, DC: American Psychiatric Association.

Americans with Disabilities Act (ADA), P.L. 101-336, 42 U.S.C. § 12101 note.

Americans with Disabilities Act. (1990, Fall). *Information from HEATH, 9*(2), 1.

Anderson, P. L. (1991). *Evaluation procedures: From diagnostic reports to program planning.* Presentation at the Sixth Annual College for Learning Disabled Students Conference, New York, NY.

Anderson, P. L. (1992, June). *Current issues and trends in diagnostic assessment: Exploring the impact on LD college programming.* Paper presented at the University of Connecticut Fourth Annual Postsecondary Training Institute, Farmington, CT.

Anderson, P. L. (1993). *Continuum of LD assessment services for postsecondary institutions.* Unpublished material. University of Connecticut, A. J. Pappanikou Center on Special Education and Rehabilitation, Storrs, CT.

Anderson, P. L. (1993). *The assessment process for students with learning disabilities.* Unpublished material. University of Connecticut, A. J. Pappanikou Center on Special Education and Rehabilitation, Storrs, CT.

Anderson, P. L. (1993). *Referral questions to ask a diagnostician regarding college students with learning disabilities.* Unpublished material. University of Connecticut, A. J. Pappanikou Center on Special Education and Rehabilitation, Storrs, CT.

Anderson, P. L. (1993). *Areas to be addressed during the screening process.* Unpublished material. University of Connecticut, A. J. Pappanikou Center on Special Education and Rehabilitation, Storrs, CT.

Anderson, P. L. (1993). *Tests frequently used for diagnosing adults with learning disabilities.* Unpublished material. University of Connecticut, A. J. Pappanikou Center on Special Education and Rehabilitation, Storrs, CT.

Anderson, P. L., & Brinckerhoff, L. C. (1989). Interpreting LD diagnostic reports for appropriate service delivery. In J. J. Vander Putten (Ed.), *Proceedings of the 1989 AHSSPPE national conference* (pp. 92–100). Columbus, OH: Association on Handicapped Student Service Programs in Postsecondary Education.

Anderson, P. L., & McGuire, J. M. (1991). *Connecticut Postsecondary Learning Disability Technical Assistance Center: Annual report, 1990–91.* Storrs: A. J. Pappanikou Center on Special Education and Rehabilitation: A University Affiliated Program, University of Connecticut.

Ariel, A. (1992). *Education of children and adolescents with learning disabilities.* New York: Macmillan.

Association on Higher Education and Disability. (1991). *College students with learning disabilities* (2nd ed.). Columbus, OH: Association on Higher Education and Disability.

Aune, E., & Ness, J. (1991a, July). *Inservice training for students with disabilities in the Minnesota Technical College system.* Paper presented at the AHSSPPE National Conference, Minneapolis, MN.

Aune, E., & Ness, J. (1991b). *Tools for transition: Preparing students with learning disabilities for postsecondary education.* Circle Pines, MN: American Guidance Service.

Ballard, J., Ramirez, D., & Zantal-Wiener, K. (1987). *Public Law 94-142, Section 504, and Public Law 99-457: Understanding what they are and are not.* Reston, VA: Council for Exceptional Children.

Barr, M., & Fried, J. (1981). Facts, feelings, and academic credit. In J. Fried (Ed.), *Education for student development: New directions for student services* (No. 15). San Francisco: Jossey-Bass.

Bashook, P. G., & Dockery, J. L. (Eds.). (1992). *Handbook on board certification and the ADA.* Evanston, IL: American Board of Medical Specialists.

Beatty, L. S., Madden, R., Gardner, E. F., & Karlsen, B. (1984). *Stanford Diagnostic Mathematics Test* (3rd ed.). San Antonio, TX: Psychological Corporation.

Beirne-Smith, M., & Deck, M. D. (1989). A survey of postsecondary programs for students with learning disabilities. *Journal of Learning Disabilities, 22,* 456–457.

Bender, L. (1946). *Bender Visual Motor Gestalt Test.* New York: American Orthopsychiatric Association.

Biehl, G. R. (1978). *Guide to the Section 504 self-evaluation for colleges and universities.* Washington, DC: National Association of College and University Business Officers.

Bigler, E. D. (Ed.). (1990). *Traumatic brain injury: Mechanisms of damage, assessment, intervention, and outcome.* Austin, TX: PRO-ED.

Biller, E. F., & White, W. J. (1989). Comparing special education and vocational rehabilitation in serving persons with specific learning disabilities. *Rehabilitation Counseling Bulletin, 33,* 4–17.

Blalock, J. W. (1981). Persistent problems and concerns of young adults with learning disabilities. In W. M. Cruickshank & A. A. Silver (Eds.), *Bridges to tomorrow: Vol. 2. The best of ACLD* (pp. 35–56). Syracuse, NY: Syracuse University Press.

Block, L., Burke, L., Carlton, P. M., Knapke, D., Walkenshaw, D., Porter, D., Beaulieu, C., Marin, K., & Runyan-Brown, K. (1986). Making sense of diagnostic tests and accommodations for students with learning disabilities. In J. S. Opliger (Ed.), *Charting the course: Directions in higher education for disabled students* (pp. 61–66). Columbus, OH: Association on Handicapped Student Service Programs in Postsecondary Education.

Bloland, P. A. (1991). Key academic values and issues. In P. L. Moore (Ed.), *Managing the political dimension of student affairs* (pp. 27–41). San Francisco: Jossey-Bass.

Borich, G. D., & Nance, D. D. (1987). Evaluating special education programs: Shifting the professional mandate from process to outcome. *Remedial and Special Education, 8,* 7–16.

Brandenberger, C., McGuire, J. M., Milliron, D., Pollack, R., Stewart, A., & Tomlan, P. (1989). Highlights of selected service delivery models for students with learning disabilities. In *Support services for LD students in postsecondary education: A compendium of readings* (Vol. 2, pp. 153–164). Columbus, OH: Association on Handicapped Student Service Programs in Postsecondary Education. Also in D. Knapke & C. Lendman (Eds.), *Proceedings of the 1988 National AHSSPPE Conference* (pp. 81–90). Columbus, OH: Association on Handicapped Student Service Programs in Postsecondary Education.

Brinckerhoff, L. C. (1985). Accommodations for college students with learning disabilities: The law and its implementation. In J. Gartner (Ed.), *Proceedings of the eighth annual AHSSPPE conference* (pp. 89–95). Columbus, OH: Association on Handicapped Student Service Programs in Postsecondary Education.

Brinckerhoff, L. C. (1986). *The McBurney Resource Center Student Inventory.* Madison, WI: University of Wisconsin–Madison.

Brinckerhoff, L. C. (1989). Diagnostic considerations for students with learning disabilities at selective colleges. In *Proceedings of the next step: An invitational symposium on learning disabilities in selective colleges* (pp. 114–136). Cambridge, MA: Harvard University.

Brinckerhoff, L. C. (1990). Section 508: Expanding computer access to students with learning disabilities. In support services for LD students in postsecondary education: A compendium of readings (vol. 2, pp. 237–239) Columbus, OH: AHSSPPE.

Brinckerhoff, L. C. (1991). Establishing learning disability support services with minimal resources. *Journal of Postsecondary Education and Disability, 9,* 184–196.

Brinckerhoff, L. C. (in press). Self-advocacy: A critical skill for college students with learning disabilities. *Journal of School and Community Health.*

Brinckerhoff, L. C., & Anderson, P. L. (1989). *Northeast Technical Assistance Center for Learning Disability College Programming, Progress Report 1988–90.* Storrs: University of Connecticut.

Brinckerhoff, L. C., & Eaton, H. (1991, Spring). Developing a summer orientation program for college students with learning disabilities. *Postsecondary LD Network News, 12,* 1–3, 6.

Brinckerhoff, L. C., Shaw, S. F., & McGuire, J. M. (1989). Implementing regional consortia for postsecondary learning disability personnel. In J. J. Vanderputten (Ed.), *Proceedings of the 1989 AHSSPPE conference* (pp. 147–150). Columbus, OH: Association on Handicapped Student Service Programs in Postsecondary Education.

Brinckerhoff, L. C., Shaw, S. F., & McGuire, J. M. (1992). Promoting access, accommodations and independence for college students with learning disabilities. *Journal of Learning Disabilities, 25,* 417–429.

Brinckerhoff, L. C., Shaw, S. F., McGuire, J. M., Norlander, K. A., & Anderson, P. L. (1988). Critical issues in learning disability college programs. In D. Knapke & C. Lendman (Eds.), *Celebrate in '88* (pp. 19–40). Columbus, OH: Association on Handicapped Student Service Programs in Postsecondary Education.

Brown, A. L., & Palinscar, A. S. (1982). Inducing strategic learning from text by means of informed, self-control training. *Topics in Learning and Learning Disabilities, 2,* 1–17.

Brown v. Board of Education of Topeka, 347 US 483, 74 S. Ct. 686 (1954).

Bruck, M. (1987). The adult outcomes of children with learning disabilities. *Annals of Dyslexia, 37,* 252–263.

Bryan, J. H. (1983). The relationship between fear of failure and learning disabilities. *Learning Disabilities Quarterly, 6*(2), 217–222.

Bryan, T. H. (1989). Learning disabled adolescents' vulnerability to crime: Attitudes, anxieties, experiences. *Learning Disabilities Research, 5*(1), 51–60.

Bureau of National Affairs. (1990). *The Americans with Disabilities Act: A practical and legal guide to impact, enforcement, and compliance.* Washington, DC: Bureau of National Affairs.

Bursuck, W. (1989). A comparison of students with learning disabilities to low achieving and higher achieving students on three dimensions of social competence. *Journal of Learning Disabilities, 22*(3), 188–194.

Bursuck, W. (1991). *Learning strategies: Module Two. Specific intervention strategies.* De Kalb: Project TAPE, Department of Educational Psychology, Counseling and Special Education, Northern Illinois University.

Bursuck, W. D., & Jayanthi, M. (1993). Programming for independent study skill usage. In S. A. Vogel & P. B. Adelman (Eds.), *Success for college students with learning disabilities* (pp. 177–205). New York: Springer-Verlag.

Bursuck, W., Rose, E., Cowen, S., & Yahaya, M. (1989). Nationwide survey of postsecondary education services for students with learning disabilities. *Exceptional Children, 56,* 236–245.

Byron, J., & Owen, B. (1990, Winter). Metacognitive training: Bridging the gap between content and learning strategies. *Postsecondary LD Network News, 8,* 1–3.

Cabrillo College v. (CA) (1 NDLR 307).

Campbell A. Dinsmore v. Charles C. Pugh and the Regents of the University of California. Berkeley (N.D. Cal., Sept. 23, 1990).

Campbell, D. T., & Stanley, J. C. (1966). *Experimental and quasi-experimental designs for research.* Chicago: Rand McNally College Publishing Co.

Campbell, P., & Shaw, S. F. (1992). *Final Report: The Connecticut Symposia on Special Education in the 21st Century.* Storrs: A. J. Pappanikou Center on Special Education and Rehabilitation: A University Affiliated Program, University of Connecticut.

Canadian Charter of Rights and Freedoms: Constitution Act, 1982, Schedule B of the Canada Act, 1982 (U.K.) C. 11 (1982).

Carlisle, J. F., & Johnson, D. J. (1989). Assessment of school-age children. In L. B. Silver (Ed.), *The assessment of learning disabilities: Preschool through adulthood* (pp. 73–110). Austin, TX: PRO-ED.

Carlson, S. (1985). The ethical appropriateness of subject matter tutoring for learning disabled adolescents. *Learning Disability Quarterly, 8*, 310–314.

Carlton, P. M., & Knapke, D. (1991). Case history factors that correlate with a learning disability diagnosis. In *Proceedings of the 1990 AHSSPPE national conference* (pp. 54–55). Columbus, OH: Association on Handicapped Student Service Programs in Postsecondary Education.

Carlton, P. M., & Walkenshaw, D. (1991). Diagnosis of learning disabilities in postsecondary institutions. *Journal of Postsecondary Education and Disability, 9*, 197–206.

Cawley, J. F. (1985). Cognition and the learning disabled. In J. Cawley (Ed.), *Cognitive strategies and mathematics for the learning disabled* (pp. 1–32). Rockville, MD: Aspen Systems Corp.

Centra, J. (1986). Handicapped student performance on the Scholastic Aptitude Test. *Journal of Learning Disabilities, 19*, 324–327.

Chalfant, J. C. (1989a). Diagnostic criteria for entry and exit from service: A national problem. In L. B. Silver (Ed.), *The assessment of learning disabilities: Preschool through adulthood* (pp. 1–25). Austin, TX: PRO-ED.

Chalfant, J. C. (1989b). Learning disabilities: Policy issues and promising approaches. *American Psychologist, 44*, 392–398.

Chalfant, J. C., & Pysh, M. (1989). Teacher assistance teams: Five descriptive studies on 96 teams. *Remedial and Special Education, 10*, 49–58.

Champlin, J. (1987). Leadership: A change agent's view. In L. T. Sheive & M. B. Schoenheit (Eds.), *Leadership: Examining the elusive* (pp. 49–63). Washington, DC: Association for Supervision and Curriculum Development.

Civil Rights of Students with Hidden Disabilities under Section 504 of the Rehabilitation Act of 1973 (Document No. ED 309 595). (1989). Washington, DC: U.S. Office of Civil Rights.

Civil Rights Restoration Act of 1987, 29 U.S.C. § 794(a)(2)(A).

Clark, D. M. (1990). *National assessment of handicapped student services programs in postsecondary education: Survey of programs*. Buffalo, NY: National Association for Industry-Education Cooperation.

Clary, L. M. (1984, February). *Identifying metacognitive skills in young adults.* Paper presented at the 21st Convention of the Association for Children and Adults with Learning Disabilities, New Orleans, LA. (ERIC Document Reproduction Service No. ED 249 705)

Clerc, J. (1985). The legal obligation to learning disabled and handicapped allied health students. *Journal of Allied Health, 14,* 203–211.

Cohen, J. (1984). The learning disabled university student: Signs and initial screening. *NASPA Journal, 3*(2), 22–31.

Cohen, J. (1985). Learning disabilities and adolescence: Development considerations. In S. C. Feinstein (Ed.), *Adolescent psychiatry, development and clinical studies* (Vol. 12, pp. 177–195). Chicago: University of Chicago Press.

Collins, T. (1990). The impact of microcomputer word processing on the performance of learning disabled students in a required first year writing course. *Computers and Composition, 8* (1), 49–68.

Cook, T. D., & Campbell, D. T. (1979). *Quasi-experimentation: Design and analysis issues for field settings.* Chicago: Rand McNally College Publishing Co.

Cooper, R. (1986). Personal counseling for the learning disabled college student. In *Support services for LD students in postsecondary education: A compendium of readings* (Vol. 1, pp. 109–111). Columbus, OH: Association on Handicapped Student Service Programs in Postsecondary Education.

Cordoni, B. K. (1982). Postsecondary education: Where do we go from here? *Journal of Learning Disabilities, 15,* 265–266.

Cordoni, B. K., & Goh, D. (1989). A comparison of the performance of college students with learning disabilities on the Stanford-Binet Intelligence Scale, Fourth Edition, and the Wechsler Adult Intelligence Scale–Revised. *Learning Disabilities, 1,* 35–39.

Cormier, W. H., & Cormier, L. S. (1991). *Interviewing strategies for helpers.* Pacific Grove, CA: Brooks/Cole.

Cowen, S., Bursuck, W., & Rose, E. (1989). Efficient strategies. In W. D. Bursuck (Ed.), *Specific intervention strategies, participants' manual,* Project TAPE. De Kalb: Northern Illinois University.

Crimando, W. (1984, April–June). A review of the placement-related issues for clients with learning disabilities. *Journal of Rehabilitation, 50,* 78–81.

Cronin, M., & Gerber, P. J. (1982, October). Preparing the learning disabled adolescent for adulthood. *Topics in Learning and Learning Disabilities*, pp. 55–68.

Cruickshank, W. M., Morse, W. C., & Johns, J. S. (1980). *Learning disabilities: The struggle from adolescence to adulthood.* New York: Syracuse University Press.

Dalke, C. (1986). *The effects of precollege transition intervention with learning disabled students.* Unpublished manuscript, Project ASSIST, University of Wisconsin–Whitewater, Whitewater, WI.

Dalke, C. (1988). Woodcock-Johnson Psycho-educational Test Battery profiles: A comparative study of college freshmen with and without learning disabilities. *Journal of Learning Disabilities*, *21*, 567–570.

Dalke, C. (1991). *Support programs in higher education for students with disabilities: Access to all.* Gaithersburg, MD: Aspen.

Dalke, C., & Franzene, J. (1988). Secondary-postsecondary collaboration: A model of shared responsibility. *Learning Disability Focus*, *4*, 38–45.

Dalke, C., & Schmitt, S. (1987). Meeting the transition needs of college-bound students with learning disabilities. *Journal of Learning Disabilities*, *20*(3), 176–180.

D'Amico, R. (1989). Learning disabilities and legal responsibilities under Section 504. In *Proceedings of The Next Step: An invitational symposium on learning disabilities in selective colleges* (pp. 20–35). Cambridge, MA: Harvard University Press.

Davila, R. R. (1991). Clarification of policy to address the needs of children with Attention Deficit Disorders within general and/or special education. *LDA Newsbriefs*, *26*(6), 1, 6–8.

Davila, R. R., Williams, M. M., & MacDonald, J. T. (1991, September). *Clarification of policy to address the needs of children with attention deficit disorders within general and/or special education.* Washington, DC: U.S. Department of Education.

Davis, W. E. (1993). At-risk children and educational reform: Implications for educators and schools in the year 2,000 and beyond. Orono, ME: Institute for the study of at-risk students.

Decker, K., Spector, S., & Shaw, S. (1992). Teaching study skills to students with mild handicaps: The role of the classroom teacher. *The Clearing House*, *65*, 280–284.

Decker, T., Polloway, E., & Decker, B. (1985). Help for the LD college student. *Academic Therapy, 20,* 339–345.

Denckla, M. (1986). The neurology of social competence. *ACLD Newsbriefs, 16*(5), 15, 20–21.

Denton, P. H., Seybert, J. A., & Franklin, E. L. (1991). Ideas in practice: A content-based learning strategies program. *Journal of Developmental Education, 11*(3), 20–24.

Derry, S. J. (1990). Remediating academic difficulties through strategy training: The acquisition of useful knowledge. *Remedial and Special Education, 1*(6), 19–31.

Deshler, D. D., Schumaker, J. B., Lenz, B. K., & Ellis, E. (1984). Academic and cognitive interventions for LD adolescents: Part II. *Journal of Learning Disabilities, 17,* 170–179.

Dexler v. Tisch, 660 F. Supp 1418 (D.C.D. Conn, 1987).

Dinklage, K. T. (1971). Inability to learn a foreign language. In G. Blaine & C. McArthur (Eds.), *Emotional problems of the student* (2nd ed.). New York: Appleton-Century-Crofts.

DragonSystems. (1991). *DragonDictate User Manual.* Newton, MA: DragonSystems.

duChossois, G., & Brinckerhoff, L. C. (1992, June). *Developing summer orientation programs.* Paper presented at the University of Connecticut Fourth Annual Postsecondary Training Institute, Farmington, CT.

Dunn, L. M. (1968). Special education for the mildly retarded—Is much of it justifiable? *Exceptional Children, 35,* 5–22.

Dunn, L., & Dunn, L. (1981) *Peabody Picture Vocabulary Test-Revised.* Circle Pines, MN: American Guidance Service.

Eastern Paralyzed Veterans Association. (1991). *Understanding the ADA.* Jackson Heights, NY: Eastern Paralyzed Veterans Association.

Education for All Handicapped Children Act, (EHA), P.L. 94-142, 20 U.S.C. § 1401 *et seq.* (now known as Individuals with Disabilities Education Act (IDEA), P.L. 101-476).

Ellis, E. S. (1990). What's so strategic about teaching teachers to teach strategies? *Teacher Education and Special Education, 13,* 59–62.

Epstein, M. H., Cullinan, D., & Neiminen, G. (1984). Social behaviour problems of learning disabled and normal girls. *Journal of Learning Disabilities, 17*(10), 609–611.

Fasas, L. A. (1989, Winter). Predictors of transition problems among learning disabled adults. *American Rehabilitation.*

Field, S. L., & Hill, D. S. (1988). Contextual appraisal: A framework for meaningful evaluation of special education programs. *Remedial and Special Education, 9,* 22–30.

Fisher, E. (1985). Educator examines myths, realities of LD students at the college level. *Hill Top Spectrum, 3*(1), 1–5, 8.

Fleischner, J. E., & O'Loughlin, M. (1985). Solving story problems: Implications of research for teaching the learning disabled. In J. Cawley (Ed.), *Cognitive strategies and mathematics for the learning disabled* (pp. 163–181). Rockville, MD: Aspen Systems Corporation.

Fonosch, G., & Schwab, L. (1981). Attitudes of selected university faculty members toward disabled students. *Journal of College Student Personnel, 22,* 229–235.

Fourteenth Annual Report to Congress on the Implementation of the Education of the Handicapped Act. (1992). Washington, DC: U.S. Department of Education.

Fox, C. L., & Forbing, S. E. (1991). Overlapping symptoms of substance abuse and learning handicaps: Implications for educators. *Journal of Learning Disabilities, 24*(1), 24–31, 39.

Fradd, S. H., Figueroa, R. A., & Correas, V. I. (1989). Meeting the multicultural needs of Hispanic students in special education. *Exceptional Children, 56,* 102–103.

Frankenberger, W., & Harper, J. (1987). States' criteria and procedures for identifying learning disabled children: A comparison of 1981/82 and 1985/86 guidelines. *Journal of Learning Disabilities, 20,* 118–121.

Freils, L. (1969). Behavioral changes in students. *Journal of School Health, 39*(6), 405–408.

Gajar, A. H. (1987). *Programming for college students with learning disabilities.* Columbus, OH: Association on Handicapped Student Service Programs in Postsecondary Education.

Gajar, A. H., Salvia, J., Gajria, M., & Salvia, S. (1989). A comparison of intelligence achievement discrepancies between learning disabled and non–learning disabled college students. *Learning Disabilities Research, 4,* 119–124.

Ganschow, L., Myer, B., & Roeger, K. (1989). Foreign language policies and procedures for students with specific learning disabilities. *Learning Disabilities Focus, 5,* 50–58.

Geist, C. S., & McGrath, C. (1983). Psychosocial aspects of adult learning disabled persons in the world of work: A vocational rehabilitation perspective. *Rehabilitation Literature, 44*(7), 210–213.

George, M. P., George, N. L., & Grosenick, J. K. (1990). Features of program evaluation in special education. *Remedial and Special Education, 11*(5), 23–30.

Georgetown University. (1991). *Learning disabilities in higher education: A Georgetown University perspective* [Videotape]. Washington, DC: Georgetown University Educational Media.

Gerber, P. (1991, June). *Being learning disabled, a beginning teacher and teaching a class of students with learning disabilities.* Richmond: University of Virginia/James Madison University Commonwealth Center for the Education of Teachers. Manuscript submitted for publication.

Gerber, P. J., & Reiff, H. B. (1991). *Speaking for themselves: Ethnographic interviews with adults with learning disabilities.* Ann Arbor: University of Michigan Press.

Gerber, P. J., Schnieders, C. A., Paradise, L. V., Reiff, H. B., Ginsberg, R. J., & Popp, P. A. (1990). Persisting problems of adults with learning disabilities: Self-reported comparisons from their school-age and adult years. *Journal of Learning Disabilities, 23*, 570–573.

Gillespie-Silver, P., Vincent, L., Mercaitis, P., Baran, J., & Fldrych-Puzzo, H. (1992, July). *Interdisciplinary assessment for students with learning disabilities in higher education.* Paper presented at the AHSSPPE national conference, Long Beach, CA.

Gillung, T. B., Spears, J., Campbell, P., & Rucker, C. N. (1992). Competencies for administrators of special education. *Journal of Personnel Evaluation in Education, 6*, 71–90.

Goldhammer, R., & Brinckerhoff, L. C. (1992). Self-advocacy for college students. *Their World*, 94–97.

Goldhammer, R., & Brinckerhoff, L. C. (1993). *Implementing an effective test-taking strategy in a competitive postsecondary setting for students with learning disabilities.* Boston: Boston University, LD Support Services.

Golick, M. (1988). *Learning disabilities in postsecondary education.* Fredericton, N. B., Canada: Maritime Provinces Higher Education Commission.

Greenspan, S., Apthorp, H., & Williams, P. (1991). Social competence and work success of college students with learning disabilities. *Journal of Postsecondary Education and Disability, 9*, 227–234.

Gregg, N., & Hoy, C. (1990). Identifying the learning disabled. *Journal of College Admissions* (129), 30–33.

Grove City v. Bell, 465 U.S. 555, 104.S. CT. 1211 (1984).

Hall, C. W., & Haws, D. (1989). Depressive symptomatology in learning disabled and nonlearning disabled students. *Psychology in the Schools, 26*(4), 359–364.

Hallahan, D. P., & Reeve, R. E. (1980). Selective attention and distractibility. In B. K. Keough (Ed.), *Advances in special education* (Vol. 1, pp. 141–181). Greenwich, CT: JAI Press.

Hammill, D. (1972). Training visual perceptual processes. *Journal of Learning Disabilities, 10,* 39–46.

Hammill, D. D. (1990). On defining learning disabilities: An emerging consensus. *Journal of Learning Disabilities, 23,* 74–84.

Handicapped Requirements Handbook. (1985, September). Washington, DC: Thompson Publishing Group.

Handicapped Requirements Handbook. (1990, October). Washington, DC: Thompson Publishing Group.

Handicapped Requirements Handbook. (1991, November). Washington, DC: Thompson Publishing Group.

Handicapped Requirements Handbook. (1992, April). Washington, DC: Thompson Publishing Group.

Handicapped Requirements Handbook. (1993, January). Washington, DC: Thompson Publishing Group.

Harper, G. F., Maheady, L., & Sacca, M. K. (1988). Classwide peer tutoring with mildly handicapped high school students. *Exceptional Children, 55,* 52–59.

Hartman, R. C. (1992). Foreword. In C. T. Mangrum & S. S. Strichart (Eds.), *Peterson's guide to colleges with programs for students with learning disabilities* (pp. v–vi). Princeton, NJ: Peterson's Guides.

Hartman, R. C., & Redden, M. R. (1985). *Measuring student progress in the classroom.* Washington, DC: Higher Education and the Handicapped Resource Center.

Hasazi, S. B., Gordon, L. R., & Roe, C. A. (1985). Factors associated with the employment status of handicapped youth exiting high school from 1979 to 1983. *Exceptional Children, 51,* 455–469.

Hawks, R., Minskoff, E., Sautter, S., Sheldon, K., Stidle, E., & Hoffman, J. (1990). A model diagnostic battery for adults with learning disabilities in vocational education. *Learning Disabilities, 1,* 94–101.

Hayes, M. L., & Sloat, R. S. (1988). Learning disability and suicide. *Academic Therapy, 23*(5), 469–475.

Heisler, A. B. (1983). Psychosocial issues of learning disabilities. *Annals of Dyslexia, 33,* 303–310.

Henderson, C. (Ed.). (1992). *College freshmen with disabilities: A statistical profile.* Washington, DC: American Council on Education.

Henteleff, Y. M. (1990, December). *Recent judgments of the Supreme Court of Canada: New hope for the learning disabled.* Paper presented to the Learning Disabilities Association of Canada.

Henteleff, Y. M. (1991, Spring). Recent judgments of the Supreme Court of Canada: New hope for special needs children. *National.* Ottawa: Learning Disabilities Association of Canada.

Herman, J. L., Morris, L. L., & Fitz-Gibbon, C. T. (1987). *Evaluator's handbook.* Newbury Park, CA: Sage.

Herzog, J. E., & Falk, B. (1991). A follow-up study of vocational outcomes of young adults with learning disabilities. *Journal of Postsecondary Education and Disability, 9,* 219–226.

Heyward, Lawton, & Associates. (1990). *Access to Section 504.* Atlanta, GA: Heyward, Lawton, & Associates.

Heyward, Lawton, & Associates. (Eds.). (1991a). Compliance with both the Education of the Handicapped Act (EHA) and Section 504: Mission impossible? *Disability Accommodation Digest, 1*(1), 5, 7.

Heyward, Lawton, & Associates. (Eds.). (1991b). Documenting the need for academic adjustments. *Disability Accommodation Digest, 1*(3), 3. Columbus, OH: Association on Handicapped Student Service Programs in Postsecondary Education.

Heyward, Lawton, & Associates. (Eds.). (1991c). Significant court cases and OCR findings. *Disability Accommodation Digest, 1,* (1), 6. Columbus, OH: Association on Handicapped Student Service Programs in Postsecondary Education.

Heyward, Lawton, & Associates. (Eds.). (1991d). Wynne v. Tufts University, the controversy continues. *Disability Accommodation Digest, 1*(2), 6. Columbus, OH: Association on Handicapped Student Service Programs in Postsecondary Education.

Heyward, Lawton, & Associates. (Eds.). (1992a). Legal forum. *Disability Accommodation Digest, 2*(1), 9, 10. Columbus, OH: Association on Handicapped Student Service Programs in Postsecondary Education.

Heyward, Lawton, & Associates. (Eds.). (1992b). Significant court cases. *Disability Accommodation Digest, 2*(3), 7. Columbus,

OH: Association on Handicapped Student Service Programs in Postsecondary Education.

Heyward, S. M. (1992). *Access to education for the disabled: A guide to compliance with Section 504 of the Rehabilitation Act of 1973.* Jefferson, NC: McFarland.

Hill Top Preparatory School. (1988). Learning disabled adolescent viewed at-risk for drug and alcohol abuse. *Hill Top Spectrum,* 3(1–4). (ERIC Document Reproduction Service No. ED 309 602)

Houck, C. K., Englehard, J., & Geller, C. (1989). Self-assessment of learning disabled and nondisabled college students: A comparative study. *Learning Disabilities Research, 5,* 61–67.

Hudson Valley Community College Catalog. (1991–92). Troy, NY: Hudson Valley Community College.

Huestis, R., & Ryland, C. (1986, February). *Integrating learning disabilities into the life of adolescents.* Paper presented at the 23rd convention of the Association for Children and Adults with Learning Disabilities, New York, NY. (ERIC Document Reproduction No. ED 269 930)

Hughes, C., & Osgood-Smith, J. (1990). Cognitive and academic performance of college students with learning disabilities: A synthesis of the literature. *Learning Disability Quarterly, 13,* 66–79.

Hughes, C., Schumaker, J., Deshler, D., & Mercer, C. (1988). *The test-taking strategy (PIRATES).* Lawrence, KS: Edge Enterprises.

HumanWare. (1992). *New software program assists learning disabled professionals.* Loomis, CA: HumanWare.

Hynd, G. W., Marshall, R., & Gonzeles, J. (1991). Learning disabilities and presumed central nervous system dysfunction. *Learning Disability Quarterly, 14,* 283–296.

Idol, L., Paolucci-Whitcomb, P., & Nevin, A. (1986). *Collaborative consultation.* Austin, TX: PRO-ED.

Interagency Committee on Learning Disabilities. (1987). *Learning disabilities: A report to the U.S. Congress.* Bethesda, MD: National Institutes of Health.

Jackson, S. C., Enright, R. D., & Murdock, J. Y. (1987). Social perception problems in learning disabled youth: Developmental lag versus perceptual deficit. *Journal of Learning Disabilities, 20,* 361–364.

Jarrow, J. E. (1986). *Integration of individuals with disabilities in higher education.* Washington, DC: D:ATA Institute, The Catholic University of America.

Jarrow, J. E. (1990). *Multicultural diversity and learning disabilities.* Columbus, OH: Association on Handicapped Student Service Programs in Postsecondary Education.

Jarrow, J. E. (1991, Winter). Disability issues on campus and the road to ADA. *Educational Record, 72,* 26–31.

Jarrow, J. E. (1992a, June). *Legal issues.* Paper presented at the University of Connecticut Fourth Annual Postsecondary Training Institute, Farmington, CT.

Jarrow, J. E. (1992b). *Title by title: The ADA's impact on postsecondary education.* Columbus, OH: Association on Higher Education and Disability.

Jaschik, S. (1990, May 30). U.S. court rules that requiring multiple-choice tests may violate the rights of learning disabled students. *Chronicle of Higher Education,* pp. A17, A20.

Jastak, J. E., & Jastak, S. R. (1978). *Wide Range Achievement Test.* Wilmington, DE: Jastak Associates.

Jastak, S. R., & Wilkinson, G. E. (1984). *Wide Range Achievement Test-Revised.* Wilmington, DE: Jastak Associates.

Javorsky, J., Sparks, R. L., & Ganschow, L. (1992). Perceptions of college students with and without specific learning disabilities about foreign language courses. *Learning Disabilities Research & Practice, 7,* 31–44.

Johnson, D. J. (1987a). Assessment issues in learning disabilities research. In S. Vaughn & C. S. Bos (Eds.), *Research in learning disabilities* (pp. 141–149). Austin, TX: PRO-ED.

Johnson, D. J. (1987b). Principles of assessment and diagnosis. In D. J. Johnson & J. W. Blalock (Eds.), *Adults with learning disabilities: Clinical studies* (pp. 9–30). Orlando, FL: Grune & Stratton.

Johnson, D. J., & Blalock, J. W. (Eds.). (1987). *Adults with learning disabilities: Clinical studies.* Orlando, FL: Grune & Stratton.

Johnson, G. O. (1962). Special education for the mentally handicapped—A paradox. *Exceptional Children, 29,* 62–69.

Johnson, J. (1989). *The LD academic support group manual.* Columbus, OH: Association on Handicapped Student Service Programs in Postsecondary Education.

Johnson, J., Evelo, S., & Price, L. (1992). *When therapy is not enough: How learning disability specialists can work effectively with mental health professionals.* Minneapolis, MN: Project Extra. Manuscript submitted for publication.

Junkala, J., & Paul, J. (1987). Learning disabilities: An international perspective. *Paedoperisse, 1,* 1. (Special monograph issue on International Perspectives on Learning Disabilities, 1–5)

Karlsen, B., Madden, R., & Gardner, E. F. (1984). *Stanford Diagnostic Reading Test* (3rd ed.). San Antonio, TX: Psychological Corporation.

Kaufman, J. M. (1989). The Regular Education Initiative as Reagan-Bush education policy: A trickle-down theory of education of the hard-to-teach. *Journal of Special Education, 23,* 256–277.

Kavale, K. A., Forness, S. R., & Lorsbach, T. C. (1991). Definition for definition of learning disabilities. *Learning Disability Quarterly, 14,* 257–266.

Kendall, D., & Wong, B. (1987). Canadian policies, practices, and programs related to learning disabilities: An overview. *Paedoperisse, 1*(1), 29–44.

Keogh, B. K. (1987). Learning disabilities: In defense of a construct. *Learning Disabilities Research, 3,* 4–9.

Kincaid, J. M. (1992, July). *Compliance requirements of the ADA and Section 504.* Paper presented at the Association on Higher Education and Disability conference, Long Beach, CA.

King, W., & Jarrow, J. E. (1990). *Testing accommodations for students with disabilities.* Columbus, OH: Association on Handicapped Student Service Programs in Postsecondary Education.

King, W., & Jarrow, J. (1991). *Testing accommodations for students with disabilities: A guide for licensure, certification, and credentialling.* Columbus, OH: Association on Handicapped Student Service Programs in Postsecondary Education.

Kirk, S. A. (1962). *Educating exceptional children.* Boston: Houghton Mifflin.

Knight, J. (1991, March). *Learning strategies at Humber College: A preliminary report.* Paper presented at Bakersfield College Conference on Learning Strategies for Underprepared Students, Bakersfield, CA.

Kolich, E. M. (1985). Microcomputer technology with the learning disabled: A review of the literature. *Journal of Learning Disabilities, 18,* 428–431.

Kolligian, J., & Sternberg, R. J. (1987). Intelligence, information processing, and specific learning disabilities: A triarchic synthesis. *Journal of Learning Disabilities, 20,* 8–17.

Kroll, L. G. (1984). LD's—What happens to them when they are no longer children? *Academic Therapy, 20,* 133–148.

Kunkaitis, A. (1986). Fostering independence in learning disabled students: A counseling approach. In *Support services for LD students in postsecondary education: A compendium of readings* (pp. 112–115). Columbus, OH: Association on Handicapped Student Service Programs in Postsecondary Education.

Laing, J., & Farmer, M. (1984). *Use of the ACT assessment by examinees with disabilities.* Iowa City, IA: American College Testing Program.

Landi, P. C. (1991). *Problems of attention deficit disorder in adults.* Arlington, VA: P. C. Landi.

Learning Disabilities Association of America. (1990, May). LDA position paper: Eligibility for services for persons with specific learning disabilities. *LDA Newsbriefs* (pp. 1a–8a). Pittsburgh, PA: Learning Disabilities Association of America.

Learning Disabilities Association of Canada. (1988). *Survey of colleges and universities in Canada of services for students with learning disabilities.* Ottawa: Learning Disabilities Association of Canada.

Lehtinen, L., & Dumas, L. (1976). *A follow-up study of learning disabled children as adults: A final report.* Evanston, IL: The Cove School Research Office. (ERIC Document Reproduction Service No. ED 164 728)

Lendman, C. (1991). *Volunteer reader/taping service handbook.* (2nd ed.). Columbus, OH: Association on Handicapped Student Service Programs in Postsecondary Education.

Lenz, K. B., Alley, G. R., Schumaker, J. B. (1987). Activating the inactive learner: Advance organizers in the secondary content classroom. *Learning Disability Quarterly, 10*(1), 53–67.

Lenz, K. B., Schumaker, J. B., Deshler, D. D., & Beals, V. L. (1984). *Learning strategies curriculum: The word identification strategy.* Lawrence: University of Kansas.

Levinson, E. M. (1986). School psychology and college learning disabled students: Training and service possibilities. *Psychology in the Schools, 23,* 295–302.

Link, T. (1989, May 5). Dyslexic student sues UC for denying extra exam time. *Oakland Tribune,* p. B-2.

Litt, A. V., & McGuire, J. M. (1989). *Continuum of services.* Storrs: A. J. Pappanikou Center on Special Education and Rehabilitation: A University Affiliated Program, University of Connecticut.

Livingston, R. (1985). Depressive illness and learning difficulties: Research needs and practical implications. *Journal of Learning Disabilities, 18*, 518–520.

Longman, D. G., & Atkinson, R. H. (1991). *College learning and study skills* (2nd ed.). Saint Paul, MN: West Publishing.

Lynch, E. C., & Beare, P. L. (1990). The quality of IEP objectives and their relevance to instruction for students with mental retardation and behavioral disorders. *Remedial and Special Education, 2*, 48–55.

Maag, J. W., & Behrens, J. T. (1989a). Depression and cognitive self-statements of learning disabled and seriously emotionally disturbed adolescents. *Journal of Special Education, 23*, 17–27.

Maag, J. W., & Behrens, J. T. (1989b). Epidemiologic data on seriously emotionally disturbed and learning disabled adolescents: Reporting extreme depressive symptomatology. *Behavioral Disorders, 15*, 21–27.

Madaus, G. F., Airasian, P. W., & Kellaghan, T. (1980). *School effectiveness: A reassessment of evidence.* New York: McGraw-Hill.

Mamarchev, H. L., & Williamson, M. L. (1991). Women and African Americans: Stories told and lessons learned—A case study. In P. L. Moore (Ed.), *Managing the political dimensions of student affairs* (pp. 67–79). San Francisco: Jossey-Bass.

Mangrum, C. T., & Strichart, S. S. (1984). *College and the learning disabled student.* New York: Grune & Stratton.

Mangrum, C. T., & Strichart, S. S. (1988). *College and the learning disabled student* (2nd ed.). Orlando, FL: Grune & Stratton.

Mangrum, C. T., & Strichart, S. S. (Eds.). (1992). *Peterson's colleges with programs for students with learning disabilities* (3rd ed.). Princeton, NJ: Peterson's Guides.

Marchant, G. J. (1990, November). Faculty questionnaires: A useful resource for LD support services. *Intervention in School and Clinic, 26 (2)*, 106–109.

Margalit, M., & Heiman, T. (1986). Learning-disabled boys' anxiety, parental anxiety, and family climate. *Journal of Clinical Child Psychology, 15*, 248–253.

Maroldo, R. (Ed.). (1991). *Individuals with Disabilities Education Act of 1990 (IDEA).* Horsham, PA: LRP Publications.

Martin, D. C., & Arendale, D. R. (1992). *Supplemental instruction: Improving first year students' success in high risk courses.* Columbia: National Resource Center for the Freshman Year Experience, University of South Carolina.

Matthews, P. R., Anderson, D. W., & Skolnick, B. D. (1987). Faculty attitude toward accommodations for college students with learning disabilities. *Learning Disabilities Focus, 3*, 46–52.

McCarthy, M. (1992, Winter). Appropriate academic accommodations: A look at Oklahoma State University v. Pat Smith. *Latest Developments*, pp. 2–3.

McCue, M., & Goldstein, G. (1990). Neuropsychological aspects of learning disability in adults. In B. P. Rourke (Eds.), *Neuropsychological validation of LD subtypes.* New York: Guildford.

McGuire, J. M. (1990). *Comprehensive evaluation implementation plan.* Unpublished material, The University of Connecticut, A. J. Pappanikou Center on Special Education and Rehabilitation: A University Affiliated Program, Storrs.

McGuire, J. M. (1990). *University of Connecticut program for college students with learning disabilities (UPLD) program objectives.* Unpublished material, The University of Connecticut, A. J. Pappanikou Center on Special Education and Rehabilitation: A University Affiliated Program, Storrs.

McGuire, J. M. (1991, Fall). *University of Connecticut admissions application process for students with learning disabilities.* Presentation at Admissions Annual Open House. Storrs: A. J. Pappanikou Center on Special Education and Rehabilitation: A University Affiliated Program, University of Connecticut.

McGuire, J. M. (1992). *Final report of the Provost's committee on learning disabilities and the general education requirement.* Storrs: University of Connecticut.

McGuire, J. M. (1992). *Academic affairs or student affairs: Pros and cons.* Unpublished material, The University of Connecticut, A. J. Pappanikou Center on Special Education and Rehabilitation: A University Affiliated Program, Storrs.

McGuire, J. M. (1992). *A step by step approach to questions to be asked in planning a program evaluation.* Unpublished material, The University of Connecticut, A. J. Pappanikou Center on Special Education and Rehabilitation: A University Affiliated Program, Storrs.

McGuire, J., Anderson, P., & Shaw, S. (1992). *Guidlines for documentation of a specific learning disability: The University of Connecticut Program for College Students with Learning Disabilities (UPLD).* Storrs: A. J. Pappanikou Center on Special Education and Rehabilitation: A University Affiliated Program, University of Connecticut.

McGuire, J. M., Archambault, F. X., Gillung, T., & Strauch, J. D. (1989). *Connecticut's statewide followup study of former special education program graduates.* Hartford: Connecticut State Department of Education. (ERIC Document Reproduction Service No. ED 303 951)

McGuire, J. M., Hall, D., Ramirez, M., & Cullen, J. (1992, October). *Documentation submitted to validate learning disabilities in a college sample.* Presentation at the 14th International Conference on Learning Disabilities, Kansas City, MO.

McGuire, J. M., Harris, M. W., & Bieber, N. (1989). Evaluating college programs for learning disabled students: An approach for adaptation. In *Support services for LD students in postsecondary education: A compendium of readings* (Vol. 2, pp. 131–136). Columbus, OH: Association on Handicapped Student Service Programs in Postsecondary Education.

McGuire, J. M., & Litt, A. V. (1992). *Learning specialist training manual.* Storrs: A. J. Pappanikou Center on Special Education and Rehabilitation: A University Affiliated Program, University of Connecticut.

McGuire, J. M., Norlander, K. A., & Shaw, S. F. (1990). Postsecondary education for students with learning disabilities: Forecasting challenges for the future. *Learning Disabilities Focus, 5,* 69–74.

McGuire, J. M., & Shaw, S. F. (Eds.). (1989). *Resource guide of support services for students with learning disabilities in Connecticut colleges and universities.* Storrs: A. J. Pappanikou Center on Special Education and Rehabilitation: A University Affiliated Program, University of Connecticut.

McGuire, J. M., & Shaw, S. F. (1992). Note from the editors. *Journal of Postsecondary Education and Disability, 10,* 2.

McGuire, J. M., Shaw, S. F., Bloomer, R. H., & Anderson, P. L. (1992, July). *The changing role of assessment for students with learning disabilities.* Paper presented at the AHSSPPE National Conference, Long Beach, CA.

McLoughlin, J. A., & Lewis, R. B. (1990). *Assessing special students.* Columbus, OH: Merrill.

McNutt, G. (1986). The status of learning disabilities in the states: Consensus or controversy? *Journal of Learning Disabilities, 19,* 12–16.

Mellard, D. F. (1990). The eligibility process: Identifying students with learning disabilities in California's community colleges. *Learning Disabilities Focus, 5,* 75–90.

Mellard, D. F., & Deshler, D. D. (1984). Modeling the condition of learning disabilities on postsecondary populations. *Educational Psychologist, 19*, 188–197.

Mercer, C. (1987). Beyond traditional assessment. In S. Vaughn & C. S. Bos (Eds.), *Research in learning disabilities* (pp. 153–165). Austin, TX: PRO-ED.

Mercer, C. (1991). *Students with learning disabilities* (4th ed.). New York: Merrill.

Mercer, C., Hughes, C., & Mercer, A. (1985). Learning disabilities definitions used by state education departments. *Learning Disability Quarterly, 8*, 45–55.

Michaels, C. (1986). Increasing faculty awareness and cooperation: Procedures for assisting college students with learning disabilities. In J. J. Vander Putten (Ed.), *Proceedings of the 1989 AHSSPPE Conference* (pp. 78–87). Columbus, OH: Association on Handicapped Student Service Programs in Postsecondary Education.

Michaels, C. (Ed.). (1988). *From high school to college: Keys to success for students with learning disabilities.* Albertson, NY: Human Resources Center.

Mills v. the Board of Education of the District of Columbia, 348 F. Supp. 866 (D.DC 1972).

Minner, S., & Prater, G. (1984). College teachers' expectations of LD students. *Academic Therapy, 20*, 225–229.

Minskoff, E. H., Sautter, S. W., Hoffman, F. J., & Hawks, R. (1987). Employer attitudes toward hiring the learning disabled. *Journal of Learning Disabilities, 20*, 53–57.

Mirenda, P., & Iacono, T. (1990). Communication options for persons with severe and profound disabilities: State of the art and future directions. *Journal of the Association for Persons with Severe Handicaps, 15*, 3–21.

Mithaug, D. W., Horiuchi, C. W., & Fanning, P. N. (1985). A report on the Colorado statewide followup survey of special education students. *Exceptional Children, 51*, 397–404.

Mooney, J. (1992, June). *Teaching considerations for faculty.* Paper presented at the Next Step: Turning Research into Practice, Connecticut College, New London, CT.

Mooney, J., & Bashir, A. (1992). *Guidelines for professors of students with learning disabilities.* Chestnut Hill, MA: Department of Curriculum, Administration, and Special Education, Boston College.

Morris, M., & Leuenberger, J. (1990). A report of cognitive, academic, and linguistic profiles for college students with and without learning disabilities. *Journal of Learning Disabilities, 23,* 355–360, 385.

Morris, M., Leuenberger, J., & Aksamit, D. (1987). Faculty in-service training: Impact on the postsecondary climate for learning disabled students. *Journal of Postsecondary Education and Disability, 5,* 58–66.

Morse, D. (1977). Counseling the young adolescent with learning disabilities. *The School Counselor, 25*(1), 8–15.

Myers, P. I., & Hammill, D. D. (1990). *Learning disabilities: Basic concepts, assessment practices, and instructional strategies* (4th ed.). Austin, TX: PRO-ED.

National Joint Committee on Learning Disabilities. (1983, January). *Learning disabilities: The needs of adults with learning disabilities.* A position paper of the National Joint Committee on Learning Disabilities. Unpublished manuscript.

National Joint Committee on Learning Disabilities. (1985, February). *Adults with learning disabilities: A call to action.* A position paper of the National Joint Committee on Learning Disabilities. Unpublished manuscript.

National Joint Committee on Learning Disabilities. (1987a). Adults with learning disabilities: A call to action. *Journal of Learning Disabilities, 20,* 172–175.

National Joint Committee on Learning Disabilities. (1987b, September). *Issues in learning disabilities: Assessment and diagnosis.* A position paper of the National Joint Committee on Learning Disabilities. Unpublished manuscript.

National Joint Committee on Learning Disabilities. (1988a). Inservice programs in learning disabilities. *Journal of Learning Disabilities, 21,* 53–55.

National Joint Committee on Learning Disabilities. (1988b). (Letter to NJCLD member organizations)

Neault, L. (1988). *Programming for learning disabled college students: Accommodations and autonomy.* (ERIC Document Reproduction Service No. ED 245 639)

Nelson, J. R., Dodd, J. M., & Smith, D. J. (1990). Faculty willingness to accommodate students with learning disabilities: A comparison among academic divisions. *Journal of Learning Disabilities, 23,* 185–189.

Nelson, R., & Lignugaris/Kraft, B. (1989). Postsecondary education for students with learning disabilities. *Exceptional Children*, *56*, 246–265.

Ness, J. N., & Price, L. A. (1990). Meeting the psychosocial needs of adolescents and adults with LD. *Intervention in School and Clinic*, *26*, 16–21.

Newman, J. (1976). Faculty attitudes toward handicapped students. *Rehabilitation Literature*, *37*, 194–197.

Norlander, K. A., & Shaw, S. F. (1988). Competencies needed by college personnel serving students with learning disabilities: Issues in preparing and hiring. In D. Knapke & C. Lendman (Eds.), *Proceedings of the 1988 AHSSPPE conference* (pp. 248–263). Columbus, OH: Association on Handicapped Student Programs in Postsecondary Education.

Norlander, K. A., Shaw, S. F., & McGuire, J. M. (1990). Competencies of postsecondary education personnel serving students with learning disabilities. *Journal of Learning Disabilities*, *23*, 426–432.

O'Hearn, C. (1989). Recognizing the learning disabled college writer. *College English*, *5* (1), 294–304.

Oliker, N. (1991, Spring). Reflections of an LD service provider on 10 years of LD college programming. *Latest Developments*, pp. 9–11.

Olivarez, A., Palmer, D., & Guillemard, L. (1992). Predictive bias with referred and nonreferred black, Hispanic, and white pupils. *Learning Disability Quarterly*, *15*, 175–186.

Ostertag, B. (1986). *Services for learning disabled adults in California's community colleges*. Sacramento, CA: Consortium for the Study of Learning Disabilities in the California Community Colleges, Office of the Chancellor. (ERIC Document Reproduction Service No. ED 265 892)

Ostertag, B., & Baker, R. E. (1982). *Report of the California community college learning disabled programs*. Sacramento, CA: Community College Chancellor's Office.

Ostertag, B., Pearson, M. T., & Baker, R. E. (1986). Programs for the learning disabled in California community colleges. *Reading, Writing, and Learning Disabilities*, *2*, 331–347.

Parks, A. W., Antonoff, S., Drake, C., Skiba, W. F., & Soberman, J. (1987). A survey of programs and services for learning disabled students in graduate and professional schools. *Journal of Learning Disabilities, 20,* 181–187, 154.

Payne, N. (1992, June). *Transition strategies: Employment preparation essentials.* Paper presented at the University of Connecticut's Fourth Annual Postsecondary Training Institute, Farmington, CT.

Pennsylvania Association for Retarded Citizens (PARC) v. Commonwealth of Pennsylvania. 334 F. Supp. 1257 (E.D. Pa. 1972).

Percy, S. L. (1989). *Disability, civil rights, and public policy.* Tuscaloosa: University of Alabama Press.

Phillips, P. (1990). A self-advocacy plan for high school students with learning disabilities: A comparative case study analysis of students', teachers', and parents' perceptions of program effectiveness. *Journal of Learning Disabilities, 23,* 466–471.

Pihl, R. O., & McLarnon, L. D. (1984). Learning disabled children as adolescents. *Journal of Learning Disabilities, 17,* 96–100.

Poirier, D., Goguen, L., & Leslie, P. (1988). *Education rights of exceptional children in Canada: A national study of multi-level commitments.* Toronto: Carswell.

Policastro, M. M. (1993). Metacognitive attributes in college students with learning disabilities. In S. A. Vogel & P. B. Adelman (Eds.), *Success for college students with learning disabilities* (pp. 151–176). New York: Springer-Verlag.

Pollack, R., & McGuire, J. (1988). Collaborative approach to serving students with learning disabilities: The University of Connecticut interactive model. In D. Knapke & C. Lendman (Eds.), *Celebrate in '88 . . . AHSSPPE and all that jazz* (pp. 82–84). Columbus, OH: Association on Handicapped Student Service Programs in Postsecondary Education.

Posthill, S. M., & Roffman, A. J. (1991). The impact of a transitional training program for young adults with learning disabilities. *Journal of Learning Disabilities, 24,* 619–629.

Price, L. (1988a). Effective counseling techniques for LD adolescents and adults in secondary and postsecondary settings. *The Journal of Postsecondary Education and Disability, 6,* 7–16.

Price, L. (1988b). LD support groups work! *The Journal of Counseling and Human Services Professions, 2,* 35–46.

Price, L. (1990). *A selective literature review concerning the psychosocial issues of LD individuals.* Minneapolis, MN: The LD

Transition Project. (ERIC Document Reproduction Service No. ED 315 956)

Ragosta, M. (1986). *Students with disabilities: Four years of data from special test administrations of the SAT 1980–1983.* New York: College Entrance Examination Board.

Ragosta, M., & Nemceff, W. (1982). *A research and development program on testing handicapped people.* Princeton, NJ: Educational Testing Service.

Raskin, M. H., & Scott, N. G. (1993). Technology for postsecondary students with learning disabilities. In S. A. Vogel & P. B. Adelman (Eds.), *Success for college students with learning disabilities* (pp. 240–270). New York: Springer-Verlag.

Reed College Catalog. (1991–92). Portland, OR: Reed College.

Reeve, R. E. (1990). ADHD: Facts and fallacies. *Intervention in School and Clinic, 26,* 70–78.

Rehabilitation Act of 1973, Section 504, P.L. 93-112, 29 U.S.C. § 794 (1977).

Rehabilitation Act Regulations, 34 C.F.R. part 104 (1977).

Reiff, H. B., Gerber, P. J., & Ginsberg, R. (1992). Learning to achieve: Suggestions from adults with learning disabilities. *Journal of Postsecondary Education and Disability, 10,* 11–23.

Renick, M. J., & Harter, S. (1989). Impact of social comparisons on the developing self-perceptions of learning disabled students. *Journal of Educational Psychology, 81,* 631–638.

Reynolds, M. C. (1984). Classification of students with handicaps. In E. W. Gordon (Ed.), *Review of research in education* (Vol. 11, pp. 63–92). Washington, DC: American Educational Research Association.

Richard, P. A., Bloomer, R. H., Negron, E., & Lesser, E. (1991, February). *Bilingual assessment: Format for an alternative procedure for assessment of Spanish speaking limited English proficient (LEP) students.* Paper presented at Eastern Educational Research Association conference, Boston, MA.

Rogers v. Bennett, 876 F. 2nd 1387 (11th Cir. 1989).

Rooney, K. J. (1991). Controversial therapies: A review and critique. *Intervention in School and Clinic, 26,* 134–142.

Rosenthal, J. H. (1973). Self-esteem in dyslexic children. *Academic Therapy, 9,* 27–39.

Rothstein, L. F. (1986). Section 504 of the Rehabilitation Act: Emerging issues for colleges and universities. *Journal of College and University Law, 13,* 229–265.

Rothstein, L. F. (1989). Learning disabilities in selective colleges: Legal issues c. 1990. In *Proceedings of* The Next Step: An invitational symposium on learning disabilities in selective colleges (pp. 36–52). Cambridge, MA: Harvard University Press.

Rothstein, L. F. (1990). *Special education and the law.* New York: Longman.

Rothstein, L. F. (1991, September). Campuses and the disabled. *Chronicle of Higher Education*, pp. B3, B10.

Rourke, B. P. (1989). A childhood learning disability that predisposes those afflicted to adolescent and adult depression and suicide risk. *Journal of Learning Disabilities, 22,* 169–174.

Runyan, K., & Smith, J. F. (1992). Identifying and accommodating learning disabled law school students. *Journal of Legal Education, 317–349.*

Ryan, A., & Heikkila, M. K. (1988). Learning disabilities in higher education: Misconceptions. *Academic Therapy, 24,* 177–192.

Ryan, A., & Price, L. (1992). Adults with LD in the 1990's: Addressing the needs of students with learning disabilities. *Intervention in School and Clinic, 28,* 6–20.

Sachs, J. J., Iliff, V. W., & Donnelly, R. F. (1987). Oh, OK, I'm LD! *Journal of Learning Disabilities, 20,* 92–93, 113.

Salvia, J., & Ysseldyke, J. E. (1991). *Assessment in special and remedial education* (5th ed.). Boston: Houghton Mifflin.

Sandeen, A. (1989). Issues influencing the organization of student affairs. In U. Delworth, G. R. Hanson, & Associates (Eds.), *Student services: A handbook for the profession* (2nd ed., pp. 445–460). San Francisco: Jossey-Bass.

Satcher, J., & Dooley-Dickey, K. (1991). Helping college bound clients with learning disabilities. *Journal of Rehabilitation, 58,* 47–50.

Scheiber, B., & Talpers, J. (1987). *Unlocking potential: College and other choices for learning disabled people: A step-by-step guide.* Bethesda, MD: Adler and Adler.

Schell, L. N. (1988, July). *Word processing for LD students.* Paper presented at Association on Handicapped Student Service Programs in Postsecondary Education.

Schumaker, J., Deshler, D. D., Alley, G. R., & Warner, M. M. (1983). Toward the development of an interventionist model for learning disabled adolescents: The University of Kansas Institute. *Exceptional Education Quarterly, 4,* 45–74.

Schumaker, J., Deshler, D., Alley, G., Warner, M., & Denton, P. (1982). MULTIPASS: A learning strategy for improving reading comprehension. *Learning Disability Quarterly, 5,* 295–304.

Schumaker, J., Hazel, J. S., Sherman, J. A., & Sheldon, J. (1982). Social skill performances of learning disabled, nonlearning disabled, and delinquent adolescents. *Learning Disability Quarterly, 5,* 388–397.

Scott, S. S. (1990). Coming to terms with the "otherwise qualified" student with a learning disability. *Journal of Learning Disabilities, 23,* 398–405.

Scott, S. S. (1991). A change in legal status: An overlooked dimension in the transition to higher education. *Journal of Learning Disabilities, 24,* 459–466.

Secretary's Commission on Achieving Necessary Skills. (1991, April 18). *The SCANS Report.* Washington, DC: The White House.

Section 504 of the Rehabilitation Act of 1973: Old problems and emerging issues for public schools. (1991, October). *Liaison Bulletin 17*(8). Alexandria, VA: National Association of State Directors of Special Education, 1–3.

Seidenberg, P. (1986). *Getting the gist: Relating text processing research to reading and writing instruction for learning disabled secondary students* (Doc. No. 5). Greenvale, NY: Long Island University Transition Project.

Semel-Mintz, E., & Wiig, E. J. (1980). *Clinical Evaluation of Language Functions: Diagnostic battery.* Columbus, OH: Merrill.

Shapiro, E. S., & Lentz, F. E. (1991). Vocational-technical programs: Follow-up of students with learning disabilities. *Exceptional Children, 58,* 47–59.

Shaw, S. F., Brinckerhoff, L. C., Kistler, J., & McGuire, J. M. (1991). Preparing students with learning disabilities for postsecondary education: Issues and future needs. *Learning Disabilities: A Multidisciplinary Journal, 2,* 21–26.

Shaw, S. F., Cullen, J. P., & McGuire, J. M. (1992). *Independence vs. dependence: A study of service providers' intervention methods for college students with learning disabilities.* Storrs: A. J. Pappanikou Center on Special Education and Rehabilitation: A University Affiliated Program, University of Connecticut.

Shaw, S. F., McGuire, J. M., & Brinckerhoff, L. C. (in press). College and university programming. In P. J. Gerber and H. B. Reiff (Eds.), *Adults with learning disabilities.* Andover, MA: Andover Medical Publishers.

Shaw, S. F., Norlander, K. A., & McGuire, J. M. (1987). Training leadership personnel for learning disability college programs: Preservice and inservice models. *Teacher Education and Special Education, 10,* 108–112.

Shepard, L. A., & Smith, M. L. (1983). An evaluation of the identification of learning disabled students in Colorado. *Learning Disability Quarterly, 6,* 115–127.

Sheridan, H. (1990, November). *Keynote address.* Next Step: An invitational symposium on learning disabilities in selective colleges. Cambridge, MA: Harvard University Press.

Silver, A. A. (1984). Children in classes for the severely emotionally handicapped. *Developmental and Behavioral Pediatrics, 5,* 49–54.

Slavin, R. (1991). Synthesis of research on cooperative learning. *Phi Delta Kappan, 72,* 71–82.

Smith, B. K. (1986, February). *The wilted flower syndrome.* Paper presented at the 23rd conference of the Association for Children and Adults with Learning Disabilities, New York, NY. (ERIC Document Reproduction Service No. ED 270 913)

Smith, J. O. (1988). Social and vocational problems of adults with learning disabilities: A review of the literature. *Learning Disabilities Focus, 4,* 46–58.

Southeastern Community College v. Davis 422 U.S. 397, 60 L. Ed. 2nd 980 (1979).

Southwest Texas State University v. Region VI (Case No. 06902084).

Spector, S., Decker, K., & Shaw, S. F. (1991). Independence and responsibility: An LD resource room at South Windsor High School. *Intervention in School and Clinic, 26,* 159–167.

Stevenson, D. T., & Romney, D. M. (1984). Depression in learning disabled children. *Journal of Learning Disabilities, 17*(10), 579–582.

Stewart, A. (1989). *The postsecondary learning disabilities primer.* Cullowhee, NC: The Learning Disabilities Training Project, Western Carolina State University.

Straughn, C. T. (1988). *Lovejoy's college guide for the learning disabled.* (2nd ed.). New York: Monarch Press.

Strauss, A. A., & Lehtinen, L. (1947). *Psychopathology and education of the brain-injured child* (Vol. 1). New York: Grune & Stratton.

Stufflebeam, D. L. (1988). The CIPP model for program evaluation. In G. F. Madaus, M. S. Scriven, & D. L. Stufflebeam (Eds.), *Eval-*

uation models: Viewpoints on educational and human services evaluation (pp. 117–141). Boston: Kluwer-Nijhoff.

Stufflebeam, D. L., Foley, W. J., Gephart, W. J., Guba, E. G., Hammond, R. L., Merriman, H. O., & Provus, M. M. (1971). *Educational evaluation and decision making.* Itasca, IL: Peacock.

Summary of major changes in parts A through H of the act. (1990, October). *Liaison Bulletin, 18*(8). Alexandria, VA: National Association of State Directors of Special Education.

Swan, W. W., & Sirvis, B. (1992). The CEC Common Core of Knowledge and Skills Essential for All Beginning Special Education Teachers. *Teaching Exceptional Children, 25,* 16–20.

Swanson, H. L. (1987). Information processing and learning disabilities: An overview. *Journal of Learning Disabilities, 20,* 3–7.

Swanson, H. L. (Ed.). (1991a). *Learning Disability Quarterly, 14*(4) [Special Issue].

Swanson, H. L. (1991b). Operational definitions and learning disabilities: An overview. *Learning Disability Quarterly, 14,* 242–254.

Swanson, H. L., & Cooney, J. B. (1991). Learning disabilities and memory. In B.Y.L. Wong (Ed.), *Learning about learning disabilities* (pp. 103–127). San Diego, CA: Academic Press.

Swanson, H. L., & Watson, B. (1982). *Educational and psychological assessment of exceptional children.* Saint Louis, MO: Mosby.

Tenth Annual Report to Congress on the Implementation of the Education of the Handicapped Act. (1988). Washington, DC: U.S. Department of Education.

Thirteenth Annual Report to Congress on the Implementation of the Education of the Handicapped Act. (1991). Washington, DC: U.S. Department of Education.

Tomlan, P., Farrell, M., & Geis, J. (1990). The 3 S's of staff development: Scope, sequence, and structure. In J. J. Vander Putten (Ed.), *Proceedings of the 1989 AHSSPPE Conference* (pp. 23–32). Columbus, OH: Association on Handicapped Student Service Providers in Postsecondary Education.

Torgeson, J. K. (1982). The learning disabled child as an inactive learner: Educational implications. *Topics in Learning Disabilities, 2,* 45–52.

Trainor, R. (1992, Spring). New hope: Nova Scotia's new human rights act provides protection for the learning disabled. *National.* Ottawa: Learning Disabilities Association of Canada.

Trapani, C. (1990). *Transition goals for adolescents with learning disabilities.* Austin, TX: PRO-ED.

Trueba, C. M. (1991, Spring). LD assessment within a disabled student service office: One campus's dilemma and response. *Latest Developments,* 5–6.

Tucker, B. P., & Goldstein, B. A. (1991). *Legal rights of persons with disabilities.* Horsham, PA: LRP Publications.

Turnbull, A. P., Strickland, B. B., & Brantley, J. C. (1982). *Developing and implementing individualized education programs.* Columbus, OH: Merrill.

Unger, K. (1991, Summer). Providing services to students with psychological disabilities: Clarifying campus roles. *Psychological Disabilities.* Columbus, OH: Association on Higher Education and Disability.

U.S. Department of Education. (1977). Definition and criteria for defining students as learning disabled. *Federal Register, 42* (250), 65083. Washington, DC: U.S. Government Printing Office.

U.S. Department of Education. (1980, May 9). Section 504: Rehabilitation Act of 1973. *Federal Register, 45*(92), 30936–30954.

U.S. Department of Education. (1990). *Twelfth annual report to Congress on the implementation of the Education of the Handicapped Act.* Washington, DC: U.S. Government Printing Office.

U.S. Department of Education. (1992). Individuals with Disabilities Act (IDEA): Rules and regulations. *Federal Register, 57* (189), 44794–44852.

United States v. Board of Trustees of the University of Alabama, 908F.2d 740 (11th Cir. 1990).

University of California at Berkeley. (1990). *Model for accommodating the academic needs of students with disabilities.* Berkeley: University of California.

University of Connecticut: General Catalog. (1992–93). Storrs: University of Connecticut.

University of Georgia: Undergraduate Bulletin. (1991–92). Athens: University of Georiga.

Valdés, K. A., Williamson, C. L., & Wagner, M. M. (1990). *The National Longitudinal Transition Study of Special Education Students: Statistical almanac* (Vol. 2). Washington, DC: U.S. Department of Education, Office of Special Education Programs.

Van Reusen, A., Bos, C., & Deshler, D. (1987). *The educational planning strategy (I-PLAN)*. Lawrence, KS: Edge Enterprises.

Vogel, S. (1982). On developing LD college programs. *Journal of Learning Disabilities, 15,* 518–528.

Vogel, S. A. (1985). Learning disabled college students: Identification, assessment, and outcomes. In D. D. Duane & C. K. Leong (Eds.), *Understanding learning disabilities: International and multidisciplinary views* (pp. 179–202). New York: Plenum.

Vogel, S. A. (1986). Levels and patterns of intellectual functioning among LD college students: Clinical and educational implications. *Journal of Learning Disabilities, 19,* 71–79.

Vogel, S. A. (1987a). Eligibility and identification considerations in postsecondary education: A new but old dilemma. In S. Vaughn & C. S. Bos (Eds.), *Research in learning disabilities: Issues and Future Directions* (pp. 121–137). Austin, TX: PRO-ED.

Vogel, S. A. (1987b). Issues and concerns in LD college programming. In D. J. Johnson & J. W. Blalock (Eds.), *Adults with learning disabilities: Clinical studies* (pp. 239–276). Orlando, FL: Grune & Stratton.

Vogel, S. A. (1989). Special considerations in the development of models for diagnosis of adults with learning disabilities. In L. B. Silver (Ed.), *The assessment of learning disabilities: Preschool through adulthood* (pp. 111–134). Austin, TX: PRO-ED.

Vogel, S. A. (1990). *College students with learning disabilities: A handbook* (3rd ed.). Pittsburgh, PA: Learning Disabilities Association of America.

Vogel, S. A., & Adelman, P. B. (1990). Extrinsic and intrinsic factors in graduation and academic failure among LD college students. *Annals of Dyslexia, 40,* 119–137.

Vogel, S. A., & Adelman, P. B. (1992). The success of college students with learning disabilities: Factors related to educational attainment. *Journal of Learning Disabilities, 25,* 430–441.

Wade, S. E., & Reynolds, R. E. (1989). Developing students' metacognitive awareness may be essential to effective strategy instruction. *Journal of Reading, 33,* 6–15.

Walker, J. K., Shaw, S. F., & McGuire, J. M. (1992). Concerns of professionals and consumers regarding postsecondary education for students with learning disabilities. *Learning Disabilities, 3,* 11–16.

Walker, M. L. (1980). The role of faculty in working with handicapped students. In H. Z. Sprandel & M. R. Schmidt (Eds.), *Serving handicapped students*. San Francisco: Jossey-Bass.

Wang, M. C., & Palinscar, A. S. (1989). Teaching students to assume an active role in their learning. In M. C. Reynolds (Ed.), *Knowledge base for the beginning teacher*. Elmsford, NY: Pergamon Press.

Wechsler, D. (1955). *Wechsler Adult Intelligence Scale*. San Antonio, TX: Psychological Corporation.

Wechsler, D. (1974). *Wechsler Intelligence Scale for Children-Revised*. San Antonio, TX: Psychological Corporation.

Wechsler, D. (1981). *Wechsler Adult Intelligence Scale-Revised*. San Antonio, TX: Psychological Corporation.

Weinberg, W. A., McLean, A., Snider, R. L., & Nucklos, A. S. (1989). Depression, learning disability, and school behavior problems. *Psychological Reports, 64*(1), 275–283.

Weinstein, C. E., Palmer, D. R., & Schulte, A. C. (1987). *Learning and Study Strategies Inventory*. Clearwater, FL: H & H Publishing Company.

White, W. J. (1992). The postschool adjustment of persons with learning disabilities: Current status and future projections. *Journal of Learning Disabilities, 25*, 448–456.

White, W. J., Alley, G. R., Deshler, D. D., Schumaker, J. B., Warner, M. M., & Clark, F. L. (1982). Are there learning disabilities after high school? *Exceptional Children, 49*, 273–274.

Whyte, L. A., Kovach, K., & Vosahlo, M. (1991). *Identifying and diagnosing postsecondary students with learning disabilities*. Edmonton, Alberta, Canada: Office of Services for Students with Disabilities, Program for Students with Learning Disabilities, University of Alberta.

Wiener, J., & Siegel, L. (1992). A Canadian perspective on learning disabilities. *Journal of Learning Disabilities, 25*, 340–350, 371.

Wilchesky, M., & Minden, H. A. (1988). A comparison of learning and nonlearning disabled university students on selected measures. In D. Knapke & C. Lendman (Eds), *Proceedings of the 1988 AHSSPPE conference* (pp. 116–118). Columbus, OH: Association on Handicapped Student Service Programs in Postsecondary Education.

Wong, B. Y. (1987). How do the results of metacognitive research impact on the learning disabled individual? *Learning Disability Quarterly, 10,* 189–195.

Wong, B. Y. (1991). *Learning about learning disabilities.* San Diego, CA: Academic Press.

Wong, B. Y., & Jones, W. (1992). Increasing metacomprehension in learning disabled and normally achieving students through self-questioning training. *Learning Disability Quarterly, 5,* 228–238.

Woodcock, R. (1987). *Woodcock Reading Mastery Tests–Revied.* Circle Pines, MN: American Guidance Service.

Woodcock, R. W., & Johnson, M. B. (1977). *Woodcock-Johnson Psycho-Educational Battery–Revised.* Allen, TX: DLM Teaching Resources.

Woodcock, R. W., & Johnson, M. B. (1989). *Woodcock-Johnson Psycho-Educational Battery–Revised.* Allen, TX: DLM Teaching Resources.

Woods, P. A., Sedlacek, W., & Boyer, S. P. (1990). Learning disability programs in large universities. *NASPA Journal, 27,* 248–256.

Worcester, L. H. (1981). *The Canadian Franco-American learning disabled college student at the University of Maine at Orono.* Paper presented at the Council for Exceptional Children Conference of the Exceptional Bilingual Child, New Orleans, LA. (ERIC Document Reproduction Service No. ED 204 881)

Worthen, B. R., & Sanders, J. R. (1987). *Educational evaluation: Alternative approaches and practical guidelines.* New York: Longman.

Wright, B. (1960). *Physical disability: A psychological approach.* New York: HarperCollins.

Wright, L. S., & Stimmel, T. (1984). Perceptions of parents and self among college students reporting learning disabilities. *Exceptional Child, 31,* 203–208.

Wright State University. (1985). *Learning disabilities: Coping in college* [Videotape]. Dayton, OH: Handicap Student Services.

Wynne v. Tufts University School of Medicine, 732 F2d 19 (1st Cir. 1991); Lexis 2629 (D. Mass. 1992).

Xerox Imaging Systems. (1992). *The Reading Edge.* Peabody, MA: Xerox Corporation.

Ysseldyke, J. E. (1987). Classification of handicapped students. In M. C. Wang, M. C. Reynolds, & H. J. Walberg (Eds.), *The hand-*

book of special education: Research and practice (Vol. 1, pp. 253–271). Oxford, England: Pergamon.

Ysseldyke, J. E., Algozzine, B., Richey, L., & Graden, J. (1982). Declaring students eligible for learning disability services: Why bother with the data? *Learning Disability Quarterly, 5,* 37–44.

Index

Academic adjustments
  access to services, 227–229
  administrative issues in, 222–235
  admission procedures, 224–227
  alternative testing form, 380–381
  based on diagnostic information,
    133–136
  checklist of, 237–238
  and computers, 197, 242–243, 244,
    248–251
  in course examinations, 229–231
  course substitutions, 231–234
  court cases on, 54–55, 57–58
  examples of, 223
  grading, 235
  guidelines for, 234
  impact of Section 504 on, 30–31,
    46–47, 54–55
  instructional adaptations and
    modifications, 251–258
  negotiation of, 246–248
  note-taking modifications, 241–
    243
  overview of, 15–16
  policy statements and policy
    issues on, 236–237 335–339,
    346–347
  readers, 240–241
  and reading machines, 251
  service-delivery options and con-
    siderations, 236–238
  tape-recorded textbooks, 238–240
  techniques for provision of, 238–
    251
  testing modifications, 243–246,
    247, 376–377
Academic affairs division, 173–176
Access to services, 227–229
Accommodations. See Academic
  accommodations
ACE. See American Council on Education (ACE)
Achievement tests, 122–123, 311–
  312
ACT. See American College Test
  (ACT)
ADA. See Americans with Disabilities Act (ADA)

ADD. *See* Attention deficit disorder (ADD)

ADHD. *See* Attention deficit-hyperactivity disorder (ADHD)

Administrative issues
in academic adjustments, 222–235
access to services, 227–229
admission procedures, 224–227
course substitutions, 231–234
financial assistance, 235
grading, 235
guidelines for academic adjustments, 234
housing, 235
in program development, 170–178

Administrators
getting support from, 182–191
personnel development for, 217–218
training needs of, 213–214

Admission procedures, 54–55, 224–227

AHEAD. *See* Association on Higher Education and Disability (AHEAD)

Alcoholism, 26, 33, 147

American Association of Social Workers, 165

American College Test (ACT), 225, 227

American College Testing Program, 227

American Council on Education (ACE), 2

American Printing House for the Blind, 239–240

American Psychological Association, 165

American Speech-Language-Hearing Association, 71

Americans with Disabilities Act (ADA)
compared with IDEA and Section 504, 44–45, 47–50

eligibility criteria in, 33
employment provisions in, 34–35
impact on college campuses, 39–41, 64
passage of, 4, 9, 32–33
provisions of, 33–39
public accommodations provision in, 36–38
public services and transportation provisions in, 35–36
telecommunications relay services provision in, 39

Anxiety, 144–145

Apple Office of Special Education Programs, 349

Application process
and alternative admission procedures, 224–227
application forms, 324–325
follow-up letter to prospective applicants, 328–329
impact of Section 504 on, 30

Assessment. *See also* Tests
areas of diagnostic testing, 118–121
complexity of adult assessment, 95–97
components of, 109–111
constraints of instrumentation and qualified diagnosticians on, 97–99
controversial nature of, 90–91
and definition of learning disabilities, 91–92
and diagnostic report, 126–130
diagnostic testing, 118–126
difficulty in assessment of adults, 91–103
and eligibility determination, 10–11, 92–95
funding sources for, 131–132
guidelines for documentation of learning disabilities, 315–317

interpretation and application of
diagnostic information, 132–136
methods of evaluation in, 121–122
multicultural assessment, 99–101
process of, 103–111, 119
purposes of, 101–103
referral for diagnostic assessment,
126–132
and referral procedures, 111–113
resources on, 295–300
role of postsecondary institutions
in, 104–106
screening options in, 113–118
state of the art on campus, 106–109
tests frequently used for, 309–314
Assistive technology. *See* Auxiliary
aids and services
Association of Counselors and Family Therapists, 165
Association on Higher Education
and Disability (AHEAD), 71, 72,
183, 218, 256, 283, 349
Attention deficit disorder (ADD),
24, 84–86
Attention deficit-hyperactivity disorder (ADHD), 84, 85–86
Auxiliary aids and services
availability of, 232
computers, 197, 242–243, 248–251
court cases on, 58–60, 200
note-taking modifications, 241–
243
readers, 240–241
reading machines, 251
tape-recorded textbooks, 238–240
technological aids, 232, 238–240,
242–244, 365–366
testing modifications, 243–246

Ball State University, 256, 373
Barnard College, 256
Basic and Supplemental Educational
Opportunity Grants, 56

Behavior Problem Checklist, 144
Bender Visual Motor Gestalt Test,
123, 310
Boston College, 388–389
Boston University
academic adjustments at, 236,
346–347
application form from, 324
summer transition program at,
193, 194–196
Brown University, 257
*Brown v. Board of Education of
Topeka,* 21

Cabrillo College, 63
California Community College sys-
tem, 92, 116, 350
*Campbell A. Dinsmore v. Charles
C. Pugh and the Regents of the
University of California,* 57–58,
229, 230, 263
Canada
contact persons in, 321
legislation in, 50–54
screening methodology in, 116
Carbonless paper, 241
Certification, for professions, 37–38
Change agent, 288–289
Charter of Rights and Freedoms, 51–54
Chemical dependency. *See* Alcohol-
ism; Drug abuse
Chronicle of Higher Education, 218
CIPP model, 16, 264, 265–266
Civil Rights Act of 1964, 49
Civil Rights, Office of. *See* Office of
Civil Rights
Civil Rights Restoration Act of 1987,
56–57
Clark University, application form
from, 324
*Clinical Evaluation of Language
Functions: Diagnostic Battery,*
123

Closing the Gap, 369
Code of ethics, 165–166
College. *See also* Postsecondary services for learning-disabled students; and names of specific
colleges
differences from high school, 5–8
impact of Secton 504 on, 27–29
mission of, 170–172
organizational structure of, 172–
176
role in assessment, 104–106
state of the art in LD assessment
on campus, 106–109
College students with learning disabilities. *See also* Postsecondary services for learning-
disabled students
assessment of, 10–11, 90–136
faculty attitudes toward, 257–258
integration of, into postsecondary
community, 286–288
psychosocial characteristics of,
12, 138–167, 252
resources for, 365–366, 370–371
statistics on number of, 2, 20
technological aids for, 197–198,
232, 365–366
Compensatory services, 205–206
Comprehensive services, 205, 206
Computers and computer software,
197, 242–243, 244, 248–251, 365–
366
ConnSense Bulletin, 370
Contact persons, 319–321
Council for Exceptional Children,
283, 349
Council for Learning Disabilities,
71, 350
Counseling. *See* Psychosocial services
Course substitutions, 231–234,
341–344

Course syllabus, 256–257, 388–389
Court cases
access to services, 227–228, 263
auxiliary aids and services, 58–60
and Civil Rights Restoration Act,
57
determination of what is "otherwise qualified," 54–55
and Public Law 94–142, 21
scope of Section 504 in higher
education, 55– 56
testing modifications, 57–58,
60–64, 229–231

Dependency issues, 143–144
Depression, 146
Dexler v. *Tisch*, 46
Diagnosis. *See* Assessment
Diagnostic testing. *See* Tests
Disability Accommodation Digest,
218
Disabled students, statistics on, 2.
See also College students with
learning disabilities
Discrimination complaints, 48–49,
291–294
Documentation of learning dis-
ability, 315–317
Dole, Robert, 32
DragonDictate, 249–250, 366
Drug addiction, 26, 33, 147
Due process, 23, 64

Education Act amendments of 1973,
56
Education for All Handicapped Chil-
dren Act. *See* Public Law 94–142
Education Department, 56
Education Department, regional
civil rights offices, 291–294
Educational Testing Service, 225
EEOC. *See* Equal Employment Op-
portunity Commission (EEOC)

Eligibility
in Americans with Disabilities
Act, 33
determination of, 10–11, 92–95
in Individuals with Disabilities
Education Act, 93–94, 102
in Public Law 94–142, 22
in Rehabilitation Act of 1973,
25–26, 68–69, 102, 104–105, 229
Employment
in Americans with Disabilities
Act, 34–35
competencies for, 150–151
underemployment of persons with
learning disabilities, 261
Equal Employment Opportunity
Commission (EEOC), 48, 49, 350
Ethics code, 165–166
Evaluation. *See* Assessment; Program evaluation
Exams and tests
academic adjustments in, 229–231,
243–246, 247
alternative testing form, 380–381
exam testing assistance procedures, 376–377
modification of format of, 60–64
providing additional time for,
57–58

Faculty
attitude toward learning-disabled
students, 257–258
and instructional adaptations and
modifications, 251–258
negotiation of academic adjustments with, 246– 248
office hours of, 256
personnel development for, 219–220
resources on learning disabilities
for, 352– 357
and tape recording of lectures,
242, 373

and testing modifications, 243–243
training needs of, 212–213
Financial assistance, 56, 235
Follow-up letter to prospective applicants, 328–329
Foreign language learning, 231–232,
297, 341–344
Formative versus summative evaluation, 266–267
Funding
for assessment, 131–132
for LD services, 190–191
for summer transition program, 193
Future directions
change agents, 288–289
fostering of successful outcomes,
281–282
integration into postsecondary
community, 286–288
knowledge base, 285–286
overview of, 17, 280
proactive versus reactive service
delivery, 284–285
professional standards, 282–283

Goals and objectives, 268–273
Grading, 235
Groups. *See* Support groups
Grove City v. *Bell*, 55–56

Handicapped Children's Protection
Act of 1986, 46
Handouts. *See* Instructional handouts
HEATH Resource Center, 2, 183, 350
High school
differences from college, 5–8
impact of Section 504 on, 27
statistics on learning-disabled stu-
dents graduating from, 3
Higher education. *See* College;
Postsecondary services for learn-
ing-disabled students
Housing, 235

HRA. *See* Human Rights Act (HRA)

Hudson Valley Community College, 171

Human Rights Act (HRA), 53–54

Hyperactivity. *See* Attention deficit-hyperactivity disorder (ADHD)

IBM National Support Center for Persons with Disabilities, 350

ICLD. *See* Interagency Committee on Learning Disabilities (ICLD)

IDEA. *See* Individuals with Disabilities Act (IDEA)

IEP. *See* Individualized Education Program (IEP)

Individualized Education Program (IEP), 7, 23, 24, 94, 194, 224, 225

Individuals with Disabilities Education Act (IDEA)

compared with Americans with Disabilities Act, 44–45, 47–50

compared with Section 504, 42–50

eligibility requirements in, 93–94, 102

importance of, 3, 22, 64, 229

provisions of, 24

Information from HEATH, 369

Information processing, 76–78, 123, 233, 310

In-service training. *See* Personnel development

Instructional adaptations and modifications, 251–258. *See also* Academic accommodations

Instructional handouts, 256–257, 384–389

Instrumentation. *See* Tests

Interagency Committee on Learning Disabilities (ICLD), 72–73

Journal of Postsecondary Education and Disability, 285–286

Justice Department, 48, 350

Kirk, Sam, 68

KRM. *See* Kurzweil Reading Machine (KRM)

Kurzweil Reading Machine (KRM), 251, 366

Labeling, 86–87

Labor Department, 12, 150

Landmark College, 193, 194

Language ability, 312–313

LDA. *See* Learning Disabilities Association of America (LDA)

Learning disabilities. *See also* College students with learning disabilities; Postsecondary services for learning-disabled students

assessment of, 10–11, 90–136

attention deficit disorder compared with, 84– 86

definition of, 9–10, 68–80, 87, 91–92

differentiated from other disabilities, 81–86

documentation of, 315–317

guidelines for documentation of, 315–317

and high school graduation, 3, 20

and interest in postsecondary education, 3, 20

labeling of, 86–87

long-term effects of, 95–96, 167

mental retardation compared with, 81–82, 83

operational definition of, 73–80, 87

psychological disorder compared with, 82

and psychosocial characteristics, 12, 138–167

resources for professional development, 349– 371

slow learners compared with, 83, 84, 85

statistics on, 2, 3, 20, 92
traumatic brain injury compared with, 85, 86
and underemployment, 261
Learning Disabilities Association of America (LDA), 3, 99, 189, 350
Learning Disabilities Association of Canada, 50, 351
Learning Disabilities Postsecondary Training Institute, 183
Learning strategies, 252–255, 310–311
Least restrictive educational placement, 23
Legislation. *See also* names of specific laws in Canada, 50–54
comparison of major laws, 42–50
impact of, 20
overview of, 2–4, 7, 8–9
practical guidelines based on, 64
provisions of major laws, 21–41
Letters, to prospective applicants, 328–329
Library of Congress, 351
Licensing, for professions, 37–38
Locus of control, 143–144, 252

Maslow, Abraham, 12, 148–150
Mathematics, 232–233, 341–344
Megacognitive skills, 252–253
Mental retardation, 81–82, 83
Microcomputers. *See* Computers
Middlesex County College, 189
Mills v. *The Board of Education of the District of Columbia*, 21
Mission, of postsecondary institutions, 170–172
Multicultural assessment, 99–101

National Association of School Psychologists, 71
National Center for Learning Disabilities (NCLD), 351

National Joint Committee on Learning Disabilities (NJCLD), 9–10, 14, 71–73, 87, 91–92, 104, 120, 121, 215, 283
National Longitudinal Transition Study of Special Education Students, 261
National Network of LD Adults (NNLDA), 351
NCLD. *See* National Center for Learning Disabilities (NCLD)
Negative behaviors and feelings, 145
New York University, 194, 208
Newsletters, 218, 369
NJCLD. *See* National Joint Committee on Learning Disabilities (NJCLD)
NNLDA. *See* National Network of LD Adults (NNLDA)
Nondiscrimination statement, 332–333
Note-taking modifications, 241–243

Objectives for program, 268–273
OCR. *See* Office for Civil Rights (OCR)
ODS. *See* Orton Dyslexia Society (ODS)
Office of Civil Rights (OCR), 4, 48–49, 63, 215, 218, 285, 291–294
Office of Federal Contract Compliance Programs, 49
Office of Special Education and Rehabilitative Services (OSERS), 4, 48, 285
Ohio State University, 208, 245, 376–377
Oklahoma State University, 228
Orton Dyslexia Society (ODS), 351
OSERS. *See* Office of Special Education and Rehabilitative Services (OSERS)
"Otherwise qualified," determination of, 54–55

Parents, 7–8, 23

Peabody Picture Vocabulary Test-Revised, 123

Pennsylvania Association for Retarded Citizens (PARC) v. *Commonwealth of Pennsylvania*, 21

Periodicals, 369–370

Personnel development
for administrators, 213–214, 217–218
competencies identified as training needs, 210–211
for faculty, 212–213, 352–357
future directions in, 282–283
needs assessments for, 215–216
needs for, 208–214
recommendations for, 215
resources for, 349–371
for service providers, 209–212, 216–217, 358–359
for student affairs and related personnel, 218–219
videotapes for, 361–364
for volunteer and peer tutors, 359–361

Planning
for LD support services, 182–185
for program evaluation, 267–268

Policy statements
academic accommodations policy statement, 235–237, 335–339, 346–347
course substitution policy statement, 341–344
nondiscrimination statement, 332–333
tape-recorded lecture policy agreement, 373

Postsecondary LD Network News, 218, 369

Postsecondary services for learning-disabled students. *See also* College students with learning disabilities

academic adjustments in, 15–16, 30–31, 54–55, 57–58, 133–136, 222–258, 335–339, 346–347, 376–377, 380–381
access to services, 227–229
administrative issues, 170–178
administrative support for, 182–191
admission procedures, 54–55, 224–227
beginnings of, 2
in Canada, 50–54
challenges in, 199–201
compensatory services, 205–206
comprehensive services, 205, 206
continuum of service-delivery models, 180–182, 273
court cases related to, 54–64
eligibility for, 10–11
funding for, 190–191, 193
future directions in, 17, 280–289
goals and objectives of, 268–273
initiating LD support services, 182–188
and institutional mission, 170–172
integration into postsecondary community, 286–288
legislation supporting, 2–4, 8–9, 20–54
maintenance and enhancement of, 188–191
model programs on, 4–5
and organizational structure, 172–176
personnel development for, 13–15, 208–220
planning for, 182–185
practical guidelines for, 64
program development for, 12–13, 170–201
program evaluation of, 16–17, 260–278
psychosocial services, 148–167
remedial services, 204–205

research needs on, 285–286
service delivery, 178–182, 272, 273, 284–285
services versus programs, 178–180
significant factors in, 2–4
staffing for, 13–15, 190, 204–208, 282–283
statistics on, 2, 50, 106–107, 173
successful outcomes for, 281–282
summer transition program, 191–199
tutoring, 205, 206
President's Committee on Employment of People with Disabilities, 351
Professional licensing and certification, 37–38
Professional standards, 282–283
Program development
administrative issues in, 170–178
challenges in, 199–201
continuum of service-delivery models, 180–182, 273
model of support services, 172
overview of, 12–13
service delivery, 178–182, 272, 273, 284–285
services versus programs, 178–180
summer transition program, 191–199
Program evaluation
challenges in, 277–278
CIPP model of, 264, 265–266
evaluation plan and methods, 271, 274–275
example of, 268–276
formative versus summative evaluation, 266–267
and goals and objectives, 268–273
impetus for measuring program effectiveness, 260–264
overview of, 16–17
planning for, 267–268

results from, 276
selection of evaluator for, 264, 266–267
of summer transition program, 198–199
Program goals and objectives, 268–273
Psychological disorder, compared with learning disabilities, 82
Psychosocial characteristics
caveats regarding, 163–166
chemical dependency, 147
definition of, 141–147
dependency issues, 143–144, 252
depression, 146
examples of, 138–139
importance of, 139–141, 167
and individual counseling, 160–161
limitations in current research on, 147–148
negative behaviors and feelings, 145
overview of, 12
and referrals, 152–158
and resistant students, 162–163
self-concept, 142
socialization skills, 142–143
stress and anxiety, 144–145
suicide, 146
and support groups, 158–159
and team approach, 152–158
tests of, 313
theoretical rationale for psychosocial service delivery, 148–152
Psychosocial services
and code of ethics, 165–166
individual counseling techniques, 160–161
and limits of professional expertise, 163–165
rationale for, 148–152
referrals for, 152–158
for resistant students, 162–163

support groups, 158–159
team approach to, 152–158
Public accommodations, 36–38
Public Law 100–259. *See* Civil Rights
    Restoration Act of 1987
Public Law 94–142 (Education for All
    Handicapped Children Act)
    definition of learning disabilities
        in, 70–71, 81
    eligibility criteria in, 22
    passage of, 2–3, 7, 260, 278
    provisions of, 21–24
    purpose of, 21–22
Public Law 99–372. *See* Handicapped
    Children's Protection Act of 1986
Public services, 35–36
Public transportation, 35–36

Readers, 240–241
Reading Edge, 251
Reading machines, 251
Reagan, Ronald, 57
Recording for the Blind (RFB), 238–
    239, 352
Reed College, 171–172
Referrals
    for assessment, 111–113
    for psychosocial services, 152–158
Regional civil rights offices, 291–294
Regional learning disability contact
    persons, 319–321
Rehabilitation Act of 1973
    and academic adjustments, 236–
        237
    and admission procedures, 224
    and assistive technology, 248
    compared with Americans with
        Disabilities Act, 44–45, 47–50
    compared with Individuals with
        Disabilities Education Act,
        42–50
    and determining what is "other-
        wise qualified," 54–55, 81, 231

eligibility criteria in, 25–26, 68–69,
    102, 104–105, 229
impact on elementary and second-
    ary settings, 27
impact on postsecondary settings,
    27–29
passage of, 4, 7, 8, 278
potential areas for litigation under,
    30–32
provisions of, 25–26
scope of, regarding higher educa-
    tion, 55–56
Relaxation, 161
Remedial services, 204–205
RFB. *See* Recording for the Blind
    (RFB)
Rochester Institute of Technology
    Bookstore, 241

SAT. *See* Scholastic Aptitude Test
    (SAT)
SCANS Report, 150–51
Scholastic Aptitude Test (SAT), 225,
    227
Screening, 113–118, 298, 301–308
Section 504. *See* Rehabilitation Act
    of 1973
Self-actualization model, 12, 148–152
Self-concept, 142
Service delivery, 178–182, 272, 273,
    284–285. *See also* Postsecondary
    services for learning-disabled stu-
    dents; Program development
Sheridan, Harriet, 257–258
Slow learners, 83, 84, 85
Socialization skills, 142–143
*Southeastern Community College
    v. Davis*, 54
Southern Illinois University, 194
Southwest Texas State University,
    63
Staff development. *See* Personnel
    development

Staffing
  and expansion of LD services, 190
  future directions in, 282–283
  needs for, 204–208
  overview of, 13–15
  and personnel development, 13–15,
    208–220
  and professional standards, 282–
    283
Standards, professional, 282–283
*Stanford Diagnostic Mathematics
  Test*, 123
Stanford Diagnostic Reading Test,
  123
Stress, 144–145
Structure, of postsecondary institu-
  tions, 172–176
Student affairs division, 173–176,
  218–219
Students. *See* College students with
  learning disabilities; Postsecond-
  ary services for learning-disabled
  students
Study skills, 252–255, 310–311
Substance abuse. *See* Alcoholism;
  Drug addiction
Substitutions. *See* Course substitu-
  tions
Summative versus formative evalua-
  tion, 266–267
Summer transition program, 191–199
Support groups, 158–159
Syllabus. *See* Course syllabus
Synthesized speech, 249, 366

Tape-recorded textbooks, 238–240
Tape recorders, 365
Tape-recording agreement form, for
  lectures, 242, 373
TBI. *See* Traumatic brain injury
  (TBI)
TDDs. *See* Telecommunications
  devices for the deaf (TDDs)

Team approach, to psychosocial services, 152–158
Technological aids. *See* Auxiliary
  aids and services; Computers
Telecommunications devices for the
  deaf (TDDs), 39
Telecommunications relay services,
  39
Test Anxiety Scale, 144–145
Tests. *See also* Assessment; Exams
  and tests; and names of specific
  tests
  achievement tests, 122–123, 311–
    312
  as admission requirements, 225,
    227
  areas of diagnostic testing, 118–121
  caveats regarding, 123–126
  and diagnostic report, 126–130
  diagnostic testing, 118–126
  frequently used tests for diagnos-
    ing adults with learning disabil-
    ities, 11, 122–123, 309–314
  guidelines for documentation of
    learning disabilities, 315–317
  of information-processing skills,
    123, 310
  of intelligence and general ability,
    120, 122, 309–310
  of language ability, 312–313
  of learning styles and study skills,
    310–311
  of psychosocial characteristics,
    120–121, 313
  resources on, 298–300
  technical inadequacy of, for adults,
    97–98
  of vocational interests and apti-
    tudes, 313–314
Textbooks, tape-recorded, 238–240
Therapy. *See* Psychosocial services
Training. *See* Personnel development
Transition services, 3, 24, 94, 191–199

Transportation. *See* Public transportation
Traumatic brain injury (TBI), 85, 86
Tufts Medical School, 60–62
Tutoring, 205, 206, 253, 255–256, 359–361

United States v. *Board of Trustees of the University of Alabama,* 58–60
Universities. *See* Postsecondary services for learning-disabled students; and names of specific universities
University of Alabama, 58–60
University of Alberta, 116
University of California, Berkeley, 57–58, 230–231, 335–339
University of Connecticut
access to services at, 228
application form from, 325, 225–226
course substitution policy statement, 341–344
documentation of learning disabilities at, 315–317
newsletter from, 218
nondiscrimination statement from, 332–333
program evaluation at, 268–276
screening process at, 114, 115
testing modifications at, 245
training at, 183, 208
University of Connecticut Program for College Students with Learning Disabilities (UPLD), 16, 225, 268–276, 315–317, 341–344
University of Georgia, 108, 171
University of Kansas, 197, 253
University of Massachusetts, 114, 115
University of Minnesota, 249
University of Nebraska, 212–213
University of Oregon, 208
University of Vermont, application form from, 325

University of Wisconsin-Madison, 108–109, 114, 245
University of Wisconsin-Whitewater, 194, 195
University of Wisconsin System, 236
UPLD. *See* University of Connecticut Program for College Students with Learning Disabilities (UPLD)

Videotapes, 198, 361–364
Voice-recognition system, 250–251

WAIS-R. See Wechsler Adult Intelligence Scale–Revised (WAIS-R)
Webb, Gertrude, 2
Wechsler Adult Intelligence Scale–Revised (WAIS-R), 11, 122, 123, 124, 310
Wechsler Intelligence Scale for Children–Revised (WISC-R), 122
Western Carolina State University, 384–386
Wide Range Achievement Test–Revised (WRAT-R), 122
WISC-R. See Wechsler Intelligence Scale for Children–Revised (WISC-R)
WJPEB-R. See Woodcock-Johnson Psycho-Educational Battery–Revised (WJPEB-R)
Woodcock Reading Mastery Tests–Revised, 123, 312
Woodcock-Johnson Psycho-Educational Battery–Revised (WJPEB-R), 11, 122, 123, 310, 312
WRAT-R. See Wide Range Achievement Test–Revised (WRAT-R)
Writing assessment, 300
Wynne v. *Tufts University School of Medicine,* 60–62, 229, 263

Xerox Imaging Systems, 251

About the Authors

Loring C. Brinckerhoff is the director of the Learning Disability Support Services office at Boston University and is a member of the special education faculty. Previously, he served as the project coordinator on a 3-year U.S. Department of Education grant at the University of Connecticut. The focus of the grant was to assist 2- and 4-year institutions throughout the Northeast in developing learning disability services. He received his doctorate in learning disabilities at the University of Wisconsin–Madison and initiated support services to college students with learning disabilities on that campus in 1983. Dr. Brinckerhoff is currently a consulting editor for *Intervention in School and Clinic*, a member of the executive council of the Association on Higher Education and Disability, and secretary of the National Joint Committee on Learning Disabilities. He has provided technical assistance to over 200 colleges and universities in the United States and Canada on topics related to the transition from high school to college, programming for college students with learning disabilities, legal rights of adults, and program evaluation.

Stan F. Shaw is a professor and coordinator of special education at the University of Connecticut. He is co-director of the Postsecondary

Education Unit of the A. J. Pappanikou Center on Special Education and Rehabilitation at the university. He was a special education teacher in New York and Colorado prior to receiving his doctorate at the University of Oregon. In 1988, Dr. Shaw was a visiting professor at Henan Normal University, Xinxiang City, People's Republic of China. He is currently co-editor of the *Journal of Postsecondary Education and Disability* and is on the editorial boards of *Exceptional Children,* and *Teacher Education and Special Education.* He has authored journal articles in the areas of postsecondary learning disabilities, secondary and transitional programs, teaching students with disabilities in the regular classroom, and teacher stress and burnout.

Joan M. McGuire is the director of the University of Connecticut Program for College Students with Learning Disabilities and is an associate professor in the educational psychology department at the University of Connecticut. Dr. McGuire also directs the Connecticut Postsecondary Learning Disability Technical Assistance Center at the university and serves as co-director of the Postsecondary Education Unit. She has been involved in service delivery for college students with learning disabilities since 1978 in 2- and 4-year public and private institutions. She is currently co-editor of the *Journal of Postsecondary Education and Disability.* Dr. McGuire's research interests include postsecondary learning disability program development and evaluation, staff training, and strategies to promote independence among college students with learning disabilities.